Judgment at Istanbul

Judgment at Istanbul

The Armenian Genocide Trials

by

Vahakn N. Dadrian and Taner Akçam

Berghahn Books
New York • Oxford

Published by

Berghahn Books

www.berghahnbooks.com

Turkish-language edition

"Tehcir Ve Taktil." Divan-ı Harb-ı Örfî Zabıtları: Ittihad Ve Terakki'nin Yargılanması 1919-1922
By Vahakn N. Dadrian and Taner Akçam

English-language edition

Library of Congress Cataloging-in-Publication Data

Judgment at Istanbul : the Armenian genocide trials / edited by Vahakn N. Dadrian and Taner Akçam. — English language ed.
p. cm.
Includes bibliographical references and index.
ISBN 978-0-85745-251-1 (hardback : alk. paper) — ISBN 978-0-85745-286-3 (e-book)
1. Trials (Genocide)—Turkey—Istanbul. 2. War crime trials—Turkey—Istanbul. 3. Armenians—Crimes against—Turkey. 4. Armenian massacres, 1915–1923. 5. Genocide—Turkey. 6. Genocide—Armenia. I. Dadrian, Vahakn N. II. Akçam, Taner, 1953–
KKX43.J83 2011
345.566'20251—dc22

2011014734

British Library Cataloguing in Publication Data

A catalogue record for this book is available from the British Library

Printed in the United States on acid-free paper

ISBN 978-0-85745-251-1 (hardback)
ISBN 978-0-85745-286-3 (ebook)

To Hrant Dink:

This book, which you wanted very much to be published, is dedicated to you. Even in your eternal silence, your voice is still heard in the struggle to bring truth, justice, and reconciliation to both our peoples.

CONTENTS

OTTOMAN-TURKISH WORDS AND NAMES

Transcription and Pronunciation of Ottoman-Turkish Words and Names

Letter	English Transcription and Pronunciation
c	*j* as in *jargon*
ç	*ch* as in *church*
ğ	*gh* as in *though*, or *w* as in *sowing*
ı	short *e* as in *often*, or *o* as in *second*
j	*zh* as in *gendarme*
ö	*oe* as in *Goethe*, or *i*, as in *girl*
ş	*sh* as in *shut*
ü	high *u* as in *fortune*
v	*w* as in *weary*
y	*y* as in *young*

Major Abbreviations

CUP	Committee of Union and Progress (Ittihad ve Terakki)
CC	Central Committee (Merkezi Umumi)
S.O.	Special Organization (Teşkilâtı Mahsusa)
T.V.	*Takvim-i Vekâyi* (the official organ of the Ottoman Parliament, special annexes [*Ilâve*] of which served as the legal gazette of the Turkish Military Tribunal court-martialing of the authors of the wartime Armenian deportations and massacres.)

Family Names

Names in parentheses that are inserted following regular, traditional names denote, as a rule, "family" names (*soyadı*) that were adopted by a vast majority of citizens of the Turkish Republic in line with the Law of Family Names enacted on 21 June 1934 (Law no. 2525) and put in effect on 2 July 1934. In other cases, they usually denote nicknames.

Alternative Spellings of Nouns, Names, Cities, and Institutions

Ahmed	Ahmet
Cemal	Djemal
Chamber of Deputies	Assembly
Court sittings	Court sessions
Diyarbekir	Diyarbakır
Ferid	Ferit
Fuad	Fuat
Hamid	Hamit
Mahmud	Mahmut
Mehmed	Mehmet
Meclis-i	Meclisi
Midhad	Midhat
Reşid	Reşit
Senators	Notables
Sıvas	Sivas
Şükrü	Shükrü
Talat	Talaat
Vehib	Vehip
Yozgad	Yozgat

Introduction

Vahakn N. Dadrian and Taner Akçam

The present volume is a study of the World War I Armenian Genocide as documented through the Ottoman Special Military Tribunal's criminal prosecution of the perpetrators involved. The ostensible aim of these post–World War I courts-martial was the exposure and punishment of the organizers of the crime. However, two ancillary considerations were also at play. Wary of the gravity of that crime and the widespread outrage it touched off, the new leaders of the defeated and almost prostrate Ottoman Empire were well disposed to accommodate the victorious Allies, especially the predominant British. Having the Ottoman capital under their control at the time, the Allies proceeded to militarily occupy the capital in March 1920 when a surge of Kemalist nationalism threatened to unhinge their control and thereby obviate their punitive schemes. This development gave new impetus to the prosecutorial vigor of the sitting courts-martial. The other consideration was the postwar Ottoman leaders' acutely felt need to dissociate the Turkish nation from the crime, thereby deflecting the scourge of the attendant mega-stigma. The ensuing series of trials was reflective of this general disposition. As the courts-martial unfolded over nearly three years (1919–1922), the near omnipotent role played in the organization of the genocide by the top leaders of a militarized political party, the Young Turk junta—along with their governmental subalterns—became all too evident. That party was the Ittihad ve Terakki, or the Committee of Union and Progress (henceforth CUP).

As detailed in the main body of this work, the trials did not proceed completely unencumbered. In addition to obstructions by the remaining partisans of the defunct CUP, the emergence and steady ascendancy of insurgent Kemalism was a factor that progressively threatened to undermine the prosecutorial task at hand. As a result, the tribunal gradually lost its effectiveness, especially with respect to the principal task of retributive justice. In other words, the principle of impunity emerged here as a kind of negative reward for the perpetrators, many of whom embraced the emerging nationalist movement and joined its ranks.

In the performance of an equally important task, however, the same military tribunal redeemed itself, notably and consequentially. Namely, it was able to assemble and classify a mass of documentary evidence affording the establishment of the facts of a centrally organized mass murder enacted against the Ottoman Empire's Armenian population. More important, that documentation was rendered both incontestable and verifiable by a distinct legal procedure the tribunal adopted: when on the witness stand, the principal defendants were invited to examine and confirm the authenticity of the many secret and top secret documents bearing their own signatures. Most of these documents had been secured and authenticated during the pretrial investigations by officials from the ministries of Interior and Justice. The authentication formula used was, "it conforms to the original."

In their core element these findings of the courts-martial famously prefigure, in summary form, in the Allies' historical proclamation some four years earlier on 24 May 1915, which had condemned the perpetration of the then ongoing "massacres" and warned "the Ottoman government" of dire consequences. The government was accused of "connivance and often assistance" in the organization of these massacres. More important, these threats subsequently proved instrumental in legally enshrining the international criminal code of "crimes against humanity," which the Allies had embedded in the 24 May proclamation. By incorporating this very formula in the Nuremberg Charter (Article 6c) and in that of Tokyo (Article 5c), the post–World War II prosecutors of Nazi crimes not only gave impetus to the process of its eventual codification within the framework of emerging international criminal law, but at the same time explicitly recognized the historical relevance of the antecedent character of the Armenian case, thereby assigning to it the attribute of a kind of legal precedence in international criminal law.

Throughout modern history that case remained intertwined with the career of the moribund Ottoman Empire. The steady decline and ultimate disintegration of the centuries-old Ottoman Empire at the end of World War I was a process that was intimately connected with the ongoing and turbulent problems besetting that empire in its relations with its ethnically and religiously diverse subject nationalities. These problems reached their apex in the 1912–1913 period, when the armies of Bulgaria, Greece, and Serbia, in a joint military undertaking, decisively defeated the empire's armies. They thereby not only achieved complete independence from their erstwhile rulers, but at the same time also managed to practically end Ottoman-Turkish dominion in Europe.

The resulting shock gripping the Ottoman-Turkish elites was such as to impart to the historically persistent—and at the time especially inflamed—Turko-Armenian conflict an almost existential significance. The European powers' revival of the lingering Armenian Reform issue, coinciding as it did with the massive military debacle in the Balkans, was sufficiently critical for these elites to define the new phase of the conflict as existential indeed. The quest for a radical remedy inevitably ensued, and some argue that the wholesale wartime liquidation of the Armenians became that sought-after radical remedy.

Countless volumes in several languages have been produced about this event; they all deal, however, with the various political aspects of the perpetration itself. The need to examine the problem in a legal-criminal context thus emerges as a pressing one. This study proposes to undertake such an examination in terms of a principal focus. In doing so it will inquire into the specific conditions surrounding the prosecutorial initiative, the trenchant obstacles that needed to be overcome, and most important, the series of verdicts that inevitably ensued.

Owing to the eventual debacle of the regime of the then reigning Ottoman sultan and with it the attenuation of the leverage of these postwar courts-martial, the verdicts associated with this period of decline proved unenforceable. The rise of a new Nationalist regime in Ankara, however, proved debilitating. Nevertheless, these verdicts—along with the Key Indictment, which is suffused with dozens of certified, official legal documents—inherently possess inestimable legal value. Furthermore, as noted above, these criminal legal trials ended up inaugurating a new legal concept in international criminal law—that of "crimes against humanity." This reference to "humanity" was repeatedly used by several Ottoman authorities involved in the prosecution under review here. This legal principle first reached the level of established international criminal law at Nuremberg, as well as Tokyo, when it was embedded in the texts of the respective indictments. In brief, the Istanbul series of criminal prosecutions did mark a legal-criminal milestone by embedding the new term "crimes against humanity" in the corpus of incipient international criminal law.

The foremost significance of this study derives from the fact that unlike previous studies, it systematically utilizes a whole series of original and authenticated Ottoman-Turkish documents dealing with the World War I Armenian deportations and massacres. These are the type of documents that punctuate the foremost significance of the very trial proceedings for which they were sought and purposively marshaled. As a result of these trials, wartime cabinet ministers, Young Turk party chieftains, otherwise identified as CUP potentates, and a number of other accessories inculpated in these crimes were court-martialed by a military tribunal in the 1919–1922 postwar period. Covering thirteen trial cases that are predicated upon such essential primary sources as the texts of the Key Indictment, the respective court records of the series of sittings, and the array of verdicts, these crucial documents are bound to be of considerable help in the task of lifting the fog that continues to obscure the catastrophe of 1915 and the circumstances surrounding it.

It is worth observing in this respect that the most acute problem in Turkey today, as far as this catastrophe is concerned (a catastrophe that domestically, in Turkey, is identified as "the Armenian question" but internationally is known as "genocide") is the near-total ignorance about the existence of these documents. Even though the event in question is almost a hundred years old, certain archives in Turkey that have holdings on this subject are in part still inaccessible to scholars and researchers; a whole series of primary sources either remain unpublished or their whereabouts are unknown. No one knows, for example, the location of the files containing countless pretrial interrogatories and voluminous trial records of the courts-martial. This is the military tribunal whose indictments and pertinent trial proceedings and verdicts—in terms of available copies—are the focus of this study. It is difficult to believe, however, that the missing documents are likely to surface in the foreseeable future, if ever. By the same token, because of the heavy restrictions imposed by Turkey's General Staff authorities, the latter's ATASE archives (Askeri Tarih ve Stratejik Etüt Başkanlığı Arşivi) containing historical material pertinent to this study can hardly be regarded as open and accessible archives.[1]

Another important archive is the Prime Minister's Archive in Istanbul—despite the possibility that during the war and the ensuing armistice it may have been purged extensively. Several recent, very positive changes in the procedures of this archive have met with appreciation from local as well as foreign researchers. However, a major problem persists: thousands of documents and other pieces of evidence are still not classified, and unlike the material lodged in the Interior Ministry's Cipher Office, the pertinent documents are not available in published form. This condition continues to be a very serious obstacle to research.

There is another issue as well: the holdings of foreign archives that deal with this subject are yet to be made available in Turkish. Foremost among these are the German,[2] Austrian,[3] and American[4] archives; next are the Russian,[5] French,[6] and British archives.[7] Containing thousands of incriminating documents about Ottoman authorities—especially CUP, accused of what the judges of the military tribunal termed as centrally organized mass murder by way of "deportations and massacres"—these European and American archives are open and thus are accessible to researchers. Yet readers in Turkey by and large are not even aware of the existence and the wealth of the material they contain. Furthermore, there is a vast literature dealing with topic-specific diplomatic correspondence involving these very same countries. Another important archive that, by reason of its direct bearing on the subject, cannot be viewed as "foreign," is the Dashnak party's Armenian archive in Boston in the US.[8] Until recently, access to that archive was granted only by special permit.

The gravity of the problem that is being confronted here becomes even more evident when the abundance of this material is viewed against the background of a single fact: the negligible, and sometimes even distorted, knowledge that Turkish readers possess on the subject. Equally important is the fact that relevant Turkish academic publications almost completely ignore the rich source-material available outside Turkey. This serious discrepancy points to the origin of the problem: the deficiencies of contemporary historiography in Turkey. It appears that the task of serious research, predicated upon detached inquiry and reliable documents, is significantly compromised owing to the imposition of a state-authorized viewpoint. What is remarkable about this is that typically it is the handiwork of dogmatic state officials, entrenched bureaucrats who, relying on a method of extreme selectivity in the use of domestic sources, are trying to validate this state-authorized viewpoint. This fact bespeaks the gravity of the problem of ideologically tainted historiography, perfunctory observations, notes, and incidental commentaries by some dissident Turkish authors notwithstanding.

The paucity of available period-specific primary sources, and the scattered and disorganized nature of those that are available, are prevailing conditions in Turkey today, posing acute problems that encumber research and discourse. If one tries to subsume all of the relevant facts and knowledge under the label of "a common body of knowledge," the fact remains that such an urgently needed common body on the Turko-Armenian conflict has yet to materialize. Unless the requisite conditions are created for its development toward affording a general dialogue, the gap will not only persist but will also be filled with legends, myths, and tainted speculation. Instead of welcoming a condition attesting to the gradual growth of a healthy body of knowledge and documentation, attended by a parallel growth of serious dialogue, one is presently forced to breathe the suffocating air of partisan strife. It is precisely for this reason that the foremost task of academics engaged in this area of research and scholarship is to offer to the public, in a systematic way, the type of primary sources and related documents that not only afford an analytical approach but also lend themselves to fostering a solid discourse and debate. An important function of such a projected common body of knowledge would be the contribution it could make to the dissipation of the existing Turko-Armenian cleavage. People in general can have a dialogue on issues only when they have access to the material that is necessary to define and comprehend the issues at hand. Otherwise, one may be facing a so-called "dialogue among the deaf," a condition that reflects the contemporary state of Turko-Armenian tensions.

Given this lacuna of tested knowledge, the array of documents and associated facts produced in the 1919–1922 period by the postwar Ottoman courts-martial in connection with the pretrial investigations, as well as the trials themselves, emerge as prima facie evidence and as such are of inestimable value. As noted above, the whereabouts and the fate of the massive volume of pretrial investigative papers and the trial records are unknown. In November 1922, Istanbul, the capital of the Ottoman Empire, passed into the sphere of hegemony of the new government set up in Ankara. There is, therefore, a strong possibility that these court-martial archives of Istanbul's martial law authorities have been transferred for purposes of safekeeping to the jurisdiction of the Chief of General Staff in Ankara. The fact that after a lapse of almost 100 years these archives are still kept secret and thus inaccessible to the public suggests the degree of importance the military authorities seem to attach to their contents.

The court records of the trial proceedings, as can be seen in Chapter 12, cover over sixty cases. The more important ones among these have been published, as "annexes," in *Takvim-i Vekâyi*, the Ottoman parliament's official gazette. As mentioned above, for the first time ever, and for the benefit of the public, many series of trial proceedings, along with the associated sets of documents, are being adduced in this volume as material for legal and historical scholarship. Specifically, these records consist of the transcripts of two separate sets of trials, each comprising fifteen court sittings, and of another set of thirteen trials comprising three sittings for one case, plus ten separate cases of trials, along with copies of verdicts occasionally including evidence of ratification by the sultan. The incidental punishment of some of the perpetrators for ancillary reasons by both CUP and the successor Kemalist regime is treated separately in Chapter 9.

An adequate understanding of the documentary evidence contained in this volume requires an appreciation of the fact of prosecution by a court-martial, and in turn, an understanding of that court-martial itself as a by-product of inordinate historical circumstances. Accordingly, it was decided to prepare a rather extensive introduction in which Vahakn N. Dadrian offers an overview of the period's general political and military atmosphere, a detailed description of trial preparations, an analysis of the court procedures themselves, and a summary of the ensuing series of verdicts. Taner Akçam, having combed through the hitherto totally unexplored Istanbul press dealing with the 1919–1922 period, compiled a detailed list of the trials in question. One can readily infer from this list that in terms of both sheer number and the scope of jurisdiction involved, the trials were quite extensive; as such, they represent one of the period's politically most important but judicially rather constrained undertakings. Moreover, the book confronts and deals with certain objections that have been raised in the past and continue to be raised in the present regarding the general validity of the trials and, hence, of the findings and verdicts themselves. Because the proceedings and the diverse circumstances surrounding them were handled in a number of separate segments of this book, certain repetitions were inevitable.

The first transcription of the relevant texts of the *Takvim-i Vekâyi* issues from Ottoman to modern script was undertaken from 1991–1994 by Hayrettin Aydın as part of a project sponsored by the Hamburg Institute for Social Research. Two expert teams subsequently set up in Ankara and Istanbul examined this first draft of the transcriptions, made some corrections, and added some new transcriptions to take care of the respective missing parts. Moreover, due to Ottoman sentence structure, the sentences are unusually long, and we had to divide them into separate sentences.

The principle of objectivity in science and scholarship is naturally coterminous with the cardinal principle of respect for facts—regardless of the ramifications of these facts and of the identity of the fact-finder. As stated at the beginning of this introduction, this study is almost entirely anchored on original and authenticated documents. The evidence these documents yield is by no means ordinary in nature, but as emphasized above, it is rather a kind of evidence that is legally characterized as "evidence-in-chief." In other words, one is dealing here with what one might call compelling evidence where several paramount attributes converge. Being of wartime origin, for example, they preclude any intrusion of post–World War I politics or even propaganda. As repeatedly emphasized, they all have been authenticated by competent Turkish officials; therefore, they all possess the requisite imprimatur of incontestability. Indeed, as underscored throughout this work, each and every one of the official documents comprising the main corpus of this evidence has been subjected to scrutiny and to the test of double verification. They were first authenticated by Turkish officials of either the Interior or Justice Ministry before being marshaled as prosecutorial evidence. Second, and perhaps even more important, during the trials the defendants were afforded a chance to examine documents bearing their own signatures, and in the end to verify their authenticity—a rare latitude, if not privilege, extended to defendants in a court-martial proceeding. These are conditions that not only attest to the legal establishment of the fact of the wartime capital crime, but also by the same token effectively invalidate its denial in any form or manner. Meanwhile, this study invites analysis that may be undertaken jointly with those scholars who, for one reason or another, tend to persist in their denial or in their equivocations but nevertheless are willing to have their denials subjected to critical scrutiny.

However, as the crime in question inevitably has manifold consequences, the fact remains that its denial is no less consequential. As was pointed out at the outset, for a variety of reasons the legal establishment of the fact of the Armenian Genocide did not produce a measure of retributive justice that, in scope and severity, would be commensurate with the magnitude of the crime. Addressing this problem, an American author recently went so far as to declare that "[t]he Constantinople (Istanbul) war crimes trials, had they not fallen apart, would have been remembered as comparable only to Nuremberg and Tokyo."[9] Another author deplored the fact that "this first tentative step toward defining and punishing genocide failed because of Turkish nationalism and Allied indifference."[10] Going one step further, he and the noted legal scholar C.M. Bassiouni attributed the perpetration on a larger scale of many of the subsequent cases of state-organized mass murders to the relative abortiveness of the Turkish courts-martial.[11]

To conclude, denial emerges here as a potent by-product of impunity. This is a form of negative reward that for decades has been accruing to the perpetrators. When transposed to the domain of the precepts of law and legality, however, the ultimate benefits of such denialism are seen as readily jettisoned. As Frederick Pollock, the noted British expert on international law, observed when commenting on the atrocities committed during World War I: "Law does not cease to exist because it is broken or even broken on a large scale."[12]

Acknowledgments

The authors would like to express their thanks to the Zoryan Institute and its President, K. M. Greg Sarkissian, for the institute's support and assistance in the translation, editing, and publishing of this book. The typing of the manuscript, including multitudes of cumbersome Ottoman texts, was initially carried out by Narreh Ghazarians, and continued diligently by Narini Badalian, and Patil Halajian, all three administrative assistants at the Zoryan Institute. Many sincere thanks go to Prof. Maria Frangos, University of California, Santa Cruz, who assisted with the editing of the manuscript. Special thanks are due to George Shirinian, Executive Director of the Zoryan Institute, who edited the manuscript and oversaw the technical details of its preparation. Finally, we extend our thanks to Berghahn Books, which was meticulous in the copyediting of a complex manuscript.

Notes

1. These restrictions are clearly intended to exercise strict supervision and control over who may do research in these archives. The fact that these archives do not have a standard application form is in itself a prime method of such control. Any scholar who wants to do research there is obligated to fill out the same application form the General Staff requires of its own personnel. Scholars are forced to answer tens of questions that have nothing to do with their research, including the question whether any of the applicant's relatives were ever convicted in a court of law. The failure to see a difference between a scholar-applicant, on the one hand, and a General Staff employee, on the other, is not only an exceedingly bizarre aspect of the procedure but also a condition that raises serious doubts about its purpose of service to scientific inquiry and knowledge. Moreover, it is a known fact that even when permission for research is granted, the final determination whether a requested document is in line with the scholar's indicated area of research is made by archive personnel.
2. A significant part of the German archives can be accessed, in German entirely and partly in English via http://www.armenocide.net. Moreover, Wolfgang Gust, with an extensive introduction, has published a sizeable portion of these documents in *Der*

Völkermord an den Armeniern 1915/16: Dokumente aus dem Politischen Archiv des deutschen Auswärtigen Amts (Springe: Klampen, 2005).

3. A substantial part of the Austrian archives, comprising some twelve volumes, has been published by Artem Ohandjanian, *Österreich-Armenien 1872–1936: Faksimiliesammlung Diplomatisher Aktenstücke* (Vienna: Ohandjanian,, 1995). Using a broad perspective, the author offers a wide array of documents, thereby illuminating some of the more obscure aspects of the Armenian Question.
4. The US archives, which are readily accessible even via the Internet, have been published through two separate venues. One is Ara Sarafian, *United States Official Records on the Armenian Genocide 1915–1917* (Princeton and London: Gomidas Institute, 2004). The other venue involves 396 microfiches, each comprising some 100 documents that Rouben Adalian gathered and compiled in *The Armenian Genocide in the U.S. Archives, 1915–1918* (Alexandria, VA: Chadwyck-Healey, 1994).
5. The holdings of Russian archives consist mainly of accounts that Armenian survivors provided, and of reports and observations that Russian commanders supplied during the years of occupation of Eastern Turkey, 1916–1917. Unfortunately this very rich material has yet to appear in print in a systematic way.
6. There exists a collection of period-specific diplomatic reports and additionally a selection of pertinent documents in Arthur Beylerian, *Les Grandes puissances, l'Empire Ottoman et les Arméniens dans les archives françaises* (1914–1918), (Paris: Universite de Paris I, Panthéon-Sorbonne, 1983).
7. The period-specific documents are being systematically published by Ara Sarafian. The volume identified as the "Blue Book" tops the list: James Bryce and Arnold Toynbee, eds., *The Treatment of the Armenians in the Ottoman Empire, 1915–1916* (Princeton, NJ: Gomidas, 2000), documents presented by Viscount Grey of Fallodon by Viscount Bryce, with a preface by Ara Sarafian, and uncensored originals of the documents. This work also appeared as a two-volume set in Turkish: James Bryce and Arnold Toynbee, *Osmanlı Imparatorluğu'nda Ermenilere Yönelik Muamele 1915–16,* with prefaces by Ayhan Aktar and Taner Akçam (Istanbul: Pencere, 2005). It should be noted that most of the documents contained in this volume are not British documents but rather US diplomatic reports and testimonies by missionaries. If one disregards Vartkes Yeghiayan's *British Foreign Office Dossiers on Turkish War Criminals* (Pasadena, CA: American Armenian International College, 1991), a work with some serious factual errors, there has yet to emerge a systematic compilation of post-1918 British documents that constitute an important source on the subject under review.
8. Because of faulty knowledge, there exists in the press and in the public mind a conviction, promoted by politicians, especially by Prime Minister Tayyip Erdoğan, that "Armenian archives are closed." It is necessary to understand that there is not, nor can there be, an archive in Armenia holding direct evidence and documents on the events of 1915. The fact is that these events predate the establishment of an Armenian state entity possessing requisite state archives. As noted above, Boston's Dashnak archive operates on the basis of restrictive access. As to the other holdings of Armenia's state archives, they are open to researchers.
9. Gary J. Bass, *Stay the Hand of Vengeance: The Politics of War Crimes Tribunals* (Princeton, NJ: Princeton University Press, 2000), p. 106.
10. James F. Willis, *Prologue to Nuremberg: The Politics and Diplomacy of Punishing War Criminals of the First World War* (Westport, CT: Greenwood Press, 1982), p. 163.

11. Ibid.; C. M. Bassiouni, "The Time has Come for an International Criminal Court," *Indiana International and Comparative Law Review* 9, no. 1 (Spring 1991): 2–4; idem, "The Normative Framework of International Humanitarian Law: Overlaps, Gaps and Ambiguities," *Transactional Law and Comparative Problems* 8, no. 2 (Fall 1998): 204.
12. Quoted in James W. Garner, *International Law and the World War*, vol. 2 (London: Longmans, Green and Co., 1920), pp. 483–501.

PART I

The Conditions Surrounding the Trials

CHAPTER 1

History of the Turko-Armenian Conflict

Vahakn N. Dadrian

Even though this study has a legal-criminological framework and thus a rather narrow focus, its extralegal underpinnings and ramifications nevertheless require a broad perspective. A proper definition of the term "genocide" is necessary to such a perspective. Presently that definition is anchored in four basic determinants. Genocide presupposes:

1. A protracted perpetrator-victim conflict that has a history and that persists in defying a resolution.
2. A substantial disparity in power relations between perpetrator and victim, yielding the correlative victim vulnerability factor.
3. The opportunity factor: even a most adept criminal must know how to bide his time until the moment when a suitable opportunity presents itself. This is the foremost condition—in fact precondition—for eventual success. The operative formula for such success is minimum risk for optimum result. Wars, especially global wars, do afford such opportunities, as attested by the spectacular success of two of the twentieth century's three major genocides, the Armenian and the Jewish.
4. The drive for a radical resolution of the lingering conflict reaches its climactic and terminal stage by the eradication of the targeted victim group through the actual act of genocide.

Within this framework, a brief review of the historical antecedents of this Turko-Armenian conflict is in order. Such a review will inevitably have to reflect the theocratic underpinnings of the Ottoman Empire and the Islamic thrust of that theocracy. As discussed in the main body of this study, the religiously dogmatic and imperious denial of the right of equality to the non-Muslim subjects of the empire rendered that empire ripe for perennial conflicts. This was due in part to Islamic theocracy but to an equal degree to another totally different and totally disconnected condition: demography. Half of the population of the empire consisted of a plethora of non-Muslim subject nationalities, almost all of them Christians of various denominations. Their statutory inferiority, which was dictated by the canon laws of Islam, led to a host of legal inequalities and the consequent social practices of prejudice and discrimination. In brief, demography clashed with religion, thereby producing unabating domestic conflicts. In time these conflicts transformed themselves into international conflicts as European powers intermittently intervened in attempts to protect their coreligionists, who were suffering from bouts of prosecution that often degenerated into serial massacres.

The end result of all these conflagrations was that the subject nationalities in the Balkan Peninsula eventually managed to emancipate themselves from Ottoman-Turkish dominion. The decisive factor in this series of emancipatory movements was, however, the factor of external—specifically European—intervention, as well as active European political and occasionally military support. In a belated and almost desperate effort to emulate the emancipatory initiatives of these European nationalities, some of the political leaders of the Ottoman Empire's Armenian population decided to likewise adopt revolutionary goals and tactics. But they failed disastrously, mainly if not only because, unlike their European counterparts, they had absolutely no effective external support. This total absence of external patronage not only produced repeated failures but, most critical for the destiny of the entire people, also produced repeated calamities. Fully aware of the abiding vulnerability of these Armenians, the Ottoman-Turkish authorities pounced upon them again and again with a vengeance. It seemed that all the cumulative bitterness and frustration associated with the woes of a steadily declining empire were being discharged and channeled into deadly outbursts against the discontented but highly vulnerable Armenians. The Armenian Reform movement, which had succeeded the Armenian Revolutionary movement, became the catalyst, and the Ottoman Empire's Armenian population at large was consequently reduced to the status of a perennial shock absorber. The shocks would only increase in scope and intensity.

With the outbreak of World War I, the Turko-Armenian conflict reached its apogee due to the February 1914 Reform Accord that was finally imposed upon Turkey by the combined exertions of the European powers—Germany and Russia in particular. The contemporary reactions of CUP leaders leave no doubt that this particular episode was the critical turning point in the steady escalation of the Turko-Armenian conflict. This Reform Accord provided not only the institutional changes ensuring actual equality for the Armenian subjects, but also a faint degree of local autonomy that infuriated these CUP leaders and at the same time filled them with anxiety about the future ramifications of the statutory changes. At this very juncture of political development, the die was cast for the Armenians. Utterly resolved to prevent a repetition of the Balkan Syndrome—i.e., the road to projected independence via equal rights, semi-autonomy, and autonomy—CUP authorities systematically proceeded to pave the ground for a radical solution to the problem. Radicalism meant the adoption of the Hamidian formula: to solve the Armenian question by way of eliminating the Armenians themselves.

The outbreak of world war was deemed to be the long-awaited ideal opportunity for this endeavor. In stages, starting with the military conscription of most able-bodied Armenian men, the Armenian population of the empire was completely uprooted, dislocated, deported, and through attendant massive massacres all but eliminated. The exigencies of war and warfare provided all the requisite opportunities to consummate this end. The military, with all its organizational resources, executive discipline, and proficiency, served as the mainstay of the lethal enterprise. The same war context was utilized by the ruling CUP leadership to effect the release of thousands of convicts from the various prisons of the empire—all for massacre duty.

The vastness and intensity of this exterminatory undertaking is matched and even exceeded by the singular boldness attending it. And in examining the conditions underlying this boldness, one's attention is drawn to the contagiousness of the successes of previous Armenian massacres, such as those identified with the regime of Sultan Abdulhamit II. What stands out throughout these past episodes of massacres is the constancy, and hence the predictability, of impunity accruing to the whole gamut of organizers, supervisors, and implementers of these serial massacres. As a rule, such impunity serves to embolden the perpetrators not only to deny their crimes, and deny them vehemently when needed, but also to seriously consider repeat performances when challenged, provoked, or otherwise motivated. It is, therefore, almost impossible to fully understand the World War I Armenian Genocide without fully taking into account the cumulative history of impunity attending the episodes of Armenian massacres perpetrated in the decades preceding World War I.

It is worth observing that when responding to the calamity of the wartime Armenian experience, Winston Churchill, the foremost contemporary British statesman, did not limit himself to merely castigating the mass murder in question in terms that in contemporary legal language are coterminous with "genocide." He used, for example, such language as "a crime" resulting from a "deliberate policy" that "was planned and executed," with the result that "the clearance of a race from Asia Minor was about as complete as such an act on a scale so great, could well be." At the operational level, however, Churchill, in "a final attempt to break through Turkish defenses at the Dardanelles," ventured to offer to the War Cabinet an inordinate plan that is rarely mentioned, much less discussed, in history books. Namely, he proposed to the Cabinet in December 1915 that poison gas be used against the Turkish defenders, in part in retaliation for "the massacre of Armenians" that was then still going on.[1]

The present study explores the World War I Armenian Genocide in a particularly significant legal context, namely, prosecution through legally validated documentation. This significant context is further accentuated by several other aspects. For the first time in modern Ottoman-Turkish history, for example, the highest-ranking governmental and ruling party authorities were subjected to criminal prosecution. Likewise, for the first time Armenian victims of centrally organized massacres were legally represented by Ottoman Turkish authorities bent on punishing the perpetrators. For the first time also, multitudes of Turks, civilian and military, of all ranks and stations of life, volunteered to publicly testify on behalf of the Armenian victims, in the process putting themselves at great risk. Notwithstanding these individuals' contributions, the successive courts-martial in charge of the criminal prosecution, when reaching and framing the series of verdicts, relied mostly on authenticated wartime official documents, only occasionally taking into account courtroom testimony. This fact alone imparts to the proceedings, and especially to the verdicts, inordinate substance and value, the more so since each one of the documents had two particular attributes. First, as noted in the Introduction, every one of them was examined and authenticated by competent officials, most of them holdover partisans of the defamed CUP regime attached to the Ministries of Justice and Interior; they then would affix on top or at the bottom of each document the formula "It conforms to the original" (*aslına muafıkdır*). Second, in nearly all cases the defendants were asked to examine the documents bearing their signatures and verify their authenticity. This iron-clad procedure of document verification by the defendants themselves renders these courts-martial an invaluable source of historical scholarship, above and beyond their legal-criminal import.

Transcending these confines of domestic penal law, however, are the broader parameters of emerging international criminal law that form the general framework of this study. As noted in the main body of this work, in the immediate aftermath of the war, the highest authorities identified with the postwar Ottoman government raised their voices to severely condemn the wartime treatment of the Armenians. In doing so, they remarkably used the term "crimes against humanity." The sultan, the supreme Ottoman-Turkish authority, for example, used exactly these words when denouncing the crime (*kanuni insaniyete karşı ika edilen ceraim*). When introducing a motion in the parliament to launch an investigation of the crimes committed during the war, Deputy Fuad, referring to the atrocities involved, invoked in the parliament the principle of "the rules of humanity" (*kavaidi insaniye*). And the preeminent Ottoman statesman Reşit Akif, the first postwar president of the Council of State, a supreme judicial organ, in a speech in the Senate on 21 November 1918, likewise invoked "the world's sense of humanity" (*cihani insaniyeti*) when decrying the massacres perpetrated against the Armenians. Moreover, in the Yozgat court-martial verdict, the condemned perpetrators of the Armenian massacres were accused of having violated the principle of "human sentiment" (*hissiyatı insaniye*).

This principle of international law came into special prominence on 24 May 1915, when the Allies—Great Britain, France, and Russia—jointly warned Ottoman Turkey about the legal criminal consequences of the ongoing wartime massacres against the Armenians. In doing so they introduced, and thus promulgated for the first time as a general principle of law, the term "crimes against humanity." Equally significant, this norm of "crimes against humanity," with a special reference to the Armenian case, was embedded as a legal precedent in Article 6 (c) of the Nuremberg Charter and Article 5 (c) of the Tokyo Charter. Moreover, Article II of the Control Council Law No. 10, applied to Germany under occupation, stipulates also "crimes against humanity" as a basis for prosecution against individual Nazis.

The Commission of 15—the post–World War I Sub-Commission III on the Responsibility for the Violation of the Laws and Customs of War—made a reference in its final report of 29 March 1919 to the "customs of war, laws of humanity, and clear dictates of humanity." In doing so it embraced the so-called Martens clause, which had become part of the Preamble of the 1907 Hague Convention IV, formally introducing for the first time the norm of "laws of humanity" to be applied to civilian populations trapped in the vortex of warfare.

The significance of these initiatives ushering in a new principle of international criminal law is that they exude a transnational or universal ethos in the application of criminal justice, which, as will be seen later, was administered strictly in terms of a subtext of Ottoman national, rather than international, penal codes. By doing so they helped set the broader parameters of such justice: what stands out here is that all three branches of the Ottoman government, the executive, legislative, and judicial, configure in this unique resolve to prosecute and punish the perpetrators involved. Equally significant, these international legal initiatives, providing for a new set of principles of criminal law—ones that target state and governmental officials and that essentially emerged in connection with the Armenian Genocide—in which war crimes, crimes against humanity, and genocide are inextricably entwined, also signal the prosecution of that genocide as a telling precedent for Nuremberg.

Apart from defining justice and to some extent even exercising a measure of punitive justice (though without actually delivering the requisite justice), these legal proceedings stand as the most formidable bulwark against all attempts at denial, irrespective of their persistence and state-sponsored arrangements of institutionalization. The array of attested documents, showcasing the magnitude of the crime, is in this sense the most potent antidote against such denial. The paramount fact is that a crime does not dissipate or disappear because it is denied, or even because it is denied for a long time by some individuals or entities identified with the perpetrator camp. Remarkably, the deniers themselves, often entrapped in the vortex of the turbulence of the crime, unwittingly end up attesting to that crime, thereby rendering any subsequent denials not only specious but even more incriminating. A recently uncovered official wartime Ottoman document punctuates this fact, albeit in veiled language. In the thick of the criminal operations, Talaat, the principal taskmaster, is quoted as saying, "the aim of the Armenian deportations is the final solution of the Armenian Question" (*Ermeni meselenin suret-i katiyede halli*).[2]

Notes

1. Winston Churchill, *The World Crisis: The Aftermath.* Vol. 5 (London: Thornton Butterworth Ltd., 1929), p. 405.
2. Interior Ministry Archives, D.H. Cipher Office, SFR File 54.426, 13 July 1915 report.

CHAPTER 2

Military Defeat and the Victors' Drive for Punitive Justice

Vahakn N. Dadrian

External Pressures: The Imposing Will of the Victors

Within days after signing the Armistice Agreement with Turkish authorities on 30 October 1918, the victorious Allies, led by the British, entered Istanbul, the capital of the then militarily defeated Ottoman Empire, whose leaders had sued for cessation of hostilities and for an armistice. Even though the terms of the armistice were not as harsh as might be expected, the anxiety enveloping a succession of postwar Turkish governments was considerable, relative to the final terms of the impending peace treaty. That anxiety was shared by large segments of the Turkish public. The dire conditions of the postwar economy and the political despair accompanying it further aggravated this condition of general malaise. But superseding all this was a more pervasive anxiety that had a specific reference to postwar punitive justice. The uncertainty of the specific conditions of postwar reckoning to be imposed by the Allies gripped both the government and Turkish society at large with apprehension. The problems involved both external and domestic liabilities.

Externally, the liability pertained to the Ottoman Empire's daring act of joining the Central powers, which were opposed by the Entente powers. That recklessness stems from the manner by which the empire entered World War I—by a preemptive attack in the Black Sea against Russian warships and coastal installations, with the encouragement of and active naval support from Imperial Germany. The gravity of this act of aggression was particularly compounded during the war, when thousands of British prisoners were reportedly mistreated and often terribly abused, causing substantial casualties. Acutely aware of the ramifications of this fact, Winston Churchill described Turkey (as was customary then, many others, like Churchill, used Turkey as an alternative to "Ottoman"[1]) as being "under the spell of defeat, and of deserved defeat." And British Foreign Minister Lord Curzon denounced Turkey as "a culprit awaiting sentence."[2]

Far more consequential, however, were the problems surrounding the wartime deportations and wholesale massacres of the Armenians of the empire.

The ever-growing body of revelations concerning the scope, intensity, and consequences of the mass murder in question accented the imagery of culpability noted above. That portrayal acquired special significance when placed in a historical context; the Ottoman Empire's past record of Armenian massacres—for example the massacres of the era of Sultan Abdulhamit II (1894–1896)—were thus cast in relief. Lloyd George, wartime prime minister of Great Britain (1916–1922), mercilessly gave expression to that imagery when denouncing the Turks as "a human cancer, a creeping agony in the flesh of the lands which they misgovern … a long record of infamy against humanity."[3] Indeed, long after the war ended, public opinion in Europe and especially in the United States was agitated by unending tales of atrocities that detailed the horrors of the Armenian massacres. The *New York Times* alone published 194 news articles on the subject, 70 percent of which appeared in the first four pages.[4]

The impact of such universal concern and consternation over the wartime treatment of the Armenians was quite evident in the emerging attitudes of many postwar politicians and officials. In a sense, these attitudes were significantly conditioned by the widespread revulsion emerging in worldwide public opinion. This universal public opinion would soon find expression in an array of organizational activities involving relief, philanthropy, political activism, and compilation of data on the atrocities involved. The following brief portrayal by Churchill sums up the picture:

> The earlier miseries and massacres of the Armenians have been made familiar to the British people, and indeed to the Liberal world, by the fame and eloquence of Mr. Gladstone … the Armenians and their tribulations were well known throughout England and the United States. This field of interest was lightened by the lamps of religion, philanthropy and politics. Atrocities perpetrated upon Armenians stirred the ire of simple and chivalrous men and women spread widely about the English-speaking world.[5]

Given its power, wealth, and resources, the United States became a critical factor for Ottoman politicians trying to reckon with and cope with these developments. The active intervention of US President Woodrow Wilson in the war and in subsequent peace negotiations, epitomized by his famous Fourteen Points, served to impart added value to public opinion in the US. Postwar Ottoman authorities could ill afford to ignore or minimize the significance of such opinion. In fact the tremendous surge of sympathy and compassion for "martyred Armenia" found dramatic expression in a host of public initiatives, which in terms of their thrust, weightiness, and extent were unprecedented in US history. The widespread grassroots movement was supported by 20,000 Protestant and Catholic churches, 40 governors, a cardinal, 85 bishops, and 250 university and college presidents, including Harvard's Charles Eliot, Chicago's Harry Pratt Judson, Princeton's John Grier Hibben, Catholic University of America's Bishop Thomas J. Shahin, and University of Michigan's James Rowland Angell. In the arena of national and international politics, the movement was endorsed by such American luminaries as three former ambassadors to the Ottoman Empire, namely, Oscar Straus, Henry Morgenthau, and Abram Elkus; J. W. Gerard, wartime ambassador to Germany, likewise actively supported that movement. In addition, Charles Evans Hughes, who later became secretary of state and chief justice of the US Supreme Court, General Leonard Wood, Labor leader Samuel Gompers, and Rabbi Wise joined the ranks of this burgeoning pro-Armenian movement. It eventually culminated in a fundraising campaign that netted some 115 million dollars—a vast sum of money for that period.[6]

Perhaps the most potent sources that energized American public opinion in support of Armenia by disseminating concrete and heartrending evidence on the wartime mass murder of the Armenians were two publications bearing the stamp of two high-ranking American officials. In 1918, the above-cited Ambassador Henry Morgenthau published a book that was more or less a compact reproduction of the daily entries of his wartime journal. In it he detailed the specifics of the Armenian Genocide, to which he bore witness while on ambassadorial duty in the Ottoman capital. An important chapter in that book was titled "The Murder of a Nation."[7] His wartime "confidential" and "secret" reports to Washington exactly mirror the data contained in both the diary and the book. In one of his reports, dated 18 November 1915 and marked "Private and Confidential," Morgenthau describes the war as "a great opportunity to put into effect their long cherished plan of exterminating the Armenian race."[8] His successor, Abram Elkus, likewise reported to Washington about "the continuation of massacres" and "the unchecked policy of extermination" applied against the Armenians.[9]

Major General James Harbord, wartime US Chief of General Staff and the head of the American "Mission to Armenia," a fact-finding mission, in the final report of 16 October 1919 submitted to the US Congress, stated, among other things, "Mutilation, violation, torture and death have left their haunting memories in a hundred beautiful Armenian Valleys … the evidence of the most colossal crime of all the ages."[10]

Fully cognizant of the pitfalls inherent in these damning revelations made by high-ranking American officials well acquainted with the facts on the ground, postwar Turkish authorities were becoming increasingly eager to placate the victors by recourse to criminal proceedings against the organizers and perpetrators of the Armenian Genocide. Clearly, the underlying main purpose was to create a semblance of judiciousness complete with pomp and circumstance but with little concern for genuine retributive justice. Aware of the prevalence of this fundamental motivation, US High Commissioner Lewis Heck felt compelled to admonish these authorities about the need to substitute the ideals of supreme justice for political expediency. He explicitly warned them not to pursue justice for the sake of relief and mitigation of the severity of the impending peace terms they expected the victorious Allies to impose upon them.[11] In fact, British High Commissioner Vice Admiral Sir S. A. Gough Calthorpe had warned the Ottoman foreign minister that "His Majesty's Government are resolved to have proper punishment inflicted on those responsible for Armenian massacres."[12] Ten days later, on 28 January 1919, Calthorpe wired London as follows: "It was pointed out to the [Ottoman] Government that when [the] massacres became known in England, British Statesmen had promised [the] civilized world that persons connected would be held personally responsible and that it was [the] firm intention of H. M. Government to fulfill [that] promise."[13] The Ottoman stance in favor of a less stern treatment at the peace conference was grounded on the argument that the Turkish nation could not be held responsible for the wartime crimes of a political party and the government it controlled.[14]

The Allies, however, at the very inception of the Armenian Genocide initiative on 24 May 1915, had solemnly declared that the massacres were being carried out with "the connivance and often assistance of Ottoman authorities." They then declared, "In view of these new crimes of Turkey against humanity … the Allied governments announce publicly … that they will hold personally responsible … all the members of the Ottoman government and those of their agents who are implicated in such massacres."[15] This declaration was noteworthy in several respects: it was a public and a joint commitment to prosecute, after the war, those responsible for the crimes perpetrated; it acknowledged the complicity of Ottoman authorities in terms of their "connivance and often assistance"; it acknowledged the historical legacy involving an established record of past massacres; it created a new framework of international criminal law by ushering in the codification of the legal norm of "crimes against humanity," the concept that was later to serve as a legal yardstick to prosecute, under an emerging international law, the top strata of Nazi leadership at Nuremberg;[16] it was fully embraced by the United Nations, forming the preamble of its Convention on the Prevention and Punishment of Genocide (9 December 1948).

Yet Turkish military defeat, like almost any other military defeat, had even greater ramifications domestically. On top of all other difficulties and crises, the problem of filling the gap that fugitive and residual wartime leaders had created needed to be addressed with dispatch and effectiveness. All kinds of maneuvers and jockeying for leadership positions, blame-targeting, settling old scores, and not least the quest for remedies and recovery were factors animating the ambitions of a whole gamut of politicians, publicists, and educators. What follows is an exploration of the problems resulting from this overall condition as they impinged upon the arch problem: namely, the handling of the matter of criminally prosecuting and punishing the authors of the Armenian Genocide.

The Outcry and Agitation of the Ottoman-Turkish Press

Human experiences usually acquire meaning through the way they are interpreted and defined by those experiencing them. This is the essence of what social psychologists call the theory of "symbolic interaction." In other words, responses to certain human experiences are shaped by the manner in which they are interpreted and are accordingly assigned a meaning. Ottoman-Turkish military defeat was not any ordinary defeat, as noted above. It was preceded by four years of warfare that had acquired an existential character and entailed inordinate hardships, deprivations, and losses. It was also a crippling blow to the proverbial Ottoman pride, which had been forged through centuries of martial tradition involving a legacy of military successes and attendant glory. The resulting sense of despair was exceeded only by the paralyzing sense of overall national humiliation, which the manifest presence of the combined might of the victors in and around the Ottoman capital rendered especially exacerbating. Ill-prepared for the consequences of such a major debacle, Ottomans in different stations of life responded differently. This was most evident in the declarations some leading figures in national political life made in the wake of that defeat. But underlying all those declarations was not only a sense of resignation to defeat but also a pervasive sense of guilt. The massive calamity of the wartime Armenian Genocide beset most of these people even as they were trying to cope with the apprehension issuing from the overall consequences of defeat.

It is under such circumstances that people in general are least inclined to indulge in the vagaries of denialism. Compunction is, more often than not, an attribute of those who are defeated, impotent, or weak and therefore devoid of the motivation or the resources to exercise denialism. In this sense one might even suggest that the overall political climate in Turkey immediately after the end of the war was not much different from that of Nazi Germany in the aftermath of World War II. This state of mind typically was evident in the attitude of wartime Ottoman-Turkish omnipotent leader Talaat, the architect of the Armenian Genocide. A few days before his flight to Germany at the end of the war he had an exchange with wartime naval hero Rauf Orbay, who described him as dejected, adding, "For the first time I saw him in a condition of despair." In that meeting Talaat conceded that multitudes of innocent Armenians had fallen victim to the "evil deeds" of provincial authorities about which, he pleaded, he had little knowledge. "Having admitted this," he went on to say, "I find it unconscionable to blame me and other high ranking governmental officials for having failed to prevent these atrocities.... Rest assured, and I confess that I am deeply saddened and pained that we failed to prevent the murder of these Armenians who had no involvement in rebellious activities."[17] Such a display of belated chagrin and remorse is not only a function of defeat and impotence, but it is also adaptive in that it tries to cope with that condition by way of identifying with a category of victims he maintains were innocent. In other words, it is a post-crime attempt at exhibiting a measure of humanity.

Other national leaders, ostensibly less implicated in the crime, or not implicated at all, relied on other forms of coping. Mustafa Kemal Atatürk, for example, denounced the mass murder of the Armenians as a "scandal," a "lowly act" (*fezahat*),[18] while an editorial in a newspaper he had cofounded with a cohort likewise condemned "the massacre against the Armenians" (Ermeni milletine karşı ... kırmak sevdası).[19] Another national leader who helped Atatürk usher in and establish the Republic of Turkey, Ismet Inönü, gave expression to his despair by declaring (on 29 November 1918) that he "would want to retire to the country and become a farmer, for everything is lost, is ruined ... it is hopeless ... our tragedy actually comes from within ... all are against us ... we will be liquidated"[20] (her şey mahvoldu ... hiç bir ümidim kalmadı ... asıl felâket bizim içimizden ... artık bize her şey düşman ... tasfiye yapacaklar tasfiye).

This pervasive atmosphere of gloom and doom was dramatically accented by the carefully organized, stealthy escape from Istanbul that was successfully carried out, with the help of the German military, by the seven top leaders of the ruling CUP. After elaborate but highly secretive preparations they fled around midnight on 1 November 1918 aboard the destroyer *RI*, a captured Russian warship that took them to the port city of Odessa on the Black Sea following a number of diversionary movements and the use of decoys. The seven fugitives included the ruling triumvir Mehmet Talaat, Ismail Enver, and Ahmet Cemal, plus two physicians, Bahaeddin Şakir and Mehmet Nazım, and the chiefs of Police Directorate and Public Security, Osman Bedri and Hüseyin Azmi, respectively.[21] With the exception of Cemal, they all were held to be the principal perpetrators of the crime under review. This problem of complicity was conceded by Talaat himself, who hours before the flight expressly spoke of "the burden of responsibility" relative to the wartime massacres; haunted by them, the fugitives were merely fleeing from them.[22] Moreover, CUP Secretary-General Midhat Şükrü, to whom Talaat had made the statement, concurred in a subsequent exchange with CUP leader, editor, and publicist Hüseyin Cahid. Sükrü stated the opinion that the escape of the seven meant that the fugitives "were admitting the truth of the accusations of complicity which their very escape served to certify them" (iftiraları kabul edip onaylamak).[23] Almost all of these suspects eventually ended up in Berlin, Germany, whose government at that time, claiming legal obstacles, steadfastly refused to surrender them, especially Talaat, to the postwar Turkish authorities. As then Foreign Minister

Wilhelm Solf retorted, "Talaat stuck with us faithfully, and our country remains open to him."[24]

However, the escape, and particularly the utmost secretiveness with which it was executed, provoked great dismay and anger among several segments of the public. Particularly agitated were those who had opposed the vanquished regime and as a result had endured various hardships, including incarceration and exile. This consternation was often entwined with elements of contempt, because the escape was generally defined as an act of damnable cowardice. All this reinforced the common resolve to identify the fugitive CUP leaders with wartime crimes and the attendant sense of urgency to prevent further similar escapes. The publicity generated by the press played a major role in galvanizing this sense of urgency. Many of the newspapers involved were entirely new outfits; others were well-established publications. Their near-uniform condemnation of the fugitive CUP chieftains stood in stark contrast to their wartime attitudes—which at best may be termed as deafening silence, and at worst, endorsement—with regard to the then unfolding genocide.

Prominent publicist Ahmet Emin (Yalman) explained the silence: "It was impossible to criticize the war-oriented policy … we couldn't in any conceivable way utter a word on such matters as the Armenian deportations. Nobody dared to oppose the modus operandi of CUP."[25] For his part, the equally prominent CUP partisan and advocate Yunus Nadi, who subsequently became an ardent Kemalist, in an editorial published near the completion of the wartime genocidal operations against the Armenians, wrote: "the policy of multiethnic harmony in the Ottoman Empire had become bankrupt and is now finished, and the era of cleaning up [*Säuberung* in German translation] has begun."[26] Now, however, the same Yunus Nadi, in the wake of the flight of his cohorts, wrote in another editorial the following: "For four years the country had to endure the nightmare, imposed on it by 3–5 people, thereby experiencing so many troubles. We can barely contain ourselves from seeing these fugitives off with our curse accompanying them. With apprehension, disgust and shudder are we now face to face with a CUP whose reputation they have soiled with their own hands."[27] Five days later in another editorial, he went one step further when approving the legal proceedings against the same men charged with the crime of "deportations and massacres."[28]

In many respects the array of the accusations and assaults hurled against the fugitive CUP chieftains by the Turkish-language press immediately at the end of the war was a measure of aggressiveness born out of immense frustration. Crushing defeat and the manifold apprehensions associated with it emboldened this press; with hardly any exception, the newspapers involved pounced at them. As British Rear Admiral and Deputy High Commissioner at Istanbul Richard Webb wired to the then British Foreign Secretary Arthur James Balfour, "There is hardly an organ of the press which is not vehemently attacking those men … for their share in the massacres."[29] These denunciations, their amplitude and forcefulness, attested to the reality of the grim aftereffects of the just-completed genocide; at the same time they also cast in stark relief the avalanche of subsequent denials of the crime by successive generations and authorities. Given the inordinate significance of this fact, a review of the components of this press and its campaign against the perpetrators is in order. Initially the bulk of the newspapers were decisively in the anti-CUP camp. Foremost among these were the following:

1. *Sabah* (Morning), a morning paper, was the voice of the anti-CUP opposition Itilaf party, run by editor Ali Kemal with the help of Dr. Riza Tevfik. In December 1919 it merged with *Peyam,* thus becoming *Peyam-Sabah.*
2. *Alemdar* (Standard Bearer) started publication on 15 December 1918. It was run by the virulently anti-CUP editor Refi Cevad, the son of Ankara province's postwar governor-general (*vali*) Ali Muhiddin Paşa. While occupying the post of *mutasarrif* of Yozgat during World War I, the latter had opposed the massacres there and consequently was soon thereafter forced into early retirement. It was shut down by the censors for six days, 6–12 February 1919.
3. *Hadisat* (Events) was edited by Süleyman Nazıf, a statesman and literary figure, and Cenab Şahabeddin, a poet and writer, both pronounced opponents of CUP; it started publication in October 1918.
4. *Ileri* (Forward) was launched in 1918 with the name of *Ati* (Future); it became *Ileri* on 11 February 1919. A morning paper, it was run by Celal Nuri, who tirelessly criticized CUP power-wielders, and was twice shut down by the censors.
5. *Yeni Istanbul* (New Istanbul) started on 9 November 1918 but became *Türkce Istanbul* on 8 December 1918. It was established by Sait Molla, a pro-British partisan politician.
6. *Ikdam* (Perseverance) was a morning paper run by Ahmet Cevdet, who had founded it in 1894 and was opposed to the CUP throughout. It had the largest circulation, some 12,000, even though it went through several periods of political crisis spanning the eras of Abdulhamit and CUP. On 1 November 1918 Cevdet founded *Içtihad* (Interpretation) daily, and in a major editorial in *Yeni Istanbul* (6 December 1918), he declared the Turkish people innocent of the crime of Armenian massacres, thus blaming CUP and its leaders.
7. *Zaman* (Period) was a morning paper that contained virulent attacks against the CUP, mostly by Refik Halid (Karay), a veteran opponent of the CUP regime whose leaders had exiled him to Sinop during World War I. His editorial "Where to, Gentlemen?" (*Efendiler Nereye*) on 5 November 1918, is a severe indictment of the seven CUP leaders who had fled the country a few days earlier.

8. *Yeni Gazete* (New Newspaper) denounced the atrocities against the Armenians as the work of "phony Turks" (*sahte Türkler*), as opposed to the "real" Turks.

Among those who were more moderate in their posture in this respect were *Akşam* (Evening), run by Necmeddin Sadak and Falih Rıfkı (Atay), who later joined him; *Vakit* (Period), run by Ahmet Emin (Yalman) and Ahmet Şükrü (Esmer); *Minber* (Pulpit) run by Fethi Okyar and Mustafa Kemal (Atatürk). The latter paper had a very short lifespan, namely 1 November–21 December 1918. On 8 February 1919, *Istiklal* (Independence), a small paper that had started on 23 December 1918, raised the issue of extending the criminal trial against the guilty Armenians as well. As for diehard CUP partisans, *Yeni Gün* (New Day) stood out in this respect. Published by ardent CUP exponent Yunus Nadi, it started its career on 2 September 1918 (during World War I Nadi had been editor-in-chief of *Tasvir-i Efkâr*, or Mirror of Thought, a paper fully identified with the aims and goals of the wartime ruling CUP party). *Yeni Gün* was closed down several times, and Nadi was forced to flee to Ankara, where he resumed its publication in 1920 as the first daily there. It eventually became the mouthpiece of Mustafa Kemal, the leader of the postwar Turkish liberation movement. Another maverick newspaper was *Söz* (The Word), which reacted strongly to schemes of anti-Turkish vendettas that were being proposed and hatched by the former "enemies of the Ottoman Empire."

The prevailing mood in Turkey immediately after the end of the war, as described above, could not fail to find its reflection in the Turkish press, which almost in concert echoed that mood. In that brief period there was no trace of Kemalism, nor any evidence of discord among the victorious Allies occupying the Ottoman capital and other strategically important territories of the empire. As a result, for the first—and, as events would subsequently demonstrate, the last—time in contemporary Turkish history, the Armenian Genocide, subsumed under the twin terms of "deportations and massacres" (*tehcir ve taktil*), would be openly discussed, detailed, narrated, analyzed, and almost unanimously condemned. In the process various categories of perpetrators would be identified, exposed, and chastised. Above all, however, the insistent demand for criminal prosecution and ultimate severe punishment would permeate these postwar reactions to the Armenian calamity. What follows is a sketch of the various categories under which these reactions may be subsumed and reviewed.

Inveighing against the Collective Escape

Ati, 5 November 1918: "They fled after having drowned thousands of people in the rivers and having murdered them in the mountain passes; they fled after thus engulfing the fatherland in fire and blood … they enlisted the meanest elements of the people to become brigands.... 'If you are innocent why do you find it necessary to flee like deceitful criminals, and disguised as women?'"

Zaman, 5 November 1918. Refik Halid (Karay) wrote: "Where to, gentlemen? Where to, bedbugs? Where to, satiated maggots? Where to, Paşas, carrying sticks in your hands, scimitars on your waists and carrying blood in your eyes? Where to, as you are running from prison to prison?"[30] As if to confirm the underlying motivation of the collective escape, fear of criminal prosecution, both Talaat and CUP Secretary-General M. Şükrü are on record recognizing the connection between this collective escape and the facts of the wartime Armenian deportations, as described in note 23 above.

The Facts of the Mass Murder

Sabah, 11 and 14 December 1918. Based on ciphers postwar Turkish authorities obtained in a variety of ways,[31] *Sabah*, in the first of the two issues mentioned above, published an article titled "Two Inculpatory Documents" (*Iki Vesaiki Töhmet*). The censors prevented these newspapers from publishing the full texts of these ciphers but allowed them to cite certain parts and disclose the overall thrust of their contents, which, in today's parlance, might be termed "directives for genocide." As noted above, Yunus Nadi, the editor of the pro-CUP newspaper *Yeni Gün*, challenged *Sabah* for publishing what it called "fake" documents and shaming it.[32] *Sabah*, three days later, i.e., on 14 December, reiterated its stance on Talaat's genocidal decision-making. In that cipher-telegram Talaat is seen issuing an explicit order for the extermination (*imha*) of the Armenians of Malatya while assuming for it both "moral and material responsibility," with the newspaper reproducing in full that part of the cipher.[33]

Hadisat, 28 November 1918. Süleyman Nazıf's article states: "Under the guise of deportations, mass murder was perpetrated. Given the fact that the crime is all too evident, the perpetrators should have been hanged already."

Vakit, 21 October 1918. Feminist writer Halide Edip's article states: "We massacred an inoffensive [Armenian] population.... Indeed, we tried to destroy the Armenians through methods characteristic of the Middle Ages.... We are living today the saddest and darkest times of our national life."

The Employment of Criminals for Massacre Duty

Hadisat, 4 November 1918. For the first time the Special Organization (Teşkilâtı Mahsusa) was mentioned as a principal instrument of wartime massacres.

Sabah, 8 November 1918. The role of convicts was identified and explained. In an open letter the paper challenges wartime Justice Minister Pirizade Ibrahim as follows:

> Did you not order the release of convicts from the prisons of the Empire, these bloodthirsty criminals who were either condemned to death or to life in prison? Were they not assembled below your office, i.e., the office of public prosecutor of the Intermediate Court of Appeals (*Istinaf*)? Did not the chiefs of these killer bands convene in the Conference Room of the Criminal Court and the Chambers of the above mentioned public prosecutor, where they were tasked to supervise the barbarically executed mass murder of the Armenians?

Hadisat, 21 October 1918 (originally appeared on 4 March 1917). Süleyman Nazıf's article states: "Not merely five centuries but even after the lapse of 50,000 years nobody could be in a position to believe it possible that we would sink so low.… We would need a comprehensive investigation to assess the scale of the moral devastation these five centuries produced."[34]

The Matter of Responsibility

Tasviri Efkâr, 29 November 1918. "Those responsible are so many as they are to be found in the highest echelons of our body politic. They include the ministers, governors-general, the parliament, especially the 250 members of the Chamber of Deputies, and civil servants."

Yeni Istanbul, 30 November 1918: "We are all perpetrators" (*fail*).

Zaman, 23 November 1918: "Turkey is in the shadow of an indictment."

Ikdam, 29 December 1918. An article by Ahmet Refik (Altınay) asks: "With rare exceptions the *valis* [governors-general] were complicit. Who directed the atrocities in fulfilling their criminal penchants?"

Söz, 28 December 1918: "They, the guilty ones, may be grouped around seven categories: 1. principal perpetrators, 2. their accomplices, supporters, especially the provincial party chieftains and CUP's Central Committee members, 3. those involved in secret missions and operations comprising low-ranked officers and convicts released from prisons, and swashbucklers, 4. compliant Deputies engaged in profiteering activities, 5. journalists and sycophants, 6. those engaged in war-profiteering and hence supporters of the regime, 7. those sycophants who circle around paşas, notables and profiteers."[35]

The Call for Draconian Measures of Punishment

Sabah, November 5, 1918. Ali Kemal, editor since 14 October 1918, portrayed, by way of analogy, the image of the typical mass murderer:

> He operates in the 20th century of civilizations as a rascal with a background embodying meanness, ordinariness, lack of education and culture. He is, pardon the expression, a rascal, who is ignorant of the ideals

> of justice, liberty and government. He is wild, and insolent, a criminal rascal, who, teaming up with other rascals—and he can do that with ease for this country abounds with them—proceeds to commit acts of madness and crimes that defy the comprehension and conscience of this century.... By adoring these hoodlums as our leaders and rulers we ended up consigning God and Monarch to oblivion for many years. We forgot everything and anything that is sacred in the world. If as a result we are suffering the effects of one calamity after the other, we will have to endure them for they are punishment for our conduct.

Some three weeks later, on 27 November, Kemal defended his stance in the same paper by declaring that his campaign of justice for the crime committed against the Armenians was being misconstrued as "a campaign against the Turks." He went on to say that by doing so, "we are inculpating ourselves by appearing to be the protectors of the criminals. The truth is that the Turkish nation is blameless and its conscience is pure and clean."[36]

A more ferocious call for punishment came from the editors of two other Turkish newspapers.

Yeni Istanbul, 9 November 1918. Under the title "The Press and the Duty to Fight," the editor proposed the following.

> They have imperiled the entire nation and the state for the sake of the most lowly and deceitful goals. These monsters should be taken in iron cages to the same Istanbul bridge to be hanged there at the same gallows where they had executed thousands of innocent people. On their chests should be placed the following signboard of warning, 'the death verdict is rendered by the court of national conscience and the spirits of the nation's martyrs who are resting in our land.' ... These people are ordinary and wretched criminals. They deserve to be hanged three times in a row.

Alemdar, 20 February 1919. Editor Refi Cevat (Ulunay) pleaded for what he called "administrative justice," arguing that the crime was obvious, the punishment was available and ready, and the matter should be disposed of through "swift and administrative handling." "The deportations and massacres are not a complicated matter; the matter is very simple. The CUP brigands [*çete*] destroyed an entire nation. They hanged some of them, massacred others, and burned to death still others. The brains that hatched up the plan and the executioners presently are in the claws of justice. Therefore, there is no need to undertake strange investigations."

On 24 April 1919, the same editor complained that the very slow pace and the tediousness of the courtroom examinations and cross-examinations were conditions that belied the idea of a court-martial, which is supposed to be swift and goal-directed. The editor of this newspaper was most virulent, if not savage, in his attack against the CUP leaders in the 12 March 1919 issue of the paper: "these are men who should be decapitated by placing their heads on a tree stump then chopping them off" (koparılması lâzım gelen bu kafalar kütükler üzerinde kesilip). He then suggested that the severed heads should be put on display in the Topkapı obelisk as a sign of warning to others. His rationale for this preference was that "these men were not worthy of the gallows" (sehpalar bu adamlara layik değildir). A day later, on 13 March, in another editorial Cevat harped on the theme of severity of punishment by calling for "greater hardness" (daha ziyade şiddet), repeating it three times.[37]

Transfer of Blame to "Fake, Bogus Turks"

Yeni Gazete, 14 December 1918. The paper declared that the atrocities against the Armenians were not committed by "real" (*halis*) Turks, but "phony" (*sahte*) Turks. At the fourth sitting of the postwar Ottoman Chamber of Deputies (period 3, session 5) on 19 October 1918, Trabzon Province Deputy Hafız Mehmet bitterly complained that Turks were always blamed for all the misdeeds and crimes committed by Ottomans who were either converts to Islam and belonged to other nationalities, or were non-Turks. "Nobody bothered to inquire into their national identity … and people were apt to shout 'jackass Turk,' thus helping to sustain the blemish on the reputation of the Turks. Yes, it is a fact. Yet, upon a careful investigation, it could be established that only 5 percent of the total of the atrocities can be attributed to the Turks."[38] Two high-ranking Turkish officials at the time of the armistice expressed themselves in a similar vein. Responding to the charges of mass murder against the Armenians, Grand Vizier (October 1918) and Foreign Minister (1921) Ahmet Izzet Paşa (Furgaç) and Minister of Education (November 1918) and President of the State Council (May 1919) Riza Tevfik (Bölükbaşı) issued passionate denials. Likewise, Ahmet Izzet, commenting on the Armenian deportations and massacres, asserted that "the majority of criminal perpetrators were not of the Turkish race" (bu cani azınlığın çoğu Türk ırkından değildir).[39] Interim Interior Minister (Kambur) Izzet declared, "The murderers are not real Muslims but are converts to Islam [*dönme*].[40]

Alemdar, 11 July 1920. Perhaps the most pungent defense of "real," "genuine" Turks came from the pen of Riza Tevfik (Bölükbaşı), MD, philosopher, and eminent poet. While discussing the civil war aspects of the Kemalist War of Independence, Tevfik made an allusion to the wartime Armenian genocide by making a reference to "the general massacre." Here is the entire segment of his denunciation:

> I beg the attention of all my countrymen and of the Europeans who maliciously are linking all the offenses, crimes, and insolent acts with the Turkish name. How many of these Anatolian brigands, brigand chieftains and their recruits can be identified as real [*hakiki*] Turks? Indeed what proportions of them belong to the Turkish race? We have to take this into account … the fact is that many among them, having been transplanted there, have seen Anatolia for the first time. The majority of the heedless and blind authors of the general massacre and the deportations, and especially of the brigand chieftains, perhaps 99½ percent of them are not Turks, at least are not Anatolian Turks.[41]

In an earlier interview with the Turkish newspaper *Tasviri Efkâr* in November 1919 Riza Tevfik had described the Turkish nation as "magnanimous," "humane," "noble," and "truth-loving."

It is to be noted that amid this avalanche of charges, denunciations, and pushing for severe punishment of the culprits, there emerged at this very period of collective self-incrimination some solitary voices demanding parity in retributive justice. They suggested namely that those Armenians who, by way of vendetta or otherwise, were guilty of similar atrocities against the Turks should likewise be prosecuted and punished. In defense of his adamant insistence on harsh punitive measures against the perpetrators of the Armenian Genocide, Refi Cevat granted that such Armenians should receive similar treatment for the sake of impartial and universal justice in *Alemdar* on 10 April 1919. On 8 February 1919 the editor of the newspaper *Istiklal* declared the necessity of parity in justice along the same lines.

Transcending all these more or less partisan clamors for justice was the voice of a retired Turkish general who also had some experience in European diplomacy. General of Cavalry Izzet Fuat Paşa, the grandson of the venerable Ottoman statesman Keçecizade Fuad Paşa, one of the architects of the era of Tanzimat Reforms, had also been ambassador to Spain at one time. While distancing himself from the atmosphere of acrimony and bitterness permeating the debate in the Turkish press about the issue of Armenian deportations and massacres, he offered the following observation: "We have no choice but to admit the criminal nature of the conduct of the CUP. It is a crime that was committed against humanity and that can't be denied. This being the case, we should publicly acknowledge it without hesitation, and in an honorable and noble way. This is today's most urgent task as it befits the gloriousness of a great people."[42]

This lively albeit bitter debate in the press could not fail to have an impact upon a public that for more than four years had been subjected to the CUP regime's straitjacket controls of the press. Even more significantly, the Allied authorities now in control of the Ottoman capital were getting a glimpse of the nature of the turmoil besetting the postwar government and public in Turkey. In fact they had a share in the genesis of that turmoil, in terms of the developing pressures and demands for prosecution and retributive justice besetting a defeated and vanquished country. How did the legislative and executive branches of the Ottoman government, and not least the reigning sultan, handle these developments? The next section will treat the respective response of the legislative branch.

Ottoman Legislative Response

When the revolutionary CUP leadership managed to topple the autocratic regime of Sultan Abdulamit II with very little bloodshed on 23 July 1908, the slogans it used were those used during the French Revolution of 1789, namely, freedom, equality, and brotherhood (*hüriyet, müsavat ve uhuvvet*). Accordingly, one of the first steps these leaders took was the restoration of the 1876 Ottoman Constitution, which the now-disenfranchised sultan had abrogated during the Russo-Turkish War in 1877. The idea was to return to constitutional monarchy. In line with this initiative, those very same leaders displayed great zeal in returning to the system of parliamentary government.

The last of the three periods of this new parliamentary regime was ushered in on 10 October 1918 following the completion of corresponding parliamentary elections. The opening ceremonies, attended by the new Sultan Mehmet VI Vahdettin, involved members of both houses of the parliament, i.e., the Chamber of Deputies and the Senate. In this bicameral system the deputies were chosen through the election process, whereas the senators, venerable old dignitaries and public servants, were appointed for life by the reigning sultan. Given the oppressive atmosphere of postwar debacle and distress, this new parliament from its very inception was enveloped by turmoil and acrimonious debate, the particulars of which will be explored below. As we will see, the specter of the wartime Armenian genocide would continue to cast a grim shadow on the unfolding debates.

The Debates in the Chamber

As in most other countries, in terms of legislation and especially legislative initiative, the Ottoman Chamber of Deputies was assigned a prominent role. In fact, in this respect it had precedence over the Senate. Aware of the prevailing grim situation, the sultan, in his opening speech—which was directed at both the deputies and the senators, who were jointly assembled in the Chamber of Deputies on 10 October 1918—uttered a prayer, soliciting God's benevolence and ending with the peroration, "May he favor you with a measure of success in the difficult task [*müşkül mesaimizde*] you are facing." Thus began the work of parliament's Fifth Assembly Period (Içtima Senesi), identified as it was with the Third Election Phase (Dönem) of that parliament.[43] With the formal termination of the duties of Hacı Adil (Arda), the deputies elected a prominent CUP leader, wartime Foreign Minister and subsequently Justice Minister Halil Menteşe, as their new president (i.e., Speaker of the House). A renowned publicist and likewise a notable CUP leader, Hüseyin Cahid (Yalçın), was elected first vice president. Only 156 out of 256 deputies were able to attend.

The Chamber was confronted with many issues, problems, and tasks as it embarked upon its work in the following days and weeks. But a particular motion (*takrir*) made by an Arab member of the Chamber, Deputy Fuat from Divaniye, a district near Baghdad, served to shift the debate to the wartime misdeeds of the collapsed CUP regime. He proposed to launch an investigation as a preliminary step. Under the terms of Article 31 of the Ottoman Constitution, the matter could then be brought before the High Court (Divan-ı Âli) for final trial and adjudication if the absolute majority of two-thirds of the deputies voted in favor of such adjudication. However, this could happen only after the Chamber's preliminary panel, by a simple majority, voted to remit the matter to the entire Chamber for such voting. Deputy Fuad's motion revolved around ten questions, of which numbers five and ten directly and indirectly dealt with the wartime deportations and massacres. Number ten had, for example, a special reference to "the terrible crimes" perpetrated by the "brigands." The allusion here is to the Special Organization, whose brigands carried out most of the massacres. Number five, on the other hand, assailed the CUP practice of taking refuge in "Temporary Laws, which subverted all precepts of law and humanity and were entirely inimical to the essence and explicitness of our Constitution." Fuad added, "They created regulations and issued orders and thereby transformed the country into a whirlpool of tragedies."[44] The allusion here is to the 26 May 1915 Temporary Law that set the stage for the Armenian deportations and massacres.

The difficulty Fuad encountered in having this motion promptly processed foretold the Chamber leadership's reluctance to bring the matter of wartime deportations and massacres up for debate. Halil, its president, was hereby conveying the general sentiment of the Chamber, which still was dominated by an overwhelming majority of residual CUP partisans. The motion was prepared on 28 October but met the resistance of Halil when submitted on 2 November; the latter tried to temporize with it, but upon Fuad's stubborn insistence felt obligated to finally yield. Thus, on 4 November the motion was read into the record as the deputies present listened to "[t]his grim-sounding motion with a heavy spell of silence."[45] Fuad's motion thus paved the way for subsequent initiatives in the same Chamber, whereby the wartime Armenian deportations and massacres gradually crystallized as a focal point of attention and debate.

Whereas Deputy Fuad's motion had indirectly—and therefore implicitly—broached the subject, there subsequently emerged a willingness to confront the issue head-on. Supported by two other Greek deputies—Smyrna's (Izmir) Vanel Mimaroğlu and Çatalca's Tokinidis—Aydın's Emmanuelidi brought forth his own motion, which contained eight items. The first was framed as follows: on the sole ground that they belonged to the Armenian nation, and for no other reason of culpability whatsoever, one million people, women and children not exempted, were murdered and destroyed. The fifth dealt with the liquidation of the two prominent Armenian deputies of the Ottoman Chamber, Krikor Zohrab and Vartkes Serengulian.[46] Deputies Hafız Mehmet (Trabzon) and Ilyas Sami (Muş) rejected the accusations insofar as they were directed at the Turks in general and, as the latter protested, stained the national honor by maintaining that "one million people were savagely murdered without any reason."[47]

Despite efforts by some Turkish deputies to terminate it, the debate was resumed by the introduction of a new motion, first by an Armenian deputy. Kozan Deputy Mateos Nalbandyan wanted to understand the government's thinking about the atrocities committed in connection with the officially ordered deportations and the ensuing confiscation of the properties and goods of the victims. What will be done, he further inquired, to the perpetrators involved?[48] The motion was co-signed by the following five other Armenian deputies: Hagop Khirlakyan (Maraş), Onnik Ihsan (Izmir), Artin Boşgezenyan (Aleppo), Hovsep Madatyan (Erzurum), and Dikran Barsamyan (Sivas). It should be noted that all of these men had run for office as CUP candidates and accordingly did not represent Armenian constituencies as such. In fact Nalbandyan, in support of his motion, stressed the fact that he had submitted it "in the name of the general Ottoman nation." He then intoned,

> I have seen many colleagues whose eyes were filled with tears when expressing their sorrow.... In the name of humanity I am appealing to your conscience ... these past events made us all weep ... the smoke is still rising from the ruined homes, and multitudes of women are aimlessly wandering here and there.... I beg my esteemed government to approach this very important crisis with a carefully drafted plan.... We want to embrace our government with purity of heart.... Please join me in the same spirit. The entire civilized world and even the Almighty God, the Lord of all of us, expect this from us.[49]

Interior Minister Fethi Okyar, a former, albeit moderate, CUP leader, rose to answer all these requests and pleas. His responses suggested that the government intended to pursue justice by criminally prosecuting and punishing the perpetrators "irrespective of rank or position," and that it would take time and require patience, given the huge material limitations of the postwar government, to rehabilitate and, whenever possible, to compensate the surviving Armenian victims.

One of the most signal aspects of this sitting, from both a moral and a political-legal standpoint, was the "voiding" (*refi*) or rescinding of the catastrophic Temporary Law of Deportation of 26 May 1915—belatedly, to be sure, as the law had already pushed the victim population to the brink of near extinction. The minister asked the deputies to treat this draft law on the rescindment as a matter of "urgency." During the ensuing discussion two deputies proposed an explanatory note, in the form of an addendum, to be attached to the bill. Tokat deputy Tahsin Riza suggested the following addition: "The Temporary Law in question was in violation of Article 36 of the Constitution," which stipulates "the existence of danger against the State and the need to guard public security" as condition for the enactment of temporary laws.

For his part, Aleppo Deputy Boşgezenyan insisted that a mere rejection of the law was not adequate, given the gravity of its consequences. The rejection should contain an explanation and provide reasons. Using a metaphor, the Armenian deputy likened the proposed new bill to an act of blunting the knife. But, he objected, "you cannot undo the untold atrocities, you cannot suppress them, by just rendering the tool useless." Continuing, he pointed out that under Article 113 of the Ottoman Constitution, for the deportation and exile even of one person "you need an imperial order from the monarch. By what logic or right then can a mere major or colonel be empowered to decide solely to deport thousands of people and eradicate untold villages and townships?" In brief, he was pleading for an account to be embedded in the new law. But in the end the Chamber ignored these amendments, and by the disposition of the body's president the old law was rescinded by a voice vote. Instead of voting in favor of a new bill denouncing and substituting the old law, the Chamber was asked if anyone was in favor of the old Temporary Law. Because there was no majority saying "yes," the Temporary Law of 26 May 1915 was declared invalid![50]

The debates taking place on November 18, 1918, had a special focus on the wartime Armenian deportations and massacres, with three Armenian deputies leading that debate. Their main antagonist was Muş Deputy Ilyas Sami who tried to explain the atrocities committed in the course of the deportations. Three major themes were explored in these exchanges. Aleppo's Armenian deputy tackled one of them when he insisted that the crimes perpetrated against the Armenians could not be attributed to the Turkish people in general, eliciting shouts of "bravo" from his Turkish colleagues. He then castigated the CUP regime as a regime of "brigands" that had become identified with the Special Organization, which was seen as a principal instrument of the massacres in question. When his Armenian colleague Barsamyan joined him by cursing the CUP leaders as the real culprits, he was chastised by cries of "You too belong to that group." Indeed, as an ardent CUP man, he had been elected almost exclusively by the Turkish constituents of his district. A second striking feature in these debates was the display of a confessional mood highlighting the principle of "conspiracy by silence." Trabzon's Deputy Hafiz Mehmet declared: "We misbehaved by remaining silent for four years. But we had no other choice." Aleppo's Boşgezenyan concurred and expressed regret that "all of us were forced to remain silent."[51]

The third signal feature of this sitting was the bitter exchange between the Armenian deputies and the Muş deputy Ilyas Sami, who subsequently would be prosecuted by the Ottoman Military Tribunal for his principal role in the wholesale extermination of the Armenian population of both the city of Muş and the Muş plain, the heartland of historic Armenia; it is estimated that this segment of the Armenian mass murder alone involved between 90,000 and 100,000 victims.[52] In contesting the arguments of his Armenian colleagues, Sami—who was of Kurdish extraction, belonged to the Kotan Kurdish dynasty, and was his area's regional CUP inspector—raised the rhetorical question "Was it a massacre, or was it reciprocal massacres [*mukatele*]?"

In answering this question he asserted that during the early stages of World War I the government had come into the possession of highly incriminatory evidence comprising seven or eight items of Armenian conspiracy. In this connection he argued that these Armenians purportedly made demands on the Ottoman government and threatened to seize lands and positions inside Turkey to join the Russian enemy at the front. Sami then intoned, "I swear in the name of Ottomanism that 70 percent of the Muslim population perished as a result of these Armenian undertakings." What happened to the Armenians subsequently, which "I loath and detest," he said, was the consequence of these treacherous acts, adding, "the heads of all those involved, on both sides, should be chopped off." He concluded that the government's actions against the Armenians were "a response to treason, and this is my understanding of justice." Deputy Barsamyan then interjected: "How about the massacres of 1895 and 1909 in Adana? Here it is, for all to see, the spirit of a massacrer." To which Sami retorted, "I am asking for the punishment of all perpetrators." Deputy Nalbandyan stated in response: "Even if we accept Sami's charges, by what norm of justice were all the Armenians of the Empire robbed, plundered, deported? By what rule of law, under which Article of the Penal Code, was such a widespread, comprehensive extension of punishment allowed and carried out? Shouldn't Ilyas Sami instead berate the wholesale destruction of a nation?"[53]

The 9 December sitting of the Chamber was punctuated by the reading into the record of the motion of the Armenian deputy of Muş, Kegham Der Garabedyan, who, near death, had written up this motion as a sort of testament, but who by the date of the sitting was already dead. When Deputy Barsamyan put it on the agenda, Hüseyin Cahid, who as first vice president of the Chamber was chairing the sitting, tried to block the reading of the entire text; he wanted to offer instead a brief summary. Upon Barsamyan's insistence Cahid still refused, saying that he would present the main points of the motion and then send the full text to the appropriate body, i.e., the Interior Ministry. When the Armenian deputy persisted in his request, arguing that the motion in question was something "extraordinary," the chair relented, allowing its full presentation. The use of the term "extraordinary" refers not only to the death of the deputy but in all likelihood also to the fact that of the ten Armenian deputies of the Ottoman Chamber—including the most two noted ones, Vartkes and Zohrab—Kegham was the only one who was elected almost entirely by the Armenians of his district.

The highlights of his motion, written up on 5 November 1918, may be summed up as follows:

> The main issue here is the fact that a great injustice was committed by the government by allowing the killing and dispersal of the multitudes of innocent Armenians. Taking issue with the estimate of 100,000 Armenian victims some of his colleagues had made, with a sense of indignation he asked the government "how was it possible that such vast numbers of innocent Armenians, people not involved at all in any crime were killed? Declaring Cihad [*jihad*], more than 1.5 million people were killed, dispersed and in the end destroyed. As if not content with the major mass murder in Turkey proper, one year later the surviving remnants of the victim population were likewise destroyed in Deir Zor and Ras-ul-Ain. In my own district embracing Muş, Bitlis, and the adjoining areas, the mass murder was carried out with a savagery hitherto unexampled in history [tarihin şimdiye kadar emsalini kayıt etmediği sureti vahşiyanede]. The population of Muş Valley villages and of the town of Muş, along with the other people brought in from the outside and adjoining areas, was destroyed through such methods as cannon fire, and burning alive. These crimes were compounded by resort to massive plunders of the movable and immovable properties of the victim population and the desecration of their sacred monuments. As I raise my voice with all the strength I possess to protest, I request to know as to what the government is going to do about all this.[54]

Two Turkish deputies with two diverse approaches and assessments dominated the debates of 11 December 1918 as they too tried to come to grips with the problems associated with the Armenian deportations and massacres. The eminent poet and writer Mehmet Emin (Yurdakul), deputy of Musul (Mosul), delivered a long speech, a written essay that captivated friend and foe alike, eliciting repeated applause and bravos. It was an eloquent effort to apply to these problems what American sociologist Charles Horton Cooley termed the art of "sympathetic introspection." This was done in a manner meant to accommodate both the Armenians and the Turks, thereby lifting the latter from the denigrating image of villains. As he recognized the cultural merits of the Armenians and their contributions to civilization, he granted that they had been victimized by evil perpetrators, "against whom I offer myself in the role of a prosecuting attorney, regardless who these perpetrators may be, yes, even if they should include my son." He then launched his oration, detailing what he considered to be the manifold and manifest virtues of the Turkish people such as "fear of God," "ethics," "possession of conscience," "love of justice," "mercy," "humanness." He further declared, "We too are aware that the power that rules the world is the ideal of justice, and that it is a greater and more abiding victory to abide by one's conscience and to conquer a nation through logic and love rather than through the sword." Therefore, he argued, it was a great shame that Turks were being recklessly slandered for the criminal misdeeds of a few whose Turkish origin and nationality he too questioned, even though, he added, these perpetrators "may include those who bear Turkish names.... However, the complicity of a few people can never be sufficient ground to inculpate the entire Turkish nation [shouts of 'Bravo']. The evil deeds alluded to here are inimical to the spirit, to the heart, to the conscience, to the ethos of the Turkish nation [shouts of "very true"]."

Emin then briefly outlined the atrocities imputed to Armenian brigands, seen as men resorting to killing operations against civilian Turkish populations, at the same time underlining the heartrending barbarities he claimed accompanied these murderous acts. As he put it, these acts "were perpetrated by individuals who in no way were connected to the Armenian nation." Moreover, Emin sang the praise of "Armenian preachers who," as he put it, "as the disciples of Jesus Christ, do embody the ideals of compassion and mercy." Further elaborating on this general theme, he declared: "The poets of this nation are vocalists who through their golden musical instruments sing the praise of ideals of justice. I know well this nation. She is one that has experienced injustice, tears, and bloodshed" (Ben bu Milleti bilirim, O, kanın, gözyaşının, mazlumiyetinin ne olduğunu bilir). He terminated his speech with this plea, "Gentlemen, allow me to juxtapose for your consideration the plight of these esteemed, unjustly treated, and innocent citizens for whom I have vouched, with that of the plight of innocent Turks. I request from our government a response in this regard."[55] In assessing the import of this intervention in the matter it should be borne in mind that Emin was not just a poet; beyond that he was, to use Aristotle's metaphor, "a political animal" (*zoon politikon*) as well. Indeed, in the 1909–1911 period alone he had successively served as governor-general of the provinces of Hicaz (Hejaz), Sivas, and Erzurum. In 1913 he was elected deputy of Mosul. He played a significant role in the ushering in and strengthening of the new Republic of Turkey, in the process becoming a cohort of Mustafa Kemal (Atatürk), the principal founder of that republic.

When Greek deputies insisted on bringing up the matter of persecutions and expulsions of hundreds of thousands of Greeks from many parts of the empire as evidence of a largely anti-Christian undertaking by the CUP government, Trabzon deputy Hafiz Mehmet intervened. He observed that all deputies should be allowed latitude and scope to freely and openly air their legitimate grievances. But, like some other deputies, he complained that the topic of persecution and massacre had been unduly consuming the time of the Chamber, at the same time monopolizing the attention of the press, the Senate, and everybody else.

> Let us bring out the truth of the matter and then let us be done with it.... It is my belief that in dealing with traitors the government was discharging its duties, but in doing so it acted somewhat aggressively. Today everybody, including the entire nation, the deputies and senators, the press, all of them, is for punishing those who violated the law, who perpetrated such atrocities and crimes. But I feel it is inappropriate to continuously bring up the matter while holding the entire nation responsible for these crimes.... With feelings of anguish, the people of Trabzon, when pained over the anti-Armenian atrocities, were saying "God will punish us for this crime."

He then related an incident that represents one of the rarest corroborations of the fact of the complicity of governmental officials in the organization of the mass murder of the Armenians—corroborations afforded by a member of the Ottoman Parliament's Chamber of Deputies, and a lawyer at that. He stated that he had been an eyewitness of a scene of such mass murder at a Black Sea port city, Ordu, one day when Armenian women and children were squeezed into a barge and then drowned in the high sea. Equally important, he further revealed that "Cemal Azmi, Trabzon province's governor-general [*vali*], carried out similar drowning operations. For three years I tried to have the *vali* taken to task, but I failed."[56]

The last animated exchanges in the series of debates took place on 12 December 1918; nine days later the Chamber would be dissolved by the monarch's issuance of a preemptive decree. From its very inception the debate became acrimonious when Tekirdağ's Greek deputy Dimistakli Efkalidis, bitter about the prewar wholesale expulsion of the Greek population of his district, located in the European part of Turkey, launched an attack against the CUP regime, which he held responsible for that disaster. Countering Turkish arguments that Turks too sustained heavy losses, he stated that losses due to warfare bear no relationship to, and hence cannot be compared with, the losses due to expulsions, massacres, and other forms of atrocities a government may inflict upon its citizens. During the prewar years Efkalidis had had an exchange about the then occurring expulsion of the Greeks with his Armenian colleague Vartkes, who told him and his Greek colleagues: "Brother, don't misunderstand me but I am glad you are being treated the way you are. When they are done with you, it will be our turn. These people consider the act of destroying [people] an important task" (imhayı akdemi vezaif addediyorlar). The Greek deputy then observed that his Armenian colleague's prediction did in fact materialize, not only for his people but also for Vartkes himself, adding, "a calm has descended upon the provinces [where Armenians used to live] but it is the calm of a cemetery."[57] Deputy Vartkes, along with his colleague Zohrab, despite their privilege of parliamentary immunity,[58] were arrested on 20 May (2 June by the Western calendar) 1915 and murdered on the road from Urfa to Diyarbekir in the third week of July 1915.

The rest of the sitting was consumed by the bitter exchange between the Armenian deputy Nalbandyan[59] (Kozan) and the Turkish (Kurdish) deputy Ilyas Sami (Muş). The Armenian deputy began his speech stressing the overall gravity of the situation, but especially the critical condition of the Armenians who were "trapped in the throes of death" and as such engaging the attention of the entire world. "They have no one but us, deputies, to address their plight and their needs." He then resumed the narration of the wartime calamity that had produced these postwar conditions. "I beg my colleagues to indulge me, for the situation requires careful deliberation and pondering so that we may be able to deal with it. This is urgent business and I feel constrained to briefly outline the stages of this crime without intending to offend particular individuals." His outline referred to particular elements of the Armenian Genocide to conclude that these "events" (for which he used the Turkish-Arabic word *vukuat*, which up to the present day continues to be employed as an evasive euphemism to denote the organized mass murder in question) were organized and carried out in a systematic way. As a result "these places were transformed into a cemetery."

In the process the nation's age-old institutions and their contents were destroyed, defiled, and plundered. This unnecessary sweep of destruction resulted in the obliteration of the wealth of the nation. "Under the guise of carrying out 'southward deportations,' the Armenians of Anatolia were butchered in Anatolia's valleys that during that season were exuding an air full of gentle breeze. Yes, gentlemen, sucklings whose mothers and older siblings were killed, whose sisters were abducted, and who still were crying, were thrown into the vortex of the waves of the Black Sea and the Euphrates and Tigris rivers, the perpetrators thereby resorting to barbarities that overshadow the frightful and evil deeds of Nero." He further provided details of scenes he had observed on his trip from Adana to Istanbul. These included portrayals of children, and old men and women, gasping their last breath in desolate bushes. "It is in these places that I witnessed so many varieties of death and dying.... In brief, gentlemen, this crime was perpetrated by way of murdering a nation, a crime that spread in all corners of the land."

Deputy Nalbandyan's final statements touched on the very delicate issue of the level of responsibility for the crimes perpetrated. After reviewing the conditions of elective and representative government, he went on to say that such a government was bound to "proceed to act in the name of the people it represents … and the resulting operative principle of sovereignty is but Turkish sovereignty that heretofore splendidly has reigned supreme in this land. Even though many Turks have been opposed to the recurrent anti-Armenian atrocities, the fact, however, is that these atrocities were carried out in the name of Turkish nationhood." (Fakat yapılan mezalim Türklüğün namına yapılmıştır). Hereupon poet-deputy Mehmet Emin interjected: "God forbid, God forbid; they were carried out in the name of oppression. Accursed be the tyrants." The response from Nalbandyan was as follows:

> We are told that the perpetrators involved only three to five people. I fail to understand this for three to five people in no way can carry out such an undertaking.… The fact is that these perpetrators were out loud declaring that they were exercising a sovereignty that was Turkish. They were further bragging that their power derived from their bonds to their Turkish bayonets. We cannot deny this fact, and I regretfully must state that the perpetrators were people who belonged to the Turkish nation [Bunu yapanlar Türk Milletine mensup eşhastır]. This is a fact that should serve as a warning. Only the wheels of justice will reveal the actual identity and specific number of these perpetrators. The general public and the innocent people expect this from the Turks. Those Turks who claim that their hands are not stained can then compile a balance sheet, and punish those who, irrespective of status, rank, or position, ought to be punished; only thus can the requisite measure of justice be administered. Only then is it possible to present the truth to the world and to humanity at large.

Deputy-poet Emin interjected in response, "We expect this line of conduct from the righteous government." Nalbandyan concluded that it was imperative that those rights that had been trampled underfoot be restored (*istirdat*) and that thereafter the government should declare to the entire world that the criminals, be they 100,000 in number, had been duly punished. "I believe," he stated, "that it is then possible to obtain acquittal, and this is the sound and right remedy in my opinion. Please rest assured that I am offering these proposals with a purity of heart."[60]

The entire debate was terminated with the final response of Muş deputy Ilyas Sami. Here is a summary:

> For five years we have been engaged in a bloody war that caused us untold miseries, enormous casualties, tragic experiences, including the mourn-

> ing of the deaths of thousands, a hundred thousand, millions of our heroic martyrs. And yet we are not being allowed to succor these wounds and to repair the enormous damage. Several nationalist elements are annoying us by their exaggerated claims and destructive attitudes. My [Armenian] colleagues should know that parallel to their murdered victims there exist the millions of Ottoman martyrs who for eight centuries had coexisted with you without harming you in any way. I will try to explain to you the occurrences that transpired in my own district—as I have witnessed them and as my conscience dictates. At the same time, however, I have a request. With a resolve never to return to it for discussion again, we should close this chapter for good, while maintaining our other resolve to inflict punishment on the guilty ones with the severity of a thunderbolt ["Yes, yes!" shouts]. While they [the Armenians] keep mentioning this tragedy that happened on Ottoman territories, they are never raising the question of "why." I beg you. Consider this too. [Deputy Nalbandyan interjects, "No act warrants such a [murderous] response."]. The name of the Turk has been defiled by the use of many adjectives. In the process even Islam has been blamed… [Sami then digressed and brought up the episode of the Kurdish uprising in Bitlis: on 11 March 1914, Kurdish Mullah Selim had threatened, and three weeks later, on 1 and 2 April, had risen up against the CUP regime, only to be crushed with great severity]. My compatriots, stemming from my Kurdish race, were crying "revenge" from the depths of their tombs, eager to pay back the sufferings and the bloody crimes CUP had inflicted upon them.

Returning to the genocidal fate of the Armenians, Sami offered the following rationale:

> Turkey at that time resembled a man who was on his way to the slaughterhouse, desperate and despairing. Facing the threat of an attempt at his life and of aggression, he delivered a powerful punch. This is how the deportations started. Rest assured, however, that I join my colleagues in expressing my disgust about the atrocities inflicted upon the innocent people and in demanding appropriate punishment.… As a result of this ignorant decision our [Armenian] citizens were deported and destroyed [*ifna*], but 80 percent of this victim population were innocent people [böyle bilmiyerek verilen bir kararın neticesi … kurbanı masumu olarak içlerinde yüzde seksen bigünah insanı vardır]. This is how I perceive the situation, as I am echoing the voices of my conscience.

Before he concluded, Sami once more reviewed the circumstances of what he called Armenian treachery as revealed to him in so many words, he claimed, by Muş Armenian deputy Vahan Papazyan (Koms). According to his account,

Papazyan had loose lips, as evident in his divulging of the tentative plans of his coopting fellow Dashnak leaders, which involved a wait-and-see attitude. Namely, in the event of a Russian victory, they were to join the Russian army units and take control of the areas containing large clusters of Armenian populations.[61] Deputy Sami continued, "Three or four months later the central government made available to me the evidence it had gathered, I do not know how the government was able to get hold of the evidence and I can assure you that this was not fabricated evidence; I swear on my honor." Deputy Sami then pleaded, repeatedly, for putting an end to this debate, declaring, "We should be content with this much of it" (Bu kadarla iktifa edelim).

The final words were spoken by Mustafa Arif (Deymer), interior minister at the time and a former Saloniki judge and lawyer:

> Even though I do not wish to interfere in your deliberations, yet, I find it necessary to say a few words. I see no purpose and no benefit in dwelling over the events of the past with the use of such general phrases. Your Chamber and the government concurrently have confirmed that certain events [*ahval*] did in fact occur. Nobody is denying it. I am willing to act when apprised that this or that complicit person has managed to escape punishment. Even if we admit that 100,000 people from among millions of Turks were thus implicated, it is incorrect and unacceptable to hold an entire race responsible and then denounce it. I am sure you agree with me [voices of "undoubtedly"]. Moreover, such debates not only cannot benefit the various nationalities but can even create cleavages among them. This is my belief but nonetheless, the decision is yours [voices of "we have debated enough"].[62]

It should be noted that in light of the active and conspicuous participation in the debates of the Armenian deputies, the Mixed Council of the Armenian National Assembly of Turkey issued a statement on 4 December 1918 that declared that the Armenian deputies of the Ottoman Parliament did not actually represent the Armenian people.[63]

Deputy Fuad's 4 November motion, aiming at the establishment of the High Court to try the Ottoman Cabinet ministers, did not come to fruition. The Chamber of Deputies, which had engaged in all these debates with a view to ultimately voting for the establishment of such a court, as required by Article 31 of the Ottoman Constitution, was abruptly dissolved on 21 December 1918 by an imperial rescript (*Irade*). Article 7 of the constitution empowered the monarch to do this.[64] Several Turkish authors indicate that this was a preemptive move by the sultan, who was advised by Grand Vizier Tevfik Paşa that the CUP leadership, in pursuit of its own designs, was about to engineer a no-confidence vote and topple the government. Aware of the controlling power of the CUP, the sultan was more than glad to comply and thereby deal a blow to its authority.[65] In fact Fethi Okyar, the prominent CUP leader who later joined the Kemalists, reveals in his memoirs that two days earlier, i.e., on 19 December 1918, the CUP had convened a secret meeting to decide the delivery of a no-confidence vote, for which they had already assembled fifty votes.[66] According to Gökbilgin, the monarch was apprised of this too.[67]

Unaware of this plan, the deputies on 21 December began their purposeful interpellations. After answering them one by one, Foreign Minister Mustafa Reşit Paşa yielded the podium to Interior Minister Mustafa Arif (Deymer). After declaring that "the atrocities against the Armenians reduced our country to a gigantic slaughterhouse," Arif read the text of the imperial rescript amid deafening noise made by the CUP deputies, who, taken by surprise, were left totally confounded. The same interior minister about a week earlier had made the following declaration in an interview with a Turkish newspaper:

> Surely, a few Armenians aided and abetted our enemy, and a few Armenian deputies committed crimes against the Turkish nation. But, it was the duty of the Turkish government to arrest and to punish only these … it is incumbent upon a government to pursue only guilty ones. Unfortunately our wartime leaders, imbued with a spirit of brigandage, carried out the law of deportation in a manner that would surpass the proclivities of the most bloodthirsty brigands. They decided to exterminate the Armenians, and they did exterminate them. This decision was taken by the Central Committee of the Young Turks and was implemented by the Government.[68]

Before inquiring into the conditions that this imperial coup against the most important branch of the legislative sector the Ottoman government would create, it is necessary to examine the developments in the Senate, the upper chamber of the Ottoman Parliament, as they relate to the handling of the issues arising out of the wartime Armenian deportations and massacres.

In the Senate

For the bicameral setup of the Ottoman parliament, Article 60 of the Ottoman Constitution stipulated that the sultan himself choose and appoint the individual members of the upper chamber of that body, i.e., the Senate, provided their total number did not exceed one-third of the members of the lower chamber, i.e., the Chamber of Deputies. Even though there were 256 deputies at the time, for the third election period, coinciding with the 1914–1918 parliamentary era, the corresponding number of the senators was only 48, and only 45 of them were actually serving. As will be seen below, absenteeism in both Houses would result in a substantial diminution of these numbers. It was noted in the preceding segment of this chapter that the members of the two chambers had gathered together on 10 October 1918 for the parliament's opening ceremonies. Even though he had formally resigned three days earlier, Talaat, the residual grand vizier at the time, read into the record the sultan's inaugural speech because the cabinet formation of his successor, Ahmet Izzet, would be delayed another four days. The deputies and the senators present, while still on their feet, then recited out loud the oath of allegiance.

Following his election as the new president of the Senate, the former longtime CUP leader Ahmet Riza delivered his inaugural speech. The new role somewhat underscored his daring wartime opposition to Talaat's anti-Armenian policy of deportation and destruction. As the Ottoman parliamentary records reveal, Ahmet Riza had valiantly challenged Talaat's wartime treatment of the Armenians on four different occasions during the October–December period of 1915, when the senate was in session. In the first of these, on 4 October (Ottoman calendar 21 September) 1915, he pleaded for mercy for "the hundreds of thousands of children, women, and old men who in misery and despair are facing the rigors of winter while being deported." In this spirit he proposed that the deportees be allowed either to return to their homes or to relocate as they wished. He then submitted a legislative bill requesting the postponement of the application of the Temporary Law—which provided, in so many words, for the confiscation of the so-called "abandoned goods" (*Emvalı Matruke*) of the deportees—declaring it both "illegal" and "immoral." But his cowed and timid Senate colleagues temporized with regard to his bill, thereby consigning it to oblivion.[69]

In his 4 November 1915 communication to the US State Department, Ambassador Morgenthau confirmed the occurrence of these debates. He further disclosed that Talaat himself exerted the greatest pressure upon Senator Riza by threatening to initiate even more severe measures against the Armenians should Riza continue his agitation on their behalf: "From other sources it is stated that the cabinet promised to modify their attitude towards the Armenians if Ahmet Riza and his friends would agree not to interpellate the government. This Ahmet Riza and his friends did."[70] All this is further accented by the fact that when the Chamber of Deputies first convened in the wake of the overthrow of Sultan Abdulhamit's regime on 27 December 1908, Riza was elected president, while Talaat, who subsequently ascended to the position of CUP boss, was subordinate to him as first vice president.

In his inaugural speech Riza invoked the memory of "the Armenians who were savagely [*vahşiyane*] murdered."[71] Two days later when retired Marshal Osman challenged him for having neglected to include Turks and Kurds in his list of victims, Riza went one step further in his denunciation, explaining that the Armenians were destroyed as part of an "official" (*resmen*) policy that was carried out by the organs of "the state" (*devlet eli ile*).[72] In the same sitting, another senator, Damad Ferit, objected to the use of the Turkish term *tehcir*, arguing that it denoted the idea of "migration elsewhere." He proposed instead the term *tebid*, denoting the idea of "exile," of "banishing." In the same vein, he allowed that the resulting tragedy cost the lives of "800,000 of our Armenian citizens."[73]

The 4 November 1918 sitting of the Senate was both remarkable and memorable in several respects. It coincided with the legislative initiatives undertaken in the Chamber of Deputies the same day and more or less along the same lines. Once more, the focal point of deliberations and debate was the wartime Armenian deportations and massacres, and the matter of how the postwar Ottoman governments should deal with the problems created by them. The two motions that were brought forth indirectly but meaningfully requested explanations about them from the government, setting the stage for further action by the Senate. One of these motions came from retired General Çürüksulu Mahmut, former minister of public works. While demanding an account for the criminal abuses—which, he said, imperiled the Turkish army and therefore called for prosecution—he at the same time referred to the need to restore "the requisite security and confidence that are so needed for the external but also the internal well-being of the country."[74] This indirect reference to the Armenian issue was replicated by the second motion made by wartime Grand Vizier and Foreign Minister Sait Halim. In it he referred to "the problems associated with the war," which, in line with the stipulations of the Constitution, he proposed to submit to the High Court for adjudication.[75] Sait Molla Zade Ibrahim, the wartime minister of justice, rose up thereafter and in a quavering voice protested his innocence. Complaining that as a wartime cabinet minister he was being treated as an accomplice and disdained by his colleagues, he invoked the glory of his membership in a family noted for its patriotic services that spanned, he said, five centuries. He then intoned, "I am prepared to pull the rope [for my hanging] myself should it be established that I have committed any crime."[76]

In compliance with Senator Mahmut's motion, the senators decided to create a new Special Committee beyond the existing seven committees, which in turn were formed from among five larger departments (*şube*). The selected eight members of this new body were charged with almost the same task as the corresponding body in the Chamber of Deputies, namely the Fifth Investigative Department's Inquiry Commission (Beşinci Şube Tahkikat Komisyonu), which likewise was created on the same day, 4 November 1918 (to be discussed in the next segment). Since three out of forty-five Senators had died and seventeen were absent, the eight were chosen from the remaining twenty-five senators. In the 6 November sitting, General Mahmut, who had become vice chairman of the Senate, provided the Special Committee with some details about his 4 November motion, especially with respect to the misinformation that CUP and Foreign Minister Halil Menteşe had given concerning Turkey's intervention in World War I. He then spoke about "the shameful and grievous disaster that was perpetrated in complete disregard of the principles of right and justice" (fezayih ve fecayi-i elime irtikâp).[77] When castigating the phenomena of the same Armenian deportations and massacres Mustafa Kemal (Atatürk) used the same word, *fazayih,* i.e., *fazahat.* He had done this in his inaugural speech, delivered at the Grand National Assembly on 24 April 1920, the day he was elected president of that body, and one day after that body had convened for the first time, 23 April.[78] It was at this sitting of the Senate's Special Committee that the decision was made to forward Sait Halim's motion to the Chamber of Deputies for consideration; only the Chamber's previously mentioned body was competent to decide whether it should be remanded to the High Court (Divanı Âli). Senator Mahmut then provided details about Article 31 of the Constitution dealing with this matter. He reviewed and summarized his proposals under three points, the last of which dealt with Armenian deportations and massacres, which once more were indirectly described as *facia* and *fazayih.*

Yet the Senate persisted in its respective efforts as it embarked upon new initiatives. On 21 November, its president, Ahmet Riza, introduced a new motion. Complaining that legal proceedings through the High Court would consume too much time, he opted in this motion for swift prosecution under the rules of public law. Otherwise, he said, evidence is bound to dissipate over time. The crimes, he argued, involved not only political offenses but also "massacres, brigandage, assaults against people and properties." He singled out the subject nationalities as victims, including the Armenians, who, he said, were "subjected to atrocities that are unparalleled in Ottoman history." In this connection, he asserted that the crimes in question involve "personal crimes"; therefore "the criminals ought to be tried under 'public law' so that they are delivered to 'the claws of justice.'"[79] Osman, a retired marshal, raised again the issue of role reversals, namely the inclusion of Turks not as perpetrators but as victims, and the Armenians among the perpetrators, with Osman thereby blaming almost entirely the CUP leadership for the massacres and excluding all other Turks. In response, Riza stated that the blame went to the executive branch of the government: a secret political party could have instigated it, but the responsibility for the actual act of perpetration remained with the central government for allowing it to happen. Since that government regrettably was in essence Turkish, "I deemed it proper to exclude from my motion the Turks as victims," he added. Ex–Justice Minister Ibrahim vehemently rejected the accusation leveled against the central government, allowing instead that the crimes in question were "personal" crimes, and that they may have been committed in connection with the deportations.[80]

Damad Ferit in his statement revealed that during the war the CUP had distributed to the members of both houses "a large book" in which was printed the following rationale for "the atrocities they perpetrated:"

> If we expelled one million Armenians from their homes and their villages, and if hawks and other winged birds devoured their bones while they were being deported to Baghdad, it is because they would otherwise be blocking our roads and transportation routes, the rear of our army, and thereby imperil the very existence of the state.

Continuing, Ferit described how convicts were released from the prisons and tasked with massacring the Armenians. "Humanity, civilizations are shuddering, and forever will shudder, in face of this tragedy, this calamity." In an effort to exculpate the Turkish nation Ferit then saw fit to confine the blame to "a few tramps."

Perhaps the most revelatory and therefore incriminatory declaration came from veteran and venerable statesman Reşit Akif Paşa. He stated that when he occupied the office of President of State Council in the aftermath of the war, he came across two cipher telegrams. One of them was an order by then Interior Minister Talaat that instructed the provincial authorities to be solicitous towards the Armenian deportees and provide them with olives and bread. The other cipher, issued by the Central Committee of CUP, was a top-secret circular instructing the brigand chieftains deployed in the interior of the country to proceed with their killing operations as soon as the deportee convoys were sufficiently removed from population centers. He then cursed "the deceitful clique" for desecrating Islam and all of humankind.[81]

During the 2 December sitting Senator Ferit questioned the viability of the alternative of referring the matter to the High Court by arguing that out of 256 deputies, 100 were absent or missing; the respective numbers for the senate were 48 and 16. Thus, neither of the two chambers was truly representative, and the High Court could not be formed, nor could it properly function without such representation. Moreover, he went on to argue, the overwhelming majority of the deputies were either members of CUP or its ardent partisans. He then declared, "you cannot simultaneously be both a defendant and a judge," adding that the High Court solution was a CUP stratagem to gain time and that the era when it was possible to resort to such "heedless maneuvers" was over. Ferit, therefore, proposed the postponement of the High Court line of procedure until such time when new elections could be organized, offering instead the route of the court-martial. All this was to be effected within the framework of his new motion, which bore the date of 2 (15) December 1918. In defending his stance, Ferit pointed out that there were two types of crimes at issue here: those committed in violation of official duties, and those committed in violation of public law. The latter did not fall under the category of crimes that were within the purview of the High Court; rather, they belonged to the sphere of regular criminal courts. Accordingly, regular courts and courts-martial should be in charge, and the public prosecutor's office should immediately initiate the requisite steps.[82]

When responding to the proposal of his colleague, Senator Mahmut reiterated once more, this time explicitly, that the crimes ascribed to the cabinet ministers were not merely "political" in nature. They involved, he said, other crimes inflicted upon non-Muslim elements, including the Armenians. These crimes were "decided upon and organized" by certain members of the cabinet and were carried out by the Special Organization's brigands. His argument was that since the arch organizers of all these crimes were cabinet ministers, the jurisdictional competence devolved upon the High Court. As an example he cited the mass drowning operations of Trabzon province on the Black Sea. Evidently, the Muslim population and the notables of Ordu, a port city on the Black Sea, vainly tried to intercede on behalf of the Armenian victims scheduled to be liquidated by drowning, vouching for the victims' innocence. But reportedly the governor-general of the province, Cemal Azmi, not only briskly rebuffed them but even threatened them with retaliation should they persist. The ensuing wholesale extermination of that province's Armenian population was thus carried out with the active support of the province's CUP representative, Yenibahçeli Nail. Senator Mahmut's main point was that these local perpetrators received their orders from the center, which was controlled, he said, by Talaat and his CUP cohorts. His conclusion was that both types of courts were needed, the High Court and the regular courts.

Two other senators joined the debate. Aristidi, of Greek extraction, clarified an important point. It was argued earlier that the Senators were co-responsible because they fully cooperated with the central authorities, i.e., the executive branch. He pointed out that it was the Chamber of Deputies that delivered the vote of confidence; the Senate was never asked to deliver such a vote, nor did it ever do so. Senator A. Şeref for his part concurred with the view that while cabinet ministers should be tried by the High Court, all other subordinate government and civil service officials should be prosecuted by regular courts.

At this juncture Senator Ferit raised—for the first time, and ominously—the specter of dissolving the Chamber if and when it should fail in its duties as provided, he said, by the Constitution. The senators then voted to transmit Ferit's motion to the Civil Affairs (Mülkiye) Committee of the Senate. The sitting ended with the reading into the record of Senator A. Riza's new motion. In it, he inquired about what the Justice Ministry intended to do about his 21 November motion and which motion was approved by voice vote.

The 9 December sitting was mostly taken up by the detailed explanations Justice Minister Haydar Molla supplied in response to A. Riza's 2 December motion referred to above. The minister identified three types of offenses calling for prosecution: (1) those committed by officials while performing their duties as officials, (2) those committed by officials but outside the realm of their official duties, and (3) offenses committed by ordinary people. Of these, he said, only the first belonged to the jurisdiction of the High Court, but the pertinent legal proceedings were time-consuming. He then outlined a plan, worked out between the Interior and Justice Ministries, for sending a number of teams of civil inspectors and legal experts to ten selected regions to investigate and pave the ground for legal action. In arguing for this plan, the minister directed attention to a certain conflict of interpretation of the law by virtue of which the Council of State, on the one hand, and the Court of Appeals and the Justice Ministry, on the other, were at odds with each other. It appeared that an existing temporary law stipulated an internal, preliminary trial for civil servants, as opposed to trial by an established bona fide court. The Civil Service offender was investigated by his superior in the office, and the case was then remanded to an administrative council identified with that Civil Service office. "The decision of that council has equal validity with the verdict an examining magistrate [*müstantık*] may reach." In other words, at that time the proposed formulas for prosecution and punishment were all but exploratory.[83]

In frustration, the senators ended the debate by expressing their various concerns about the outcome of all this. Ferit wanted "justice" in three weeks; otherwise, he said, "because of our defective justice system, we incur the risk of being subjected to a very severe judgment, and being belatedly sorry will be of no avail." He stuck to his argument that the perpetrators of the crime and of the related atrocities were but "a few tramps." Senator Hüseyin Hüsnü Paşa invoked the example of the nineteenth-century Ottoman Foreign Minister Keçecizade Mehmet Fuat Paşa as an example of resoluteness for swift justice. In dealing with a similar crime of anti-Christian massacre in Lebanon in 1860, he promptly had had the 167 perpetrators executed by hanging and through firing squads, and one year later he was promoted to the highest office, i.e., grand vizier.[84] A. Riza rejoined, saying that the crimes in question could not fail to affect everyone, for "we are the owners, the masters of this land. Hence, the responsibility devolves upon all Ottomans. Our reputation has been stained and it is incumbent upon us to purge ourselves from this stain." Prior to adjourning, the report of the Senate's Civil Affairs Committee was read; in it, it was proposed that, if a crime did not fall within the purview of the Constitution relative to official duties, the offenders should be remanded to regular courts or to a court-martial.[85]

Among the many revelations of this series of debates in the Ottoman Senate was one whose text was relayed by one of the Armenian senators. When Reşit Akif Paşa had finished reporting the discovery of a secret cipher telegram ordering the massacre of Armenian deportee convoys (during the 21 November sitting), Armenian Senator Azaryan rose to relate his exchange with Osman

Bedri, director-general of police in the Ottoman capital during World War I. In the presence of Zareh Dilber, another Armenian senator, the police chief is quoted as saying the following to Azaryan:

> Do you, Armenians, really think that we would bother to separate the innocent from the guilty? With one clean sweep we disposed of all of them [Hepsini bir sudan yıkadık].[86]

The Special Committee of the Senate had wound up its work on 9 November. It reported its findings to the full Senate, which met on 14 November, and decided to have some of Senator Mahmut's material published. Senators Reşif Akif and Abdurrahman Şeref, ex-minister and renowned historian, respectively, insisted on such publication. However, with the prorogation of the Chamber of Deputies on 21 December 1918, all these undertakings proved abortive.

This was not the case with the other chamber of the Ottoman parliament, however. As stipulated by Article 31 of the Ottoman Constitution, the Chamber of Deputies was entrusted with the task of initiating legal action against cabinet ministers accused of misconduct in office. The first stage of such legal action was the activation of the Chamber's Fifth Investigative Department. Its formation, function, and performance will be explored in the next section, where the focus of inquiry will be the Armenian deportations and massacres: two of the ten questions around which the interrogation of the wartime cabinet ministers revolved dealt with these atrocities.

The Fifth Investigative Department of the Chamber of Deputies (Beşinci Şube Tahkikat Komisyonu)

Unlike the Senate, which had only two departments and seven committees to carry out pertinent parliamentary inquiries and investigations, the Chamber utilized over five respective departments (*şube*) and twenty-one committees (*encümen*). As the title indicates, the Chamber decided to assign the job of investigating cabinet ministers to one of its departments rather than to one of its subordinate committees. As a Turkish chronicler pointed out, the forty-five members of the investigative department "almost entirely were chosen from CUP's 1915 list of candidates."[87] In a sense this was inevitable, for from its very inception the CUP was bent on gaining optimal control in the affairs of the parliament, especially those of the Chamber. As one of the original founders of the rebellious Young Turk (later CUP) movement declaimed, "95 percent of these deputies were not elected [as claimed], but were rather appointed by the last government [i.e., the CUP]."[88] A similar appraisal, albeit in more restrained language, was made by Mustafa Kemal (Atatürk) some ten days later when he declared, "The Chamber of Deputies is not representative of the nation."[89] In arguing along the same lines Silan, one of the staff of the investigative body, likewise pointed out that "most of these deputies were CUP men despite their identification with the new brand of that party,"[90] i.e., Teceddüd. Moreover, out of the forty-five members, one had resigned and two were deceased; seventeen out of the remaining forty-two, for a variety of reasons, could not come to Istanbul to take part in the Chamber's postwar work.[91]

Another striking point was the issue of "conflict of interest." Among the members of the investigative body, chosen by drawing lots, were three wartime cabinet ministers who were expected to sit in judgment of their own misdeeds, namely, Halil Menteşe (foreign minister), Ahmet Nesimi (commerce and agriculture, subsequently foreign minister), and Mehmet Cavit (finance minister). The situation was further compounded by the inclusion in that body of Midhat Şükrü, the secretary-general of CUP and as such a partisan potentate, and of other CUP men known for their active involvement in the crime they were expected to investigate and to adjudge, such as Hüseyin Tosun, Ali Cenani, Seyfullah (Erzurum), and above all Ilyas Sami.[92] But at no time did the full complement of this body take part in the actual investigation; rather, there were at all times only 20–25 members present to perform that task.[93]

In the period stretching from 6 November to 7 December 1918, the body conducted fifteen hearings, during which eleven ministers and one Grand Vizier were interrogated. Among them, Finance Minister Mehmet Cavit was interrogated three days in a row (24, 25, 26 November), and Minister of Food Supplies Kemal, the only cabinet minister who was not a deputy at the same time, was interrogated for two days (2, 7 December). The remaining two hearings involved the reading into the record on the same day, 19 December 1918, of the written responses of the two Şeyhülislams, Ürgüplü Hayri and Musa Kâzım. Five days earlier, i.e., 14 December, the members, by an overwhelming majority (with three votes in dissent), voted to publish the proceedings in their entirety. Grand Vizier Sait Halim's written response, as a supplement to his oral testimony, was read into the record on 17 November. Of the fourteen cabinet ministers, seven claimed not to have been part of the Ottoman government during the wartime deportations and massacres. This left the ministers Molla Zade Ibrahim, Ahmet Şükrü, Ahmet Nesimi, Abbas Halim, and the two Şeyhülislams, along with the grand vizier, to confront and answer the two questions that, as noted above, dealt directly and indirectly with the deportations and massacres. They constituted numbers 5 and 10 in the list of ten questions Divaniye Deputy Fuad had submitted in his motion on 4 November; he passed away eleven days later.

It is significant that from this body of CUP members and partisans, the questions and the probing relative to Armenian deportations and massacres came almost entirely from Arab deputies, namely, Hilmi (Basra), Fuad (Divaniye, district capital in Baghdad province whose population comprised a large number of tribal Bedevis), Halit (Divaniye), but above all Ragıp Neşâşibı (Jerusalem), who kept exploring many aspects of the mass murder, such as the subversion of the principle of legality, the use of convicts, and wholesale retaliation, among others. On the other side of the equation was a young deputy from Ertuğrul (Bilecik), Şemsettin (Günaltay), then thirty-five years old, who subsequently would join the Kemalists in the War of Independence and in 1949 would become prime minister in the new Republic of Turkey. He was serving as assistant and secretary to the chairman of the investigative body, Abdullah Azmi (Kütahya); both of them were CUP men. Notwithstanding, both of them, Şemsettin in particular, played a pivotal role in shaping the direction of the overall investigation. When the CUP dissolved into a new party, Teceddüd, on 31 October 1918, Şemsettin, after a fiery speech in which he sharply criticized the CUP, was elected the second president of the new party.

Even though he had resigned at the start of World War I in protest against Turkey's intervention into the war after maintaining a three-month long "armed neutrality," Finance Minister Cavit did deem it important to offer some comments on 4 February 1917. He had joined the second wartime Ottoman cabinet, headed by Talaat—who then was promoted to the rank of grand vizier—when the Armenian genocide was all but consummated. In answering the relevant questions, Cavit declared:

> I never was agreeable to the deportation of the Armenians; furthermore, whenever the opportunity presented itself, I sensitized my associates about this fact. Moreover, after joining the Cabinet, I adopted a permissive and lenient attitude when applying the laws and regulations dealing with the goods and possessions of these deportees. I even was able to obtain Talaat's consent for their return from exile.[94]

Justice Minister Ibrahim's interrogation yielded a number of revelations about the hidden aspects of the Armenian Genocide. Even though he denied direct governmental involvement in the crime, he nevertheless inadvertently attested to it—as it so often happens in the course of such probes and interrogations. In responding to the Arab Deputy Ragıb Neşâşibı's challenge that Talaat's Temporary Law of Deportation of 13 (26) May 1915 never was submitted to the Chamber of Deputies for final approval and enactment, Ibrahim relied on the method of indirection. He pointed out that two committees of the Chamber had done so. Indeed, on 21 September (4 October) 1915, the office of the grand vizier issued a memorandum that provided "the rationale" for a draft law ordering the deportation of the Armenians. Some fifteen months later, on 4 (17) December 1916, the Chamber's Committee for Military Affairs (Askeri Encümen) approved that draft through the issuance of an official report (*mazbata*). The Judicial Committee (Adliye Encümeni) did the same on 18 (31)

January 1917. However, there is no record anywhere that the Chamber as a whole considered and formally promulgated that law as required by Article 36 of the Ottoman Constitution. That article stipulates that the temporary laws "have [only] provisionally the force of law.... [However] they should be submitted to the Chamber of Deputies as soon as this may be convened."[95] Ibrahim claimed that he had only belatedly learned about the abuses and crimes against the Armenians, with Deputy Neşâşibı countering that these problems had been going on not for one day but for a year and half. When told by Hilmi, an Arab deputy, that multitudes of Armenians far removed from the war zones were likewise deported and killed wholesale, he again retorted, "I know nothing about it" (Ondan haberim yok). When told again by Neşâşibı that "many massacres were perpetrated and there are documents at hand about them," Ibrahim then allowed that he and his colleagues were belatedly saddened about them. At this point, Ibrahim underscored the fact that the deputies of the Chamber were fully apprised about these crimes, but that none of them lifted a finger or "alerted us with a sense of urgency." He went on to say that there was no official request, "Absolutely none, to investigate, no complaint whatsoever." Even though he was investigating the Armenian massacres, he said, "all of us, nevertheless, felt constrained to maintain silence on certain matters—because of the war."

When the questions addressed the role of the Special Organization and the convicts enrolled in it, Ibrahim remarkably claimed, but simultaneously also disclaimed, knowledge about them. He offered the following explanation: a public prosecutor (*müddei umumi*) had emptied the prisons to enable the convicts to enroll in that organization. "When this came to my attention I raised hell. Only through a request to the pertinent Ministry and through an imperial rescript can a convict be freed. But then the military intervened, arguing 'we can't afford neglecting the services of a sizeable force component.' Accordingly, we framed and enacted a respective law which your esteemed assembly approved."[96] Finally, Ibrahim complained that the military was disdainful of the cabinet ministers and therefore almost completely ignored them when reaching important decisions.[97]

The thrust of the testimony of Grand Vizier Sait Halim was along the same lines, except that he added Talaat's Interior Ministry to the military powerhouse as a source of evil. The Interior Ministry was described as an agency that ignored Halim, the supreme executive authority of the empire, and when necessary pushed him around. This was significant, considering that in terms of rank he was the superior of both Enver and Talaat, the ministers of Defense and War and the Interior, respectively.

The wartime grand vizier's interrogation focused first of all on the role of the criminals enrolled in the Special Organization. He flatly disclaimed any knowledge of them, arguing that it was a military matter and outside the

Cabinet's jurisdiction. He then allowed that he was unable to control even the ministers of the Cabinet, who had a nonchalant attitude toward him. When Deputy Şemseddin reminded him that he had the power to dismiss or replace any of the ministers, the answer was that he could not force the resignation of any of them. Upon the retort, "But you could have the power to do so," Sait Halim replied "I can't, if he refuses to resign." The interrogation then shifted to the power and role of Talaat. Upon his plaint that Interior Minister Talaat was willful and acted as he pleased, Şemsettin again reminded him that he and his Cabinet had the authority to fire any governor-general (*vali*), despite their dependence upon the office of the Interior Ministry for office-holding. The answer was the same: Talaat was in charge of everything. The chair then raised the issue of the enactment of "illegal laws" relative to the Armenian deportations, which entailed the victimization of people who were uninvolved and innocent. Neşâşibı, focusing on the same issue of deportations, asked why these people, who posed no threat to the rear of the army, were nevertheless deported. Sait Halim's answer replicated that of Justice Minister Ibrahim: "If these things really happened, I was not aware of them."

The interrogation then switched to the matter of the relationship between "deportations" on the one hand, and "massacres" on the other. Arab Deputy Neşaşibı wanted to know why the law of deportations had led to "butcheries [*asıp kesme*] for which there was no law, and which were carried out by military commanders." He then intoned, "Is there any law to deport and kill women and children?" Sait Halim's answer to this aspect of the problem, specifically the deportations seen as being a stepping stone for subsequent massacres, a so-called initial phase for organized mass murder, is both revealing and confessional. In this sense, it is of paramount importance for demonstrating, through prima facie evidence, that the covert intent of the deportations was the destruction of the deportee victim population. When answering this core question, this statesman, the highest formal authority of the Ottoman Empire, explicitly and unequivocally admitted that the real goal of the deportations, as decided by the Cabinet, had been willfully twisted by the implementers to become a "killing off" (*öldürmek*) operation. In fact, when elaborating further on this point, this wartime grand vizier twice used the word "massacre" (*kıtal*) without availing himself of the twin word "deportation," thereby coming as close to the concept of "genocide" as was then conceivable under the prevalent circumstances. As if to confirm the companion concept of "crimes against humanity," the chairman of the Chamber of Deputies' investigative body, Abdullah Azmi, observed, "these are offenses that can be subsumed under the terms of 'crimes against humanity.'" It should be noted that one of the two questions at issue here, no. 5, was framed in the terms of the temporary law under which the Armenians were deported and destroyed; these temporary laws were "totally contrary to the rules of law and precepts of humanity."[98]

Wartime Grand Vizier Sait Halim further disclosed in the course of his interrogation that Interior Minister Talaat, "despite my persistence and insistence refused to make available to me the final reports of those investigators who were sent to the provinces, and where massacres were perpetrated. Clearly, he was concealing [*ketm*] them from me. For months we were being subjected to temporizing, to being put off." Returning to the topic of the Special Organization, Sait Halim reiterated that there was no formal governmental decision regarding such matters as its creation, tasks, and competence. Nor was it possible to discuss these matters with those in charge of it. His response to the question of whether he sought written clarification on all these matters from the War Ministry was: the submission of "written requests for information was an exercise in futility for either no answer would be forthcoming, or the facts at issue would be met with a flat denial." (Ya cevap verilmiyor, yahut inkâr ile geçiştiriliyor).[99]

As indicated above, none of these interrogations, nor the preceding debates in both chambers of the parliament, would serve their ultimate goal: the creation of the High Court to try the wartime cabinet ministers, as provided by the Constitution. Ironically these efforts were nipped in the bud by the terms of the same Constitution, specifically Article 7, which allowed the sultan to dissolve the Chamber and for all practical purposes thereby silence the voice of the legislative representatives of the Ottoman government.[100] After a lapse of several months, during which Senate President Ahmet Riza for some reason had withheld them, the Archives of the Ottoman Chamber of Deputies, especially of its Fifth Investigative Department, were finally handed over by Mustafa Asım, the new Senate president, to the inquiry commissions of the new court-martial. Notwithstanding, the abruptness of the move of dissolving the Chamber not only exposed the constitutionally framed vulnerability of the legislative branch of that government but, by the same token, cast into relief the scope of freedom of action that was thereby accorded the executive branch of that government. How this latitude for freedom was handled in terms of the specifics of such executive actions will be discussed next, as these executive initiatives relate to the aim of prosecuting and punishing those responsible for Armenian deportations and massacres.

The Ottoman Executive Response

The Initial Steps

Before it fell, the first post–World War I Ottoman cabinet, headed by Grand Vizier Ahmet Izzet, sent, through Interior Minister Fethi (Okyar), a vague circular to the provinces that ordered the launching of a program of prosecution for crimes committed against the Armenians during the war. The respective investigation was to be carried out "without regard to status and rank" (mevki ve rütbelere bakılmaksızın).[101] Three weeks later, on 11 November 1918, the successor government, headed by the new Grand Vizier Ahmet Tevfik, did in fact launch, through the agency of Interior Minister Mustafa Arif, the requisite formal investigation. The wheels for criminal prosecution were thus set in motion. For this purpose he convened a meeting of civil inspectors. Within days his ministry began preparing dossiers relative to the Armenian deportations and massacres; a special segment of these files comprised incriminating data on the provincial governors who were part of the civil service system: *vali*s, *mutasarrıf*s, and *kaymakam*s. The resulting mass of information was relayed to the Ministries of War and Justice.

The drive for prosecution and punishment received an impetus when on 24 November the monarch, Sultan Vahdettin (Mehmet VI), referring to the Armenian massacres, publicly declared, "Such misdeeds … have broken my heart. I ordered an inquiry as I came to the throne.… Justice will soon be done."[102] Three days earlier, Reşit Akif, the distinguished Ottoman statesman with a remarkable record of public service in the highest offices of the Ottoman Empire, had revealed in his famous speech in the Ottoman Senate (see note 81) that while serving as president of the Council of State he had uncovered incriminating documents dealing with the matter of Armenian deportations and massacres. He had determined on that occasion that the Central Committee of the CUP, along with Interior Minister Talaat, had played a decisive role in the organization of these crimes. These revelations were weighty enough to prompt the empire's chief public prosecutor to decide to launch an investigation. On 6 December he secured a list containing the names of the respective suspects, against whom a general initiative of legal prosecution was launched four days later. All these steps led to the convening on 17 December of a major conference at the Justice Ministry. It was attended by Tahir, Chief of Criminal Affairs Division of that ministry, and by Saadi, Legal Counsel at the Interior Ministry. They agreed on a draft law, consisting of a number of statutes and framed in four articles, which was to be submitted to both ministries with a request to treat it as "urgent" business in need of approval by the parliament—then in session—and by the sultan. Article 1 stipulated that verdicts by the projected court-martial could not be appealed. Thus it took about a month before the Justice Ministry could come up with a legislative bill specifying the functions and outlining the competence of the envisaged court-martial.

In the meantime the cabinet, considering the uncertainty of the set of statutes under which the suspects could be tried, had decided on 14 December, to avail itself of the provisions of the Temporary Law on the Suppression of the Armed Brigands (*çete*); the purpose was the court-martialing of these suspects.[103] The intent of this arrangement, namely, the depicting of the label of brigandage, was to emphasize the character of the defendants and underscore the nature of their crimes involved. As a rule, courts-martial presuppose the application of the rule of martial law (*idare-i-örfiye*). The first such law in modern Turkey was enacted during the Turko-Russian War (2 October 1877). It was supplemented on 20 June (3 July) 1909, and then again in 1910.[104]

These were the conditions that mandated the launching of criminal proceedings against the suspects. Accordingly, these authorities tried to muster all their resources to obtain optimal results by way of launching the requisite pretrial investigation; for that very purpose they created the redoutable Mazhar Inquiry Commission. What follows is a detailed examination of the formation, composition, function, and productivity of that commission.

The Mazhar Inquiry Commission

The above-mentioned revelations of Reşit Akif had influenced the modus operandi of the then officiating cabinet, which on 5 December accepted, as a preliminary step to court-martial, the statutes, with province-oriented subcomponents, needed to form a special inquiry commission. It was to comprise officials from both the Justice and Interior Ministries. With the active support of (Gürcü) Haydar Molla, then Minister of Justice, this commission (Heyeti Tetkikiye) was tasked with "the investigation of misdeeds" (*tetkiki seyyiat*) of officials only. Installed in the headquarters of the Directorate of Public Security (Emniyeti Umumiye),[105] it nevertheless operated as an independent agency. Headed by Hasan Mazhar[106] and hence bearing his name, the commission was charged with the task of conducting a thorough pretrial investigation.[107] The commission started its work on 13 November 1918 and ended in the second half of January 1919. The decision to formally arrest a detainee was a judicial one and could be made by a justice of the peace. The entire procedure was put in motion by the public prosecutor, who, as required by law, became convinced that criminal prosecution was warranted and forwarded to the examining magistrate a written demand for the opening of a preliminary investigation.

The Mazhar Inquiry Commission undertook other supplementary initiatives. It asked the Sublime Porte, the seat of the Ottoman government, to assemble the many accounts of wartime massacres that were appearing in newspapers at that time and transmit them to the commission via the Bureau of the Press. In addition, in December 1918 Mazhar sent the War Ministry a set of eight questions respectfully requesting answers for the sake of "clarification." Focusing on the role of the Special Organization in the organization and implementation of the Armenian massacres, Mazhar's questions included the following specifics: How many Special Organization contingents (actually he used the word "divisions" [*fırka*]) did B. Şakir, a member of CUP's Central Committee, have at his disposal? From which prisons and when were the convicts of the Special Organization released? How many lieutenant colonels,

colonels, majors, captains, etc. were in charge or in command? How many of them were trained as regular army officers? Who ordered their release and who engaged them? The sense of these queries was to emphasize the Inquiry Commission's focal interest in the major role it felt the Special Organization had played in the crimes it was to investigate and prosecute. In fact question no. 7 specifically inquired as "to the mission and number of brigands" associated with brigand chief Yakup Cemil.[108] Even though its name suggested an information-gathering mission, the Mazhar Inquiry Commission essentially functioned as a body meant to conduct a large-scale pretrial criminal investigation. As such, it immersed itself in the following four types of investigative activity.

The gathering of eyewitness accounts that were appearing in the newspapers

The commission was not only interested in accounts coming from survivor-victims but most particularly in those originating from Turkish and other Muslim eyewitnesses. Accordingly, on 4 December 1918 the office of the prosecutor, attached to the Intermediate Court of Appeals (Istinaf Mahkemesi), issued a public invitation for such witnesses to come forward and offer their testimony. It soon became evident, however, that the ensuing body of information was not always reliable or sufficient. To remedy the situation the Cabinet Council created a Special Commission of Information whose task would be to scrutinize the ensemble of individual accusations with a view to determining their overall probative value. Kemal, the associate director of public security (Emniyeti Umumiye), was appointed chairman of that commission.

The gathering of official and quasi-official documents

The work of documentation proceeded at two levels: local, i.e., in Istanbul, then the Ottoman capital; and provincial, involving the major centers of deportations and massacres in Anatolia as well as the rest of European Turkey, such as Tekirdağ (Rodosto) and Edirne (Adrianapolis). As a result, from Ankara province alone, for example, the commission received a batch of forty-two cipher telegrams that included telegraphic exchanges between two military commanders.[109] Colonel Şahabettin, deputy commander of Kayseri district's 15th division and Kayseri's military commander (*nokta kumandanı*), is seen here relaying information on details relative to the ongoing Armenian deportations and massacres to his superior, Colonel Halil Recayi, deputy commander of Ankara's Fifth Army Corps. What is significant about these cipher telegrams is the paramount fact that every one of them was scrutinized and eventually authenticated by competent officials from the twin ministries of Interior and Justice, who thereby legalized each and every one of them. Thereafter, as indicated above, they affixed at the bottom of the document the formula "it conforms to the original," or *aslına muafıkdır;* sometimes the word "mutabıkdır" was used as a substitute for *muafıkdır.* At the 9th sitting of the Yozgat trial series (22 February 1919), the public prosecutor reiterated this point of official authentication when the same Colonel Şahabettin was on trial. As he kept denying his complicity, the presiding judge ordered the court clerk to produce the ciphers, which the tribunal had secured unbeknownst to the defendant; they all bore the defendant's signature. Upon his personal inspection and confirmation of their authenticity, the colonel reversed his denial and began to narrate the details of the crimes before suffering a nervous breakdown when, as a result, he was granted a respite. This evidence-gathering operation was extended to twenty-eight provincial locations.

It was even more intensive in the Ottoman capital. Though the raid upon the premises of CUP's headquarters proved largely abortive, the raiding team—consisting of the public prosecutor of the court of the first instance (*bidayet mahkemesi*) and his support group, the judicial police—did manage to secure two residual documents, which were immediately impounded. Referring to one of them on 11 December 1918, the Turkish daily *Sabah* disclosed its provenance and content in an editorial.[110] Two days later the French language dailies *Le Spectateur d'Orient* and *Renaissance* followed suit. As stated earlier, Yunus Nadi, the nationalist-Kemalist editor of the daily *Yeni Gün*, shamed the editors of *Sabah* two days later while dismissing the document in question as "fake" (*uydurma*). On the next day, 14 December, in a retort titled "Response to *Yenigün*," *Sabah* emphatically stuck to its story, at the same time inviting *Yeni Gün* to answer six questions it posed. In the alleged cipher-telegram that was addressed to Malatya's CUP club (in Harput province), Talaat is depicted as ordering "the extermination [*imha*] of the Armenian deportees there, for which I assume responsibility."

The relative success of this operation of search and seizure, and the stimulus it provided to carry on, led to a new undertaking. Prompted by rising suspicions that the array of secret documents that were missing from the Nuriosmaniye headquarters of the CUP might be held for safekeeping by Ahmet Ramiz, on orders of the minister of police, a surprise raid at the Ramiz's residence was organized. Ramiz was not only an attorney, not only a counselor in the Defense Ministry, but above all the son-in-law of Dr. Bahaeddin Şakir, one of the arch authors of the anti-Armenian scheme. The search took place on 12 December 1918 at Sabunhane Street in Şişli, a residential section of Istanbul, yielding a suitcase full of documents that were believed to be part and parcel of those missing from CUP headquarters.[111] When it was opened four days later by court officials, among its contents were found portions of the minutes of the deliberations of top CUP leaders relative to their plans for liquidation of the empire's Armenian population. In the course of his testimony before the military tribunal that was court-martialing top CUP leaders, the party's secretary-general, Mithat Şükrü, disclosed that Dr. Mehmet Nazım, another principal architect of the Armenian genocide, had whisked all these documents away from CUP headquarters.[112] During the Ankara Independence Courts trials, which dealt with the conspiracy against the life of Mustafa Kemal Atatürk, Şükrü testified once more. He thereby indicated that Dr. Şakir carried all important CUP documents in a suitcase to the residence of Ramiz, who subsequently destroyed them, lest they fell into the hands of the British.[113] It remains unclear whether the documents handled by both Nazım and Şakir were the same documents, and whether, when, and to what extent Ramiz did destroy them.

However, the one surrendered by Harput province's wartime governor-general, Sağırzade Sabit, was most consequential. Acknowledging the possibility of Turkey losing the war, and apprehensive about the day of reckoning relative to the crimes committed in his province and under his watch, he deemed it prudent to save some ciphers with which to defend himself. The one dated 21 June (21 April) 1915 and bearing no. 2597 was such a cipher. In it Dr. B. Şakir urges his underling, Resneli Boşnak Nazım, CUP's responsible secretary in Harput province, to expedite the elimination of the provinces' Armenian deportee population by using "*tasfiye*" and "*imha,*" meaning liquidation and destruction, respectively. The authenticated version of this cipher was used in the Key Indictment and the Harput trial series verdict.[114] It is noteworthy that Hasan Tahsin (Uzer), Erzurum's wartime governor-general, likewise comported himself defensively when he declared on 11 December 1918, "I shall respond to inquires with documents and proofs."[115] In fact Tahsin is on record attempting to dissuade Interior Minister Talaat, who through a circular had ordered the deportation of the Armenians of Erzurum province on 10 (23) May 1915. In his response, sent the next day, Tahsin pleaded with Talaat to spare the Armenians of his province, for whose loyalty he vouched and whose deportation, when effected, could, he went on to argue, prove a calamity for the Turkish war effort. (Ermenilerin sevki casusluk ve ihtilâl gibi esbabe müstenid ise, bendenizce bu gayri variddir.... Ermenileri dahile sevke teşebbüs etmekle ordunun korkduğu başına gelmiş olur.... Van'da ihtilâl olmazdı ve olamazdı. Kendimiz zorlaya zorlaya şu içinden çıkamadığımız kargaşalığı meydana getirdik ve orduyu müşkül mevkiye sokduk).[116]

There was one more, final raid on CUP headquarters before the occupying Allied powers decided to impound all CUP properties and clubs. Armed with an order issued by the Finance Ministry, authorities of the office of Real Estates and Landholdings (Emlâk ve Arazi), accompanied by a squad of secret police agents, conducted yet another search. This time they uncovered a hidden basement, elegantly decorated and furnished, which contained the CUP's secret coffers (*sandık*). The new documents found there were turned over to the military governors' office (*muhafızlık*).[117]

Through a circular issued 28 December 1918, the Mazhar Inquiry Commission requested incriminating evidence from provincial authorities, and by mid January 1919 it had completed its investigation of twenty-eight provincial areas. Mazhar's success in this respect was not complete, however, as many officials, holdovers of the discredited and defunct CUP regime, did not cooperate fully, withholding incriminating evidence by stalling or ignoring the request, sometimes even showing open defiance. Some of them chose to cling to certain documents to protect themselves against future prosecution.

The recourse to interrogations and interrogatories

As indicated above, the Mazhar commission's investigation was, by Cabinet decision, to be limited to officials of any and all ranks. Its targets were mainly parliamentary deputies and provincial governors-general (*vali*). The first step in this respect was taken by arresting the *vali*s of the four provinces in which the deportation and extermination of the Armenians was most widespread. Involved were the *vali*s of Sivas (Ahmet Muammer), Diyarbekir (Dr. Mehmet Şahingiray Reşit), Harput (Sağıroğlu Sabit), and Musul (Mehmet Memduh). Of these, Dr. Reşit would manage to escape on 25 January 1919 only to be tracked down shortly thereafter; thus cornered, he committed suicide. Because officials could not be held in detention more than thirty days, and because he was intent on keeping them longer, Mazhar inquired at the Interior Ministry about the possibility of changing the statutes in question. Moreover, pursuing the case of another *vali,* Trabzon's Cemal Azmi, who had fled to Germany, Mazhar sent an investigator to Trabzon to gather evidence for prosecution. His next target being the CUP deputies of the parliament, Mazhar sought authorization to deny travel documents to twenty-six of them; he was especially interested in those of Muş, Kayseri, Erzincan, and Diyarbekir, epicenters of huge massacres. He was able to locate and arrest the latter province's two deputies, Pirinccizade Arif Feyzi and Zülfizade Zülfi.

The pretrial interrogations of these arrested officials were conducted by examining magistrates, i.e., *tahkikat hakimi* (Penal Code, Article 47). With the help of the judiciary police (*adli zabıta memuru*) they were taken into custody after being served subpoenas; failure to respond to such subpoenas incurred the risk of prison terms under Articles 75 and 87 of the penal code. Rogatory commissions (*bil istinabe*) were employed for evidence gathering in cases handled in absentia, and legal-size white foolscap (*eseri cedid*) was used for recording the evidence gathered, which then was verified and signed by the suspects. That evidence largely consisted of oral and written answers to sets of questions drawn up by the inquiry commission. Given the capital crime aspect of the pending cases, secrecy and exclusion of defense counsel at this stage of the proceedings were mandatory conditions.

Written statements and affidavits

The inquiry commission additionally collected evidence from several Muslim witnesses who for one reason or another could not come and testify in person. Foremost among these was the affidavit of Third Army Commander-in-Chief Mehmet Vehip (Kaçı), who throughout the month of December (1918) supplied the Mazhar Inquiry Commission with a steady flow of detailed information about several aspects of the Armenian Genocide operations that were consummated in his command zone, encompassing six Ottoman provinces with a heavy concentration of Armenian subjects. The written report, most detailed and damning, and dated 5 December 1918, was used in the military tribunal's Key Indictment (*T. V.*, 3540, p. 7) and the Harput verdict (*T. V.*, 3771, p. 1). Also noteworthy in this respect is the affidavit that Ahmet Avni Paşa, the wartime military commandant of the Trabzon port district, prepared for the fourth sitting (3 April 1919) of the military tribunals' Trabzon trial series; most particularly notable was the material incorporated in an ancillary affidavit he submitted before his second appearance on 5 May (16th sitting). In it Avni Paşa revealed the crimes committed by the *çete*s of the ancillary Special Organization, led by that province's *vali,* Cemal Azmi, and exempted the original Special Organization from blame for these crimes.

The final stage of this multi-level investigation involved the codification and indexing of the wealth of the evidence assembled along three categories: (1) by the name of those CUP leaders presumed to be the chief perpetrators or accomplices (*ceraim failleri*) or *ratione personae;* (2) by provenance of the acts of perpetration involving specific regions and locations, or *ratione loci;* and (3) the classification and itemization of that evidence, or *ratione materiae,* into such categories as series (*tertip*), files (*dosya*), document (*vesika*), single-leaf document (*varaka*), investigative loose papers (*evrakı istintakiye*), appendix (*merbut*), photocopy (*photograph*), deposition (*beyanatı* or *ifadatı tahririye*), remnants of the Special Organization papers (Teşkilâtı Mahsusa'nın evrak mütebakiyesi), and Talaat's papers (Talaat Bey'e ait evrak).

The resulting dossiers were clustered around the criteria by which the courts-martial were arranged, namely, categories of defendants such as cabinet ministers, CUP party chieftains, CUP's provincial representatives, delegates, and inspectors, and various sites of atrocities. Before it disbanded, the Mazhar Inquiry Commission had compiled and handed over to the court-martial authorities some 200 dossiers warranting the criminal prosecution of the suspects identified and described in them.

Pretrial Mass Arrests

Two-stage arrests were the next phase in the overall initiative bent on court-martialing the perpetrators in question. The drive received impetus from the pressure the British and French occupying military authorities were exerting upon postwar Turkish governments, especially with respect to the arrest of wartime cabinet ministers.[118] The ensuing arrests were triggered by the 8 January 1919 Tevfik Cabinet decision.[119] Officials of the First Department of the Directorate of Police raided the homes of the targeted suspects at midnight and delivered their charges in the early hours of the next day.[120] After they were detained at police headquarters for twenty-four hours, the director of police had to obtain formal arrest orders from the Interior Ministry, since the subjects had been taken into custody on orders of the Cabinet Council, which had no jurisdiction beyond the initial 24-hour limit.

The first stage of the arrests covered the period between 30 January and 4 February 1919. The cabinet had ordered the arrest of 120 suspects, but only 90 of them could be apprehended by the police agents headed by Halil. Of those, 58 were temporarily detained at the facilities of the Directorate of Police and the remaining 32 at those of the military governor (*muhafızlık*). In addition, the Ministry of War arrested some forty army officers.[121] Below is a list of various categories of suspects arrested in the first stage of the roundups, mostly on 30 and 31 January 1919. They were eventually taken to the military governor's headquarters and thence to the military prison run by the Defense Ministry.

1. CUP leaders: Mithat Şükrü (Bleda); Hüseyin Cahit (Yalçın); Mehmet Ziya Gökalp; Tevfik Rüştü (Aras); Ferit (Hamal); Mustafa Rahmi (Evranos) Aslan; Lazistan deputy Süleyman Sudi; CUP Central Committee member Dr. Rüsuhi; Public Security Chief Tevfik Hadi, Ali Münif (Yegena).
2. Military commanders and other officers: Mahmut Kâmil, major-general (*Tümgeneral*), Third Army commander; Mehmet Vehip (Kaçı), brigadier-general (*Tuğgernal*) and successor to General M. Kâmil; Süleyman Numan, colonel, head of Sanitation and Health Services of the Army; Ali Ihsan Sabis, Sixth Army commander, major general; Fahrettin (Türkkan), lieutenant-general (*Korgeneral*); Nuri Kıllıgil and Mürsel Paşa, both honorary brigadier generals serving under the umbrella of the Army of Islam in Baku; Istanbul's military governor *Kızanlıklı* Artillery Colonel Ahmet Cevat; Halil (Kut), commander in chief of the Army Groups East, lieutenant-general. According to a local daily newspaper report (*Djagadamard*, 31 May 1919) Colonel Cevat sobbed (*hüngür hüngür*) as he was taken to a steamboat at Sirkeci for transport and incarceration at Malta under British custody.

The matter of the legality of prosecuting cabinet ministers within weeks produced, however, a governmental crisis. Grand Vizier Ahmet Tevfik (Okday) failed to secure the requisite imperial *Irade* (the command of the Sultan in writing) on grounds that such prosecution was inimical to the terms of the

Ottoman Constitution. Thereupon, on 3 March 1919, Tevfik, with his cabinet, resigned.[122]

Within days after he came to power on 4 March 1919, Damad Mehmet Ferit, who was succeeding Grand Vizier Tevfik, delivered a speech to his cabinet. In it he emphasized the necessity of speeding up the criminal prosecution of the perpetrators, "whose crimes drew the revulsion of the entire humankind" (Alemi insaniyetin nefretini celbeden erbab-ı cinayet haklarında âcilen bir karar ittihaz eylemeleri).[123] Promptly responding to this call, his new interior minister, Cemal, embarked on 9 March upon a large-scale initiative of arrests; twenty prominent CUP men, including several cabinet ministers, were taken into custody on that day alone. One day earlier, an imperial *Irade* had authorized the formation of a new and strictly military court-martial. The arrests continued for several days, resulting in the apprehension of some sixty men, thus bringing the sum total of the two roundups to 300.[124] According to the Turkish chronicler Sarıhan, whose respective total figure is 200, the three high commissioners, British, French, and Italian, had handed over their own combined list of thirty-six men whose arrests they demanded.[125] Among the twenty arrestees (March 9) the following Cabinet Ministers were listed: Giritli Ahmet Nesimi (Sayman), Foreign; Sait Halim, Grand Vizier and Foreign; Ali Münif, Public Works; Ahmet Şükrü, Education; Pirizade Ibrahim, Justice; Fethi Okyar, Interior (postwar); Halil Menteşe, Foreign; Rifat, Finance; Musa Kâzım, Şeyh-ul-Islam.[126] For a historical overview of these developments, leading up to the formation of the courts-martial under review here, one may consult Taner Akçam's article.[127]

The central task of all criminal justice systems is to identify a given perpetrator and establish the type and degree of involvement in the crime at hand. The evidence of lethal violence and the victims it creates are conditions that inevitably place the criminal rather than the crime at the forefront of the criminal justice system. This is the main, if not the only, reason why the ultimate end of that system is retributive justice. The function of all pretrial investigations is precisely this: to facilitate the process of identifying the perpetrator of a crime. In brief, it is not so much the crime, but the criminal and his (or her) related circumstances that occupy center stage in the criminal justice system.

The evidence of the World War I Armenian genocide was both ubiquitous and overwhelming in the immediate aftermath of that war. But the matter of perpetrators, with all their gradations of culpability, remained to be established and documented. This is precisely the reason why Aukland Geddes, the British ambassador in Washington, D.C., responding to a request from London, stated that the U.S. National Archives contained "a large number of documents on the Armenian deportations and massacres." He added, however, that under existing conditions it was not possible to assign and charge specific culpabilities to specific Turkish suspects.[128] Yet British Foreign Office Near East Specialist W. S. Edmonds, referring to the same Turkish suspects detained by the British in Malta, stated that "there is probably not one of these prisoners who does not deserve a long term of imprisonment, if not capital punishment."[129]

The massive and multilayered archives of the Mazhar Inquiry Commission are testimony to the postwar Turkish authorities' grim resolve not only to expose the crime of the centrally organized mass murder, but to seek a measure of tangible retributive justice. The inordinate importance of the reality of these twin objectives can be gauged by bringing it into a relationship to an episode that remarkably coincides with the pretrial investigative efforts of the Mazhar commission. In an interview with the special correspondent of the British newspaper *Morning Post,* the heir apparent to the Ottoman throne, Prince Abdul Mecit, disclosed that upon hearing of the scheme of massacres, he rushed to see War Minister and de facto Commander-in-Chief of the Ottoman Armed Forces Generalissimo Enver: "I went to Stamboul and insisted on seeing Enver. I asked him if it was true that they intended to recommence the massacres which had been our shame and disgrace under Abdulhamit. The only reply I could get from him was: 'It is decided. It is the programme.'"[130]

The Constraints Bearing Down on a Timid Sultan

As stated above, before resigning, Grand Vizier Tevfik vainly tried to secure imperial authorization for proceeding against the wartime cabinet ministers held responsible for the Armenian deportations and massacres. When formulating his reasons for declining such explicit authorization, the sultan, arguing that it devolved upon the Cabinet Council to do so, nevertheless recognized the magnitude of the crime, whose planning War Minister Enver had confirmed to the heir apparent. In doing so the Turkish monarch invoked, for the first time, the principle of "crimes against humanity" (Kanun-ı insaniyete … karşı ika edilen ceraim), adding that "the arrest and prosecution of the authors of these crimes is the essential duty of a civilized government [*vezaif-i asliyesi*]."[131] Yet throughout the pretrial and trial stages of the prosecution he remained a remarkably cautious, hesitant, and even apprehensive monarch. His fears extended not only to the remaining CUP conspirators but also to other embittered nationalists increasingly becoming restive and despondent.

Within days after making this argument, the sultan ended up authorizing the establishment of courts-martial, confiding to a British intermediary that he was prepared to comply with all the demands of the British relative to the matter of criminal prosecution if he could only receive British protection in return. He let it be known that large-scale prosecutions were likely to trigger a popular uprising, his dethronement, and even his assassination. In brief, he wanted to know if he could count on the support of the victorious Allies should he proceed with severity against the offenders in question; he was painfully aware of the possibility that the latter might decline such support on the grounds that it was an internal matter.[132] On 27 January, however, he directed his anxieties toward the Allies, whom he bemoaned for being "merciless" toward him: "Only God beside myself, knows the extent of my suffering. They [the victors] do not hint but rather bluntly tell what is in their minds. Even though I am a constitutional monarch, they treat me as if I were an absolutist monarch. Whenever I remind them of the constitution, they retort with 'What constitution?'"[133]

These anxieties and apprehensions came to a head on the occasion of the death verdict the court-martial issued against Mehmet Kemal, one of the perpetrators of Armenian massacres in Yozgat, a district in Ankara province. The extraordinary sensitivity of the matter of executing a Turkish official for crimes against a non-Muslim minority led to protracted bickering between the sultan, who had to ratify the verdict, and the *Şeyhulislam,* the chief legal-religious interpreter of Islam, who had to verify that a certain governmental act of punishment was in conformity with sacred Islamic law and was, therefore, legitimate. When the sultan received the papers for signature the day after Kemal's conviction, already sanctioned by the grand vizier and the defense minister, the monarch hesitated. He wanted the *Şeyhulislam* to issue an appropriate *fetva* (authoritative opinion sanctioning an act). He correctly anticipated that Kemal was likely to be elevated to the altar of martyrdom following his execution, and he therefore believed that a *fetva* might mitigate the probability of antagonizing the masses he knew would be aroused by the execution under any circumstances.

What ensued was a protracted and tortuous exchange between the two. The sultan insisted on a Sublime Opinion that would be tantamount to legitimizing the verdict on general principles (*ifta*), averring that, as sultan, he was personally convinced of the guilt of Kemal; he added, however, that he needed the support of the *Şeyhulislam* inasmuch as he was also a caliph, i.e., a spiritual head, and therefore also responsible in a religious sense. The *Şeyhulislam,* perhaps not fully understanding the monarch's subtle concerns, composed the requested *fetva,* in which he declared the execution of a Muslim convicted of murdering non-Muslims as being compatible with Muslim sacred law. This brand of opinion was held to be not the *ifta* but the *kaza* type, amounting to a pronouncement of a verdict, therefore a kind of secular-legal performance, the difference between *ifta* and *kaza* being that of consultative vs. distributive justice. Still, the monarch not only refused to accept it but wrote a memo outlining more specifically what he wanted, which was this: the *fetva* should not dwell on the specifics of Kemal's case but be rather a general declaration of principle, stating that if the trial in question was conducted according to law and justice, then the death sentence was deemed to be in conformity with the sacred law. This version was eventually composed and incorporated in a new *fetva* bearing Şeyhulislam Mustafa Sabri's signature. By the time the sultan was finally ready to ratify the death verdict, Kemal had already been executed.[134]

Notwithstanding the apprehensions and hesitations of the sultan, the Cabinet, together with the judicial authorities, proceeded to complete the preparations for the criminal prosecution of the principal perpetrators through court-martial. The series of official acts relative to these preparations are listed below.

1. On 12 December 1918, the imperial rescript was issued for the establishment of the court-martial. It was published in the 21 December 1918 issue of *T.V.*, no. 3424.
2. On 18 December 1918, a bill for amnesty was submitted to the Chamber of Deputies, but following its dissolution by imperial rescript, the cabinet, on that same day, 23 December, enacted it as a law. It was published in the 24 December 1918 issue of *T.V.*, no. 3427.
3. The Cabinet likewise issued a decree on 25 December 1918, relative to the trial by regular courts of the suspects, and for areas not placed under martial law. It was published in the 28 December 1918 issue of *T.V.*, no. 3430.
4. On 8 January 1919, the Cabinet Council decided to install courts-martial in six regions, namely, Izmir (Ömer Yaver Paşa), Bursa (Hilmi Paşa), Tekirdağ (Osman Rifat Paşa), Edirne (Esat Paşa), Samsun (Tevfik Paşa), and Ayıntab (Mehmet Ali Paşa). The decision was published in the 14 January issue of *T.V.*, 3445.
5. On 1 February 1919, the Cabinet Council decided to declare the CUP illegal and confiscate all its properties. The decision was published in the 15 February 1919 issue of *T.V.*, 3462.
6. On 8 March 1919, Demad Ferit, the new grand vizier, issued a message to his new cabinet in which he warned all officials that henceforth "all manner of oppression, tyranny, persecution, massacre, deportation, has been banished." It was published in the 9 March 1919 issue of *T.V.*, no. 3491.

The stage was set for proceeding to the actual court-martial.

Notes

1. See the explanation in Vahakn N. Dadrian, *Key Elements in the Turkish Denial of the Armenian Genocide* (Cambridge and Toronto: Zoryan Institute, 1999), in the section on "Alternate Use of the Words 'Ottoman' and 'Turkish,'" pp. 5–6.
2. Winston Churchill, *The World Crisis. The Aftermath*, vol. 5 (London: T. Butterworth, 1929), p. 367; for Curzon, see W. Woodward and R. Butler, eds., *Documents on British Foreign Policy*, vol. 4: *(1919–1939)* (London: HMSO, 1952), p. 57, 8 March 1919.

3. Quoted in Sir John A. A. Marriott, *The Eastern Question: An Historical Study in European Diplomacy,* 4th ed. (Oxford: Clarendon Press, 1940), p. 538.
4 *The Armenian Genocide: News Accounts from the American Press: 1915–1922,* compiled by Richard D. Kloian, 4th printing (Berkeley, CA: ACC Books, 1985), viii, ix.
5. Churchill, *The World Crisis* [n. 2], pp. 406–407.
6. Many of the data contained in this segment are culled from *The Lausanne Treaty, Turkey and Armenia,* a publication by the American Committee Opposed to the Lausanne Treaty (New York: n.p., 1926).
7. Henry Morgenthau, *Ambassador Morgenthau's Story* (New York: Doubleday, 1918), chap. 24, pp. 301–325.
8. U.S. National Archives, R. G. 59.867.00/798 ½.
9. Ibid., 59.867.4016/299, 17 October 1916 report.
10. *International Conciliation,* 151. New York (June 1920), 281.
11. Interview with Istanbul's French-language daily *Journal d'Orient,* 12 April 1919.
12. British Foreign Office Archives (henceforth FO) 371/4174/118377, 18 January 1919 exchange with the minister.
13. Ibid.; FO 371/4172/16321. See also Bilal Şimşir, *Malta Sürgünleri* (Istanbul: Milliyet, 1976), p. 54.
14. Sina Akşin, *Istanbul Hükümetleri ve Milli Mücadele,* vol. 1, 2d. ed. (Istanbul: Cem, 1983), pp. 140–41; Ismail Hami Danişmend, *Izahlı Osmanlı Tarihi Kronolijisi,* vol. 4: *1703–1924* (Istanbul: Türkiye, 1961), p. 457; FO 371/4173/44216, 20 March 1919 report of W. H. Deedes.
15. U.S. National Archives, R.G. 59.867.4016/67, 28 May 1915. Once more, "Ottoman" and "Turkey" are used here interchangeably.
16. In crafting the Nuremberg Doctrine, which provided the legal framework for the prosecution of the Nazi leaders, the 24 May 1915 Allied declaration served as a guidepost for the formulation of article 6c in the Key Indictment as it referred to "a large-scale mass murder." As the framers of the doctrine of "crimes against humanity" maintained, the 24 May 1915 declaration "constitutes a precedent for Article 6c of the Nuremberg Charter." *History of the United Nations War Crimes Commission and the Development of the Laws of War,* compiled by UN War Crimes Commission (London: His Majesty's Stationery Office, 1948), pp. 35, 45, 192, 193, 194.
17. Rauf Orbay, "Rauf Orbayın Hatıraları," *Yakın Tarihimiz* 1 (1962): 81.
18. *Atatürk'ün Söylev ve Demeçleri 1919–1938,* vol. 1 (Istanbul: Ministry of Education, 1945), p. 49.
19. The newspaper had just been launched and was being jointly financed by Mustafa Kemal and Fethi Okyar. The editorial bore the title, "Ermeni Terbiye-I Milliyesi." *Minber,* 9 November 1918.
20. Kâzım Karabekir, *Istiklâl Harbimiz* (Istanbul: Türkiye, 1969), p. 7.
21. Turkish sources indicate that the escape was organized and facilitated by General Bronsart von Schellendorf, the 1914–1917 chief of the Ottoman General Staff. Cemal Kutay, *Talat Paşa'nın Gurbet Hatıraları,* 3 vols. (Istanbul: n.p., 1981), vol. 3, p. 1103; Fethi Okyar, *Üç Devirde Bir Adam* (Istanbul: Tercüman, 1980), p. 251. The details of the escape are provided by Galib Vardar, *Ittihad ve Terakki Içinde Dönenler,* ed. S. N. Tansu (Istanbul: Inkilâp, 1960), pp. 386–388. The most accurate description was provided by a young officer of the German Naval War Staff who volunteered to organize and execute the mission. The German destroyer *RI* was the vehicle of escape to

Russia. Kapitänleutnant Baltzar, "Das romantishe Ende der drei grossen Türken der Kriegszeit: Talaat, Enver und Dschemal Pascha. Eine Erinnerung an den 1. November 1918," *Orient-Rundschau* 15, no. 11 (10 November 1933): 120–121. (The rare issues of this organ of German World War I combatants of Turkey are held in the military archives of the Federal Republic of Germany, viz., Bundesarchiv-Militärarchiv, Koblenz, 4.332/1923/34.3.

22. Midhat Şükrü, *Imparatorluğun Çöküşü* (Istanbul: Remzi, 1979), p. 124.
23. Hüseyin Cahit Yalçın, *Siyasal Anılar* (Istanbul: Türkiye Iş Bankası, 1976), p. 259.
24. Vahakn N. Dadrian, *History of the Armenian Genocide. Ethnic Conflict from the Balkans to Anatolia to the Caucasus,* revised and enlarged 8th printing, (New York and Oxford: Berghahn Books, 2006), p. 391. Berlin's refusal of 16 November was a response to the extradition request made by Turkish Ambassador Rifat Paşa on 11 November 1918. For the Turkish version of this book, see *Ermeni Soykırımı* (Istanbul: Belge Yayınları, 2008).
25. Ahmet Emin Yalman, *Yakın Tarihte Gördüklerim ve Geçirdiklerim,* vol. 1: *1888–1918* (Istanbul: Yenilik, 1970), p. 266.
26. German Foreign Ministry Archives, i.e., Auswärtiges Amt (henceforth A.A.), R14093 or, Türkei 183/44, A27741, 7 October 1916, no. 1886 report. Full text of the editorial, in German translation, is Interim German Ambassador Radowitz, 9 October 1916 report to Berlin; *Tasvir-i Efkâr,* 7 October 1916, no. 1886.
27. *Yeni Gün,* 4 November 1918. Quoted in Orhan Koloğlu, *Aydınlarımızın Bunalım Yılı 1918* (Istanbul: Boyut, 2000), p. 95.
28. *Yeni Gün,* 9 November 1918.
29. FO 371/3411/210534, folio 334
30. Quoted in Koloğlu, *Aydınlarımızın;* for the excerpts from *Ati* and *Zaman,* see pp. 98, 102.
31. Accompanied by police, the public prosecutor, attached to the Lower Court (Bidayet Mahkemesi) conducting pre-trial investigations, raided the headquarters of CUP on 11 December 1918 to seize and impound all their documents and other relevant material. However, they were able to find only the two documents discussed here.
32. It should be noted that this same editor, Yunus Nadi, wrote the following, during the war when the 1915–1916 Armenian Genocide was all but consummated, in an editorial titled "Bankrupt and Cleansing": "The familiar politics of fostering the unison of the different population elements is bankrupt; we recognize this fact. Accordingly, the era of cleansing, needed for the safety of our fatherland, has arrived." The editorial appeared in the 7 October 1916 issue of *Tasvir-i Efkâr.* German Foreign Ministry Archives, A.A. R14093, Türkei 183/44, A27741, enclosure in German Legation Counsellor Wilhelm von Radowitz's 9 October 1916 report no. 626, addressed to German Chancellor Hollweg.
33. Koloğlu, *Aydınlarımızın,* p. 91. See also Zeki Sarıhan, *Kurtuluş Savaşı Günlüğü,* vol. 1 (Ankara: Öğretmen Dünyası, 1982), p. 63 covering events of 14 December.
34. Quoted in Koloğlu, *Aydınlaramızın* [n. 27], p. 93.
35. Ibid., pp. 161–162.
36. Ibid., pp. 98, 100 for the first article, p. 157 for the second.
37. Akşin, *Istanbul Hükümetleri* [n. 14], p. 201.
38. *Meclisi Mebusan Zabıt Ceridesi,* Devre 3 (3rd Election Era), Cilt 1 (vol. 1), Içtima senesi 5 (5th Assembly Period), Dördüncü Inikad (4th Sitting), 19 October 1918, pp. 32–33.

39. Ahmet Izzet Paşa, *Feryadım,* vol. 1 (Istanbul: Nehir, 1992), p. 207.
40. *Tasvir-i Efkâr,* 13 February 1919.
41. Quoted in Feritun Kandemir, *Istiklal Savaşında Bozguncular ve Casuslar.* Istanbul: Ağbaba, 1964, p. 182.
42. *Ictihad,* 26 December 1918. Quoted in Koloğlu, *Aydınlaramızın,* [n. 27], p. 155.
43. Necmeddin S. Silan, "Ikinci Meşrutiyette Divan-ı Ali Hareketleri," part 2, *Tarih Konuşuyor* 5, no. 28 (June 1966): 2469–2474, 2470.
44. Ibid., pp. 2473–2474.
45. Ibid., p. 2474.
46. *Meclisi Mebusan,* Onbirinci (11th) Inikad (henceforth "sitting"), 4 November 1918, p. 109.
47. Ibid., p. 111, right column.
48. Ibid., p. 112, left column.
49. Ibid., p. 113.
50. Ibid., pp. 114, 116.
51. Ibid., 14th sitting, 18 November 1918. For Deputy Hafız Mehmet's statement see p. 149 left column; for that of the Armenian deputy, p. 143.
52. For a detailed account of his involvement in the organization and execution of these massacres, and his subsequent involvement with court-martial authorities, see Vahakn Dadrian, *Haigagan Tzeghasbanoutyunu Chorourtaranayeen Kunnargumnerov* [The Armenian Genocide under parliamentary investigation] (Boston: Baikar Publishers, 1995,) pp. 94–94, endnote 17; Akşin, *Istanbul Hükümetleri* [n. 14], vol. 2 (1992), p. 354, n. 191.
53. *Meclisi Mebusan* [n. 38], 14th sitting, pp. 158–160.
54. Ibid., 23rd sitting, 9 December 1918, pp. 257–258.
55. Ibid., pp. 289–293.
56. Ibid., p. 300, left column.
57. Ibid., 25th sitting, 12 December 1918, p. 314.
58. Yusuf Hikmet Bayur, *Türk Inkilâbı Tarihi,* vol. 3, part 3 (Ankara: Türk Tarih Kurumu, 1957), p. 47.
59. According to official German sources, Deputy Nalbandyan managed to escape the fate of other Armenians of Adana province and stay alive, by bribing the brother of that province's governor-general, Hamdi. That bribe was in the form of surrendering half of the harvest of his landed property, namely a 7,500-Dönem stretch, which corresponds to some 1,800 acres. A.A. R14088, A30012, Adana's German Consul Eugen Büge's 1 October 1915 report.
60. *Meclisi Mebusan* [n. 38], 25th sitting, 12 December 1918, pp. 315–317.
61. In his memoirs, published in three volumes, Ottoman Parliament's Deputy Papazyan provides, while confirming some points made by Sami, a slightly different account, the thrust of which is that elements of ambivalence, confusion, and indecision permeated the attitudes of Dashnak leaders in Turkey, as distinct from those in the Caucasus. The overriding sentiment, as manifested in the leaders' faces, thoughts, and gestures, wrote Papazyan, was a premonition of an impending major catastrophe, more correctly, the specter of general massacre, hanging over the heads of the Armenian population of Turkey. In trying to deal with this overwhelming crisis, these leaders could never overcome the split that paralyzed them. One faction favored a waiting and passive attitude to see what CUP authorities would do, and responding only when in acute

danger. The other faction was in favor of facilitating the Russian victory by a variety of ways, including the supply of Armenian volunteer corps and the secret deployment of Armenian self-defense forces in the border regions. Vahan Papazyan, *Eem Housheru* [My memoirs], vol. 2 (Beirut: Hamazkayeen, 1952), pp. 277–280. For more details see Dadrian, *Haigagan* [n. 52], pp. 100–102 of endnote 75.

62. *Meclisi Mebusan* [n. 60], 25th sitting, 12 December 1918, pp. 317–322.
63. *Zhamanak* (Armenian daily in Istanbul), 14 December 1918.
64. Friedrich von Kraelitz-Greifenhorst, *Die Verfassungsgesetze des Osmanischen Reiches* [The Constitutional Laws of the Ottoman Empire] (Vienna: Forschungsinstitut für Osten und Orient, 1919), pp. 32, 55, 56. This was a dissolution (*fesh*) as opposed to suspension (*tatil*). In either case, the parliament had merely confirmed the theocratic prerogative, or "the sacred right" (*hukuk-u mukaddes*) of the sultan. The Ittihadists, bent on optimizing their control of legislation through the agency of a weak and meek monarch, had pushed the revisions through the Chamber of Deputies, at the same time doing away with Article 35, which dealt with conditions of conflict between the ministers and the Chamber regarding bills and served to encumber the monarch's clear-cut exercise of power. The complete abolition of this restrictive article was part of the 1916 Amendment of Article 7.
65. Akşin, *Istanbul Hükümetleri* [n. 14], pp. 133–135; Tayyib M. Gökbilgin, *Milli Mücadele Başlarken*, vol. 1 (Ankara: Türk Tarih Kurumu, 1959), pp. 20–21
66. Fethi Okyar, *Üç Devirde Bir Adam*, ed. C. Kutay (Istanbul: Tercüman, 1980), pp. 264–265.
67. Gökbilgin, *Milli Mücadele Başlarken* [n. 65] , p. 20.
68. *Vakit*, 13 December 1918; *Renaissance*, 14 December 1918.
69. Vahakn N. Dadrian, "Genocide as a Problem of National and International Law: The World War I Armenian Case and Its Contemporary Legal Ramifications," *Yale Journal of International Law*, 14, no. 2 (Summer 1989): 221-334, 267–269.
70. Ibid., p. 269. For A. Riza's interpellations in the Senate on behalf of the Armenian deportees see also Bayur, *Turk Inkilâbı*, [n. 58] pp. 46–47; Akşin, *Istanbul Hükümetleri* [n. 14], pp. 44–45; Tarık Zafer Tunaya, *Türkiye'de Siyasal Partiler*, vol. 1 (Istanbul: Hürriyet Vakfı, 1984), p. 577, n. 48; Johannes Lepsius, *Deutschland und Armenien* (Berlin and Potsdam: Tempel Verlag, 1919), pp. 216–218. The State Department source is R.G. (L.) 59.867.00/797½, U.S. Foreign Relations, L., p. 763.
71. *Meclisi Âyan Zabıt Ceridesi*. Devre 3, Cilt 1, Içtima Senesi 5, 2nd sitting, 19 October 1918, p. 8.
72. Ibid., 11th sitting, 21 October 1918, p. 29; Akşin, *Istanbul Hükümetleri* [n. 14], p. 43, n. 59.
73. Taner Akçam, *Insan Hakları ve Ermeni Sorunu: Ittihat Terakki'den Kurtuluş Savaşı'na* (Ankara: Imge Kitabevi, 1999), p. 418. It should be noted here with emphasis that this is the first and thus far the only comprehensive treatise in any language covering the criminal proceedings of the postwar Turkish Military Tribunal. In this context, the World War I Armenian genocide is seen as an operation preparatory for the emergence and triumph of the 1919–1922 Turkish War of Independence, thus a prelude to the advent of the modern Republic of Turkey.
74. Silan, *Ikinci Meşrutiyette* [n. 43], 6, no. 31 (August, 1966): 2569.
75. Ibid., 2570. The Constitution's relevant articles are nos. 92–95.
76. Ibid.

77. Ibid., 6, no. 34 (November 1966): 2836.
78. *Atatürkün Söylev ve Demeçleri,* [n. 18].
79. *Meclesi Âyan,* [n. 71]. 11th sitting, 21 November 1918, p. 117.
80. Ibid., pp. 119, 120–121.
81. Ibid., pp.122, 123.
82. *Meclisi Âyan* [n. 71], 13th sitting, 2 December 1918, pp. 145–147.
83. Ibid., [n. 71], 14th sitting, 9 December 1918, pp. 163–166.
84. Dadrian, *History of the Armenian Genocide* [n. 24], p. 23.
85. *Meclisi Âyan,* [n. 71], 14th sitting, 9 December 1918, pp. 170, 174–175.
86. Ibid., 11th sitting, 21 November 1918, p. 123.
87. Zeki Sarıhan, "1914–1918 Savaş Kabineleri Üyelerinin Görüşleri" *Saçak* 40 (May 1987): 24.
88. Koloğlu, *Aydınlarımızın* [n. 27], p. 166. The statement was made in *Ictihad* by Abdullah Cevdet, MD, a noted author and patriot of Kurdish extraction, on 7 November 1918.
89. Sarıhan, *Kurtuluş Savaşı* [n. 33], p. 32. Originally published in *Vakit,* 18 November 1918.
90. Silan, *Ikinci Meşrutiyette,* [n.43]: 2657.
91. Ibid., 2655.
92. Osman Selim Kocahanoğlu, *Ittihat- Terakki'nin Sorgulanması ve Yargılanması* (Istanbul: Temel, 1998), p. 31.
93. Ibid., p.34.
94. Ibid., p. 351.
95. "The Ottoman Constitution," *The American Journal of International Law* 2, supplement (1908): 372; see also Şevket Süreyya Aydemir, *Makedonya'dan Ortaasya'ya Enver Paşa,* vol. 1: *1860–1908* (Istanbul: Remzi, 1972), section "Kanuni Esası," pp. 574–575.
96. For a detailed discussion of the procedures in the Ottoman parliament by virtue of which this law was pushed through by a variety of governmental officials, see Vahakn Dadrian, "The Law Allowing Convicts to Enroll in the Special Organization," Special Edition (Collected Essays of V. N. Dadrian) of *Journal of Political and Military Sociology,* 22, no. 1 (Summer 1994): 57–62.
97. Kocahanoğlu, *Ittihat-Terakki* [n. 92], pp. 155, 159, 160, 162, 163, 167, 168, 169.
98. For the verbatim reproduction of Deputy Fuad's ten questions see ibid, pp. 52–53.
99. Ibid., pp. 79, 80, 81, 81, 84, 93, 103.
100. For the complete list of the forty-five members of the Fifth Investigative Department of the Chamber see Ibid., p. 31; for a list of only those who actually took part in the investigation; see Tunaya, *Türkiye'de Siyasal Partiler* [n. 70], vol. 3 (1989), p. 548, n. 18.
101. *Hadisat,* 22 October 1918. Quoted in Koloğlu, *Aydınlarımızın* [n.27], p. 201.
102. Gotthard Jäschke, "Beiträge zur Geschichte des Kampfes der Türkei um Ihre Unabhängigkeit," *Die Welt des Islams,* vol. 5, no. 1–2, N.S. (1958): 16.
103. Kocahanoğlu, *Ittihat-Terakki'nin* [n. 92], p. 38. For the original French text of this law, which was first enacted on 14 (27) September 1909 and then reintroduced on 19 August (1 September) 1910, see A. Billiotti and Ahmet Sedad, *Législation Ottomane depuis de la Constitution,* vol. 1 (Paris: Jouve and Co., 1912), pp. 482–483. The respective original Ottoman-Turkish sources are in *Takvim-i Vekâyi,* nos. 345 and 622.

104. Kraelitz-Greifenhorst, *Die Verfassungsgesetze* [n. 64], pp. 49, 61.
105. Generally known as Direction de la Sureté Générale, this bastion of national security was instituted on 22 July 1909 to replace its predecessor, the Ministry of Police. The Armenian-owned large Sanasarian commercial building, requisitioned by the Ottoman authorities during World War I, served as its headquarters. After occupying its fourth floor for a short while, the Mazhar Inquiry Commission moved to the edifice housing the General Directorate of Police (Polis Müdüriyeti Umumiyesi).
106. Of Albanian extraction. Hasan Mazhar had a long career of civil service in Macedonia, where he served as *vali* of Üsküb. After the Ittihadist revolution he became police chief in Smyrna (Izmir), and until April 1914 he was governor of Bitlis province; then Ittihad replaced him with Talaat's brother-in-law Mustafa Abdulhalik (Renda). In 1916, Talaat appointed Mazhar to one of the four inquiry commissions that went to the provinces ostensibly to investigate atrocities against the Armenians. But these commissions in the main confined themselves to investigating economic abuses involving the embezzlement by officials of large amounts of money and other spoils taken from the Armenian victims; their offense was that, instead of handing over the riches to the state, they appropriated them for themselves.
107. For a succinct essay on this matter see Annette Höss, "The Trial of the Perpetrators by the Turkish Military Tribunals: The Case of Yozgat," in *The Armenian Genocide: History, Politics, Ethics*, ed. R. Hovannisian (New York: St. Martin's Press, 1992), 208–221.
108. Armenian Patriarchate Archives Jerusalem, Respecting Mazhar Inquiry Commission, Series 21, File M, no. 555.
109. When forwarding this batch of forty-two telegrams, along with their ciphers, to the public prosecutor on 2 April 1919, Interior Minister Cemal indicated that in addition to these, sent to Istanbul from Ankara, the originals of another batch of cipher telegrams, sent on the previous date from the Interior Ministry to the authorities of the provinces and dealing with [Armenian] deportations, and covering the May 1915 to April 1917 period, had been secured from the offices of the Ministry of Post and Telegraph. ("Tehcir meselesine dair 331 senesi Mayıs iptidasından 333 senesı Nısanı gayesine kadar Nazaretden Vilayete yazılan şifrelerin gönderildiğini…") The number of the document is 5083/27. Ibid, Series 17, file H, no. 146.
110. Koloğlu, *Aydınlarımız* [n. 27], p. 91. The editorial was titled "Two Inculpating Documents." (Iki Vesikai Töhmet). See *Ikdam*, 13 December 1918 issue, for parts of text of the cipher. For reasons of their own, Turkish censors prevented Armenian-language newspapers from publishing any of this material by excising it and leaving blank spaces in the print sheet. *Zhamanak*, 12 December 1918. In the same editorial in *Sabah* it is further stated, "We have plenty of other information in this connection but consider publication at this juncture harmful to the task of the judiciary." Similar claims were made by *Tasvir-i Efkâr*, 3 February 1919. No newspaper was allowed to print the full text of the uncovered ciphers.
111. In its 12 December 1918 issue, the Turkish daily *Akşam* confirmed that these were indeed the documents that were whisked away from CUP headquarters.
112. *Takvim-i Vekâyi* (henceforth *T.V.*; the official gazette of the Ottoman parliament, which covered these court-martial proceedings in supplements [*ilâve*]), no. 3543, 4 May 1919, 2nd sitting of the Cabinet Ministers trials, published on 8 May 1919, p. 20, right-hand column.

113. Tunaya, *Türkiye'de Siyasal Partiler* [n. 70], vol. 2 (1986), p. 96, n. 16.
114. For the Key Indictment see *T.V.*, no. 3540, p. 6; for the Harput Verdict see *T.V.* no. 3771, p. 2; 13 January 1920, issue. Sabit had produced this cipher when he was being interrogated by members of the Mazhar Inquiry Commission in mid December 1918. In the Responsible Secretaries trials, public prosecutor Şevket, when delivering his closing arguments, described this cipher as "unimpeachable testimony" comparable to "the 2 + 2 = 4 equation." Dadrian, "Genocide as a Problem," [n. 69], p. 302.
115. *Zhamanak*, 12 December 1918.
116. Interior Minister Talaat's 10 (23) May 1915 cipher is reproduced by several Turkish authors. See Kamuran Gürün, *Ermeni Dosyası* (Ankara: Türk Tarih Kurumu, 1983), p. 218; idem, *The Armenian File* (New York: St. Martin's Press, 1985), p. 210. For a summary of the text of the same cipher, see Muammer Demirel, *Birinci Dünya Harbinde Erzurum Ve Çevresinde Ermeni Hareketleri (1914–1918)* (Ankara: Generlkurmay, 1996), p. 52. The same cipher text, in the original Ottoman-Turkish and in Armenian script, has been located in the archive of the Jerusalem Armenian Patriarchate, along with a French translation. Series 17, File, H, nos. 571–572. But, most significant, *vali* Tahsin's response to the interior minister, sent the very next day and also available in the files of the Patriarchate's archive, is nowhere reproduced in relevant official and unofficial Turkish publications. Two inferences of major significance become unavoidable: first, the authenticity of the invaluable holdings of the Patriarchate archive relative to foremost primary sources documenting the Armenian genocide; second, the systematic withholding and concealment of incriminating documents by Turkish authorities. Indeed in his response, *vali* Tahsin was disputing and objecting to the need for deportation as explained in the text above, thereby authoritatively disputing the validity of the official Turkish charges relative to Erzerum province's Armenians, and at the same time casting in relief the respective lies Talaat was disseminating in that respect.
117. *Jhogovourtee Tzain,* 3 February 1919.
118. French General Franchet d'Esperey, for example, on 12 February 1919, warned Turkish Grand Vizier Tevfik about the urgent need to arrest wartime Cabinet ministers. Sarıhan, *Kurtuluş Savaşı* [n. 33], pp. 127–128. British Rear Admiral and High Commissioner Richard Webb made a similar demand on 5 March 1919. Ibid., p.158. Their concern for the crime of Armenian massacres was subsidiary to their anger that Turkey had intervened in the war on the side of the Central powers rather than the Allies, and that British prisoners were terribly abused by the Turks.
119. Kocahanoğlu, *Ittihat ve Terakki* [n. 92], p. 38.
120. Tarık Mümtaz Göztepe, *Osmanoğullarının Son Padişahı Vahideddin Mütareke Gayyasında* (Istanbul: Sebil, 1969), p. 89.
121. *Morning Post,* 13 February 1919; Göztepe, *Osmanoğullarının,* [n. 120], p. 38.
122. Kocahanoğlu, *Ittihat-Terakki* [n. 92], p. 39; Ali Fuad Türkgeldi, *Görüp Işittiklerim,* 2nd printing (Ankara: Türk Tarih Kurumu, 1957), pp. 186–196. The crisis arose when the sultan refused to issue a special *Irade* sanctioning the prosecution of Cabinet ministers, the authorization for which, he said, fell within the purview of the executive branch, i.e., the Cabinet. The purpose of such a new *Irade* was to form a new and more rigorous court-martial. The sultan agreed to sign a new *Irade* that merely required a confirmatory signature.
123. Ali Fuad Türkgeldi, *Görüp Işittiklerim* (Ankara: T.T. Kurumu), p. 197.

124. Kocahanoğlu, *Ittihat-Terakki* [n. 92], pp. 39–40; Jäschke, "Beiträge," p. [n. 102]: 12.
125. Sarıhan, *Kurtuluş Savaşı* [n. 33], p. 113; the 200 figure is on p. 156.
126. Bilal N. Simşir, *Malta Sürgünleri*, Istanbul, Milliyet, 1976, p. 76; Sarihan, *Kurtuluş Savaşı* [n. 34], pp. 163, 164.
127. Akçam, "Divan-ı Harbi Örfi'lerin Kurulması: Istanbul Yargılamaları," *Tarih ve Toplum*, no. 137 (May 1995): 303/47–307/51. See also, Ferudun Ata, *Işgal Istanbul'unda Tehcir Yargılamaları* (Ankara: Turkish Historical Society, 2005), 323 pp. and fifteen Appendixes.
128. Dadrian, *Key Elements* [n. 1], p. 25; FO 371/6503/E6311, folio 34, 1 June 1921. Notwithstanding, Turkish denialist literature continues to misinterpret this statement by Geddes as proof of British rejection of the evidence of the wholesale massacres.
129. FO 371/6509/E8745, folios 23–24.
130. The report carries the 1 December 1918 dateline and appeared in the 7 December 1918 issue of the London newspaper.
131. Türkgeldi, *Görüp Işittiklerim* [n. 123], p. 194.
132. FO 371/4172/13592, 10 January 1919, Vice Admiral Calthorpe report to London. Two weeks later Calthorpe complained to London that the sultan's hesitations were unduly delaying the legal proceedings. FO 371/4172/13694, 24 January 1919.
133. Türkgeldi, *Görüp Işittiklerim*, [n. 123], p. 182.
134. Ibid., pp. 202–206. The entrenched attitude of placing lesser value on the lives of subordinate non-Muslim subjects came into striking relief at the funeral of Kemal, the first Turk sentenced to die at the scaffolding for his part in the 1915 Armenian massacres. In commenting on the spectacularly demonstrative procession of that funeral, British High Commissioner Admiral Calthorpe wrote to London: "The perpetrator of crimes, the nature of which would send a shudder through any civilized community, was treated as a hero and martyr amongst Moslems; but then, his victims were Christians." FO 371/4173, 72536, 21 April 1919, folio 355. No less significant are the descriptions of the funeral by two British officers reporting to the General Staff Intelligence Office at the General Headquarters. Captain E. La Fontaine wrote: "It is generally the custom for the bearers to carry the bier on their shoulders, but in order to give greater importance to the ceremony, the bier was borne at arms length above the head … more than 1000 invitations were issued [for this funeral], things which are unheard of in the Mahomedan religion." Captain H. A. D. Hoyland added: "Kemal was described [in the wreaths] not as 'innocent victim of the nation', but as 'innocent Islamic martyr.'" FO 371/4173, 72536, 21 April 1919, folios 356, 357.

CHAPTER 3

The Preparations for Courts-Martial

Vahakn N. Dadrian

The preparations coincided with the process of transition from Tevfik Paşa's cabinet to that of Damad Ferit, who, while serving five different times as grand vizier in the 4 March 1919–17 October 1920 period, played a central role throughout these courts-martial.[1] The turbulence, the limited successes, and the significant failures marking these proceedings were therefore factors that were closely linked to the personality and policies of this postwar Turkish leader. Superseding these factors in importance was a series of developments that were as precipitous as they were unsettling for the Turkish general public. The mood of abject resignation to the dire consequences of military defeat, punctuated by the unfolding grim stories of Armenian deportations and massacres, was aggravated by these developments. One may even argue that the interplay of these developments generated such a dynamic, that this mood of resignation eventually gave way to a spirit of evolving bellicosity. It seemed that terribly frustrated masses were waiting with anguish for some opportunity to discharge these frustrations via aggression. Due to the failure of Ferit's government to anticipate and control, if not prevent it, this emerging bellicosity grew in intensity and gained momentum without, however, imperiling, for a while at least, the new postwar regime. Ferit's express willingness to cooperate with the victorious Allies, especially the British, in the task of vigorously prosecuting the perpetrators served as a catalyst in this respect.

Three major events paved the way for the rise of this collective temper of bellicosity: the conviction, execution, and demonstrative funeral of Governor Mehmet Kemal on 10 April; the incursion and landing of the Greeks at Smyrna (Izmir) on 13–15 May with the approval of the Allies and under British, French, and US naval protection; and the ensuing two-week series of mass protest meetings in various parts of the Ottoman capital.[2] All these demonstrations were driven by high-pitched patriotic fervor and a measure of defiance. One important consequence of these events was the reinforcement of the remaining CUP partisans' will to sabotage and, wherever possible, to prevent, through various means of intimidation, the prosecutorial and retributive effort of the Ferit regime. What follows is a review of the manifold aspects of this countervailing movement.

The Array of Impediments to Overcome

The first signal for the source of this subculture of resistance and obstruction to a policy of retributive justice came from the pen of Cenab Şehabettin, a distinguished writer and publicist. In an editorial in the Turkish daily *Hadisat* (8 November 1918), he bitterly complained about the ubiquitousness and sway of CUP influence in postwar Turkey, declaring, "The police officer is Ittihadist [i.e., is a CUP man]; the police chief is Ittihadist, the army officer is Ittihadist, the soldier is Ittihadist, the governmental offices are Ittihadists, everyone is Ittihadist."[3] In terms of a general overview the Istanbul correspondent of the British newspaper *Morning Post* estimated that "over 500 government officials," CUP men mostly, were obstructing government's "every step."[4] The obvious reason for this condition was confirmed by one of the leaders of CUP, who bragged in his memoirs that among those who sympathized with CUP, there was one police officer who regularly, "sometimes three or four times a day," apprised him by telephone regarding measures on "implementing arrests."[5] Former Defense Minister and postwar Prime Minister General Ahmet Izzet granted that "[d]espite their setbacks and demise, the CUP in the land, especially in the Ottoman capital, was not a negligible power-group. All governmental officials were their men."[6] Several Western experts and observers uniformly seem to concur with this assessment.[7] The Turkish police in Istanbul was more than thirteen times larger than the combined numerical strength of the police officials of the three occupation forces, i.e., British, French, and Italian.[8]

Given these conditions of massive popular outbursts, the fear of a French Bastille–style storming of the notorious Bekirağa prison that would free the detainees awaiting criminal prosecution on charges of Armenian deportation and massacres was real. As a result, on 21 May the apprehensive government of Grand Vizier Ferit released forty-one high-ranking prisoners as a means of mollifying the restive and aggressive crowds.[9] Of these, twenty-six were ordered released by court-martial authorities with the observation that "there is no case against them." Commenting on all forty-one of them, British Admiral Calthorpe wired to London, "there was every reason to believe that [they] were guilty of the most heinous crimes … mainly in connection with massacres."[10] As a result of all this intimidating turmoil, the occupying powers, led by the British, decided, with the approval of Grand Vizier Ferit, to transfer the sixty-seven inmates of Bekirağa prison to Malta Island.

Ever since these high-profile prison inmates had been taken into custody and incarcerated, the prison authorities had allowed them unusual leeway, bordering on privileges. The following two British passages summarize the picture: "prisoners had friends in almost every department of State and had been allowed the utmost liberty of communication with their friends and sympathisers,"[11] and "All prisoners of whom there are 112 are allowed to walk about the prison and mix freely during the day. Except for a casual glance at their passes, individuals are not subjected to any inspection on entering the prison, and large packets are often to be seen being carried in by individuals, stated to be food, but might be anything. Women are allowed in all times during the day, and are never inspected."[12] The defendants were not assembled at secure locations or held in the close confinement ordinarily imposed in such cases. The cabinet ministers were allowed to meet in a large room as members of the prison's "Cabinet Council" and discuss defense strategy. They even invited Osman, the legal counselor of the Interior Ministry, for consultation; Osman happened to be incarcerated in a nearby room.

Civil servants who were either Ittihad partisans or sympathizers availed themselves of every opportunity to obstruct the efforts of the court. They withheld crucial documents, impeded communication with provincial authorities, and stalled when complying with court orders in order to hinder the proceedings. Thanks to this and the overall permissive atmosphere, a number of top Ittihadists were able to organize their escape from the prison. For example, Diyarbekir Governor Dr. Mehmet Reşit (Şahingiray), the Sixth Army Commander Halil (Kut), and CUP Central Committee member Küçük Talaat (Muşkara), all implicated in the Armenian massacres, were able to escape from prison,[13] and others managed to avoid arrest and detention by using government-issued *vesikas* (travel identity cards) that allowed them to leave Turkey. In the latter group were Trabzon's CUP Responsible Secretary Yenibahçeli Nail, Erzurum's Delegate-Inspector Filibeli Ahmet Hilmi, and the region's Special Organization leader Ebuhintli Cafer. The complaints continued as Justice Minister Vasfi became upset about the delays hampering the work of the courts-martial, due mainly to the frequent resignations and dismissals of the public prosecutors. Among these, Feridun, for example, complained about the lack of such simple amenities as ink, delays in responding to investigative inquiries, inadequate executive authority, and above all the endemic practice of manipulation of red tape by civil servants who were protégés of CUP, to whom they felt heavily indebted for their jobs and careers.

Nor was the office of the court-martial spared these vexations. As one Turkish newspaper enumerated them, the provincial authorities were more often than not uncooperative, as they would delay transmitting evidentiary material and delay the dispatching to Istanbul of the witnesses and the suspects demanded by the court-martial; the prosecutors, as expected, were most eager to complete their investigations and to have the requisite verdicts delivered.[14] One member of the court-martial panel complained bitterly that the investigative papers dealing with the trials of wartime cabinet ministers were handed over to that court only one day before the latters' exile to Malta.[15] On top of all this, British sources declared that over forty additional suspects held for trial had already escaped, and that in a single night forty-two others likewise escaped from the central prison by digging a tunnel underneath a prison wall.[16]

These circumstances call for a review of the Ottoman criminal justice system and its bearing on the problems surrounding the prosecution of the defendants held in prison.

The Ottoman Criminal Justice System

Any analysis of this system has to encounter and overcome the linguistic problems intrinsic to the twin domains of that system, namely, the Code of Criminal Procedure (Usulu Muhakematı Cezaiye) and the Penal Code itself (Mülkiye Ceza Kanunnamesi). As the translators of these codes conceded, these problems were considerable. The veteran British translator George Young declared in 1906: "The Turkish language is so difficult. Its vocabulary is so ill suited to express even the most simple ideas of Western legislators. Its style and its syntax lack so much clarity and conciseness. And the Arabic alphabet is so inadequate for the need to avail oneself of vocables that this part of the labor leaves much to be desired."[17] The translators of the Ottoman Penal Code in 1913 referred to "the intrinsic difficulties of the Turkish language … the awkward construction of indefinite phrasing which have to be encountered constantly," while deploring its "lack of precision."[18] These limitations inevitably tended to encumber many parts of the present study. What follows is a brief inquiry into the historical origins of the Penal Code and its evolution into a modern instrument of criminal justice, as revealed in the post–World War I prosecution of the crimes associated with Armenian deportations and massacres.

The Penal Code was first promulgated in 1863; it was revised in 1911. Two aspects of it have relevance to this study. First, it was a by-product of the 1856 Treaty of Paris by virtue of which the Ottoman Empire, a non-Christian and by and large a Muslim entity, was admitted "to participate in the public law and concert of Europe."[19] Second, the code, in its classification of criminal violations and offenses and in its organization and divisions, was modeled on the French Penal Code, notwithstanding a series of appended details bearing the stamp of distinctly Ottoman clauses. When effectively launched on June 5 (17) 1879, it typically reflected, however, the French judicial organization that was anchored in the famous law of 24 August 1790. As such it more or less mirrored the French system of courts and tribunals operating in the aftermath of the French Revolution.

Generally speaking, there were three stages in the administration of criminal justice: preparation, preliminary examination, and the actual trial. During the preparation for public prosecution a warrant of arrest was issued by the justice of peace. In the preliminary examination stage an examining magistrate (*Sorgu hakimi* or *müstantik*) issued the warrant of arrest and could decide on the expediency of continued detention of a suspect. Without a warrant, an order of arrest could also be issued by a judge during the trial when delay was adjudged to be detrimental to the cause of justice. At the end of the preliminary investigation a decision (*kararname*) was rendered for the commencement of trial. The public prosecutor relayed that decision, along with the accusation (bill of charges), to the court-martial. The nature of the offense and aggravating or mitigating circumstances relative to punishment were indicated (Art. 222 of the Penal Code).

Trial commenced with the roll call, whereby the identity of the accused was recorded (Art. 263); it was followed by the reading of the decision relative to the opening of the trial (Art. 265). The next phase involved the introduction of evidence. The defendant and his or her counsel had the right to respond to the public prosecutor. Witnesses could be held over when caught lying (Art. 281). The chief judge could separate defendants to secure separate testimony (Art. 278). If new crimes came to light during the trial and prior to the verdict, and if they merited severer punishment than the crime already under consideration, then the defendant would be prosecuted on the basis of these new charges (Art. 311). The chief judge had discretionary powers in the conduct of the hearing; accordingly, he could allow the introduction of any and all evidence he deemed critical for "uncovering the truth."

By the same token, the panel of judges reached its verdict in line with a particular brand of the law of evidence. Namely, it adhered to and practiced the principle of "intimate conviction" (*hukuku takdiriye* or *kanaatı vicdaniye*) (Art. 232). As the trier of fact, the judge considered the probative value of all the evidence submitted from the investigative phase and during the actual trial, freely attributing credence to that evidence to the best of his conscience. However, the proof of guilt had to rely on definite evidence. Such evidence comprised confession, witness testimony, writings and official records, evidence gained through discovery, judicial notice relative to national and international laws, the constitution, certain historical events, etc. As stated in another part of this study, the Ottoman criminal justice system was essentially inquisitorial. There were no fixed rules of evidence, and therefore no rules of excluding certain types of evidence, such as hearsay and non-expert opinion. The standard of the judge's "deep-seated conviction" had primacy over that of preponderance of evidence. In the final analysis the subjective factor eclipsed the objective one.

Before the rendering of the judgment, the defendant and counsel, who already during the trial had been afforded opportunities to respond to the charges, had the last word (Art. 289). The trial ended with the rendition of judgment, i.e., the verdict, consisting as it did of two parts: the judgment proper, called "the decision," and the justification of the judgment.

Throughout these procedures, the framing of the indictment, especially within the parameters of martial law, and its corollary, the state of siege, were of crucial import. Being from its very inception a more or less inquisitorial system, and of French origin, the Ottoman criminal justice system accorded a central role to the function of indictments, thereby encumbering to some extent the task of defense. In this sense the Key Indictment, which overshadowed and eclipsed all other indictments prepared in connection with several subsidiary trial series dealing with Armenian deportations and massacres, occupied a central position throughout the multifaceted court-martial proceedings.

The Bearings of the Key Indictment

In three major respects the Key Indictment was a singular phenomenon, not only in the history of Turkish jurisprudence and criminal justice but in Ottoman-Turkish history as a whole. First, for the first time ever, high-ranking Turkish officials, including two wartime prime ministers, i.e., grand viziers, and a host of cabinet ministers, were being criminally prosecuted for crimes, the likes of which, in the past, had been dismissed with disdain as insignificant mishaps. Within this historical context, this indictment is of inordinate significance. Second, Ottoman Turks themselves were demonstratively prosecuting other Turks for exterminatory violence against non-Muslim subjects. Third, the crime of centrally organized mass murder—genocide in today's terminology—was being treated as a national crime, and thus subject to municipal penal law, or Ottoman law, rather than international law. Furthermore, this Key Indictment, bent on prosecuting and punishing the highest authorities of wartime Turkey, had a unique feature. Unlike all other subsidiary indictments, it was punctuated by the embedding in it of some forty-two authenticated, official, semiofficial, and regular other documents that were of wartime provenance and that attested to the crimes under review. The attested documentary thrust of this legal instrument is of critical importance for examining and evaluating the work of the courts-martial.

Above all, one is dealing here with what criminologists call evidence-in-chief, bearing proof of certification indicating the origin, nature, and destiny of every one of the array of documents that were lodged with the Key Indictment. Many of these documents were top secret orders and coded telegrams. Others were admissions of guilt and related confessions from the accused, who were subjected to pretrial interrogatories administered by examining magistrates. Still others were written statements and depositions from a number of civilian and military officials supplying testimony on the complicity of the defendants. Except for the Armenian deputy Onnik Ihsan—who allegedly was spared the fate of his co-nationals because he belonged to Ittihad, i.e., CUP—the indictment is entirely based on evidence furnished by Muslim Turks.[20]

The trial of the wartime cabinet ministers and top Ittihadists, for which the Key Indictment was prepared, began on 28 April 1919. Following the identification of the defendants and their defense counsels, the presiding judge asked Şefik, the court clerk, to read the indictment (*iddianame*) into the record. After that, Major-General (Ferik) Mustafa Nazım, the chief judge, and Mustafa Nazmi, the procuror-general, made their observations.

At the beginning and at the end of the indictment, reference is made to "the tragedy" resulting from "the Armenian deportations" (p. 5; other page numbers are given in parentheses below), and the court identifies its "principal task" as the probing of wartime "massacres and profiteering," "crimes which the perpetrators dared to commit" (8).

After declaring that "an important portion" of the documentary material belonging to CUP's Central Committee and to the Special Organization had been "stolen" (*aşırıldığı*), the court described the evidence in its possession. Included in it were "pretrial documentary material" (*istintak*) (4), usually assembled by examining magistrates, "documents and proofs" (*delail vę berahin*), "depositions" (*beyanatı tahririye*), and other valid accounts (5). In addition, the court had special files containing "the Residual papers of the Special Organization," the "Talaat file," obtained from the Fifth Committee of the Chamber of Deputies, and a long, detailed deposition from the Third Army Commander Vehip Paşa (6). The ensemble of the evidence-in-chief in the possession of the court-martial encompassed documents obtained from, or implicating, army commanders Mahmut Kâmil, Ahmet Cemal, Yanyalı Vehip, and Halil Kut, as well as colonels Halil Recayi, deputy commander of Ankara's Fifth Army Corps, and Şehabettin, deputy commander of Kayseri's Fifteenth Division in Ankara province.

Outstanding in this collection of evidence were the documents incriminating Special Organization chiefs Drs. Mehmet Nazım and Bahaeddin Şakir, Major Yusuf Riza, Colonel Kızanlıklı Cevat (Halil's successor in the post of military governor of Istanbul [*Muhafiz*]), "Kambur" Atıf, and the Special Oganization's infamous anti-Armenian field operations chief, Major Yakup Cemil. The indictment places Interior Minister Talaat in the forefront of all the initiatives directed against the Armenians. Seven governors-general (*valis*)—Mazhar (Ankara), Mehmet Celal (Aleppo, Konya), Hasan Tahsin (Uzer) (Erzurum, Damascus), Mehmet Reşit Paşa (Kastamonu), Dr. Mehmet Reşit (Diyarbekir), Süleyman Nazıf (Baghdad), and Münir (Akkaya [postwar Erzurum])—are also mentioned as sources of legal evidence. These sources are supplemented by documents relating to *mutasarrıfs* Sabur Sami (Antalya), Ali Suat (Deir Zor), and Müfit (Bolu). Among the sets of documents lodged with the indictment were twelve coded cipher telegrams, four telegrams, and nine statements obtained from governors through pretrial interrogatories. As underscored earlier, before being introduced as exhibits by the prosecution, the documents were authenticated by competent officials from the Ministries of Justice and Interior with the notation, "it conforms to the original" (*aslına muafık* or *mutabık*).

The task of substantiating the charges comprised in the indictment was difficult for several reasons. The Ittihadists, particularly Dr. Nazım and new Director General of Public Security Erzurumlu Hüseyin Aziz (Akyürek) (Emniyeti Umumi Müdürü), had carried off loads of documents in the days prior to the armistice. The court had to make do with what was left and with anything else that was beyond the reach of the agents of Ittihad who were bent on removing as much incriminating evidence as they could. But the main impediment was that since the CUP anti-Armenian scheme had had to remain secret, records and written orders were kept to the barest minimum. The CUP maintained "an external and public" façade while it engaged in "covert and secretive operations," relying on the use of "oral and secret instructions" (4), that were carried out "through oral and secret orders" (5). These criminal actions were made possible by the workings of an operative "secret network" (5).

Another aspect of the prosecution's conspiracy charges had a Nurembergian touch as the CUP was accused of "aggression" with the intention to exploit the war for its own ends. "The intervention in the World War I was rendered an accomplished fact by resort to a number of vile tricks and deceitful means ... the idea was to take advantage of the fact that Europe was preoccupied with the general war" (5). Hiring brigands for massacre duty was part of this conspiracy. "The idea was broadcast that these *çetes* were to be assigned war duties. An effort was made to persuade well-intentioned and gullible people of this purport. Taken together the documents and other pieces of evidence demonstrate, however, that subsequently [these *çetes*] were employed for the end of massacre and destruction of deportee convoys" (6).

Conspiracies require appropriate decision-making by the conspirators regarding the course of action being contemplated. That point is underlined by the statement that "the massacre and destruction of the Armenians were the results of decisions taken by the Central Committee of CUP" (7). These decisions were the result of "extensive and profound deliberations" (ariz ve amik düşünülerek karar verilmiş) (8). By the same token, the covert aspects of the conspiratorial intent were revealed in the actual outcome of the conspiracy itself. When alluding to the implementation of anti-Armenian measures, the indictment refers to "carrying out in a secret way the intent of the leadership of Ittihad" (5). Speaking of Interior Minister Talaat as the arch conspirator, the indictment cites a particular coded telegram betraying Talaat's "secret intent" about the Armenian deportations. The Deir Zor *mutasarrıf* Ali Suat, the recipient of the cipher, is instructed to "destroy" the evidence after reading it (6). In another instance, the indictment adduces evidence of a case in which a high-ranking deportation official, Abdulahad Nuri, admits to having been told by Talaat that "the purpose of the deportation was extermination" (tehcirin imha manasına müstenit bulunduğunu). He is quoted as saying, "I … personally received the orders of extermination" (imha emirlerini bizzat aldım) (5). The entire undertaking was expected "to solve the Eastern [i.e., the Armenian] question" (8). In fact, Ittihad is accused of having tried a kind of final solution resulting from its propensity to seek remedies that "through terror could solve once and for all lingering problems" (ilkai dehşetle hall ve fasl sevdasına düşerek) (4), as revealed in Talaat's 13 July 1915 cipher confirming his goal of a "final solution" of the Armenian Question.

The charges asserted that the massacre was accomplished with the cooperation of the central authorities. The indictment dismisses arguments that the anti-Armenian measures were a reaction to certain incidents, or were limited to certain localities, and insists instead that these measures were sweeping, organized, and directed "by a unanimously acting central body" (5). The indictment further asserts that the deportations had very little to do with wartime exigencies, citing the case of Bolu, a city located some 72 miles inland on the Istanbul-Adapazar-Ankara main road and thus far removed from "the war zone." The deportations represented "the goals and desires of the Cemiyet; they were neither a measure of military necessity nor of discipline or punishment" (ne tedbiri askeri ne tedbiri inzibatı cümlesinden olmayıp) (6).

That there was an overall scheme of wholesale destruction is asserted by the statement that "the use of the method of massacres is only a part of the activities and actions of the leaders of the Cemiyet as they seem to appear to be merely operations subsidiary to a centrally conceived plan" (7). The repeated references to Talaat and his Interior Ministry are such as to portray him as the mastermind devising the plan that subsequently was carried out by that ministry in tandem with the party's operatives. This joint involvement is "evident," for example, in the recruitment of "the *çete*" cadres (Dahiliye Nezareti ile Cemiyetin bu çetelerle meşgul olduklarını iraye eder) (6). Talaat is further singled out as being in secret communication with Şakir, the director of the Special Organization operating in the eastern provinces; the court got hold of a cipher telegram sent by Şakir to the CUP Central Committee via Talaat (8). In another document Talaat shelves a report informing him of the massacres, and in another piece of evidence his ministry is depicted as having hidden a notorious massacrer through administrative fiat (7).

Two groups organized and supervised the details of the killings. One was comprised of the CUP leaders who were in charge of the Special Organization (S.O.) units committing the massacres. Halil (Kut), the military governor (Merkez Kumandan) of Istanbul (January–December 1914), his successor, Colonel Ahmet Cevat, Security Chief Erzurumlu Hüseyin Aziz (Akyürek), *fedayi* executioner Atıf (Kamçıl), Artillery Major Yusuf Riza, and Drs. Bahaeddin Şakir and Mehmet Nazım were mentioned by name. Colonel Cevat is described as "having supplied" Dr. Şakir with "code keys, automobiles, explosives and ample cash" (5). The other group consisted of a coterie of ex-officers who had resigned from the military to become CUP operatives in order to undertake special missions in the provinces on behalf of the CUP. Whether called responsible secretary (*kâtibi mesul*), delegate (*murahhas*), or inspector (*müffetiş*), they were vested with enormous powers, including power to veto the decisions of the provincial governors-general. These commissars were the actual authority running the operations of the S.O. units. The indictment generally describes them as functionaries that the CUP "deployed in the provinces" to facilitate "the massacres" (5). It cites specifically Inspector Musa (Balıkesır), and Responsible Secretaries Mithat (Bursa), Rüştü (Samsun) (6), Cemal Oğuz (Çankırı), Necati (Ankara), Hasan Fehmi (Kastamonu) (7), and Yenibahçeli Nail (Trabzon) (8).

Overall, three overlapping groups of perpetrators are mentioned. The first are the gendarmes or provincial police. According to a 15 July 1915 cipher telegram, cited in the indictment and sent by Erzurum Governor Hasan Tahsin to the Interior Ministry, "the gendarmes, attached to the Special Organization," launched "criminal attacks and committed atrocities against the Armenians" in Erzurum province (6).

The second group consisted of the brigands who operated under the name of "Special Organization." Their objective was "the destruction of the deportee convoys, for which purpose the S.O. maintained close contact with the CUP" (imha vazifesiyle meşgul olarak Cemiyetle irtibatı müekked vesaikdendir) (6). As evidenced in the *çete* operations organized by Bahaeddin Şakir, the means used were massacre and plunder (B.Ş. beyin tertip etmiş olduğu çete efradı… katl ve garete maruz kaldıkları) (7).

The third group, used to carry out the massacres, were convicts released from imperial prisons. The indictment identified S.O. leaders Halil (Kut), Dr. Nazım, Kambur Atıf, and Erzurumlu Aziz, who "emptied the prisons" of gangs of criminals (*caniler*, *şakiler*) (6) and integrated them into the command and control system of the Special Organization (5). Elsewhere, they are described as "butchers of human beings, consorting gallowbirds, and gendarmes with bloody hands and eyes" (ipten ve kazıkdan kurtulmuş yaranını…eli gözü kanlı jandarmalar) (7).

In organized mass murder, the organizers have to reckon with a certain amount of reluctance, or resistance, that ordinary people are likely to muster. Success required its suppression. The indictment cites several instances of officials who resisted respective orders as having been removed from office or, in some instances, put to death in order to ensure the compliance of others. The evidence supplied by Hamit, the director-general of the Civil Service Inspectorate, cites the murder (by hanging) of two *kaymakams* (county executives) who had "objected to the atrocities and executions perpetrated against the Arabs, and who had taken issue with the Diyarbekir governor's method of handling the Armenian deportations" (Araplara icra kılınan mezalim ve idamlara…) (8). Two governors—General Hüseyin Celal from Aleppo province, and Mazhar from Ankara province, were dismissed for objecting to the massacres (8). The court, relying on evidence it had obtained through investigation, declared that those who "vehemently rejected, and refused to get involved" in these operations were regarded "as traitors to the fatherland." The threat of these sanctions played no small role in securing "docile and submissive officials" (*muti ve münkad*) as evidenced in Dr. Bahaeddin Şakir's operational zone, where "government officials submitted to his orders and directives" (7).

The same severity was applied to ordinary Muslims who might have been tempted to help imperiled Armenians by providing them refuge. The indictment cites an order issued by Third Army Commander General Mahmut Kâmil that threatened Muslims with death by hanging in front of any house in which an Armenian might be sheltered, at the same time ordering that the house itself be torched. If the offender happened to be an official or belonged to the military, the order provided for court-martial (Bir Ermeniyi tesahüp edecek bir Müslümanın hanesi önünde idam ve hanesi ihrak) (7).

The indictment also reproduces the text of a 21 June 1915 cipher telegram in which Şakir inquires of Harput's Responsible Secretary Resneli Nazım whether the Armenians were being destroyed, or were merely being deported and exiled (imha ediliyor mı yoksa yalnızca sevk ve izammi olnuyor?) (6).

The indictment refers to large-scale massacres (5–7) and mass drownings, particularly in the coastal areas of the Black Sea where "the Armenians were being put on board caïques and drowned," according to the testimony of Trabzon Deputy Hafız Mehmet (7). It also spells out a number of ancillary offenses that might have eventually hastened the death of other victims, such as "gutting houses" (5), "rape," and "all sorts of tortures and shameful acts" (5).

The indictment charges members of the two wartime cabinets that were headed by Grand Viziers Sait Halim (1913–1917) and Mehmet Talaat (1917–1918). Among the defendants present at this sitting of the tribunal were Sait Halim, party General Secretary Mithat Şükrü, Ittihad Central Committee member Küçük Talaat, Foreign Minister and President of the Chamber of Deputies Halil Menteşe, party ideologue Ziya Gökalp, Head of National Security Office Ismail Canbolat, Şeyhülislams Musa Kâzım and Mustafa Hayri Ürgüplü, Foreign Minister Ahmet Nesimi, Minister for Food Supplies Mustafa Kemal, Special Organization Administrator Kambur Atıf, and Ittihad Central Committee member Yusuf Riza. Those being tried in absentia were warlord Ismail Enver, party boss Mehmet Talaat, Fourth Army Commander Ahmet Cemal, Special Organization Directors Drs. Bahaeddin Şakir and Mehmet Nazım, and National Security Chief Erzurumlu Aziz.

The Supplementary Indictment

The chief public prosecutor argued that the investigation of the cabinet ministers was not yet completed, and that therefore their trial should be deferred. They would be tried in the next round of seven sittings (3 June 1919–26 June 1919); unfortunately, however, only three were present, others having opted to become "fugitives from justice."

The trial of the rest—two wartime cabinet ministers along with Ittihadist leaders and Special Organization chiefs—had to be again postponed due to the fact that sixty-seven of them had been seized by the British on 28 May and were being held in Malta for future trial. Upon the motion of District Attorney Feritun, the trials of many of them, including those of Sait Halim, Halil Menteşe, Ahmet Nesimi, Ali Münif (Talaat's deputy in the Interior Ministry and later Public Works Minister), and Ahmet Şükrü (a top Ittihadist and wartime Minister of Education), were rescheduled, and the court proceeded without them.

The investigation of the misdeeds of the cabinet ministers, which shortly after the start of the trials was found to be incomplete, prompted the public prosecutor's office to notify the court on 3 May 1919 that new offenses had been discovered by the examining magistrates. Accordingly, on 3 June at the opening of the second series of seven trials, a new, amended indictment was read into the record. Since the defendants had been moved from Istanbul's Bekirağa prison to Malta, only three cabinet ministers as defendants were present at these trials: Minister of Post Hüseyin Haşim, Minister of Finance and Senate President "Topal" Rifat, and Şeyhülislam Musa Kâzım. At the sitting of 12 June 1919, a fourth suspect, Şeyhülislam Esat, was added to the roster. Even though the deportations and massacres were the main focus, District Attorney Feritun enlarged the scope to include the charge of "overthrowing of the government." The defendants were accused of having created a "fourth instance of power" in the governmental system of the Ottoman state. The preamble of the new indictment spoke also of "the extermination of an entire people constituting a distinct community," and of "the admission and confession" of the defendants (*kabul ve itiraf*). The initial indictment also had asserted that the deportations had not been dictated by military necessity, and that they had not constituted a disciplinary measure. The amended text of the indictment was even more explicit on this point. These deportations, "conceived and decided upon by Ittihad's Central Committee," had "tragic consequences ... in almost every corner of the Ottoman Empire" (Memaliki Osmaniyenin hemen her tarafinda) (For ease of reference, this publication is again cited within the text as follows: *T. V.*, no. 3571, p. 130).

Perhaps the most significant aspect of the new indictment was its reinculpation of the Special Organization as the main instrument of the genocide, particularly in the eastern provinces: "The Special Organization was set up by the leaders of the Ittihad Party." The pivotal role of Dr. Bahaeddin Şakir is once more underlined, for "he presided over the activities of the Organization, for the success of which he put to use the Responsible Secretaries and Inspectors of the party." To emphasize premeditation and central organization, the indictment pointed out the "uniform patterns" (*yeknesak harekâtı*) in the perpetration of the crimes, especially the utilization of local party organizations by way of recruiting their "central committees."

The amended version of the indictment refers to the crimes of "massacre," "plunder of properties," "torching of corpses and buildings," "rape," and "torture and torment" (*T. V.* 3571: 128–132). Furthermore, the amendment also charged that these crimes were committed "in a particularly organized way." They were perpetrated "in the capital as well as in the provinces." The preamble to the new indictment also spoke of the existence in the evidentiary material of "the admission and confession" of the defendants (*T. V.* 3571: 131). The original indictment had maintained that these measures were due to neither specific incidents, nor were they merely limited to certain localities (*T. V.* 3540: 5).

However, the mere defining of a task does not always ensure task attainment, given the contingencies associated with task performance. These contingencies concern the prosecutorial endeavor to achieve as smooth a transition as possible from indictment to conviction and a corresponding guilty verdict. That prospect in no small measure confounded and even agitated large segments of the Turkish public. These sentiments were echoed by two prominent national figures reacting to the first of a series of verdicts pronounced at the end of the Yozgat trials (8 April 1919), during which two relatively low-level, minor officials were prosecuted. CUP's powerful Secretary-General Midhat Şükrü (Bleda) indignantly labeled this verdict and other ensuing verdicts as a "self-condemnation by the Government and the Court, and a condemnation of the Turkish nation."[21] An exgrand vizier, both during the armistice and at the inception of the Kemalist regime, Fethi Okyar, described the same verdict as "a concession and certification of guilt by our own governments."[22]

The chapter to follow will explore the legal processes through which a military tribunal sought to administer criminal justice according to the terms of the Key Indictment, described above. The series of trials that ensued, which one contemporary Turkish newspaper headlined as "historical"[23] and another described as "the most important trials in Ottoman history,"[24] deserve utmost attention in terms of their precedence in the history of both national and international criminal justice.

Notes

1. His dates of appointment and reappointment are: (1) 4 March, (2) 19 May, (3) 21 July 1919, (4) 5 April, (5) 31 July 1920.
2. (1) at Istanbul University, 18 May, (2) Fatih, 19 May, (3) Üsküdar, 20 May, (4) Kadıköy, 22 May, (5) Sultan Ahmet, 23 May, (6) Sultan Ahmet, 30 May. Kemal Arıburnu, *Milli Mücadelede Istanbul Mitingleri* (Ankara; Yeni Desen, 1975).
3. Quoted in Orhan Koloğlu, *Aydınlarımızın Bunalım Yılı 1918* (Istanbul: Boyut, 2000), p. 145.
4. 10 February 1919 issue.
5. Yunus Nadi, *Kurtuluş Savaşı Anıları* (Istanbul: n.p., 1978), p. 19.
6. Cited in Ibnülemin Mahmut Kemal Inal, *Son Sadrazamlar,* vol. 4 (Istanbul, n.p., 1982), p. 1983.
7. Edgar Pech, *Les Alliés et la Turquie* (Paris: Les Presses Universitaires de France, 1925), on pp. 14–15 describes CUP's influence during the armistice as ubiquitous; Paul Helmreich, *From Paris to Sèvres: The Partition of the Ottoman Empire at the Peace Conference of 1919–1920* (Columbus, OH: Ohio State University Press, 1974), p. 107; A.A. Cruickshank, "The Young Turk Challenge in Postwar Turkey," *The Middle East Journal* 22, no. 1 (Winter 1968): 17.
8. The number of Turkish police deployed in 32 police stations was 3,470. The respective distribution of police officials among the three Allies was as follows: British, 67; French, 99; Italian, 93. Tevfik Çavdar, *Milli Mücadele Başlarken Sayılarla* (Istanbul: Milliyet, 1971), pp. 147, 150.
9. Bilal N. Simşir, *Malta Sürgünleri,* Istanbul, Milliyet, 1976, pp. 112–113. Sina Akşin reveals that on 15, 17, and 18 May, a series of similar mass demonstrations took place in several cities in the interior of Turkey. Sina Akşin, *Istanbul Hükümetleri ve Milli Mücadele,* vol. 1, 2d. ed. (Istanbul: Cem, 1983), p. 306.
10. Quoted in Vahakn N. Dadrian, "Genocide as a Problem of National and International Law: The World War I Armenian Case and Its Contemporary Legal Ramifications," *Yale Journal of International Law,* 14, no. 2 (Summer 1989): 284, n. 228.
11. FO 371/4173/84878, folio 487.
12. Ibid., 4174, folio 149. "The Prison Had Become a CUP Club," *Halil* [n. 13], 271.
13. Hüsamettin Ertürk, *Iki Devrin Perde Arkası,* ed. S. N. Tansu (Istanbul, Nurgök, 1957), p. 327; Halil Paşa; *Bitmeyen Savaş,* ed. M.T. Sorgun (Istanbul: Yedigün, 1972), pp. 281-282. See also *T.V.* nos. 3731 and 3480. For the respective roles of Cafer, Hilmi, and Dr. Reşit, see Doğan Avcıoğlu, *Milli Kurtuluş Tarihi,* vol. 3 (Istanbul: Ertu, 1974), pp. 1142, 1183.
14. *Ileri,* 7 July 1919.
15. *Nor Giank,* 1 June 1919.
16. FO 406/41/132278, 7 September 1919, report to London.

17. *Corps de Droit Ottoman,* vol. 7, comp., trans., and ed. George Young (Oxford: Oxford University Press, 1906), p. xvi.
18. *The Imperial Ottoman Penal Code,* trans. J. A. S. Bucknill and H. A. S. Utidjian (Nicosia, Cyprus, 1913), p. xvi.
19. Charles Fenwick, *International Law,* 2d ed., vol. 2 (New York, 1934), p. 83.
20. Beginning with the no. 2540 issue, *Takvim-i Vekâyi,* the official organ of the Ottoman parliament, started to publish many of the portions of these proceedings. The specifics of the indictment detailed here are excerpted from the supplementary issue (*ilâve*) of *Takvim-i Vekâyi,* no. 3540, which, along with other supplementary issues, served as a quasi-judicial journal irregularly covering the court-martial proceedings involved. Pages 4–8 of that issue (in which 27 April is a misprint for 28 April, the opening day of the trial) comprise the text of the indictment. The Jerusalem Armenian Patriarchate Archive and the Bibliothèque Nubar in Paris have the original issues. For a comprehensive analysis through the method of breakdown and reconstruction of the entire text of the Key Indictment in which columns of English translations of segments of the indictment are placed alongside those containing original but Latin-script Ottoman segments of the indictment, see Vahakn N. Dadrian, "A Textual Analysis of the Key Indictment of the Turkish Military Tribunal Investigating the World War I Armenian Massacres," *Armenian Review* 44, 1 (Spring 1991): 1–36.
21. M. Bleda, *Imparatorluğun Çöküşü* (Istanbul: Remzi, 1979), p. 62.
22. Fethi Okyar, *Üç Devirde Bir Adam* ed. C. Kutay (Istanbul: Tercüman, 1980), p. 280.
23. *Alemdar,* 29 April 1919, pp. 1 and 2.
24. *Hadisat,* 26 April 1919.

CHAPTER 4

The Initiation of Courts-Martial

Vahakn N. Dadrian

The Statutory Conditions of Military Justice

There were two fundamental reasons why the recourse to military justice was more efficient and more promising. First, the statutes of state of siege (*idare-i-örfiye*), which were first instituted on 2 October 1877 in connection with the Russo-Turkish War and were twice supplemented on 2 July 1909 and 1 September 1910, were still in force. Hence, martial law was applicable at the time. Second, Article 3 of that law transferred law-and-order functions from the purview of the Cabinet Council to that of military authorities while providing that respective decisions and administrative measures be carried out by local police. Moreover, Ottoman penal law, as a rule, considered a defendant guilty until proven innocent. In other words, at that time martial law prevailed. Equally significant, the subjects to be prosecuted through such courts-martial, mainly cabinet ministers and high-ranking CUP leaders, were generally identified as prosecutable "brigands." This kind of labeling issued from the terms of the statutes in question, described as the Temporary Law on the Suppression of the Armed Brigands (Müsellah Çetelerin Tenkili).[1]

Before the Ottoman monarch had suspended the Ottoman parliament on 21 December 1918, there was a lively debate in the Chamber of Deputies relative to the type of jurisdiction to be applied to the prospective suspects. The quest for suitable criminal prosecution led to a set of probing constitutional arguments that were advanced by several deputies. Deputy Ali Haydar (Saruhan district), for example, pointed out that in the existing statutes there were no penal codes, nor codes on criminal procedures, on the basis of which the cabinet ministers, the prime suspects in question, could be prosecuted. While concurring, Interior Minister Fethi (Okyar) pointed, however, to the problem of the illegality of retroactivity, should the Chamber comply with deputy Haydar's proposal to enact a new law for this purpose. Deputy Hamit (Aleppo) proposed instead the application of existing principles of law, more specifically, of existing municipal penal law, inasmuch as the crimes to be prosecuted were ordinary crimes; he therefore objected to enacting new laws. As a remedy to the absence of any specific law in this regard, Deputy Mehmet Fuad (Antalya) argued in favor of applying existing municipal penal law, as provided, he said, by the Constitution. Deputy Mehmet Sadık (Denizli) objected, invoking Article 32 of the Constitution, which stipulated, "A special law shall determine the procedure to be followed for the trial of Ministers." He also argued that the Constitution was silent on the matter of the terms of punishment. This meant, he went on to say, that existing penal codes were adequate for determining punishment. He concluded by reiterating the need for a new law on the matter of procedure.[2] This last point was indeed warranted by the terms of Article 15 of the Ottoman Penal Code, which declared that "Punishment is not to be effected in accordance with a subsequent law." (nulla poena sine lege).

Given the suspension of the Chamber and the resulting irrelevance of the idea of constituting a High Court (Divan-ı Âli) to try the cabinet ministers and deputies as provided for by the Constitution, these debates proved academic. By the same token, also rendered irrelevant were Article 85 ("every affair shall be judged by the tribunal to which this affair shall belong") and Article 89 ("Besides the ordinary tribunals there cannot be instituted under any denomination whatever extraordinary tribunals or commissions for judging certain special affairs").[3] All these issues were touched on in the text of the executive decree that the cabinet issued on 14 December 1918, which announced the intention of the courts-martial to prosecute and punish the crimes related to the Armenian deportations and massacres. It was signed by the grand vizier and the cabinet ministers.[4]

The exceptional authority of the courts-martial issued from several additional attributes. First, it was formally characterized as "extraordinary" (*fevkâlade*). It was likewise formally sanctioned by an imperial rescript or edict (*Irade*) that fully legitimized the recourse to criminal justice by means of courts-martial. Most important, it secured and used as evidence-in-chief an array of official wartime documents not obtainable or found in any other Turkish venue or source. As the Turkish author of a major work dealing with the documentary treatment of the criminal prosecution of the Armenian deportations and massacres declared, "In establishing a linkage between the CUP and the Special Organization, the Courts-Martial through its [key] Indictment and Verdict integrates important historical facts not found in other books dealing with the Special Organization."[5]

When the defense tried to challenge, on constitutional and other grounds, the competence of the court-martial during the second and fourth sittings, the chief judge ordered the reading of the court's written response rejecting these challenges. One of the principal grounds of that rejection was, as noted above, the reliance on Article 2 of the Temporary Law on State of Siege, whereby constitutional guarantees and civil statutes became temporarily suspended. The court further noted that the accused themselves used this clause to commit their crimes during their rule.[6] Three major imperial rescripts were issued to render the courts-martial operational. The first was issued on 16 December 1918 (published in *T.V.* 3424). The second, providing for jurisdiction for existing criminal courts involving areas not under siege by martial law and dealing with public officials, was issued on 25 December 1918 (*T.V.* 3430). Article 88 of the Constitution, setting forth the conditions of venue and jurisdiction, thus found its application. A third *Irade* of 8 January 1919 (*T.V.*, 3945) declared the extraordinary court-martial ready to prosecute the crime of deportations and massacres (*tehcir ve taktil*).

The Problems of Administering Court-Martial Justice

The turbulence attending the advent of successive postwar Turkish governments inevitably spilled over, creating a host of problems for the operating military tribunals. These problems were particularly acute for the ever-changing prosecutorial teams and their support personnel. Of the three postwar governments involved, two are identified with the various governments of Grand Vizier Damad Ferit Paşa, an ardent advocate of prosecution. The first coincided with the two-tier tenure of Grand Vizier Ahmet Tevfik (Okday), 11 November 1918–3 March 1918. Several series of trials, including those of Yozgat and Trabzon, were launched during his tenure but completed during that of his successor, Damad Ferit. The most important series of trials coincided, however, with Ferit's first period of office, 4 March–30 September 1919. Ferit's second period of office lasted from 5 April 1920 to 17 October 1920.[7]

As stated above, the military tribunal was severely handicapped by the instability of a succession of district attorneys comprising the prosecutorial team. Some resigned, others were induced to resign, and still others were simply dismissed and replaced. The following details may provide a glimpse into the type of conditions under which the tribunal was forced to labor. The first formation of the court-martial was completed on 16 December 1918; Major-General (*Ferik* or *Tümgeneral*) Mahmut Hayret Paşa, retired, was the chief judge. As provided by the terms of martial law and stipulated in the 14 December 1918 executive decree (see note no. 4), of the other four members of the panel, two were likewise to be military. They were Brigadier-General (*Mirliva* or *Tuğgeneral*) Ali Nadir (who in 1912 had the city of Saloniki surrendered to the Greeks), retired, Struma Army Corps commander of the Eleventh Division, and Süleymaniyeli "Nemrud" Kürd Mustafa, retired commander of the Twenty-Seventh Division. The two civilian members of the panel were Judge Şevket and Artin Mosdiçyan, an Armenian; both of them were from the Appeals Court and were allowed to retain these judgeship posts while serving in the court-martial.

The public prosecutor was Nihat, a first deputy of the chief prosecutor of the Court of Cassation. The four examining magistrates (*müstantik* or *sorgu hakimi*)—Moiz Zeki, Misak Magaryan, Nazıf, and Abdüssamed—were all members of the Beyoğlu Court of First Instance (Bidayet), except the last one, who was from the Istanbul Court (*T.V.* 3424, 21 December 1918). However, after a short while the prosecutor Nihat and the examining magistrate Nazıf resigned, citing health reasons. They were replaced by Sami, examining magistrate at Beyoğlu's Court of First Instance and, to deputize for him, by another Sami, a substitute member of Istanbul's Court of Appeals. Additionally, Dimitraki, from the Court of Commerce, was appointed as alternate member of the court.

More changes were in evidence in the next two court-martial panels. Headed first by retired Staff Brigadier-General Ali Fevzi and subsequently by retired Staff Major-General Mustafa Nazım of the Office of Military Materials Procurement, who had served as war minister in July and August 1919, these military tribunals were even more beset by additional personnel changes. No longer comprising civilians, the first new panel of judges included retired Brigadier-General Ali Nazım (later replaced by Nemrud Kürd Mustafa), Mustafa Zeki Paşa, and Colonel Recep Ferdi. The public prosecutor was Yusuf Ziya, head of the Court for Maritime Commerce. He was aided by examining magistrates Nazıf, Artin Boşgezenyan, Misak, and Dimitraki; his assistants were Haralambos and Kudretullah and counsel Ibrahim Reşat.[8] This new, fully militarized panel also relinquished the term "extraordinary" and added two new elements to the set of charges: namely, dragging the country into war and provoking internal strife.

The changes in the prosecution team were even more frequent and rapid in this period. Yusuf Ziya lasted only a few weeks and was replaced by Captain Cevat, who in short order was himself replaced by Mustafa Nazmi after daring to abruptly release from prison some defendants awaiting court-martial.[9] When ex–Aleppo Deputy Artin Boşgezenyan offered to resign from his post, he was turned down. The resignation of his colleague, Magistrate Nazıf, was accepted; he was replaced by Sait Molla from Mülga's State Council Appeals Court (Şurayı Devlet Mülga Mahkemeyi Istintakiye), which was then abolished. Due to his discord with Chief Judge Nazım, however, Sait Molla was dismissed within weeks. A similar conflict with the panel of judges had prompted the resignation of Yusuf Riza.[10] On the other hand, Haralambos was restored to his old post as first deputy director of legal affairs at the Justice Ministry (Adliye Nezareti Umuru Hukukiye Müdür Muavini). He was replaced by Talaat, Galata's Justice of the Peace (Sulh Hakimi). At the same time, Feridun, Simav's prosecutor, was appointed second deputy to the public prosecutor (Müddei Umumi Muavin) at the court-martial.[11]

The third period of prosecution occurred during the full occupation of Istanbul by the Allies, precipitated as it was by a new surge of pro-Kemal activities in the Ottoman capital, and especially in the new Chamber of Deputies. Intoxicated with the results of the irregularly held October–November 1919 parliamentary elections, nationalist Turkish politicians began to assert themselves as new leaders. The onset of this new regime of occupation led to a new initiative of mass arrests. As a result, Damad Ferit, with the support of the monarch and the British as the leading occupying power, reclaimed the post of grand vizier. There thus began a new period of courts-martial. Chaired by Kürd Mustafa as chief judge, the new tribunal's charter under Article 3 stipulated punishments for crimes that—beyond the regular offenses of deportation and massacre—included the anti-Kemalist clauses of "rebellion" and assaults against "the internal and external security of the Ottoman State." The trials were held in secrecy and would exclude defense counsel (Art. 4). Death verdicts could be reached either unanimously or by a two-thirds majority (Art. 5) (as recorded in *T.V.* 3837). This new military tribunal also obtained, at the instigation of the new cabinet, the monarch's validating signature. The bylaws of the tribunal were thus signed into law on behalf of the cabinet by the grand vizier and the war minister on 10 April 1920 (*T.V.* 3829, 17 April 1920). In a period of some six months, this court-martial issued sentence renditions and delivered a whole gamut of verdicts ranging from death to various prison terms; these verdicts will be dealt with separately in the sections that follow.

The Constitutional and Related Defense Arguments

The defense arguments were crafted by a large team of lawyers led by Celaleddin Arif, president of the Turkish Bar Association and professor of law at Istanbul University. He later joined the Kemalists to become deputy and subsequently president of the fledgling parliament in Ankara, and later a cabinet minister. Below is a list of the defense lawyers and their clients, the cabinet ministers and CUP chieftains:

Defense Lawyer(s)	Client(s)
Hasan Hayri (Tan) and Celaleddin Arif	Sait Halim, Grand Vizier
Esat, Kâzım, and Tahsin	Halil Menteşe, Foreign Minister and President of Chamber of Deputies
Sâki and Esat Muhlis	Ahmet Nesimi, Foreign Minister
Sadettin Ferit	Ahmet Şükrü, Minister of Education
Mahmut Mahir, Yusuf Cemal, and Kadri	Ibrahim, Minister of Justice

Sadettin Ferit, Ahemt Ramiz, Mahmut Mahir	Mithat Şükrü, CUP Secretary-General
Haydar Rifat, Ismail Tevfik	Ziya Gökalp, CUP's chief ideologue
Mişon Ventura	Cevat Paşa, Military Commandant of the Ottoman capital
Ali Haydar	Şeyhulislam Musa Kâzım, Minister Haşim, and Senate President Rifat[12]

The arguments advanced by this defense team, mainly by Celaleddin Arif, may be summarized as follows.

Article 31 of the Constitution set forth the procedures for bringing to trial a minister charged with misconduct, while specifying the High Court as the requisite venue for trial. The crimes charged in the indictment were not "ordinary crimes" but rather crimes associated with the implementation of the Deportation Law. That law was sanctioned by an imperial rescript and had been enacted by the government. Since the massacres in question were incidental to the deportations, they were to be viewed as an "act of state." Hence, the matter of guilt or innocence was bound up with the problem of exercising ministerial duties and authority. Accordingly, they were not subject to the terms of Article 33 but rather to Article 92, which dealt with abuses of authority and specified the composition and function of the High Court (Divan-ı Âli). Further, even if one assumed that Article 33 would apply, the law in question stipulated that, in the event misconduct was not related to official duties, existing criminal courts, not a court-martial, must have jurisdiction. Accordingly, a High Court venue was ruled out. Finally, the court-martial did not have authority to determine which Article of the Constitution should be applied in the present case, for Article 117 specified the Senate as the ultimate interpreter of the exact meaning and application of an article of the Constitution (*T.V.* 3540: 10–12).[13]

The court first rejected the "act of state" argument, allowing that even if the massacres were held to be the by-products of the official acts of deportation, massacres, being what they are, were still murders and thus were to be treated as separate and distinct acts. Further, the available evidence pointed to decisions arrived at by the defendants not as ministers conducting legitimate official work, but as members of a secret, conspiratorial group (*cemiyet*). In other words, their decisions represented not standard and legitimate government business, but rather murderous, criminal intent. Thus, criminal prosecution was held to be consistent with the indictment, whose principal purpose was defined as the prosecution of the crime of "massacres" (*taktil*). Moreover, these massacres belonged in the category of "personal crimes" (*şahsi ceraim*), as they could not be treated as legitimate state business.

The court also rejected the remaining constitutional and jurisdictional challenges. Since martial law had been imposed by the CUP itself and was still in force, neither Article 32 nor 33 could be invoked to effect a change of venue or to transfer the defendants to the jurisdiction of regular criminal courts, as suggested by the defense. Further, Article 113, dealing with martial law, provided for the temporary suspension of civil rights by declaring that "wherever martial law is in force, civil and judicial laws are entirely muted" (kavanini mülkiye ve adliye tamamile sakin), and courts-martial become the only penal recourse (*mercii ceraim*). (In 1909 the CUP itself had revised the original martial law in order to have greater authority in suspending regular laws.) Finally, "an Imperial decree vested the Court with the requisite authority and competence to conduct the trials." On 4 May 1919, at the second sitting, the court again rejected the constitutional argument and the related challenge to it, while invoking the importance, in the handling of the matter, of the fear of God and the precepts of the Koran (*T.V.* 3540: 14).

The main text of the Key Indictment of the Ottoman Special Military Tribunal ends with an avowal reaffirming the main mission of the court-martial: to prosecute the defendants charged with the twin crimes of "massacre" (*taktil*) and "economic gain through profiteering" (*ihtikâr*). It concludes by saying that "the very formation and task of the Court-Martial" (*teşkil ve vezaif*) were grounded in this mission (*T.V.* 3540: 8, left-hand column).

Apart from the obstacles created by local political resistance, the military tribunal was encountering a new challenge to its legitimacy and integrity: the rising tide of Kemalism in Anatolia. As a result, not only did the prosecutorial zeal of the tribunal slack considerably, but the sentences it meted out became progressively lighter (*hafif cezalar*).[14] It is therefore essential to examine this phase in the career of the tribunal in some detail before covering its final phase, that of renditions of judgments and verdicts.

Notes

1. Vahakn N. Dadrian, "Genocide as a Problem of National and International Law: The World War I Armenian Case and Its Contemporary Legal Ramifications," *Yale Journal of International Law,* 14, no. 2 (Summer 1989): 305, n. 331, 303, n. 316; for the original French text see A. Billiotti and Ahmet Sedad, *Législation Ottomane depuis de la Constitution,* vol. 1 (Paris: Jouve and Co., 1912), p. 195. See also Sina Akşin, *Istanbul Hükümetleri ve Milli Mücadele,* vol. 1, 2d. ed. (Istanbul: Cem, 1983), p. 141, n. 12.
2. *Meclisi Mebusan Zabıt Ceridesi,* Devre 3 (3rd Election Era), Cilt 1 (vol. 1), Içtima senesi 5 (5th Assembly Period), , 11th sitting, 4 November 1918, pp. 104–106. See also Ferudun Ata, *Işgal Istanbul'unda Tehcir Yargılamaları* (Ankara: Turkish Historical Society, 2005), p. 38.
3. "The Ottoman Constitution Promulgated 11/23 December 1876," *American Journal of International Law* Supp. (1908): 367–387, 381.

4. The complete text with an explanatory note is in *Osmanlı Belgelerinde Ermeniler 1915–1920,* Prime Minister's General Directorate for Archives, Ankara, 1994, pp. 189–191.
5. Osman Selim Kocahanoğlu, *Ittihat- Terakki'nin Sorgulanması ve Yargılanması* (Istanbul: Temel, 1998), p. 43.
6. *T. V.*, 3543, p. 16, left-hand column; *T. V.*, 3549, p. 55, right-hand column.
7. The specific dates for both grand viziers are as follows: Tevfik, a. 11 November 1918–12 January 1919; b. 13 January–3 March 1919. Ferit, a. 4 March–15/16 May 1919; b. 19 May–20 July 1919; c. 21 July–30 September 1919. Ferit's second tenure involves the following periods: a. 5 April–31 July 1920; b. 31 July–17 October 1920. Succeeding him, Tevfik once more and for the last time became grand vizier from 21 October 1920 to 4 November 1922, only to see the Kemalists abolish that office, along with the sultanate.
8. Akşin, *Istanbul Hükümetleri* [n. 1], p. 141; Tarık Zafer Tunaya, *Türkiye'de Siyasal Partiler,* vol. 3 (Istanbul: Hürriyet Vakfı, 1989), p. 561, notes 83, 84.
9. Akşin, *Istanbul Hükümetleri* [n. 1], p. 201, n. 21.
10. Ata, *Işgal Istanbul'unda* [n. 2], pp. 129–131.
11. Nejdet Bilgi, *Ermeni Tehciri ve Boğazlıyan Kaymakamı Mehmet Kemal Bey'in Yargılanması* (Ankara: Kök, 1999), pp. 130, 134, 135.
12. Tunaya, *Türkiye'de* [n. 8], vol. 3, p. 562, n. 88.
13. Saadettin Ferit, another principal defense counsel, sustained Arif's arguments (*T. V.* 3540: 13–14). Moreover, Mahmut Mahir and Cemal Molla, the other defense counsel, joined the defense with ancillary arguments (*T. V.* 3540: 14).
14. Bilal Şimşir, *Malta Sürgünleri* (Istanbul: Milliyet, 1976), p. 147.

CHAPTER 5

Emergent Kemalism and the Courts-Martial

Vahakn N. Dadrian

The crucial significance of the new challenge posed by the Kemalist movement, which had been gathering strength in Anatolia in the 1919–1920 period, is revealed in the eventual demise of the sultan's government. Grand Vizier Damad Ferit's growing inability to confront and eliminate the threat issuing from that movement proved fatal. The rise of the Defense of Rights movement, culminating in the victory of the new Turkish nationalists in the October–November 1919 parliamentary elections, and these nationalists' ensuing sway in the new Chamber of Deputies convening in Istanbul in January 1920,[1] as well as the fact of Mustafa Kemal having been elected as a deputy of Erzurum in these elections, set the stage for a new era of political changes in postwar Turkey.

The Rudiments of Reactive Turkish Nationalism

The Kemalist challenge to the sultan's government was essentially fueled by a new thrust of Turkish nationalism. Several factors converged in this development. Foremost among these was the projected Allied plan to exact a heavy price from defeated Turkey in terms of drastically curtailing its territories while carving up new national entities in those areas. A new Armenian state entity would be accorded a lion's share in this plan. The two new regimes of grand viziers Ali Riza (2 October 1919–3 March 1920) and Salih Hulusi (8 March–2 April 1920), especially the former's, embarked on a two-track national policy. While acknowledging the enormity of the crime against the Armenians, a special effort was made to exonerate the Turkish people as a whole. For example, Ali Riza, barely a month in office, issued a statement on 30 October 1919 in which he generally acknowledged the deportations and massacres and the associated casualties "involving hundreds of thousands of people"; he vowed at the same time to launch a criminal prosecution against the perpetrators and court-martial them. However, he went out of his way to declare that "the Turkish nation [is] completely uninvolved in these crimes, for that noble nation is impervious to the shameful blot involving any and all kinds of savagery." He deplored the fact that despite months of criminal investigations, no justice had yet been attained.[2]

Moreover, Ahmet Reşit (Rey), who twice served as Interior Minister (1912–1913 and 1920) in the Ottoman cabinet, in a memorandum issued on 25 February 1919 likewise declared "the Ottoman and Muslim nation's purity and innocence to be evident." He blamed the CUP leaders "who, as the organizers of the crimes, have taken refuge in Berlin," and emphasized that the Greeks were somehow spared "this type of violence that was inflicted upon the Armenians."[3] The other grand vizier, Salih Hulusi, reached an accord with Mustafa Kemal while serving as marine minister in Ali Riza's cabinet. They agreed to a plan to institute criminal prosecution against those Malta exiles who were believed to be implicated in Armenian deportations and massacres and who might be surrendered to Ankara authorities by the British. This was part of a secret agreement reached in Amasya between the Kemalists and the Istanbul government.[4]

One of the important decisions of the new Chamber of Deputies was to rescind the wartime Law on Abandoned Goods that the CUP government had enacted on 26 September 1915, thereby confiscating and appropriating on a massive scale the properties of the Armenians who were being deported.[5]

The Sultan's Regime in Conflict with Incipient Kemalism

That conflict found its first expression in the imposition of reinforced military control in the Ottoman capital, and elsewhere, by the Allied occupation forces. Having been pressured to comply, the officiating Ali Riza cabinet resigned; it was replaced by Salih Hulusi's,[6] which lasted, however, less than a month. Shortly thereafter, 150 nationalist Turks were arrested as martial law was declared; on pain of death, people were forbidden to assemble, and Istanbul, having been fully occupied, was declared under de jure Allied military control. In retaliation, Mustafa Kemal took British hostages in the interior of Turkey. All this provoked the sultan to dissolve the Chamber, which thus had its final session on 18 March 1920.

The conflict with the Kemalists began to take shape when the Istanbul government's War Minister Şevket Turgut ordered Kemal, still a military officer, back to Istanbul. The sultan followed suit with his own order and with an imperial rescript that was co-signed by the new War Minister, Damad Ferit, and Deputy Grand Vizier Sabri.[7] On 8 July 1919 Sabri officially terminated Kemal's duties as inspector of the Third Army.[8] Some seven weeks later War Minister Nazım ordered Army Commander Kâzım Karabekir, at that time headquartered in Erzerum, to arrest Kemal,[9] who had been formally expelled from the army some three weeks earlier.[10]

Intensification of the Conflict

With the onset of the fifth round of Damad Ferit's premiership in the summer and early fall of 1920, the antagonism, and the attendant hostilities with the Kemalists, progressively intensified. They reached their climax when Ferit finally had to yield, resigning on 17 October 1920. Because of their relevance to the outcome of the courts-martial, these hostilities deserve a brief overview.

The impetus for this intensification had become manifest when Durrizade Abdullah, the reigning Şeyhulislam at the time, issued a *fetva*—an authoritative opinion—on 11 April 1920, sanctioning "the killing of the rebels," i.e., the Kemalists, whose actual murder would thus be a matter of religious duty.[11] A week thereafter, Istanbul's regime instituted and deployed its forces of repression (Kuvayı Inzibatiye) to confront and demolish the national forces—the Kemalist National Independence Army (Kuvayı Milliye)—with Ferit thereby taking over the Ministry of War as well.[12] Within days, namely on 23 April 1920, the Kemalists inaugurated the Grand National Assembly in Ankara as a vehicle for a functioning provisional government. One of the first acts of that body was to institute a court-martial that was vested with extraordinary powers. About a week later a law concerning the punishment of "treason committed and directed against the nation" was enacted. In retaliation, a court-martial in Istanbul convicted Mustafa Kemal and issued a death sentence against him on account of the latter's creation of the Kuvayı Milliye. The sultan ratified this verdict some two weeks later.[13] Twelve days later, on 6 June 1920, Istanbul's series of death verdicts extended to the other leaders of the Kemalist insurgency: Ismet, B. Sami, Riza Nur, Fahri Paşa, Yusuf Kemal, C. Arif.[14] Ankara retaliated again by enacting Law No. 7, whereby all agreements and treaties signed by the sultan's government since 16 March 1920—the termination of the pro-Kemalist parliament in Istanbul—were declared null and void.

Throughout these developments the court-martial in Istanbul, now led by its new president, Staff Brigadier-General (*Mirliva* or *Tuğgeneral*) Ahmet Esat, charted, or intended to chart, a new course: the courts-martial, hitherto proceeding at a terribly slow pace, were to accelerate markedly. It was therefore decided to restructure court proceedings in late September 1919. The changes involved both statutes and prosecutorial procedures, such as the complete elimination of the system of pretrial inquiry commissions and a reliance only on the performance of examining magistrates. Verdicts could be appealed, including death verdicts. The panel of judges would again be entirely military.

Kemalism and the Issue of Armenian Massacres: Changing Tactics and Strategy

While still in its evolving stages, Kemalism, as shaped by its founder Mustafa Kemal, assumed a posture of reasonable judiciousness. That posture found its expression in a most restrained way on 24 April 1920, the second day of the inauguration of the new Kemalist parliament in Ankara, when Kemal made a very furtive allusion to the wartime Armenian massacres, which he gently denounced as a "shameful act" (*fazahat*). Twelve days later in a communication to Army Commander Kâzım Karabekir he explicitly used the word "massacre" when conveying his apprehension about the possibility of "a new Armenian massacre" (*yeniden bir Ermeni kıtalı*). He was even more emphatic when discussing the matter with foreigners, such as the Swiss journalist Emile Hildebrand and French journalist Maurice Prax. He went so far as to tell the latter that the perpetrators of these massacres, whom he denounced as "rascals," should be hanged forthwith.[15]

But his acknowledgement of these massacres to Major-General James G. Harbord, wartime US Army chief of staff, acquired special significance when Kemal explicitly cited the figure of 800,000 as the number of Armenian victims of the massacres.[16] Still uncertain of a favorable, final outcome, Kemal, as the leader of an insurgent movement, displayed all the requisite skills of political pliability and appropriate adaptive compromise. The result was a series of accommodations on the matter of dealing with the delicate issues of the Armenian massacres. The oath of allegiance the Kemalists instituted in the Sivas Congress on 6 September 1919, like the Amasya Protocol,[17] was fashioned in such a way as to dissociate Kemalism from its CUP connections and sympathies, thereby distancing from the CUP's crimes against the Armenians.[18] In the period from March to September 1921, the Kemalists made three distinct pledges, directly and indirectly, that they would prosecute those guilty of the crime of massacres against the Armenians.[19]

However, that very same year, when Mustafa Kemal was conveying his annual report to the Grand National Assembly on 1 March 1921, he indicated that out of 350 deputies, 68 were actually ex-deputies from Istanbul and 12 were former Malta detainees. This fact would prove to be the forerunner of a host of subsequent developments whereby Kemalism became more and more entwined with the residual anti-Armenian CUP leaders, many of whom had played leading roles in the organization and implementation of the wartime Armenian Genocide.[20] To crown a series of governmental measures glorifying the memory of past CUP leaders, with Law No. 318 on 31 March 1923 Ankara declared a general amnesty for all who had been convicted by courts-martial as well as by municipal criminal courts.

Allied efforts to have the Ottoman authorities deliver the suspects involved to their jurisdiction proved fruitless. Not only did the foreign minister of the Istanbul government object to surrendering Turkish nationals to the Allies, but Mustafa Kemal, the head of the antagonistic Ankara government, rejected the very idea, considering it tantamount to "recognizing a kind of right of jurisdiction on the part of foreign government over a Turkish subject's acts in the interior of Turkey."[21] Instead, the Kemalists offered to launch internal criminal proceedings against the war criminals. On 11 June 1921 the Ankara government informed the British that as soon as the Malta internees were released in exchange for British civilian and military persons, "those accused of crimes would be put on impartial trial at Ankara—in the same way as German prisoners were being tried in Germany."[22] This, as well as subsequent similar assurances, proved rather to be negotiating ploys, however. Beyond the exertions of nationalist politics, a legal issue worked in Turkey's favor: the ex post facto character of the relevant provisions of the Sèvres treaty, which were not predicated on existing national or international law. Indeed, Article 15 of the Ottoman Penal Code explicitly prohibited that type of procedure ("punishment is not to be effected in accordance with a subsequent law"). Furthermore, these provisions of the Sèvres treaty did not specify the jurisdiction and laws by which conviction and sentence rendition could be effected.

All these developments acquired, however, a particular irony, bordering on sarcasm, through the exceptionally boastful way in which many of the court-martialed and convicted perpetrators in question, from the highest to the lowest in rank and position, were celebrated and memorialized by the Kemalists in subsequent years. The Kemalist parliament granted Mehmet Kemal, one of those who were executed by hanging, a family pension on 19 December 1920; Mehmet Nusret, likewise, was rewarded with the allocation of a family pension on 25 December 1920.[23] Both men were declared "national martyrs" (*milli şehid*) by the same parliament, and additionally, large sums of money were raised for their families through public subscription. Moreover, by Law No. 478 on 13 April 1924, the Kemalist parliament allocated pensions to the families of the two arch organizers of the Armenian Genocide, Talaat and Dr. Bahaeddin Şakir.[24] Not satisfied with such periodic and fragmentary arrangements to benefit the families of these men, the Kemalist government made a final dispensation two years later. Through its parliament it enacted Law No. 882, by virtue of which each member of the families of the following "victims" would receive compensation in the form of expropriated Armenian properties: Talaat Paşa; Cemal Paşa; Cemal Azmî; Bahaeddin Şakir; Süreyya, Adjutant of Cemal Paşa; Nusret, Adjutant of Cemal Paşa; Sait Halîm Paşa; Servet, District Governor of Muş; Nusret, District Governor of Urfa; Kemal, County Executive of Boğazlıyan; Dr. Reşit, Governor-General of Diyarbekir; and Hafız Abdullah of Erzincan. There were, however, two stipulations attached to this arrangement: first, the value of property to be given was not to exceed TP 20,000; second, that property could not be sold for a period of ten years.[25]

The ground is now prepared for proceeding to the actual phases of criminal prosecution, involving the documentary establishment of the crime. The next chapter will attempt to cover and explore these phases.

Notes

1. Tarık Zafer Tunaya, *Türkiye'de Siyasal Partiler,* vol. 1 (Istanbul: Hürriyet Vakfı, 1984), pp. 14–15.
2. Gökbilgin, *Milli Mücadele Başlarken* Ankara: Türk Tarih Kurumu, 1959. Istanbul: Analiz Basım, 2004, vol. 2, p. 135.
3. Ibid., pp. 212–213.
4. Bilal Şimşir, *Malta Sürgünleri.* Istanbul: Milliyet, 1976., pp. 158–159. The author maintains in this connection that by this agreement Kemal was not necessarily conceding the culpability of the Malta detainees; moreover, he wanted to have guilty Armenians prosecuted as well.
5. *T.V.* 3747. When enacting this new law the new Chamber comprised seventy-four deputies.
6. *T.V.* 3796.
7. Turgut's order was issued on 5 June, the sultan's on 2 July, and his rescript on 8 July 1919.
8. *T.V.* 3596, 13 July 1919.
9. That was on August 30, 1919.
10. *T.V.* 3621.
11. *T.V.* 3834, 11 April 1920.
12. *T.V.* 3883, 21 June 1920.
13. *T.V.* 3864, 24 May 1920.
14. *T.V.* 3883, 21 June 1920.
15. Vahakn N. Dadrian, "The Documentation of the World War I Armenian Massacres in the Proceedings of the Turkish Military Tribunal," *International Journal of Middle East Studies* 23 (November 1991): 551–552.
16. Orbay, "Rauf Orbay' ın Hatıraları," *Yakın Tarihimiz* 3 (1962): 179.
17. Kemal Atatürk, "Nutuk," in *Vesikalar,* vol. 3, 7th printing (Istanbul: Milli Egitim, 1963), p. 1112.
18. Gotthard Jaeschke and Erich Pritsch, "Die Türkei seit dem Weltkriege 1918–1928" *Die Welt des Islams* 10 (1927): 20, 23.
19. The first pledge was made on 10 March 1921 by Ankara's Foreign Affairs Minister Bekir Sami, FO 371/6499/E3110, folio 190; the second was made on 11 June 1921 on behalf of the Ankara government by Safa, the Foreign Affairs Minister of the sultan's government in Istanbul, FO 371/6504/E9112, folio 47, p. 2; the third was made by Rafet Paşa, Ankara's Interior Minister, on 14 September 1921, FO 371/6504/E10411, folio 130.
20. For a partial list of these leading men see Dadrian, "The Documentation of the World War I Armenian Massacres," [n. 15], pp. 575–576, notes 64 and 65.

21. *A Speech Delivered by Mustafa Kemal Atatürk* (Istanbul: Ministry of Education, Istanbul, 1963), p. 497.
22. FO 371/6504/E9112, folio 47.
23. Zeki Sarıhan, *Kurtuluş Savaşı Günlüğü* , vol. 3 (Ankara: Öğretmen, 1986), p. 333. For Kemal alone the amount raised through subscription was 20,000 Turkish pounds (TP); the vote in parliament regarding Nusret was 35 against, 64 for; Jaeschke and Pritsch, *Die Türkei* [n. 18], p. 84, Law No. 478.
24. Jaeschke [n. 18], (1927), p. 84. See also Edgar Pech, *Les Alliés et la Turquie* (Paris: Les Presses Universitaires de France, 1925), pp. 46–47. In commenting on the significance of a pension for Talaat's family, Sir Andrew Ryan, a British expert on Turkey, noted that not only was this bill welcomed by the Turkish parliamentarians when it was introduced in the parliament, but they "vehemently applauded the chief speaker who … justified the tragic deportations of Armenians generally." *The Last of the Dragomans* (London: Geoffrey Bles, 1951), p. 219.
25. Enacted on 20 May 1926, the law was published in the official gazette *Resmi Ceride* on 27 June 1926. The details of the enactment of the law are in *The Transcripts of the Grand National Assembly,* II/25, 30 May 1926, pp. 645–646. It should be noted that there is no credible evidence of Servet having being assassinated by an Armenian. Rather, there is indication of some source of sickness as cause for death.

CHAPTER 6

The Series of Major Trials and the Related Verdicts

Falsification of the Arguments of "Relocation," "Civil War," and "Intercommunal Clashes"

Vahakn N. Dadrian

The court-martial proceedings may be divided into three major categories: (1) geographic areas and related middle-level and minor officials; (2) cabinet ministers and CUP's Central Committee members (recognizing the fact that the top leaders of the latter group, especially Talaat and Enver, were at the same time identified with the former group), and (3) responsible secretaries and delegates. When assessing the key role this latter group played in executing CUP's overt and covert major schemes, which included the Armenian deportations and massacres in particular, Tunaya, the late dean of Turkish political scientists, described them as "most dependable" party functionaries; "the spirited bearers" (*taşıcılar*) of CUP's missions; CUP's "source of energy"; "more powerful than government officials," they constituted "a state within the state."[1] Their inordinate leverage of power derived from the simple fact that that power was informal rather than formally grounded; hence, transcending as it did the power and authority of a regular government, it was circumventive power.

The geographic areas of operative courts-martial specifically involved the cities Yozgat (Ankara province), Bayburt and Erzincan (Erzurum province), and the provinces of Harput and Trabzon. Moreover, some of these trial series were concurrent, thus creating conditions in which several of them overlapped. The first of the Yozgat series began, for example, on 5 February 1919; the rest of the series stretched over a period of eighteen months, to end on July 1920. The start of the Trabzon series coincided with the 14th sitting of the Yozgat series (26 March 1919), with the latter ending at the 18th sitting (7 April 1919). Between the 14th and 15th sittings of the Trabzon trials (26 and 30 April 1919), the major cabinet trial series was started (28 April). The Trabzon series ended at the 20th sitting (17 May 1919), and after several interruptions that were caused mainly by the transfer to Malta of most of the CUP ministers, the trial of the cabinet ministers ended on 15 July 1919.

The cabinet ministers' and CUP chieftains' trial series occupy a central place in the trials conducted by the Special Military Tribunal, for those facing prosecution included cabinet ministers, two grand viziers, two *Şeyhülislams*, and several army and army group commanders. The severity of the charges was matched by the fact that, as pointed out above, such trials were unprecedented in Turkish history. As if to underscore this, the chief public prosecutor lodged with the Key Indictment the most incriminating documents in the possession of the court. The goal was to highlight the pivotal role of the central authorities in the organization and execution of genocide, focusing, therefore, on the decisive role of the CUP, particularly its Central Committee. The defense strategy that had been agreed upon among the defendants during the consultations in Bekirağa prison was that all the principal defendants uniformly would deny the charge that there had been Armenian massacres. This prompted the celebrated writer Aka Gündüz (Enis Avni) to poke fun at them in an article imitating their defense style. "Oh alas, oh alas. We didn't see, we didn't know, we didn't hear" (Vah-vah, vah-vah, görmüyorduk, bilmiyorduk, işitmiyorduk).[2] As Tunaya observed, all of them in concert and in unison were to emphatically deny the perpetration of the crime of "massacre."[3]

To counter this defense strategy, the Military Tribunal used two principal methods: (1) it sprang one surprise after another by introducing as evidence hitherto hidden and unrevealed coded telegrams bearing the names and signatures of the defendants; and (2) it undermined their denials by introducing statements and confessions from the pretrial interrogatories signed by them. As a result, some, though not all, of the defendants amended their testimony, including Central Committee member Yusuf Riza, as well as top Ittihadist Küçük Talaat and Special Organization Director "Kambur" Atıf (Kamçıl).

What is significant about all these major trial series is that the verdicts depended almost entirely on Muslim testimony supporting the bulk of the existing documentary evidence. The courtroom testimony of dozens of Armenian survivors was summarily dispensed with in this respect. This procedure was shadowed by the initiative of the district attorney near the end of the Yozgat trials, namely, at the 16th sitting on 29 March 1919. Moreover, at the 9th, 12th, and 16th sittings of the same trial series (22 February, 6 and 29 March 1919, respectively) the district attorney (procuror general) emphasized that all the documents being introduced as evidence were, as required, validated by competent officials of both ministries, Interior and Justice, who then would append the notation, "it conforms to the original." This is a judicial fact whose paramount importance calls for emphasis.

In its ancillary verdicts, the tribunal also came to grips with the most abiding issue punctuating the controversy about the nature of the anti-Armenian measures. The perpetrators were maintaining that "relocation" was the sole purpose of the deportations. In the Yozgat Verdict this claim was refuted with the assertion that the deportations were rather a cloak for the organization of ensuing massacres. "There can be no doubt and no hesitation" about this (şüphe ve tereddüt bırakmadığından).[4]

Finally, there is the argument of "civil war" and its twin appendage, "intercommunal clashes," whereby the functional polarity between victim and victimizer is artfully collapsed into an undifferentiated form of mutual hostility. In refusing to invoke Article 56 of the Ottoman Penal Code, which the district attorney had proposed, the judges of the military tribunal in their Yozgat Verdict rejected the contention of a civil war, a case that is subsumed in Article 56. That article has reference to acts of "mutual slaughter" by communal groups poised for combat "against each other." The tribunal instead applied Article 45 for conviction and sentence rendition, thereby singling out the distinct role of the perpetrators while identifying the nature of their crimes.

With these observations as background material, the individual Verdicts may now be depicted and examined in terms of their main features. As was customary in Ottoman criminal procedures, these verdicts are spelled out as "decisions" (*kararname*) and usually have two main components: (1) the reasons underlying the verdicts, (2) the verdicts themselves.

The Yozgat Verdict

There were three principal defendants in this trial:[5] (1) Mehmet Kemal, the 35-year-old *Kaymakam* (county executive) of Boğazlıyan county in Yozgat district. For a period of some seven weeks between 6 August and the end of September 1915, he became deputy district governor of Yozgat district; (2) Manastırlı Mehmet Tevfik bini Halil Osman, a 44-year-old gendarmerie captain, subsequently promoted to major; he was in charge of the districts of Çorum and Yozgat in Ankara province; (3) Abdül Feyyaz (Ali), 40 years old, Boğazlıyan county's Pious Foundations (Evkaf) official. For a variety of reasons, however, his case was detached at the very start of the proceedings for purposes of a separate trial.

The central element in this judgment is the determination of the crime of massacre and its constant corollary, "pillage and plunder." Here are the major contentions of this judgment. The crimes were committed with a firm intention. Equally important, the method of "deportation" was a subterfuge for the ultimate objective of "exterminating the deportee population." About this "there can be no doubt and no hesitation." Referring to the method of incapacitating the male victims at the very start of the deportation operations, the verdict speaks of the standard procedure of "tying together the arms of several men." In order to intensify the scale of the atrocities, the perpetrators incited the religious hatreds "not only of Yozgat Muslims but Muslims in general." Addressing the issue of Armenian provocations, the verdict points out that their incidence was too insignificant to justify the magnitude of the crime. "Even if a fraction of the Armenian people had participated in such acts, the fact remains that the rest of the people had actually demonstrated their loyalty [*sadakat*] to the state." In his defense the suspect Kemal referred to the atrocities the Armenians were said to have committed against the Muslims of Van, Erzurum, and Bitlis. But these acts, even if true, "cannot be attributed to Yozgat Armenians who are known to have not resorted to any uprising whatsoever ... such reasoning is in accord neither with any law nor with one's conscience." The verdict further emphasized its reliance on "detailed evidence" (*delaili mebsute*), "absolute proofs" (*berahini katiyen*), and on "hand-written documents" (*hattı destiyle muharrer vesika*). In doing so it dismissed out of hand the defense arguments as being "entirely worthless." By the same token the same verdict invoked as its guidepost the "sentiments of humanity and civilization" (*hissiyatı insaniye ve medeniye*) and the canons of Islam that warn against "mortal sin" (*kebairı cinaattan*).

Having separated the trial of Abdül Feyyaz Ali from those of the remaining two defendants, Kemal was found guilty of first-degree murder and sentenced to death by hanging. The other defendant, Manastırlı Tevfik, as an accessory to the crime, was sentenced to fifteen years of hard labor. Kemal's conviction was based on Article 170 of the Penal Code, which provides for the death penalty for acts of killing with premeditation (*ta'ammüden*), and on Section 1 of Article 171 of the Military Penal Code, which also provides for the death penalty for armed or unarmed assaults and pillage by way of coercion. Tevfik's sentence, on the other hand, was predicated on Section 2 of Article 45 of the Penal Code, punishing people who are found to be accessories to a crime. That provision of the law stipulates that in the event the principal perpetrator is sentenced to death, or to perpetual hard labor, the accessory shall receive a sentence of temporary hard labor (*muvakkat kürek*) for no less than ten years.

The Trabzon Verdict

The defendants were:[6] (1) Ahmet Mustafa, an agent in the Seyri Sefain maritime company; (2) Mehmet Ali, director of Customs and trustee of Trabzon's Red Crescent Hospital; (3) Niyazi, merchant, hotel manager, and Black Sea motorboater; (4) Nuri, Trabzon police chief; (5) Talaat, lieutenant-colonel of the gendarmerie (*kaymakam*) and a member of the Commission of Military Requisitions; (6) Ali Saib (MD), director of Trabzon's Health Services; (7) Yusuf Riza, artillery major, head of Trabzon's S.O. brigand-guerilla units (his case, as well as MD Ali Saib's, would later be detached for the purpose of separate trials); 8. Manastırlı gendarmerie Major Tevfik bin Yusuf.

The absentee defendants, the principal organizers of the mass murder in Trabzon province, were Cemal Azmi, the province's omnipotent governor-general, and Yenibahçeli Nail, the province's equally omnipotent CUP representative, the so-called responsible secretary (*Kâtibi Mesul*).

As in the framing of the Yozgat Verdict, here too is the fact underscored that the term "deportation" was used by the authorities to deflect attention from the real purpose of the order for deportation, namely, the extermination of the deportee population. The defendants were described as "repeat criminals," gendarmes, and "vile elements." In order to conceal the actual crime of massacre, the brigands were deployed in such a way that they remained "as much out of sight as possible." The male and female infants were loaded in batches onto barges and boats, ostensibly for the purpose of normal sea transport. However, "as soon as they were out of sight, they were summarily drowned and destroyed." The properties of the victims were systematically plundered. Not only men were separated from women, but the latter were subsequently robbed as many of them were raped as well by bandits. These acts of sexual violation extended to many orphan girls who were being distributed among Turkish families (T.V. 3617, p. 2, right column). The verdict specifically mentions the Red Crescent Hospital, where these "rapes were perpetrated against virgins." All these crimes were committed under the supervision of the governor-general, who, together with the CUP potentate Yenibahçeli Nail, was executing the CUP's secret orders while pretending to execute the ostensible orders of deportation (T.V. 3617, p. 1, left column).

The verdict concluded that, based on credible witness testimony and the ambivalent confessions of the defendants, the defense arguments had proven to be "completely groundless." Accordingly, pursuant to the terms of Article 45 of the Penal Code, Cemal Azmi, Delegate Nail, and Mehmet Ali were found guilty. Likewise, Police Chief Nuri and Acente Mustafa were guilty of having misused their official positions. The decision was reached unanimously. The punishments and acquittals were framed as follows: Cemal Azmi and Nail were found liable to punishment pursuant to Article 45, Section 1, which identified them as principal conspirators of the first degree because of their complicity in the crimes as co-perpetrators. Accordingly they were condemned to death under the provisions of Article 171 of the Military Penal Code and of Article 170 of the Municipal Penal Code, which were stipulated for perpetrators of "murders" committed with premeditation (*ta'ammüd*) and with deliberation (*kasden*) (p. 3 right column). They were at the same time divested of their civil rights, as a result of which their pawned properties were confiscated and transferred to the Treasury. Mehmet Ali, as accessory to the crimes, was sentenced to ten years of hard labor. Acente Mustafa and Police Chief Nuri were each sentenced to prison for one year and were denied the right to office for two years. Because there was no evidence of their involvement in the massacres and plunders, Niyazi and Talaat were acquitted. Talaat's alleged misconduct relative to military confiscations fell, it was argued, outside the purview of this court. Unless other charges were pending against them, they were allowed to go free. Health Services Director Ali Saib's case was deferred for the purpose of further clarification of certain matters. These decisions were unanimously reached in the absence of Cemal Azmi and Nail; all the others were present.

The Harput Verdict

The principal defendants,[7] both of whom were tried in absentia, were Dr. Bahaeddin Şakir, Central Committee member of the CUP and chief (*reis*) of the Special Organization (East); and Resneli Boşnak Nazım, CUP's responsible secretary in Harput province. The defendants who were present were (Haci Boloşzade) Mehmet Nuri, deputy from Dersim; and Ferit, Dersim's superintendent of education (at the time Konya's superintendent of education). Once more, the verdict focused on the crime of "massacre," more specifically on "the extermination and destruction of the Armenians" (*Ermenilerin ifna ü imhası*) and the plunder of their properties and goods (1, l). And again, the verdict from the very beginning points out that it is predicated upon the composite evidence provided both by prosecution and defense, the ensemble of court papers (*evrâkı dava*), and the contents of court transcriptions. Further, the assertion is made that all of them "from head to toe have been examined and deliberated upon.… The Verdict was reached only after carefully probing into the thusly emerging picture" (1, l).

The court findings essentially revolved around the status of Dr. Bahaeddin Şakir as the chief architect of the massacres and the leader of the respective arch perpetrators. He is depicted as the principal organizer of the brigands of the Special Organization, which functioned as the main instrument of the massacres. To achieve this goal Şakir resorted to two methods. He gathered together and organized those convicts who were released from the prisons, as well as an assortment of "wicked persons," and he also relied not only on "oral" orders but also on "cipher telegrams" in order to receive and convey the requisite instructions.

The evidence adduced in the verdict is perhaps the most damning in the entire set of documents the military tribunal was able to obtain and produce. It consists mainly of two pieces of prima facia evidence. One of them is an authenticated cipher telegram dated 12 June 1915, which Şakir sent from Erzurum, his headquarters, to Harput, where his underling Resneli Nazım,

Harput's CUP representative, was stationed. In it the S.O. chieftain anxiously inquires whether Harput's Armenians are merely being "deported" or in fact are being "liquidated" (*tasfiye*) (p. 1). The second is a signed affidavit from wartime Turkish Army Commander General Mehmet Vehip, who during the war was commander-in-chief of the Turkish Third Army, deployed in the six eastern provinces with large and dense Armenian populations. In addition to Sivas, Erzurum, Harput, Bitlis, Diyarbekir, and Van, it also had jurisdiction over a seventh province, Trabzon. In his affidavit of 5 December 1918, prepared at the request of the military tribunal following a rather extensive correspondence with its prosecutors, General Vehip testified in detail to what he knew about the wartime mass murder of the Armenians. In focusing on the role of Dr. Şakir, the general, without mincing words, told the court-martial that Şakir had mobilized "butchers of human beings" (*insan kasabları*) to carry out the CUP Central Committee's goal, which was "the mass murder and extermination of the Armenians and the pillage of their properties" (katl ve imhası ve mallarının yağma ve gasbı) (p. 2, right column).

Dr. Şakir was found guilty under the terms of Article 181 of the Penal Code, which designates instigation and pillaging as felonies accompanying the killing operations and other forms of violent acts. He was sentenced to death pursuant to Article 170 of the same code, which particularly stipulates "premeditation" as a required condition. Resneli Nazım, who at the time remained in hiding in Istanbul, was found guilty as an accessory under Section Two of Article 45 of the Penal Code and accordingly was sentenced, likewise in absentia, to five years of hard labor. Defendants Mehmet Nuri and Ferit were acquitted by unanimous decision for want of reliable and convincing evidence against them. In the case of Nazım, three of the judges—Süleyman Şakir, Ismail Hakkı, and Esat, a majority of the panel—disagreed with the other two judges, declaring that he had been not only an accessory but, like Dr. Şakir, a principal perpetrator. For unexplained reasons, however, the judgment of the minority held.

The Bayburt Verdict

Mehmet Nusret, son of Behram, age 44, was county executive (*kaymakam*) of Bayburt county in Erzurum district, part of the province bearing the same name.[8] In the month of September 1915, he was promoted to district governor for the Erzincan district (Sancak). On 13 November 1915, he was appointed district governor of Ergani district in Diyarbekir province. The verdict again focuses on "the massacres perpetrated in connection with the Armenian deportations, and the related plunder of the possessions of the victims." It cites several cases of rape of minors by Nusret himself and his acolytes. In dismissing defense arguments as groundless, this verdict too singles out the paramount role of CUP Central Committee member Dr. Bahaeddin Şakir, his Special Organization bands of killers, and CUP's Erzurum delegate Filibeli Hilmi. The orders of CUP were conveyed through the S.O. functionaries. Nusret is depicted as a "head brigand" who, with these other brigands, accompanied the deportee convoys, participated in the plunders of the victims, and personally observed the ensuing massacres. Among several Muslim eyewitnesses testifying to the vehemence of the atrocities, Ergani mining engineer Abdullah Husrev stands out. He revealed that Nusret's nickname was "the governor of the iron paws" (*demir pençeli mutasarrıf*). The verdict determined that Nusret and reserve officer Mehmet Necati, also called Pire Mehmet, were the principal organizers of the mass murder of the Bayburt Armenians and of the attendant plunder of the latter's goods and properties.

Reiterating the point that the court had in its possession "undeniable proof and documentary evidence," the judges declared that they had reached the verdict with "an all-clean conscience." They "unanimously decided that the defendants are guilty." Once more the verdict invoked Section One of Article 45 of the Penal Code to determine and spell out the nature and gravity of the crimes. For the purpose of specifying the relevant penalties, the verdict made reference to Article 170 of the Penal Code and Article 171 of the Military Penal Code. Accordingly, the two principal defendants, Nusret and Necati, were sentenced to death, with the latter being deprived of all his civil rights; all his possessions were to be confiscated and disposed of according to the terms of the law. Furthermore, the verdict set forth a plan to initiate criminal proceedings against twenty-six other individuals whose complicity was indicated not only in the deportations of Armenians of Bayburt and Ergani Maden, but also of those of Erzurum. This verdict was passed in the presence of Nusret and in the absence of Necati, unanimously.

The Erzincan Verdict

The defendants were:[9] (1) 44-year-old Mehmet Memduh bin Tayyar, born in Muğla and presently in detention in Malta; he was *mutasarrif*, or district governor, of Erzincan; (2) Hafız Abdullah Avni bin haci Hüseyin, 45 years old, in the hotel business; (3) former Erzincan deputy Halet, at that time a fugitive; (4) Haci Vahitzade Riza from Erzincan; (5) KırmoYusuf, Dersim, tribal chief and notorious brigand; (6) Aslan, gendarme sergeant from Erzincan; and (7) Kako, head of Danzig township from Plumer county in the Erzincan district. Implicated in the events cited in the No. 27 official report (*mazbata*) of 26 June 1920, the offenses of these defendants were sufficiently established in the court proceedings and the companion investigations. Hafız Abdullah Avni, Halit,

Kırmo, Yusuf, Aslan, and Kako among them were found guilty pursuant to the terms of Section One of Article 45 of the Penal Code and accordingly were punishable pursuant to Article 170 of the Penal Code and Article 171 of the Military Penal Code. Accordingly, Hafız Abdullah Avni, Halit, Kırmo, Yusuf, Aslan, and Kako were condemned to death. Vahtizade's case was eliminated (*sükut*), since he had passed away. Memduh's case was to be detached since he was detained in Malta. For nine other suspects, newly identified in this verdict, criminal investigations were to be initiated. For Abdullah Avni, the verdict was issued in his presence; the others were issued in the absence of the offenders, who were to be retried upon apprehension.

The minister of war was authorized to execute the imperial rescript.

The Verdict against Responsible Secretaries and Delegates

This trial series, which started on 21 June and, after an interruption at its third sitting, reconvened on 6 October 1919, comprised thirteen sittings and ended with a verdict issued on 8 January 1920.[10] The indictment, which was read into the record at the first sitting, charged thirty defendants (not all of whom were responsible secretaries) with crimes against the Armenians. The centerpiece of it was the accusation that the defendants had gained control of the state apparatus and consequently had imposed their party objectives upon the government. They treated the Central Committee as the supreme instance for governmental decision-making. The promulgation of the Temporary Law of Deportation was the result of these developments. The deportees were "annihilated," and their goods and properties were "plundered and pillaged" by brigands and gangs of outlaws the Central Committee had engaged for this purpose.

Among the accused were prominent Ittihadist leaders, including physician Ahmet Midhat, the party's secretary for Bolu, a district in the province of Kastamonu, who did yeoman's work in inciting the Muslim populations of other provinces through inflammatory speeches. Another was Edirne Province Inspector Abdülgani. Still another was Kastamonu's Responsible Secretary Hasan Fehmi, whose powers had exceeded those of the governor-general of the province. Even though the prosecution was primarily directed against the responsible secretaries of the CUP, the indictment did extend the bill of charges to a variety of other officials, functionaries, and parliamentary deputies, including War Minister Enver's father. Of the 29 cited as indicted men, only 11 responsible secretaries appeared; the other 18 remained absent.

One of the more notable features of the second sitting of the trial series was the admission by Edirne CUP Inspector Abdülgani that "the Armenians of Edirne were very honorable people. During the occupation of the city by the Bulgarians they offered protection to the Turkish families." He nevertheless, admitted that there was some deportation from Edirne, at the same time denying, however, that the victims' goods and possessions had been pillaged. In the third sitting, Dr. Besim Zühdi, delegate-secretary of Eskişehir, argued that the crimes "were not the work of the Ittihad Party, but that of the government which was executing the law on deportation."

Notwithstanding, these repeated denials by the accused of any complicity in the crimes were consistently belied by the testimony of Muslim witnesses, including high-ranking civilian and military officials. Here is a list: Retired Major Ismail Hakkı; late Marshal Asaf Paşazade Cemal; Ninth Regiment Commander Colonel Hurşit; and Silifke Gendarmery Commander Major Mustafa Şerif, who quoted a confession from Gendarmerie Colonel Izzet. The civilian officials included: Kastamonu Administrative Council (Meclisi Idare) Secretary Besim; Kaymakam Celal; and Bolu Deputy Mutasarrıf Ali Ilmi (dismissed for objecting to deportations). In addition, the War Office sent a memo regarding Abdülgani's offenses. Muslim civilians who testified included: Vahid; Cevdet; Salim; Kastamonu notable Tevfik; Medrese hoca Mehmet; and the attorney Izzet. The defendants present at the trial were: Dr. Besim Zühdi, Bursa's responsible secretary; Avni, Manisa's; Abdülgani, Edirne's, Mehmet Cemal, Aleppo's; Hüseyin Cevdet, Mirgün's deputy responsible secretary; Hasan Salahattin, Beyoğlu (Istanbul's); Dr. Mithat, Bolu's; Abdülkadir (deputy), Konya's; Münir (deputy), Kastamonu's; Agâh, ex-chairman of Karahisar's Liquidation Commission; and Hayrettin, Karahisar Liquidation Commission member.

As the verdict underscored, "the defendants participated in the CUP's Central Committee's criminal decisions, especially on the matter of deportations and massacres and plunders." They abused the 14 (27) May Temporary Law of Deportation for the purpose of pursuing personal interests. Using the CUP's provincial branches, they organized and paved the ground for massacre and annihilation of the Armenians. These party potentates showed excessive zeal with respect to "pillage" (p. 4, right column). Transgressing the law, they extended the deportations to all corners of the land. The pursuit of the goals of acquisitiveness and personal enrichment (*iddihârı servet*) played a major role (p. 4, right column). The massacres were organized, with the help of the Special Organization, by the CUP's Central Committee in order to prepare and facilitate these criminal missions (p. 4, left column).

Among these party potentates Hasan Fehmi from Kastamonu was most influential in the organization and direction of the actions against the Armenians in Kastamonu. As a member of the Commission on Abandoned Goods, he brought sacks into stores and, with the help of his men, gathered everything he needed. Only after completing this thievery did he order the opening of these stores and declare the auction open for the people. He was more powerful than the province's governor-general. No one dared to stop his thievery.

Similar misdeeds were committed by other responsible secretaries, especially Edirne's Abdülgani (p. 5, left column).

The verdict in effect reaffirmed the thrust of the indictment, at the same time underscoring a number of relevant facts. The court established that in at least three cases provincial responsible secretaries had been able to effect the dismissal of governors who resisted orders for massacres. One of them was Ankara's Hüseyin Necati. He had Yozgat's District Governor Cemal replaced by Mehmet Kemal, who by then had already exterminated the Armenians of Boğazlıyan county in Yozgat district; Cemal refused to take informal orders for massacre from Necati, who, being a CUP man, did not represent the government but would read an order from a piece of paper, saying that it was issued by CUP's Central Committee. Necati adamantly refused to allow Cemal to read the order himself. Another such dismissal was engineered by Kastamonu's Responsible Secretary Hasan Fehmi, who had that province's Governor-General Mehmet Reşit Paşa removed from office. The latter had denounced Hasan Fehmi as "a nefarious creature" and had refused to permit the Armenians to be massacred, saying, "I cannot stain my hands with blood" (ben elimi kana boyamam). Hasan Fehmi then denounced Reşit Paşa as "the protector of the Armenians, or more accurately … the governor-general of the infidels" (Ermenilerin hâmisi, daha doğrusu kâfirlerin vâlisidir).

The third case involves the above-mentioned Dr. Midhat, Bolu's responsible secretary, who managed to bring about the dismissal of Ali Ilmi, Bolu's deputy-governor, who also had resisted the deportations in the district. To effect that dismissal Midhat went all the way to Istanbul to lodge his complaint. He had also agitated among the Muslims in order to arouse them against the Armenians. Bolu's Armenians were finally deported by Atıf, the replacement of Kastamonu province's Governor-General Reşit Paşa. The verdict pointed out that these secretaries were vested with such powers as to be able to compel any agency of the government to submit to their extralegal levers of executive operations. The verdict indicated that Abdülgani was caught lying about the number of convoys deported from Edirne; in pretrial testimony he had admitted to three, but in court he admitted to only one. The defendants relied on and engaged criminal gangs and mobs to enact their crimes. Some of them, after pretending to be helping the deportees, tricked the latter into transferring to them their abandoned goods.

The court refrained from issuing any death verdicts as it considered most of the accused merely accessories to the crime. Most of them were found guilty of robbery, plunder, and self-enrichment at the expense of the victims. Two of the five-judge panel, Staff Brigadier General (Mirliva) Ihsan and Infantry Colonel Şakir, objected even to the conviction of the four principal defendants, Hasan Fehmi, Dr. Ahmet Midhat, Abdülgani, and Avni. One of these judges, Ihsan, was part of another panel of judges that terminated these criminal proceedings early in 1921 as Kemalism gained ascendancy and the demise of the sultan's government grew imminent.

The verdict stated that save for Hasan Fehmi, Mithat, Abdülgani, and Cevdet, the other defendants should be set free, as insufficient evidence had been produced to show that they were involved in "massacre" and "plunder." Accordingly, Hasan Fehmi, Dr. Midhat, and Abdülgani were found guilty of committing massacre, plunder, and other crimes under the pretext of organizing deportations. By majority vote it was therefore decided that Besim Zühdi, Mehmet Cemal, Münir, and Abdülkadir would go free, unless they were to be held in prison for other offenses. Ismail Hakkı and Kemal were accused of fraud, but no trials had been conducted. The district attorney could eventually launch an investigation, but at that very time they could not be held in prison. Hence, their acquittal was decided unanimously. As to Hayrettin and Agâh, their cases called for further legal examination. The joint cases of Hayrettin and Kosti needed to be separated, as requested by the Finance Ministry and as decided unanimously (p. 6, left column).

Hasan Fehmi and Midhat were guilty pursuant to the terms of Article 170; their punishment was determined by the terms of Section Two of Article 45 of the Penal Code. Accordingly, they were sentenced to ten years of hard labor, counting from the time of their arrest and imprisonment. The case of Abdülgani was pending in connection with the trial of the Edirne deportations. Avni's sentence was determined pursuant to the terms of Article 203 of the Penal Code, and counting from 17 February 1919, the day of his incarceration, he was sentenced to only two months of imprisonment. Having thus completed the term of his sentence, however, he was set free, as decided by a majority vote. These verdicts were reached in the presence of all the defendants, except for the defendant Agâh. The verdict was signed as follows:

> Provided that our rationale is registered in the proceedings of the trial, we oppose the judgment issued against Zühdi.
>
> Staff Major General and Court President Esat.
> Staff Major General Ismail Hakkı.
>
> We oppose the Verdicts against Hasan Fehmi, Midhat, Gani, and Avni for three objectionable grounds:
>
> 1. the modus operandi of the proceedings
> 2. the framework within which the guilt was defined and explained
> 3. we oppose only the dispositions by which Hasan Fehmi, Midhat, and Avni were adjudged guilty of the crimes specified. The specifics of our objections shall be incorporated in the transcripts of the proceedings.
>
> General Staff General Ihsan
> Infantry Colonel Şakir

The Verdict against Cabinet Ministers and Top CUP Leaders

Before their abrupt arrest and transfer to Malta by the British, the principal defendants at the postwar Turkish courts-martial were the following wartime cabinet ministers: Grand Vizier Sait Halim, Şeyhülislams Musa Kâzım and Hayri, Halil Menteşe, Ismail Canbolat, Abbas Halim, Sait Mollazade Ibrahim, Ali Münif, Ahmet Şükrü, Mustafa Şeref, Kemal, Haşim, and Rifat.[11] Those being tried in absentia were Mehmet Talaat, Ismail Enver, and Ahmed Cemal. The group of prominent CUP Central Committee members likewise being tried included Küçük Talaat, Riza, Mithat Şükrü, Ziya Gökalp, Miralay Ahmet Cevat, and Atıf. Those being tried in absentia from the same group were Drs. Nazım, Şakir, and Rüsuhi, and Hüseyin Aziz.

The series of trials began on 28 April (*T.V.* mistakenly printed 27 April instead) and, after a number of changes in court statutes and the composition of personnel, ended on 5 July 1919 when the Key Verdict and related sentences were pronounced. There were altogether fourteen sittings; they proceeded on the basis of two separate but essentially interrelated indictments. The first seven of these sittings covered the trial of a large number of prominent and top CUP leaders and S.O. chieftains (28 April–17 May 1919). The second series of seven sittings, essentially covering wartime cabinet ministers, who were present, and involving the period between 3 June and 26 June 1919, was broken into two periods. The first four of the sittings took place in the period from 3 to 12 June 1919; the second period, covering the remaining three, lasted from 24 to 26 June 1919.

The central theme of the Key Verdict is that "the crime of mass murder" against the Armenians was "organized and carried out by the top leaders (*erkân*) of CUP" (T.V. 3604, p. 219, right column). "Posturing as lawful people, they created a sham group of administrators whom they could easily mislead and deceive, and then gradually took over the government, only to finally have cabinet ministers to bow to their views and decisions" (T.V. 3604, p. 218, right column). They ended up creating "a menacing fourth branch of government" (*dördüncü bir kuvveyi tehdidiye*) (T.V. 3604, p. 219, left column). These crimes were such as to readily identify them as being associated with "CUP's moral personality; hence they are to be viewed as personal offenses" (Cemiyetin şahsi manevisine atf ve isnad olunan cinayatı şahsiyeyi) (T.V. 3604, p.218, left column). As testified by Şeyhulislam Musa Kâzım (T.V. 3604, p. 219, left column), the CUP leadership even went so far as to insist that abandoning the CUP was tantamount to abandoning Islam. One of the consequences of all this was that the Armenian nation experienced disillusion about "the non-realizability of the ideals of our revered Constitution as it relates to the principles of security and justice" (T.V. 3604, p. 218 left column).

The verdict determined that Talaat, Enver, Cemal, and Dr. Nazım, all of them cabinet ministers but at the same time also top CUP leaders, were guilty of "paramount crimes" (T.V. 3604, p. 220, right column). Accordingly, these offenses fell under the terms of Section One of Article 45 of the Penal Code and their perpetrators were subject to the punishment provided by that Code: the death sentence. As for Cavit, Mustafa Şeref and Musa Kâzım, who were subject to punishment by the terms of Section Two of the same Article 45 and the last section of Article 55 of the Penal Code, they were sentenced to fifteen years of hard labor. Ex-Ministers Rifat and Haşim were acquitted, provided such acquittal did not preclude the possibility of a future trial, the holding of which would be decided by a High Court. As to ex-Post and Telegraph Minister Oskan and ex-Commerce Minister Süleyman El-Büstani, the investigation indicated that they had been in Europe for a long time and were unaware that they had been subpoenaed to appear before the court, and that even if they were aware they were highly unlikely to be able to show up, which led the court to decide to separate their case.

The verdicts, reached in the absence of Talaat, Enver, Cemal, and Dr. Nazım and in the presence of Rifat, Haşim and Musa Kâzım, were reached unanimously, but with the following two qualifications:

> Even though I participated in the reaching of this unanimous Verdict, I nevertheless am of the opinion that Haşim is guilty of the crime of accessory of second degree.
>
> Colonel Mehmet Zeki

> The Court believed Musa Kâzım to be not guilty of the crimes committed by the CUP. However, he was subservient to the cited offenses of its Central Committee, never objected to its evil deeds. He, therefore, is a principal perpetrator. As to Haşim, by his own admission, he was at heart a partisan of the CUP, faithful to it and he never took a stand against its crimes and until the days of the Court Martial he held the CUP to be clean.
>
> Staff Colonels Mustafa bin Aziz and Süleyman.

Some Subsidiary Trials and Convictions

Büyükdere

The Büyükdere court-martial, after a series of eight sittings that started on 23 April 1919, the court-martial reached its verdict on 24 May 1919.[12] The two principal defendants, Kerim, who was engaged in police work, and civil servant Refik were charged with looting the properties of the Armenians (as well as of the Greeks) in the Bosphorus area. Kerim was convicted and sentenced to one year of prison, and Refik was likewise convicted and sentenced to two years. The other two defendants were acquitted.

Izmit[13]

The defendants were Hüseyinoğlu Mehmet, Mehmet Celil, and Hasanoğlu Hüseyin. They were charged with brigandage, highway robbery, and assisting and facilitating the escape from prison of Army Commander Halil (Kut), who was the uncle of War Minister Enver, and of Talaat (Muşkara), otherwise nicknamed Küçük Talaat, who at one time was a member of CUP's Central Committee. These two prominent Young Turk leaders were being detained for criminal prosecution on account of their roles in the Armenian genocide. Hüseyin was convicted and sentenced to six years of hard labor; Mehmet Celil was likewise convicted and sentenced to six months of prison. Hüseyinoğlu, who was legally a juvenile, received a statutory sentence of nine years of prison that was reduced to six months as provided by Article 40 of the penal code.

Drs. Bosnalı Ismail and Ahmet Midhat

Charges were brought in relation to Dr. Mithat's escape from prison, Dr. Ismail's facilitating role in that escape, and the pair's subsequent joining "the rebels," or the Kemalists. Midhat had played a crucial role in the area of propaganda and agitation against the Armenians in several provinces and thus helped pave the way for the ensuing organized mass murder against them.[14] As a result, he was convicted and sentenced to ten years of prison by the court-martial prosecuting CUP's responsible secretaries. He ended up, however, in a hospital for some treatment. Under the terms of paragraph 1 of Article 45, paragraph 4 of Article 55, and Article 56, both defendants were convicted and sentenced to death in absentia.

Cemal Oğuz and Major Nurettin

Çankırı's CUP Responsible Secretary Cemal Oğuz was a key member of the secret committee in charge of streamlining the exterminatory operations against the area's Armenians.[15] He was also a member of Kastamonu province's Commission on Abandoned Goods, which dealt with the expropriation and confiscation of the vast properties of the deported Armenians. Nurettin, formerly the director of Trabzon's gendarmerie school, was a fugitive from justice.

Oğuz was arrested on 3 April 1919. He is cited in the Key Indictment of the military tribunal. For some reason, however, he was let go after a few months of detention—conceivably owing to "lack of evidence." He was accused of having organized the ambush and ensuing massacre of five Armenians, members of a group of hundreds of Armenian elites whom the Turkish authorities had arrested on and around 24 April 1915 as prelude to the wholesale liquidation of the Ottoman Empire's Armenian population. What was so inordinate about the murder of these five Armenians was that two of the victims, Daniel Varoujan and Dr. Rupen Sevag, were the foremost rising stars in the field of Armenian literature and poetry. The impact of their loss was further accentuated by the fact that they were subjected to especially gruesome murders. The date was 13 (26) August 1915. As a result of the personal intervention of Talaat, however, the criminals and their cohorts, some ten of them, were released from prison about a year later.[16]

Upon the order of Esat Paşa, the new president of a new court-martial, Cemal Oğuz was rearrested on 27 October 1919. This date coincides with the particular sitting of the responsible secretaries trial series when the case of Cemal Oğuz was merged with this series. Feigning madness throughout December 1919 and January 1920, during which period he repeatedly clashed with the chief judge and attempted suicide, in the end he forced the court to have his mental state examined by a physician; he was trying to have the court consign him to a mental hospital. His request was granted and he was taken to Gümüşsu Hospital, Central Prison's annex for health services. On 27 May 1920 he was released from that hospital and handed over to Central Prison again. However, at the request of the British high commissioner, Cemal Oğuz was surrendered to British authorities on 2 August 1920. On 30 September 1920 the British transferred him for detention to Malta, where dozens of other Turkish suspects were being held for future prosecution on charges of crimes committed against the Armenians.

As it evolved over a period of time, however, the criminal prosecution of Cemal Oğuz took strange, at times even bizarre, turns. Before his case was merged with those of the responsible secretaries, his indictment had been based upon the murder of the five Armenians described above. The indictment declared that along with Major Nurettin, Oğuz paved the way for and facilitated the commission of the crime and therefore was an accessory (*ferenzi-methal*) to that crime.[17] In the end the military tribunal convicted him and Nurettin. His initial sentence of eight years and four months was reduced to five years and four months; Captain (later Major) Nurettin, on the other hand, was sentenced to six years and eight months of prison.

Notwithstanding, the Court of Cassation some six weeks later, on 23 March, reportedly overturned this verdict, arguing that Cemal Oğuz had already been tried and convicted by Ankara's military tribunal during the war. The court-martial, it further argued, neither had jurisdiction in the case, nor could legally undertake to try a defendant a second time. It developed that Oğuz had engaged in a variety of illicit financial activities, misappropriating very large amounts of money and funds, largely at the expense of his Armenian victims. During the third sitting of the Responsible Secretaries trial series on 28 June 1919, Dr. Ahmet Midhat confirmed the complaints made about the fiscal abuses of Oğuz. He saw fit, however, to spiritedly defend his fellow responsible secretary by way of shifting the blame to the latter's subordinates.[18] British Intelligence indicated that "through the deportations Oğuz had amassed much wealth"; for their part, Armenian sources estimated that, when arrested by the British, he was in possession of a fortune of half a million TP (Turkish gold pounds), the approximate equivalent of some two million dollars.[19]

The Istanbul court-martial flatly rejected the arguments of the Court of Cassation, declaring that the Ankara trials were not only not completed but that Oğuz himself had not been a defendant at that trial, and that his court-martial in Istanbul had involved not a single offense but an array of offenses resulting from his role as CUP responsible secretary. Furthermore, the court maintained, these offenses were of the type that constituted the core of its jurisdictional competence. In consequence, the court-martial reinstated the verdict that the Court of Cassation had quashed.[20]

It should be noted that the most compelling evidence against Oğuz was provided by a number of Turks, including Haci Tevfik, Ziya, and Osman Efendis. Especially critical was the testimony of another Turk, Cemal Asaf, who depicted defendant Oğuz as the arch culprit in the crimes perpetrated against the Armenians and hence identified him as the principal organizer of the Tüney murder of the five Armenians—in close cooperation with Kurd brigand Alo. As mentioned above, this fact is recorded in the Key Indictment and attested by the attachment to that indictment of Document No. 18.[21]

Notes

1. Tarık Zafer Tunaya, *Türkiye'de Siyasal Par*tiler, vol. 3 (Istanbul: Hürriyet Vakfı, 1989), pp. 209, 210.
2. *Alemdar,* 10 May 1919.
3. Tunaya, *Türkiye'de* [n. 1], pp. 210, 281.
4. *T.V.* 3617, p. 2, left column.
5. *T.V.* 3617: 1–2. The verdict was issued on 8 April 1919 and published in *T.V.* on 7 August 1919.
6. *T.V.* 3616: 1–3. The verdict was issued on 22 May 1919 and was published in *T.V.* on 6 August 1919.
7. *T.V.* 3771: 3–6. The verdict was issued on 13 January 1920 and was published on 9 February 1920, substituting the words "Mamuret ül Aziz" for Harput.

8. *Tereüman-ı Hakikat* (Dragoman of Truth), 5 August 1920. The verdict was issued, however, on 20 July 1920. See also Ali Çankaya, *Yeni Mülkiye Tarihi ve Mülkiyeyiler,* vol. 3 (Ankara: Mars Editors, 1968–1969), pp. 797–801. The sultan's ratification of the verdict is in *T.V.* 3923, 8 August 1920.
9. *T.V.* 3917, 31 July 1920. The verdict was issued on 27 July 1920.
10. *T.V.* 3772: 1–6. The verdict was issued on 8 January 1920 and was published on 10 February 1920.
11. *T.V.* 3604: 217–220. The verdict was issued on 5 July 1919 and was published on 22 July 1919.
12. *T.V.* 3618, 9 August 1919. The verdict was issued on 24 May 1919.
13. *T.V.* 3900, 11 July 1920. This issue contains both the text of the verdict as well as that of the requisite ratification by the sultan.
14. *T.V.* 3944, 1 September 1920. The verdict was issued on 19 July 1920. See also *Vakit,* 22 July, and *Alemdar* 22 and 23 July, 1920 editions.
15. *T.V.* 3867, 31 May 1920. The verdict was issued on 8 February 1920, with the sultan ratifying it on 27 May 1920.
16. The details of these horrors were subsequently revealed by one of the Turkish drivers of the two horse-drawn carriages in which the victims were being transported, a twenty-year-old youth. According to his testimony, by pre-arrangement with Cemal Oğuz, four Kurdish brigands led by Alo (Tunaya [n. 1], p. 284) ambushed the convoy at Tüney. Easily casting aside the initial, feeble resistance of the accompanying gendarme officer, the butchers went to work. In order to secure their clothes undamaged and intact, they first ordered the victims to undress. The carnage that followed involved mutilation by multiple sword-strikes and cutting off of forearms and feet. For having dared to resist, the illustrious poet Varoujan was accorded special treatment: his eyes were gouged out and he was disemboweled. Still shaken by the spectacle of this crime, the young driver is reported to have cursed his job with a vow to end it. Grigoris Balakian, *Armenian Golgotha: A Memoir of the Armenian Genocide, 1915-1918. Translated by Peter Balakian with Aris Sevag,* (New York: Albert Knopf, 2009), chap. 14, pp. 100-102. See also item VII in same chapter, p. 356, n. 43. For Talaat's personal involvement, see Taner Akçam, *'Ermeni Meselesi Hallolunmuştur' Osmanlı Belgelerine Göre Savaş Yillarinda Ermenilere Yönelik Politikalar* (Istanbul, Iletişim: 2008), pp. 196–199.
17. Kararname Sureti, No. 35, Aslına Muafıkdır, Armenian Patriarchate Archives Jerusalem, Series 11, File J., no. 623.
18. *T.V.* 3596, p. 214, left column, and p. 215, right column.
19. FO 371/6501/76270, folio 228/726.
20. Ibid., folio 225/723.
21. *T.V.* 3540, p. 7, left column.

CHAPTER 7

Legal Proceedings as a Conceptual Framework

Vahakn N. Dadrian

As underscored in the introduction to this study, the prosecution of the crime of the wartime organized mass murder of the Armenians of the Ottoman Empire was an unprecedented event in several respects. Foremost among these was the fact that a postwar Turkish government not only officially acknowledged it, but more important—and defying an entrenched tradition of impunity in such cases—it ventured to investigate and punish the crime and its perpetrators. Equally if not more significant was the fact that the suspected perpetrators belonged to the highest echelons of the government and to the monolithic political party, the CUP, which dominated that government throughout the 1913–1918 period. These twin facts alone were sufficient to impart extraordinary significance to the projected criminal proceedings. The military tribunal that was to undertake this task was coincidentally labeled "The Extraordinary Court-Martial."

The specter of the military defeat of the Ottoman Empire and the ensuing belligerent presence of the victorious Allies in the Ottoman capital were omnipresent facts. Turkish authorities were therefore hard pressed to dispel concerns about a looming "victor's justice" imposed by a "kangaroo court." Accordingly, they took two unusual steps. Departing from established court-martial practice, they decided to hold open trials, allowing access to the media and the public. Moreover, they allowed defense lawyers to be present and to argue when required. Such arguments materialized especially at the start of the trials with respect to matters such as court jurisdiction, the Constitution, the admissibility of certain types of evidence, and closing arguments.

The launching of the courts-martial was foreshadowed in several respects by the parliamentary debates that preceded these trials. The first signposts appeared in the Ottoman Senate, i.e., the Upper Chamber of that parliament. As already discussed, two senators through their respective speeches set the stage for the launching of the prosecution. When responding to his critics, for example, Ahmet Riza, the newly elected president of the Senate, asserted on 21 October 1919 that the extermination of the Armenians, pursuant to "official" policy, was quite centrally organized. Implicit in this assertion was the charge that there was deliberate intent, and possibly even premeditation, by the central authorities involved. In the same Senate, on 21 November 1918, distinguished veteran statesman Reşit Akif revealed that immediately after the end of World War I, in his office as president of the Council of State, he had come into possession of two documents. One of them was the overt, official order of deportation; the other was a secret circular, issued by CUP's Central Committee, ordering the annihilation of the deportee convoys as soon as they were sufficiently removed from population centers. In other words, there was in place a system of a two-track transmission of orders whereby a political party was seen exercising its informal and superordinate authority to order mass murder while relying on ex-convicts. The third parliamentary revelation came on 11 December 1918 from a deputy of the Ottoman Chamber of Deputies. Hafız Mehmet, a lawyer, disclosed in his speech that he had been an eyewitness to an exterminatory operation at the port city Ordu on the Black Sea during which Armenian women and children were thrown onto barges that then set sail and dumped their trapped victims into the high sea to drown.

These accounts are indicative of the nature and scale of the lethal operations that in short order would engulf the bulk of the empire's Armenian population. As explained above, prima facie evidence obtained in the Lower Chamber of the Ottoman Parliament tended to confirm the radically lethal nature of these undertakings. There too an official investigation revealed that some wartime cabinet ministers remarkably anticipated the subsequent major findings of the military tribunal when responding to the queries of the members of the Fifth Investigative Department of the Chamber of Deputies. Justice Minister Ibrahim, for example, disclosed that he had been forced by War Minister Enver to order, against the law, the release of thousands of convicts. On the other hand, the special law authorizing such an act was enacted when these convicts had all but completed their operations of mass murder against the Armenians. Furthermore, Grand Vizier Sait Halim revealed that the cabinet was not informed about the enlistment of convicts into the Special Organization, and that the cabinet's decision relative to the treatment of the Armenians did not include the provision that they be "killed," but rather was limited to an order that they be deported.

For all of these reasons, these pretrial parliamentary initiatives acquire inordinate significance, not just in terms of evidence gathering and documentation, but also in terms of examining and ascertaining the principal determinants of the crime of the World War I Armenian Genocide. Calling for a review and reevaluation, four such determinants emerge. They are not only germane to a thorough understanding of the Armenian case of genocide, but may also have wider significance for the study of other cases of genocide, including that of the World War II Jewish case. These determinants involve:

(1) Premeditation and special intent (*dolus specialis*);
(2) The Special Organization (the main instrument for the on-the-spot implementation of the crime);
(3) Responsible secretaries and delegates (the local CUP organizers and supervisors of the implementation phase and mechanics);
(4) The central authorities, i.e., the CUP Central Committee (the brain trust for decision-making and authorization).

Before proceeding to explore this matter, however, it is necessary to identify and describe the corpus of evidentiary material upon which the courts-martial predicated the prosecution and on the basis of which they rendered their verdicts.

The Legal Evidence: The Crux of Prosecution and Verdict Rendition

Reexamining the Documentary Evidence

As stated above, a substantial part of the evidence was stolen—whisked away at the end of the war by some of the major organizers of the crimes. However, given the vast scope, organizational problems, and manifold categories of the crimes in question, it would be a gargantuan task to manage to completely, or even near completely, remove or destroy all traces of such evidence. Indeed, almost inevitably a handful of pieces of evidence randomly end up surviving. As such, they often prove sufficient to successfully prosecute a case. Moreover, as happened in the present case, when anticipating military defeat and subsequent probable criminal prosecution, some potential defendants, in sheer pursuit of self-protection, often try to be of help by saving and later producing for the prosecution some critically incriminating documents. The massive pretrial investigations of the Mazhar Inquiry Commission yielded a significant volume of assorted documents and proofs in this respect. They were supplemented by those secured by the military tribunal's own inquiry commissions.

Perhaps the greatest advantage accruing to the courts-martial issued from the fact that the Ottoman-Turkish criminal justice system, modeled after its French counterpart, was inquisitorial. Defense lawyers were barred from access to their defendants while the latter were in custody, and thus were barred from access to pretrial styled evidence: this is in sheer contrast to the Anglo-Saxon practice of "discovery," which allows defense lawyers full pretrial access to the evidence in the possession of the court. As a result, the tribunal was in a position to spring surprise after surprise by producing an avalanche of documents, not before but during the trial, thereby rendering defendants and counsel alike confounded, often catching them unawares. Some of these pieces of evidence were secured through search and seizure operations.

Superseding all these aspects of assembling evidence was a condition that is almost always invaluable in any effort to render such evidence both incontestable and irrefutable. As repeatedly disclosed during the Yozgat trial series, at the 9th (22 February 1919), the 12th (6 March 1919), and the 16th (29 March 1919) sittings, each and every official document that was introduced as prima facie evidence was authenticated beforehand by competent officials from either the Justice or the Interior Ministry, who then appended to the document in question the notation "It conforms to the original" (*Aslına muafıkdır,* or, *mutabıkdır*). This fact alone should impart to the proceedings—and particularly to the verdicts of the courts-martial—uncommon legitimacy.

It is worth noting once more that attached to the Key Indictment were more than forty such documents, including twelve cipher telegrams, four regular telegrams, and ten signed statements that were secured following the pretrial administration of oral and written interrogatories; secured were also "several" documents dealing with the Special Organization. In the third section of Chapter 3 the itemization of these documents is described. Many other cipher telegrams were introduced in the course of some three dozen subsequent major court-martial sittings. In the course of the fifth sitting alone, targeting CUP's Central Committee members, some sixteen cipher telegrams and regular telegrams were introduced by the prosecution.

The Incidence of the "Stealing" and Destroying of CUP and War-Related Documents

Near the end of World War I a large body of secret CUP documents were whisked away from the main CUP headquarters by three men who were deeply involved in the organization of the genocide. They were Drs. Bahaeddin Şakir, Mehmet Nazım, and National Security Chief Erzurumlu Hüseyin Aziz (*T.V.* 3543 p. 27, right column). CUP's Central Committee boss Midhat Şükrü, during his interrogation, confirmed this theft by Dr. Nazım, as did Yusuf Riza, who succeeded Şükrü at the witness chair (*T.V.* 3553 (3554): 74, left column–75, right column, 89, left column). Likewise, wartime Minister of Post and Telegraph Haşim declared during his testimony that upon the orders issued by the General Headquarters, he had "absolutely" (*behemehal*) completely burned all cipher telegrams (*T.V.* 3573, p. 146, right column).

The Procedures of Verifying and Authenticating Official Documents

As stated above, it was very important for the tribunal, and the successive postwar Turkish governments supporting it, to have the defendants, mainly top-ranking party leaders and high-ranking military officers, personally inspect the ciphers bearing their own signatures and confirm their authenticity.

Without the knowledge of the defendants and their lawyers, the court-martial had succeeded in locating and securing these crucial documents. Though fully convinced that they could get away with their earlier intentional misstatements, three key defendants nevertheless felt constrained to reverse themselves in their subsequent testimonies. Given the preponderance of standard denials in such cases, a brief description of these cases is warranted.

At issue was the performance of massacre duties by hard-core criminals especially released from the prisons for this purpose. These detachments of ex-convicts were integrated in a particular branch of the Special Organization (Teşkilât-ı Mahsusa) that differed from the original main body. That body's missions included intelligence, sabotage, and spying, activities that were mostly foreign-bound or beyond the territorial boundaries of Turkey. In fact the chief judge had raised this question at the fourth sitting of the main trial when interrogating Central Committee member and S.O. leader Atıf. In doing so he informed the latter of the court's knowledge that whereas one S.O. branch was attached to the War Office, the other one was identified with CUP secret missions that were entirely criminal (*T.V.* 3549, p. 58, right column, p. 58 left column).

When Colonel Cevat, Istanbul's wartime military commandant (Merkez Kumandan) in charge of S.O. logistics and supplies, appeared on the witness stand, the chief judge reminded him that in his previous testimony he had denied any link between CUP and the S.O. Notwithstanding, Cevat repeatedly and vehemently denied again the existence of any such link (hayır hiç bir rabıta). The chief judge then ordered the court clerk to read into the record a cipher telegram signed by the S.O. chieftain and CUP Central Committee member Dr. B. Şakir; it was addressed to the party boss, Interior Minister Mehmet Talaat. When the judge then restated the question about the link, thereupon the nonplussed colonel promptly reversed himself and confirmed the link (Anlaşılır, Paşa hazretleri) (*T.V.* 3553 (3554), m. 70, left column and p. 71, right column).

A similar, almost identical, pattern of reversal of testimony occurred with Central Committee members Atıf and Riza, whose testimony followed that of Cevat. After likewise repeatedly denying any such link, and upon the chief judge's emphatic confirmation of that link through the reading into the record of additional ciphers, Atıf ended up pleading poor memory (hafızam o kadar kuvvetli değil, cevap verememem) and then proceeded to relent. He finally allowed that even though there was no link, still the S.O. organization availed itself of the services of CUP's Central Committee and provincial responsible secretaries to enlist "volunteers" for the needs of the S.O. (*T.V.* 3553, p. 86, right column–p. 86, left column).

Colonel Riza went through the same ritual of repeatedly and emphatically denying any link between the CUP's Central Committee and the S.O. (hiç bir rabıtası yoktur). Ciphers belying these denials were then again read into the record by the court clerk. Relenting, Riza finally allowed that some cooperation (müracaat ... havale) did exist. At that point the chief judge declared for the record: "It follows from your testimony [ifadenizden anlaşılıyor] that S.O. detachments were implicated in the operations of deportation and massacres [tehcir ve taktil]." Thereupon, Riza began to admit the creation of a "second" type of S.O. that was involved in the matter of Armenian deportations but insisted that it need not be confused with the other S.O. (*T.V.* 3553, p. 88, right column–p. 89, left column). When discussing Dr. Nazım's leading role, it is most significant that Cevat identified Nazım's involvement with the "volunteers" (*gönüllü*) branch of the S.O. as distinct and separate matter. He insisted that this mission of Nazım was not to be confounded with that of those who were dispatched to the Caucasus for sabotage operations, thereby differentiating the S.O.'s external and internal missions; he repeatedly described the latter as "extra-military" (*askerlik haricinde*) operations. (*T.V.* 3543, p. 26, left column, p. 27, right column, p. 28, right column).

The lengths to which these defendants were prepared to go in order to deny, disavow, or equivocate is revealed in the following exchange between the chief judge and defendant Colonel Cevat. This exchange concerned the original text of a cipher telegram sent to the S.O. in which Cevat, through a postscript, was advising the recipient to "save" it until such time when as required it could be returned to the sender.

> Chief: Is this your handwriting?
> Cevat: Let me see. It looks like the original.
> Chief: Is it not your own transmission [*havale*]?
> Cevat: The writing looks like mine, your Highness [*Paşa hazretleri*].
> Chief: Let him look at it again.
> Cevat: The writing of the original text is mine but not the cipher itself.
> Chief: I am referring to the original text of transmission.
> Cevat: I think it is my handwriting.
> Chief: Can't you recognize your own handwriting?
> Cevat: I think it is my handwriting, Sir.
> Chief: Show it to him again.
> Cevat: This is my handwriting but the converted telegraph script is not mine.
> Chief: The court has taken due note of this fact of removing and concealing documents.
> (*T.V.* 3554, p. 68, left column, p. 69, right column).

The more dramatic case of a key witness reversing himself and reframing his testimony in court was that of Colonel Şehabettin. He had repeatedly denied knowledge of cipher telegrams he had personally signed and dispatched to Colonel Recayi, his superior in Ankara, informing him of the number of Armenians deported from his district and killed shortly thereafter. First he was confronted with the evidence of massacres that were reported in two ciphers dated 22 July 1915 and 23 July 1915; both of these ciphers bore his signature. Recayi then was confronted with a new set of five cipher telegrams, all bearing his signature, and all belying his disclaimer of knowledge of any massacres against deportee Armenians in his district, Kayseri. The evidence was direct and compelling. Apprehensive about the consequences of his mendacity, Recayi ended up suffering a fainting spell (20 February 1919, 8th sitting) and was briefly excused. When he returned to the witness stand, he was more forthright and factual, flat out disputing the assertion of the two key defendants that the Armenians had rebelled.

Identifying and Locating Specific Items of Evidence, Proofs, and Documents

The various categories of evidentiary material have already been spelled out (in the third section of Chapter 3). What follows is a list of a variety of designations under which are subsumed many of the items of evidence, proofs and documents.

a. *T.V.* 3547, 42 r: "secret proofs" (*delaili mukanna*);
b. *T.V.* 3571, 130 r. "Pre-war Grand Vizier Izzet's statement" (*ifade*) "as proof" (*delail*); "absolute proof" (*delili kati*) relative to "CUP's manifold abuses";
c. *T.V.* 3586, 164 r: "pretrial interrogations" (*tahkikatı istintakiye*) "yielding manifest confessions" (vâzıhan ... ikrar ve itirafları), and "investigative papers" (*evrakı tahkikiye*) "comprise the requisite proofs" (*delail*);
d. *T.V.* 3617 ("official telegraphic communications" (*muhaberât-ı resmiye-i telegrafiye*), and 2 r and l: "the contents of investigative papers" (*evrâk-ı mevcude ve münderecatı*), "hand-written documents" (*hattı destiyle muharrer vesika*); "the proofs concerned" (*delâ'il-i mebsuta*); "above cited solid proofs" (*berâhin-i katı'a-yı mezküre*);
e. *T.V.* 3771, p. 2, right column: "the document at hand" (*evrak-ı mevcude*);
f. *T.V.* 3772, p. 4, left column: "the succinct proofs attest to" (*delalet eden karâ'in-i kâtı-a*) and "overt proofs" (*berâhin-i vâzıhadan*);
g. *T.V.* 3772, p. 3, left column: "after having thoroughly and carefully examined the charges, the defense arguments, and the transcripts of testimonies, and having taken into account in their totality the trial papers, and thus having heard both sides ..." (iddia taleb ve müdafaat ve ifadatı sencideyi mizan tetkik ve bilcümle evrakı dava ve zavabatı mahkeme serapa mütalaa ve keyfiyeti bil etraf tamik olunduktan sonar ...).

Just as it would happen at Nuremberg, wartime secret and top secret official documents constituted the principal arsenal of the prosecution. Compared to this central role, witness testimonies were merely incidental. Such testimony as essential supportive evidence was, however, most helpful in adjudicating several individual cases. The descriptions below provide a glimpse into the types of such testimony with respect to the Yozgat, Trabzon, and Harput courts-martial. They also demonstrate, however, the critical fact that the preponderance of the Turkish witnesses belonged to all stations and walks of life. Of the twelve witnesses in the Yozgat trial series, for example, five were Turks, including a parliamentarian, one lieutenant-governor, three colonels, and one customs inspector. In the thirty-eight witnesses of the Trabzon trials, twenty-nine were likewise Turks, including one ex–governor-general, one appellate court judge, one judicial inspector, one police chief, one customs inspector, three MDs, three colonels, one major, two captains, and two lieutenants. In addition, there were introduced as evidence two lengthy depositions from two army commanders. Moreover, some dozen other Turkish witnesses testified in the Harput trial series.

A final comment on the respective importance of law in general and, by implication, criminal law in particular may be in order. The legal examination of a crime does not always require that it be entwined with an examination of its legal outcome, as criminal prosecution is not always conducive to concrete and tangible retributive justice. Indeed, even when impunity is the inevitable outcome of such failure of criminal justice, the principle of the rule of law yet remains intact as it retains its timeless authority.[1] As Sir Frederick Pollock, the eminent British expert on international law, asserted in connection with World War I atrocities, "Law does not cease to exist because it is broken or even because for a time it may be broken on a large scale."[2]

Premeditation and Special Intent (*dolus specialis*)

The issue of premeditation—but particularly that of special intent relative to a centrally organized exterminatory mass murder—has critical importance for identifying such a mass murder as genocide. All studies purporting to deal with any aspect of genocide will thus have to confront this condition. It should be noted at the outset that the definition of premeditation eludes a sharp and concise formula for the simple reason that a prior resolve to commit a criminal act does not need to preexist for any specific period of time before it is carried out. Such a resolve may just be a thought that might arise and exist for any length of time without any kind of planning or preparation. Premeditation becomes relevant and significant, however, when it becomes an integral component of a specific intent to commit genocide through stages of planning. Inasmuch as this type of intent is rarely revealed or conceded by a perpetrator, it will have to be derived or inferred from a set of circumstances surrounding the crime. Foremost to consider in this respect are such factors as the scale and intensity of the mass murder, the selective and systematic targeting of the victim population, the commission of associated or subsidiary crimes directed against the same victim population, and the general context of the murderous acts.

In the Armenian case, the context of war emerges as a decisive factor. In fact it represents a classic case of the kinds of war-related crimes that would become a focal point in the formulation of the Nuremberg principles. The central idea here was that Nazi aggression and the attendant precipitation of World War II were acts that were intimately connected with the ensuing Nazi war crimes, including genocide's variant, "crimes against humanity." The parallels with the Armenian Genocide are striking. As emphasized throughout this study, the adoption in international criminal law of the new legal precept of "crimes against humanity" can be traced to the fact of the initiation of that genocide by Ottoman-Turkish authorities. When responding to it and issuing a threat on 24 May 1915 to punish, after the war, those responsible for the crimes, the Allies—Great Britain, France, and Russia—for the first time publicly and formally introduced that legal term. It subsequently was adopted by the framers of the Nuremberg Charter and was incorporated as Article 6 c in the text of the Nuremberg Indictment.[3]

Equally if not more significant is the parallel between Ottoman Turkey's preemptive initiation of war and the aggression of the Nazis, who unleashed World War II by preemptively attacking Poland in September 1939. This parallel becomes accentuated in conjunction with Hitler's reported effort to persuade his hesitant generals that there were no risks in his anti-Polish and, by extension, anti-Jewish exterminatory scheme by declaring: "After all, who remembers the annihilation of the Armenians."[4]

The matter of preemptive intervention in the war by Ottoman Turkey, whose naval forces, assisted by German naval forces, attacked Russian warships and coastal installations on the Black Sea on 29 October 1914 (thus violating Turkey's openly proclaimed neutrality), is a matter of historical record.[5] In full recognition of this fact, the military tribunal in its Key Indictment asserted that the central authorities, by this act of aggression, were pursuing "their secret designs," for which purpose they resorted to "intrigues and tricks." Indeed, the CUP leadership pursued its goals in a "secret fashion." When doing this, "they were taking advantage of the fact that Europe was preoccupied with war" (*T.V.* 3540, p. 5, right column, p. 5, left column). Moreover, the Key Indictment further asserts that "long before the outbreak of the war," they intentionally were bracing themselves for war and that the CUP deliberately pursued this goal "as attested to by Central Committee Secretary-General Midhat Şükrü's

August 17, 1914 cipher, sent to Talaat through the medium of Erzurum vali Tahsin." This fact is evidenced in the text of a memo of the Interior Ministry (*T.V.* 3540, p. 6, right column). The preemptive Turkish war initiative is most explicitly evident in the testimony of Central Committee member Yusuf Riza, who on several occasions openly "confessed" (*itiraf*) to the tribunal that "without waiting for a declaration of war" (ilânı harp beklemeksizin) he "attacked" (*saldırı*) Russia in the Caucasus "with a contingent of 4–5 officers and 600 soldiers" (*T.V.* 3557, p. 106, right column and *T.V.* 3604, p. 219, right column). In his other testimony in the Trabzon trial series, at the eleventh sitting on 4 April 1919, he testified that when war broke out he was already "in a small Russian town."

The "secret designs" propelling Turkey's unilateral intervention into the war can be more clearly understood when perceived as an allusion to, among other things, a plan for solving once and for all the lingering "Armenian Question." Dr. Nazım, one of the key organizers of the Armenian Genocide, provided a not-so-subtle hint. He is quoted in the Key Indictment as saying that the current wartime operations against the Armenians were the result of the CUP's "careful and profound deliberations" (*uriz ve amik düşünülerek*) (*T.V.* 3540, p. 8, left column). These operations involved, however, "the massacre and extermination of the Armenians resulting from the CUP's respective decision-making" (Ermenilerin katl ve imhası … Ittihad ve Terakki Merkezi Umumisinin neticei mukarreratı olup …) (*T.V.* 3540, p. 8 right and left columns).

The statements of two top CUP leaders further corroborate the plausibility of this war-related CUP decision—namely, to solve the Armenian Question by simply eliminating the Armenians themselves. Cemal Paşa—minister of the navy, commander-in-chief of the Fourth Army, and "the Viceroy" of Syria, Lebanon, and Palestine—candidly admitted in his memoirs that deliverance from what he called "the shackles" of the Armenian February 1914 Reform Accord, signed some six months prior to the outbreak of the war, and "imposed upon us," was one of the factors that pushed Turkey into the war. As he argued further, "our sole objective [*bizim yegâne gayemiz*] was to free ourselves from such shackles.… We wanted to tear up that Agreement."[6]

Remarkably, these expressions are of uncommon relevance to the quest for a basic common denominator among the array of many other declarations trying to explain the wartime scheme of liquidating the Armenian population. They are indeed remarkable because, as noted above, they basically coincide with those of Talaat, the chief architect of that scheme. After decades of suppressing this vital piece of evidence, a contemporary Turkish chronicler has ventured to publish, albeit in some modified form, the text of the official statement in which Interior Minister Talaat, the CUP party boss, is seen outlining his rationale for ordering the massive Armenian deportations. From this text we learn that the principal reason for this draconian measure had very little to do with any wartime misbehavior on the part of any group of Armenians, but instead had much to do with the launching of the prewar Armenian Reform movement. Wartime acts of disloyalty on the part of any group of Armenians, including the April 1915 Van uprising, a strictly local event, were certainly a consideration, but compared to the centrality of the perils that the CUP leadership attached to the projected Armenian reforms, they were rather of incidental significance.

Indeed, at the very outset, Talaat, in several paragraphs of his memorandum of 13 (26) May 1915, delves into the aggravating problems the 8 (21) February 1914 Armenian Reform Accord,[7] co-promulgated by the six European powers, was going to entail for Turkey; he especially argued that this act threatened the territorial integrity of the Ottoman Empire through partition and dismemberment (*inkısam ve tecziye*). With anger, Talaat altogether denounced these efforts at reform, which were secured through the intervention of European powers, as divisive and separatist. He expressed his choice of a remedy as follows: "It is necessary to eliminate in a fundamental way and completely wipe out this [source] of trouble" (bu gailenin esaslı bir suretde hal ve faslı ile külliyen izalesi). The hint here for the need of a radical solution to avert the supposed danger of Turkey's dismemberment and partition is unmistakable. Exactly two months later, however, a more confident Talaat, going one step further, declared that the goal of the Armenian deportations was "the final solution of the Armenian Question" (Ermeni meselesini'nîn suret-ı katiyede halli).[8]

Talaat's intentions for the radical solution of the Armenian question are recorded in the 3 August 1915 entry of the diary of Henry Morgenthau, the wartime US ambassador to Turkey. In it Morgenthau quotes Talaat as saying that "The CUP has carefully considered the matter in all its details and that the policy which was being pursued was that which they had officially adopted … the result of prolonged and careful deliberation."[9] The complete identity of the wording of the phrase with that used by Dr. Nazım, cited above, is most significant.

In his affidavit to the Ottoman Special Military Tribunal, another military leader, General Mehmet Vehip, the wartime commander-in-chief of the Third Army, described his personal observations about the massacre—the sites of which he had inspected in the spring of 1916. He referred to the "mass murder and extermination of the Armenians" (Ermenilerin katl ve imhası), which he characterized as "a product of the decision-making of CUP's Central Committee" (Ittihad ve Terakki Merkezi Umumisinin neticeyi mukarreratı). However, the more critical part of his testimony concerned his judgment that this undertaking was the result of "a studied program based upon a definite intention," namely, the wholesale destruction of the targeted victim population (mukarrer bir program ve mutlak bir kasd tahtında).[10]

Perhaps most important, the critical issue of premeditation was noticeably cast in relief in each of the verdicts of the Yozgat, Trabzon, and Erzincan trial series. Although the principle of "intent" (*kasden*) was referred to in the text of the verdicts, in the sentencing part of each of the verdicts, however, Article 170 of the Ottoman Penal Code was invoked. There, the term *ta'ammüden* was used, which means "by prior deliberation."

The Special Organization

One of the major findings of the Turkish court-martial pertained to the decisive role of the Special Organization in the implementation phase of the Armenian Genocide. Deployed to the major areas of the operations, the organization's killer squads, led by a whole gamut of military officers, many of them reservists, carried out their assigned deadly missions. Hard-core criminals, only recently released for this particular task from the various prisons of the Ottoman Empire, comprised the bulk of these executioners. According to Colonel Cevat, the military commandant in the Ottoman capital in charge of the logistical aspects of the Special Organization, they were sometimes described as "volunteers" (*gönüllü*), and other times as "brigands" (*çete*) (*T.V.* 3543, p. 66, right column). The text of the Key Indictment is suffused with references to the S.O., and with related supportive documentary data (*T.V.* 3540, pp. 3–8). Investigating this problem, a Turkish author stated that the Key Indictment "contains material not available anywhere else."[11] This material, dealing especially with the enlistment and enrollment of convicts in the ranks of the Special Organization, contains numerous details directly relevant to this discussion.[12]

First, the operation of enlisting convicts (*mahkümin*) would, during as well as after the war, create problems in the politically emasculated Ottoman parliament. One problem, for example, was that the convicts had been at work for almost a year and had all but completed that work when the issue belatedly came before the Senate for consideration. The debate that ensued in that body on 12 December 1916 sheds light on the extent to which the central authorities took liberties with existing laws in order to push through their schemes. Senator Ahmet Riza, the lone voice of daring dissent, objected to the bill that provided for such enlistment, on the grounds that the Constitution forbade it, that, should the released prisoners dishonor it, the presence of such felons in the army would have a corrosive effect on the morale of the other recruits and possibly even corrupt them, and that nowhere else were such convicts allowed in the military.

It is quite revealing, however, that when responding to these concerns, Colonel Behiç (Erkin), director of Department I of the Ottoman General Headquarters and at the same time deputy director of the Department of the Army in the Ministry of War, felt compelled to disclose the real purpose of the proposed bill. He informed the Senators that these convicts "will not be processed as soldiers destined for combat duty" (darülharplere doğrudan doğruya asker olarak sevkedilmiyorlar). Rather, he went on to reveal, "they will render special services through the ranks of the Special Organization." After Ahmet Riza had snapped back, by way of retort, "we are fully aware of the nature of that Special Organization," Ministry of Justice Undersecretary Yusuf Kemal followed Colonel Behiç at the podium to discuss, he said, the principle of legality and administration of justice.

The gist of his argument was that these convicts were not going to serve simply as plain soldiers, but rather as patriots to perform special missions through the Special Organization. Accordingly, "Can we not afford to want to forgive them, especially in consideration of the fact that these are not the kind of bandits [şaki] who from their very conception, i.e., in the wombs of their mothers, are already bandits [şaki anasının karnında şakidir] ... Senator Riza's argument has no merit ... Besides, the proposed law had long been put into effect and its validity had expired." The presiding senator, retired General Çürüksulu Mahmut Paşa, interjected this comment: "This draft law was approved by the Senate's Military Affairs Committee for the simple reason that the government, i.e., the CUP people, had already been executing it for some time without legislative approval." Kemal then requested a vote "on grounds of urgency" (*müstaceliyet*), and it was promptly approved, thereby ending one of the most bizarre episodes associated with the legal-criminal circumstances of the Armenian Genocide.[13] The matter of releasing convicts from the prisons was further documented, however, during the second sitting of the court-martial when the prosecution introduced a cipher telegram to that effect that had been signed by Colonel Behiç.[14]

After the war, when the Lower Chamber of the Ottoman Parliament took up the issue of the Special Organization's convicts having committed widespread wartime massacres, wartime Justice Minister Ibrahim explained the preemptory, almost coercive, nature of the release of the convicts from the empire's prisons. The question posed to him by the chairman of the Fifth Department of Investigation of the Chamber of Deputies involved the crimes perpetrated by the *çetes*, or brigands, particularly inside Turkey (*dahili memlekette*). When answering that question, Ibrahim made reference to the convicts released from the prisons, thus directly identifying them with the brigands. His answer further revealed that War Minister Enver was wont to defy normal channels for transacting official business, readily bypassing the Grand Vizier (the head of the cabinet), to whom both he and the justice minister were bound to report first when submitting any request. In so many words, Enver simply ordered another cabinet minister, in this case the justice minister, to comply with his request—despite the latter's relenting on grounds that convicts could be released only through the issuance of an imperial rescript. Minister Ibrahim was thus constrained, if not compelled, to order the release from the empire's prisons of "a considerable number of convicts" (mühim bir yeküna balig olan).[15]

The evidence is ample and compelling. The central mission of the domestic branch of the S.O. was to liquidate, through wholesale massacres and related atrocities, the bulk of the Armenian population of Ottoman Turkey. In defining its primary objective of court-martial, the postwar Ottoman Special Military Tribunal, during its second sitting, identified the principal issues to be dealt with through prosecution. Accordingly, it declared the following: the Special Organization was under the direct control of CUP's Central Committee; the S.O. consisted of aggregates of convicts and tramps whose task it was to attack the Armenian deportee convoys and kill and destroy the deportees; and the defendants would be held "personally responsible" on account of the fact that the crimes with which they were being charged were ordinary crimes (*ceraimi adideyi âdiye*) that they committed not as governmental officials but rather as executives of the CUP.

This bill of charges was read into the record in the presence of several party chieftains and wartime cabinet ministers, including Grand Vizier Sait Halim. (*T.V.* 3543, p. 16, right and left columns). Turkish author Kocahanoğlu, who is one of the very few contemporary chroniclers exploring the career of the court-martial in his latest book, affirmed that the court-martial indeed succeeded in "establishing a link between the CUP and the S.O." [16]

These links materialized and were fostered at several levels and in different directions. The court-martial, during its fifth sitting of the Cabinet and Central Committee trial series, introduced some of them (*T.V.* 3554, p. 68, right column–p. 74, left column, p. 86, right column, and p. 87, left column). As the nerve center of the network of the multiple ties to the S.O., the Central Committee (CC) of the CUP, in particular its Secretary-General Midhat Şükrü, played an essential role, especially with respect to such matters as organization, transmission of communications, and command-and-control functions. Foremost in this respect were the interactions between the CC and the two physicians Şakir and Nazım. In fact these two dominant members of the CC emerge as the key executives of the Special Organization. The former young CUP adherent Falih Rıfkı Atay, who went on to become a prominent figure in the emergence of the post-CUP Kemalist movement, provides a vivid example. In his memoirs he describes how he was eager to join the S.O. as a reserve officer at the start of the war. As he relates, upon hearing from Dr. Nazım (who was then recruiting young military officers for duties in the S.O. at Harbiye, the War Staff College) that the mission in question involved killing operations, he recoiled in disgust. He summed up his reaction saying that he would have no part in "an army of volunteer murderers" (*gönüllü katiller ordusu*).[17]

Nazım's role of recruiting this type of "volunteer" is confirmed by none other than the man in charge of taking care of the logistical aspects of those recruitment operations. He testified at the court-martial that Nazım was involved in recruiting "volunteers" whose missions were "extra-military" (*askerlik haricinde*) (*T.V.* 3543: 27 r, Colonel Cevat's testimony). In fact we learn from the same source, Cevat, that the S.O., intended for such murderous missions, was in the first place created by Dr. Nazım, along with his cohort, Dr. Şakir, and National Security Chief Erzurumlu Hüseyin Aziz. (*T.V.* 3543, p. 31, right column).

While Dr. Nazım operated primarily in Istanbul, the Ottoman capital, Dr. Şakir, his partner in the entire undertaking, was handling the on-the-spot details—even though at the very inception he had played a major role in securing the requisite decision-making from the CUP's Central Committee in Istanbul. A Turkish author, seemingly privy to some of the inner secrets of that body, explicitly confirms this central fact, at the same time revealing the protracted process of genocide-related decision-making.[18] The court-martial on numerous occasions cites and underscores the active involvement of Şakir in the very vortex of killing operations. The massacre of the convoy of Erzurum's wealthy Armenians by the S.O. brigands deployed at Dersim by Şakir himself is just one such example (*T.V.* 3771, p. 2, right column, culled "from the documents assembled in Erzurum vali Münir's file"). In the fifth sitting of the court-martial, it is further confirmed that Dr. Şakir's close cooperation with Interior Minister Talaat, the CUP boss, was afforded through the mediation of the office of the CUP's Central Committee in the person of Midhat Şükrü, its powerful secretary-general, (*T.V.* 3554, p. 71, right column, p. 73, left column, and p. 74, right column).

It is clear that the Central Committee of the CUP, in the person of Secretary-General Midhat Şükrü, was not only a principal instance of decision-making but also additionally served as a principal facilitator by discharging the function of a central transmission belt that relayed orders and instructions.[19] The cooperation of two institutions, the military and especially the Interior Ministry, stands out in this respect. A chronicler of the S.O. clearly states that Interior Minister Talaat personally prepared the operational blueprints for the S.O.[20] Another specialist on the S.O. states: "The Special Organization was created by the Central Committee, for which end Enver and Talaat, who in other matters were pitted against each other in a bitter struggle, joined hands. The Ittihadist Commanders of the Organization's brigands were chosen by Talaat and the Central Committee."[21] Talaat's Interior Ministry was also in charge of the provincial governors-general, some of whom were enrolled in the S.O. An expert in the study of that organization describes, in graphic detail, the induction ceremony of one of those *vali*s who was tried, convicted, and sentenced to death in absentia for his key role in the extermination of his province's (Trabzon) Armenian population.[22] It was Talaat who arranged for the *vali*s of Trabzon and Erzurum to be enlisted in the S.O. and actively support its missions (*T.V.* 3543, p. 32, right column, testimony of S.O. chieftain Atıf).

The involvement of the military in the creation, organization and employment of the S.O. units, in close cooperation with the Central Committee of the CUP, is described above. At issue are War Minister Enver's order to release convicts from the prisons for S.O. missions and Colonel Behiç's role in the organization and deployment of such missions, and most particularly his role in securing the ex post facto enactment of a law meant to formally legitimize that undertaking.

There remains, however, the case of Colonel Şevket Seyfi (Düzgören), who was in charge of Department II both at the Ottoman General Headquarters and at the Ministry of War. A Turkish newspaper declared during the armistice that it was Seyfi who, as director of the Political Department at the Ottoman General Headquarters, mapped the strategy of the massacres against the Armenians, mobilizing, in close cooperation with Dr. B. Şakir and under the auspices of the Ittihad party's Central Committee, the *çetes* of the Special Organization.[23] Even more significant, the German military plenipotentiary at the German embassy at Constantinople, Colonel (later Major General) Otto von Lossow, confirmed this fact. In a dispatch to the German General Headquarters dated 16 November 1916, Lossow indicated that Seyfi and his Department II at Ottoman General Headquarters were in charge of implementing "the Armenian deportations" (*Armenierverschickungen*). "He handles this matter and knows exactly about it" (der diese Sachen bearbeitet und genau orientiert ist).[24] Moreover, Colonel Fuat Balkan, one of the top leaders of the Special Organization operating in the Balkans, in his memoirs published in *Yakın Tarihimiz*, stated that Seyfi directed the overall operations of the Special Organization from his office at the General Headquarters.[25] While discussing the external missions of the other branch of the S.O., an American author implicitly conceded the existence of the other branch as one comprising an unruly "group of brigands" whom he decried as "a secret rather disreputable group."[26]

In critical assessments of the performance of the S.O., three prominent Turkish authors, two historians, and a political scientist provide helpful analyses. In the third volume of his three-volume study of Turkish political parties, Tunaya offers some relevant analytical comments. He declares that the CUP Central Committee revolved around "a nucleus" (*çekirdek*). Its composition was such, however, that the three principal architects of the Armenian Genocide—Talaat, Şakir, and Nazım—were prominently configured in it; the other two members of CUP's Central Committee, i.e., Midhat Şükrü and Ziya Gökalp, likewise figured in it as adjunct cohorts.[27] Tunaya's comment also provides a principle by which to pinpoint the military's complicity in the crime. He states that the army became politicized, actually "Ittihaticized," while the CUP men became militarized.[28] As to his views on the S.O. and its operative cadres, he portrays them conjointly in the equation S.O. = CUP,[29] while referring to "volunteers," "*çetes*," and "convicts" as the S.O.'s constitutive elements suffused with the mentality of brigands (*eşkiya*);[30] *çete*s are described as being identical to convicts but excluding "rapists" and "immoral men."[31] The selection of the convicts was carried out by committees comprising representatives of the Interior, Justice, and War Ministries, plus a Health Services official.[32] Tunaya identifies two deputies of the parliament as belonging to the S.O.[33] Finally, at one point in his discussion, while disputing the genocidal complicity of the main contingent of the S.O., described above, and when referring to the court-martial prosecution of the other branch of the S.O., he found it suitable to use the new Turkish term for genocide, *soykırım*.[34]

The second author, an American-trained sociologist-publicist (PhD, Columbia University), is perhaps the most unequivocal exponent of the view that the wartime treatment of the Armenians amounted to an attempt at wholesale extermination. What is most relevant here, however, is that this view is predicated on his evaluation of the decisive role of the S.O. in this respect. Ahmet Emin Yalman concludes: "The outfit called Special Organization, consisting of çetes, directly pursued the goal of extermination" (doğrudan doğruya bir imha hedefinin arkasından kosmuşlardır). Yalman then adduces the rationale of Dr. Şakir, identifying him as "a member of the CC and a leader of S.O., but also a passionately patriotic man." That rationale is summed up as follows:

> It is a fact that the Armenians have been living near the Russian borders in a dense and concentrated way. It is a matter of urgency, from the point of view of national salvation, to do whatever is possible, to eliminate this threat. Conceivably, the charting of such a course of action may run counter to the spirit of national and humanistic precepts. Yet, I am prepared to pay with my life the price for this sin. Whether I will succeed or not, still I am certain I will be shamed. I am aware of this, but I also know that there will emerge in the distant future those who will appreciate the fact that I have sacrificed myself in service for my country.[35]

Contemporary with the era of Armenian massacres, the account of Ahmet Refik (Altınay), a onetime professor of history at Istanbul University and by chance Mustafa Kemal (Atatürk's) history teacher at the War Staff College (Harbiye) in Istanbul, acquires a significance exceeding that of all others discussed above. This importance is further accented by the fact that immediately before as well as during the war, Ahmet Refik occupied important posts affording him rare opportunities for firsthand observation and judgment. Having attended two military schools and subsequently graduating from the War Staff College with the rank of Captain of the Navy, Ahmet Refik served as an inspector of military censorship during the 1912 Balkan war. During World War I, he was called into military service again as a captain and was assigned to the Ottoman General Headquarters as general inspector of censorship (Sansür Umumi Müfettişi). Coincidental with the Armenian deportations and massacres, in 1915 he was appointed to the post of president of Eskişehir's Commission on Deportations (Eskişehir Sevk Komisyonu Reisi), Eskişehir being a major transit point for the deportation of Western Turkey's Armenian populations. Toward the end of the war, he was part of a commission tasked to investigate, mostly in Erzincan and Erzurum, the incidental atrocities committed by Armenians during the two-month period of January–February 1918 as reprisals against the preceding mass murder of their compatriots. Many of these avengers, in their march to the interior of Turkey from the Russian border areas, had been eyewitnesses to the gruesome horrors of the mass murder. In brief, Prof. Ahmet Refik had personally seen, heard, and digested enough to write his own account.

He stated that the Armenian Van Uprising (20 April–17 May 1915) "created an important opportunity for CUP to pursue their national aims." What were these aims and how were they pursued? After stating that "a righteous and just government would have proceeded to punish only those who helped materialize such an uprising," Refik went on to write: "Yet, CUP was intent on eradicating the Armenians and thereby eliminating the [vexing] Eastern Question." As to the means employed, here was his studied verdict: "At the start of the war, many çetes were dispatched to Anatolia from Istanbul. These consisted of thieves and murderers who were released form the prisons. After training at the War Ministry's open square for one week, they would then be dispatched, through the medium of the Special Organization, to the border areas of the Caucasus. In the matter of atrocities against the Armenians, the greatest crimes were perpetrated by theses çetes" (Ermeni mezaliminde en büyük cinayetleri bu çeteler ika ettiler).[36] The author further reveals that Deputy Sudi (mentioned in note 33), was actively involved in *çete* activities in Artvin and Ardahan in November and December 1914, when thousands of Armenians were massacred months before the initiation of the actual genocide. Furthermore, in the summer of 1918 he personally verified on the spot that these were the same brigand groups who in the summer of 1915, having been transferred from the Caucasus to Bozanti in the Adana region, proved the most fear-inspiring massacrers.[37] Concluding, Prof. Refik wrote: "This entire undertaking was a crime against humanity. No government, at no time, has ever acted with such perfidy and cruelty."[38]

The thrust of the preceding discussion demonstrates the existence of twin objectives in the scheme of S.O. operations, external and internal, with the external eventually dissolving itself in the internal. Beyond that, however, it demonstrates even more amply the overarching thrust of one objective in particular, so that one is inclined to think the other objective was not a separate and distinct one, but rather was subsumed by the other. What is being suggested here is that the wholesale liquidation of the Armenians was not an end in itself but was subsidiary to a larger objective, which may best be described as a drive bent on embracing pan-Islamism and/or pan-Turkism. This is exactly what one of the best chroniclers of the wartime operations of the S.O. has maintained. According to him, "The S.O.'s espionage and brigandage operations were but a cover for Talaat's and Enver's secret objectives and thoughts relative to the CUP's future; these were all being dissipated in the purview of the ideals of Islamic union and Turkism. Superseding all other CUP pursuits, whether Enver's design of military despotism or Talaat's future projects for CUP, there was the sublime goal to infuse the entire CUP movement with the idea of the S.O. That sublime goal was Islamic union and all embracing Turkism."[39]

Another specialist of the S.O. likewise asserts that the main mission of the S.O. was twofold: to gather all Muslims under one roof—"under one flag," to use his words—and also to safeguard "the Turkish race" (*Türk ırkını*) through the anti-Armenian "deportation" initiative.[40] A similar view is expressed by another student of the S.O. He states that the chief mission of the S.O. was to "curb the separatist movements that were developing within and sweeping the Ottoman landscape, and that the securing of political unison was to be achieved through the goal of Islamic Oneness."[41] In blunt language, the operative leader of the S.O., Eşref Kuşcubaşı, also spelled out the S.O.'s mission. As he put it:

> The S.O. has been operating outside the sphere of the government but through the agencies of the War Ministry and the CUP's Central Committee. In the course of a series of secret meetings at the War ministry, the main topic that was explored was the goal of liquidating [*tasfiyesi*] the non-Turkish masses of populations which were located in strategic areas and were under foreign and negative influences.[42]

In the end the Armenians were in fact largely liquidated through wholesale deportations and massacres, mainly via the instrumentality of the S.O. This is an irrevocable fact of Ottoman-Turkish history. But that historical fact was cast in rare relief when one of the foremost leaders of that S.O., who happened to be also a member of CUP's Central Committee, finally felt constrained to recognize the criminal nature of the S.O.'s instrumentality. At the last sitting of the first seven series of the court-martial, he ended his testimony by declaring, "Under the auspices of CUP's Central Committee, the S.O. was reduced to an instrument of serial crimes."[43]

The Responsible Secretaries and Delegates

A comprehensive mass murder requires above all two principal groups of actors: centrally located and power-wielding decision-makers, and subservient and *in loco* implementers of the respective decisions. Given the enormity and the vast dimensions of the nature of the crime, however, these two groups of actors are utterly inadequate for the task. Indispensable for the performance of such a task is a group of other actors, perpetrators who are interposed between these two groups and as such play intermediary roles. The innocuous-sounding titles of these actors, in this case the responsible secretaries and delegates—Kâtibi Mesul and Murahhas, respectively—were misleading by design. As a well-informed chronicler of CUP disclosed in one of his volumes:

> The title 'Responsible Secretary' was created to avoid the appearance of overshadowing the state authority while investing the holder with such powers as may be required for the directing of the course of events. In fact, in all matters of consequence, *the last decision* [italics in the original] belonged to them. These men … in line with this practice made *final decisions.* They were selected by the Central Committee, the shadow Cabinet, on the basis of experience, age, brains and familiarity.[44]

Tunaya described them as "the bearers (taşıcıları) of CUP … CUP's real power outside the Parliament."[45]

The court-martial had anticipated these assessments decades earlier in its proceedings and especially its verdicts, which prefigure in all of them. Indeed, when framing its new indictment in the new series of cabinet members' trials on 3 June 1919, it declared that these secretaries had become "the bearers of secretive but optimal influence [*amili müessir ve nafız*] and acted as imperious lords as they bore down on local governments." This relative omnipotence manifested itself especially in the matter of "Armenian deportations which they and the delegates had organized while the plans for the respective crimes were set up by the CUP, and were carried out under the control of Bahaeddin Şakir" (*T.V.* 3571, p. 130, right column, p. 131, left column). When explaining the conditions affording such near-unlimited power, the tribunal touched on a most critical issue relative to the source and scope of that power. It declared that these men acquired and exercised the kind of power that was free from any element of responsibility and hence from any requirement of public or any other kind of accountability. They were able to establish a government within the government (hükümetin içinde bir hükümet), thereby creating a type of authority that was beyond and above the scope of official authority (ve bu suretle kuvayı resmiyeyi hükümetin fevkinde) (*T.V.* 3557, p. 158, left column).

These developments were intimately connected with those general operations that involved "the massacre and destruction of the Armenians the organization of which some of the Responsible Secretaries did facilitate." Additionally, they also helped in "the plunder and theft of the belongings and the appropriation of their "abandoned goods" (*T.V.* 3772, p. 4, left column). Having been thus left free, these men indulged in "villainous behavior" (*T.V.* 3772, p. 3, left column). They had the temerity, for example, to relay, during "the Armenian deportations, special instructions [*talimatı mahsusa*] to the valis, as attested to by Vali Tahsin." Through intervention with the authorities in the Ottoman capital, dissident *valis*, unwilling to comply with these instructions, were thus dismissed and replaced (*T.V.* 3571, p. 131, right column). Ankara's Responsible Secretary Necati, for example, had Yozgat's *mutasarrıf* Cemal promptly dismissed and replaced. Cemal had agreed to carry out the deportation of his district's Armenians but had adamantly refused to allow the massacre of the deportee population (teklif olunan imha keyfiyetine muhalefet). In doing so he had poignantly made the point that Necati had no official position and he, therefore, would not want to comply with hand-written, secret orders issuing from a political party (*T.V.* 3772, p. 4, left column).[46]

Among several of the abusive responsible secretaries and delegates, the court focused especially on the following three.

(1) Dr. Midhat was targeted for his role in the deportation of his district Bolu's Armenians. Equally significant, he too had had removed a *mutasarrıf*, namely Bolu's Ali Ilmi, for resisting Armenian deportations (*T.V.* 3772, p. 4, left column).
(2) Hasan Fehmi, responsible secretary of Kastamonu, is depicted as a man whose power exceeded that of the *vali;* accordingly it proved impossible to mount any opposition against him. As in the previous two cases, he too was able to force the removal and replacement of Kastamonu province's *vali* for likewise refusing to send away the Armenians to be massacred, for which reason Fehmi had denounced and denigrated him as "the vali of the Armenians" (*T.V.* 3772, p. 4, left and p. 5, right columns).
(3) Abdülgani, Edirne's responsible secretary, was accused of having had "ruined lots of Armenians" on account of his "influence." He was observed running around with "armed çetes" (*T.V.* 3772, p. 5, left column).

The case of Cemal Oğuz, Çankırı's responsible secretary, was explored separately above (see pp. 112–24).

The court, on the basis of these and other subsidiary charges, found these functionaries guilty as accessories to the principal crime of organized mass murder. The Ottoman Penal Code, Article 45, paragraph 3 addresses the guilt of being an accessory to a crime, as distinct from that of being a principal perpetrator. An accessory is one who knowingly assists a principal perpetrator in the commission of a capital crime. Accordingly, no death verdict was pronounced in the Responsible Secretaries and Delegates trial series.

The Central Authorities, i.e., the Central Committee of CUP

From the very inception of the genocide, a substantive documentation of the decisive role of the Central Committee ("CC") of CUP in effect was blocked by that body's calculated decision. As Bayur stated, "the most important decisions were secretly made among two or three people. It is, therefore, natural that they do not show up in the transcripts of the Cabinet Council. However, in cases of extreme importance … written records were kept."[47] Eşref Kuşcubaşı, the executive chief of the S.O., boasted that the S.O.'s operations were so secret that even the government was not apprised of them.[48] The situation is best summed up by Tunaya. He wrote:

> Ittihad was a power-wielding monopolistic clique which issued orders from behind the curtains [her şeyi perde arkasından hükmeden] … the great Empire was in the hands of these eight individuals … operating secretly behind a mysterious curtain and in an organized way … a secret oligarchy which resorted to weapons whenever it could not silence ideas.[49]

Against this background an attempt may be made now to examine the Central Committee's decisive role.

The first critical document the court-martial was able to obtain was Third Army Commander General Vehıp's affidavit, discussed previously (p. 7, n. 10). Having personally investigated the crime that was committed under the auspices of his predecessor, General Mahmut Kâmil, he prepared, upon the military tribunal's request, his famous written deposition. In the summary section he testified, explicitly and with emphasis, that "the massacre and extermination of the Armenians was the result of the decision-making of CUP's Central Committee [neticeyi mukarreratı], and that bloodthirsty felons and criminals, especially released from the prisons [eli gözü kanlı … ipten ve kazıkdan kurtulmuş yaranını], did commit these crimes."[50]

Using this deposition as a frame of reference, the tribunal proceeded to ascertain the facts relative to the CC's decision making and in the end to integrate its findings in various indictments, closing arguments, and of course verdicts. In the text of the indictment framed for the trial of the responsible secretaries, for example, it declared that "the annihilation of the deportee convoys [*kafilelerin imha*] resulted from the special law that was itself the result of a decision made by the CC" (Merkez-i Umumin'in ittihaz eylediği karara tebean) (*T.V.* 3586, p. 164, right column). The CC (*erkân*) was able to undertake such initiatives because it succeeded in establishing "a secret powerhouse that served to alter the form of the government" (şekli idareyi hükümeti tagyir) (*T.V.* 3557, p. 98, right column, p. 99, left column). According to the verdict condemning the supreme leaders of CUP, the Central Committee was able to do this because they had created a fourth instance of authority that relied on the method of issuing threats (*kuvvei tehdidiye*) (*T.V.* 3604, p. 219, left column). In the text of the Harput Verdict, the court-martial clearly stated that the headquarters of the CC were the actual locus where the decision for "massacre and extermination" (*ifna ve imha*) (*T.V.* 3771, p. 1) was made. The text of the new indictment, meant for the trial of the cabinet ministers, refers to "the massacre and extermination" (*katl ve imha*) that "the secret" outfit (*cemiyeti hafiye*), relying on the terms of the special law, had organized. The victims were "a community of people" whose convoys, through attacks carried out by specially assembled brigands, were subjected to schemes of annihilation (*T.V.* 3571, p. 129, left column). Finally, the fact of the organized mass murder of the Armenians is repeatedly cited in the Responsible Secretaries Verdict with reference to such terms as "deportation and massacre" and "massacre and extermination" (*tehcir ve taktil, taktil ü imha*) (*T.V.* 3772, p. 3, left column, p. 4, left column).

The Sidelining of the Cabinet as a Function of CUP Omnipotence

Equilibrium in any political system is, as a rule, maintained by applying the principle of distribution of power whereby various institutions interact among themselves within a framework of an established system of power relations. The accretion of extra power to one of the components of that system not only serves to increase the leverage of that component, but concomitantly and correspondingly diminishes the power leverage of the other components. An inevitable decline of status goes hand in hand with such a diminution of power. Moreover, two ancillary conditions may render this process rather lasting: the revolutionary abruptness of the change, and the progressive entrenchment of the agent of that change.

The Ittihadist Young Turk revolution of July 1908 and its subsequent phase of firm entrenchment through a coup d'état on 23 January 1913 were events that not only galvanized Turkish society but served to spread fear all around, intimidating CUP opponents. Having only just been jarred loose from one despotism, that of Abdulhamit II, Turkish elites found themselves caught in the tentacles of an emerging new variety of despotism. By the outbreak of World War I and Turkey's unilateral intervention in that war three months later, the CUP nearly completely dominated the Turkish political landscape. In other words, the whole process was essentially a CUP revolution, which meant CUP predominance and control throughout the empire. This fact was amply in evidence in the circumstances under which top CUP leaders, without consulting the rest of the cabinet, let alone lesser officials, such as deputies or senators, effected that intervention by a preemptive attack against Russia. In other words, as early as the very start of the war, the CUP, with total abandon, ignored the cabinet as a superordinate body of executive authority; in the end, the cabinet was altogether jettisoned with silent disdain. Nonetheless, the enduring humiliation inflicted upon that body through this act of exclusion from decision-making, on a matter that was central and fundamental to the jurisdiction of that body, has critical importance for the present attempt at analysis. The import of the relevant material produced by the court-martial is further enhanced by the corroborative data in the possession of the Chamber of Deputies; namely, the latter's Fifth Investigative Department had interrogated most of the wartime cabinet ministers in the weeks preceding the initiation of the courts-martial.

The practice of sidelining at issue here was most acute and consequential in the handling of the 14 (27) May 1915 deportation order, for whose pro forma legal enactment the help of the grand vizier and his cabinet was enlisted. But even here there was preemption on the part of Interior Minister Talaat. First of all, the deportations in some parts of the country were actually launched weeks before Talaat enlisted the emergency-style legislative help of the cabinet. Second, Talaat preempted the cabinet by not bothering to wait for it to collectively deliberate and formally approve the enactment of his motion as a temporary law. In any event, the cardinal issue here, about which Sait Halim complained during his postwar interrogation by the Fifth Department of the Chamber of Deputies, was that Interior Minister Talaat had recklessly abused his authority. The fundamental problem was that the formal governmental decision to deport the Armenian population en masse was illegally transformed by an informal agent of power into a decision for actual massacres. The criminality of the act is here compounded by the illegitimate character of the source authorizing it.

Intent on avoiding a precipitous war, Grand Vizier Sait Halim had tried in vain to prevent his government from being tricked or maneuvered into World War I. As the court-martial declared, it had secured "proofs and documents" and other valid records and evidence showing that the CC of the CUP ignored the cabinet and broke the law by circumventing it (*T.V.* 3571, p. 130, right column). (Sait Halim's testimony before the Fifth Department is mentioned above (pp. 55–6); that of Finance Minister Mehmet Cavit, relating to this opposition, is recorded elsewhere.)[51] The court in its Key Verdict pointed out that certain important matters of state were handled without consulting the cabinet, that the cabinet was ignored, and that on top of all this war was declared without the requisite cabinet approval (ilânı harb kararını meclisi Vükelanın arasına vazetmeyi bilüzum görmüş). (*T.V.* 3604, p. 218, left column, p. 219, left column, p. 219, right column). This point is reiterated in the testimony of CUP Secretary-General Midhat Şükrü, himself a member of the powerful CC clique, who confirmed that the cabinet had been against war. (*T.V.* 3554, p. 76, left column). Finally, the court established that the S.O. was an outfit whose existence the cabinet was unaware of; hence it could not have been approved by the cabinet (*T.V.* 3554, p. 77, right column). All the three cabinet ministers—Sait Halim, Justice Minister Ibrahim, and Finance Minister Cavit—categorically declared that they were neither consulted on, nor were they aware of, its existence and mission.[52]

Ex post facto denials or equivocations are common features in the self-serving testimonies of almost all witnesses suspected of direct or indirect complicity in crimes of all kinds, or even lesser offenses. Unless they realized that they were facing compelling evidence, all the defendants in the courts-martial under review here, with hardly any exception, went to any lengths to deny, evade, twist, or bend factual evidence. Neither Grand Vizier Sait Halim nor the other cabinet ministers were entirely innocent. But they had priorities and knew how to weigh risks while enjoying the honors and other benefits bestowed upon them by virtue of the positions they held. Some of them were misinformed and felt that some counter-measures against the Armenians were warranted. For lack of precise knowledge, others simply felt confounded. Still others were totally oblivious to the fate befalling the victims. From a strictly legal point of view, there is no evidence that they had any direct or even indirect part in any murderous decision-making save Justice Minister Ibrahim.

They were, however, complicit in the sense that they willfully, and some of them with relish, submitted to the overall illegal acts of informal, and hence illegitimate, authority. By doing so they were violating the Constitution and the sacredness of their oath of office; also, they failed to exercise their option to resign. Their main, if not only, excuse—or perhaps mitigating circumstance, given the then prevailing codes of conduct—was that the two main architects of the organized mass murder in question, in addition to being supreme CUP party potentates, were at the same time also powerful cabinet ministers: Interior Minister Talaat and War Minister Enver. But even Grand Vizier Sait Halim, the so-called prime minister and hence superior in rank to both of them, felt constrained to meekly submit to the willful acts of both.

Notes

1. Vahakn N. Dadrian, "Impunity," in *Encyclopedia of Genocide and Crimes Against Humanity*, vol. 2 (Detroit: Macmillan Reference: U.S.A., 2005): 489–491.
2. Quoted in James Wiltford Garner, *International Law and the World War*, vol. 2 (London: Longmans, Green and Co., 1920), p. 504, paragraph 595.
3. Dadrian, "Genocide as a Problem," (see Bibl.), p. 262. This fact is acknowledged in the United Nations' official publication *The Development of the Laws of War* (United Nations War Crimes Commission: London, 1948), pp. 35, 45, 194, and 196–197.
4. Vahakn N. Dadrian, "The Historical and Legal Interconnections Between the Armenian Genocide and the Jewish Holocaust: From Impunity to Retributive Justice," *Yale Journal of International Law* 23, no. 2 (Summer 1998): 503-559, 538.
5. Bayur, *Türk Inkilâbı Tarihi*, vol. 3, part 1 (Ankara: Türk Tarih Kurumu, 1953), pp. 237–241; for the events leading to the preemptive strike see pp. 229–237. See also vol. 3, part 4 (1983), p. 791, where this renowned Turkish historian condemns "this act of aggressiveness" along with its companion "institutionalized plunders" (soygunculuğu bir müessese durumuna getirip).

6. Cemal Paşa, *Hatıralar*, ed. B. Cemal (Istanbul: Çağdaş, 1977), p. 438; on pp. 413 and 443, however, Cemal in the same vein denounced the massacres against the Armenians as "revolting."
7. For details see Dadrian, *History of the Armenian Genocide*, pp. 185–202. (in Biblog.)
8. *Ati*, Turkish Daily, otherwise called Ileri, 24 February 1920 issue. For a slightly more modern Turkish version of the text see Muammer Demirel, *Birinci Dünya Harbinde Erzurum ve Çevresinde Ermeni Hareketleri (1914-1918)* (Ankara, Genelkurmay, 1996), p. 53. This latter statement, made on 13 (26) July 1915, is in the Interior Ministry Archives, Cipher Section, DH.SFR 54.426, as quoted in Fuat Dündar, *Modern Türkiye'nin Şifresi* (Istanbul: Iletişim, 2008), pp. 308–309.
9. Henry Morgenthau, *Ambassador Morgenthau's Story* (New York: Doubleday, 1918), p. 333.
10. The full text of the Vehip affidavit is in the Jerusalem Armenian Patriarchate Archive: Series 17, File H. doc. No. 171–182. This depository was read in its entirety at the second sitting of the Trabzon trial series (29 March 1919). Portions of it were incorporated in the Key Indictment (*T.V.* 3540, p. 8, right column), and the Harput Verdict (*T.V.* 3771: 2 r).
11. Osman Selim Kocahanoğlu, *Ittihat ve Terrakki'nin Sorgulanması ve Yargılanması* (Istanbul: Temel, 1998), p. 43.
12. *T.V.* 3553 (3554), p. 86, right column; *T.V.* 3557, p. 98, right column, p. 99, right column; on military officers helping in the task of recruiting and organizing them see *T.V.* 3543, p. 26, left column, and for commanding the S.O. units, see p. 28, right column.
13. Dadrian, "The Law Allowing Convicts," 57–61. (see Bibliog.)
14. *T.V.* 3543, p. 29, left column.
15. Kocahanoğlu, *Ittihat-Terakki'nin* [n. 11], p. 168, for Ibrahim's official testimony.
16. Ibid., p. 43.
17. Falih Rıfkı Atay, *Zeytindağı* (Istanbul: Ayyıldız, 1981), p. 36.
18. On p. 1135 in his massive volume, *Milli Kurtuluş Tarihi*, Doğan Avcıoğlu writes: "Within a very brief space of time [çok kısa bir sürede] the Armenians were deported en masse. The S.O. and trustworthy CUP leaders were bent on solving the Armenian question in a radical way [Ermeni sorunu temelden çözme amacını güttüyü ...] ... The sponsor of this program was Dr. Şakir who promoted the plan at CUP's Central Committee." On p. 1114 of the same book, the author reveals that the entire scheme was the result of months-long deliberations and planning at the War Ministry, where "the liquidation of the Christian elements [*tasfiye*] was decided and for which end young officers were tasked."
19. Hüsamettin Ertürk, a military officer with the rank of lieutenant-colonel and a leading figure in S.O., declared that the deportations were not only decided upon by the CC of CUP as reprisals against the Armenians, but that the S.O. was in charge of these deportations. *Iki Devrin Perde Arkası*, pp. 297–298, 306. (see Biblio.)
20. Galip Vardar (Ertürk's right hand man), *Ittihad ve Terakki Içinde Dönenler.* Ed. S. N. Tansu. (Istanbul: Inkilâp, 1960), pp. 244–246, 274.
21. Mustafa Ragıp Esatlı, *Ittihad ve Terakki Tarihinde Esrar Perdesi* (Istanbul: Hürriyet, 1975), p. 258.
22. The reference is to Cemal Azmi who, despite his escape to Germany at the end of the war, was tracked down by Armenian avengers and assassinated in Berlin on 17

April 1922. For the description of the induction ceremony see Arif Cemil (Denker), *I. Dünya Savaşında Teşkilâtı Mahsusa* (Istanbul: Arba, 1997), p. 26.

23. The newspaper was *Sabah*, from which a day or two later *Ariamard* (namesake of Dashnak newspaper *Djagadamard*) excerpted that piece of information in its 13 December 1918 issue.
24. German Foreign Office Archives, Berlin. A.A. Botschaft Konstantinopel, vol. 174, A3351.
25. Fuat Balkan, "Beş Albaylar." *Yakın Tarihimiz* 2 (1962): 297.
26. P. Stoddard, *The Ottoman Government and the Arabs, 1911 to 1918: A Preliminary Study of the Teşkilâtı Mahsusa* (University Microfilms: Ann Arbor, 1964), p. 49. For more information on Seyfi and his involvement in this matter see Dadrian, *History of the Armenian Genocide,* p. 229, notes 5 and 6, and p. 373, n. 34, and on Seyfi again, within a larger framework exploring the entire Special Organization, see Vahakn N. Dadrian, "The Role of the Special Organization in the Armenian Genocide during the First World War" in *Minorities in Wartime,* ed. P. Panayi (Oxford: Berg, 1993), pp. 50–82.
27. Tunaya, *Türkiye'de Siyasal Partiler,* vol. 3 (Istanbul: Hürriyet Vakfı, 1989), pp. 241, 243.
28. Ibid., p. 252.
29. Ibid., p. 275.
30. Ibid., pp. 280, 281.
31. Ibid., pp. 282, 285, 327.
32. Ibid., p. 285.
33. Ibid., p. 277, Seyfullah from Erzurum and Süleyman Sudi from Lazistan (Trabzon).
34. Ibid., p. 281.
35. Ahmet Emin Yalman, *Yakın Tarihte Gördüklerim ve Geçirdiklerim, vol. 1: (1888–1918)* Istanbul: Yenilik, 1970), pp. 331–332. It should be noted that this dire prediction came true: on 17 April 1922, Şakir was gunned down and killed along with Trabzon *vali* Cemal Azmi in Berlin, where both of them had taken refuge after the war, as mentioned in note 22 above. Yalman in a previous volume had already singled out the S.O. as the main instrument of the massacres. *Turkey in the World War* (New Haven: Yale University Press, 1930), p. 220.
36. Ahmet Refik Altınay, *Iki Komite, Iki Kıtal,* ed. Hamide Koyukan (Ankara: Kabikeç Publications, 1994), p. 27. The original, appearing in Ottoman script, was published in Istanbul in 1919, and before that it was serialized in the 17 December 1918–13 January 1919 issues of *Ikdam.*
37. Ibid., pp. 38–39, 41.
38. Ibid., p. 45. For more details on Refik, see Bernard Lewis, "History-Writing and National Revival in Turkey," *Middle Eastern Affairs* 4 (1953): 218–227. On p. 223, Lewis characterizes Refik "as the most distinguished among the contributors to the journal *Ottoman Historical Society*, perhaps the most distinguished." For biographical sketches of Ahmet Refik see "Ahmet Refik Altınay," in Nahid S. Özik, ed., *Yüzelli Yılın Türk Meşhurları Ansiklopedisi* (Istanbul: Ekicigil, 1953), p. 104; and Reşad E. Koçu, ed., *Ahmet Refik, Hayatı: Seçme Şiir ve Yazıları* (Istanbul: Semih L. Erciyas, 1938). When providing an overall assessment of him, Turkish Prof. Fahrettin Kırzıoglu described him as "our historian who even today remains unequalled, very productive and influential." *Belgelerle Türk Tarih Dergisi,* no. 1 (March 1985): 31.

39. Cemil, *I. Dünya Savaşında* [n. 22], p. 11.
40. Ihsan Birinci, "Cemiyet ve Çeteler," *Hayat Tarih* 2, no. 9 (1 October 1971): 20.
41. Ergün Hiçyılmaz, *Belgelerle Teşkilâtı Mahsusa* (Istanbul: Ünsal, 1979), p. 102.
42. Quoted in Celal Bayar, *Bende Yazdım: Milli Mücadeleye Giriş,* vol. 5 (Istanbul, Baha, 1967), p. 1573.
43. *T.V.* 3561, p. 124, right column, Atıf's testimony.
44. Cemal Kutay, *Celal Bayar'ın Yazmadığı ve Yazmayacağı Üç Devirden Hakikatler* (Istanbul: Alioğlu, 1982), p. 12.
45. Tunaya, *Türkiye'de Siyasal Partiler* [n. 27], vol. 3 (1989), pp. 209, 210.
46. For details of this incident see Dadrian, "The Documentation of the World War I Armenian Massacres in the Proceedings of the Turkish Military Tribunal," *International Journal of Middle East Studies* 23, no. 4 (1991): 549–576, 563.
47. Bayur, *Türk Inkilâbı Tarihi,* vol. 3, part 1 (1953), p. 484. Yalman expresses a similar view in *Turkey in My Time* (Norman: University of Oklahoma, 1956), pp. 34–35.
48. Quoted in Cemal Kutay, *Birinci Dünya Harbinde Teşkilât-ı Mahsusa* (Istanbul: Ercan, 1962), p. 18.
49. Tarık Zafer Tunaya, *Türkiyede Siyasi Partiler, 1859–1952* (Istanbul: Doğan, 1952), p. 182.
50. For full details see Vahakn N. Dadrian, "The Armenian Question and the Wartime Fate of the Armenians as Documented by the Officials of the Ottoman Empire's World War I Allies: Germany and Austria-Hungary," *International Journal of Middle East Studies* 34, no. 1 (February 2002): 84–85, n. 111.
51. Kocahanoğlu, *Ittihad-Terrakki'nin* [n. 11], pp. 58–59; Cavit's on pp. 311, 381.
52. Ibid., pp. 79, 83, 166–167, 381.

CHAPTER 8

A Summary of the Conditions Surrounding the Trials

Vahakn N. Dadrian

Generally speaking, the nature of legal prosecution is such that the verdicts resulting from it address the matter of truth in a rather restricted manner, namely, one that is consistent with "the rule of law." In this sense it is "legal" truth that is at issue here and not necessarily truth in a broader sense. Moreover, verdicts, as a matter of judicial principle, presuppose a type of evidentiary material that is probative and hence is tested for relevance as well as veracity. It is most significant that in the Istanbul court-martial proceedings two conditions prevailed—conditions that not only invaluably enhanced the significance of the respective verdicts, but more important, helped render the attendant evidence compelling. First to note is that the majority of the witnesses were Turks and other Muslims; second, and notwithstanding, the bulk of the verdicts were predicated upon authenticated official wartime Ottoman documents.

The corollary implication here is that these are documents of the type that would readily engage the attention of any historian or political scientist researching the career of the Young Turk regime, and especially the essential role of the Central Committee ("CC") of the CUP, the bearers and masters of that regime. In brief, the documentary foundations of the courts-martial, by way of extrapolation, clearly afford an analysis transcending the boundaries of law, and criminal law in particular. That analysis concerns the attempt at establishing a broader and more inclusive framework for the examination of the wartime fate of the Armenians.

The Denial Syndrome

Against the backdrop of such stringent documentation, the vehement and persistent denial of the crime during and in the aftermath of the war by the Ottoman authorities, led by Talaat himself, deserves a brief critical evaluation. As discussed earlier, denial by perpetrators who have managed to escape consequential prosecution is, as a rule, a function of that very fact of escape. But escape from effective prosecution and punishment can in no way impair an analysis of the offenses in question; on the contrary, it often renders such analysis even more expedient and significant. The significance is presently related to the crucial role Talaat played in the organization and execution of the crime under review here. Indeed, his very escape, as discussed elsewhere in the text, is intimately connected with the fact of that criminal role. Accordingly, a brief review of comments by his contemporaries, whether historians, newspaper editors, or other professionals, may offer a way to assess the value of a post-crime industry of denial, the premises of which Talaat framed and ushered in. His posthumous memoirs exemplify this pursuit of denial.[1]

Through the application of a broad perspective, Bayur on numerous occasions and in several of his volumes, decries Talaat as an unmitigated liar who deliberately distorted, subverted, misinformed, double-talked, and generally perverted truths with remarkable ease.[2] His contemporaries expressed similar and even harsher judgments in the aftermath of his flight from Turkey at the end of the war on the night of 1–2 November 1918, to be exact.[3] The most vehement decrier was one of the most renowned literary figures of the time, Cenab Şehabettin. He described Talaat as:

> Wicked in nature; his intelligence was that of a scoundrel [habis bir zekâ]. It was put to use in order to set up a net, to lay a trap, to lie in wait for ambush, to get ready to strike, to operate as a trickster, a cheat—altogether a duplicitous, treacherous intelligence.... For Talât the national fraternity merely consisted of membership in the Central Committee of Ittihad and the fatherland merely consisted of the network of Ittihadist [CUP] clubs. He was a fanatic partisan of Ittihad.... He was a komiteci, a frightening komiteci.[4]

As to Talaat's memoirs mentioned above, the plethora of inaccuracies was fully exposed by a legally trained and otherwise broadly educated (mostly European) distinguished newspaper editor, Ebuzziya Velit.[5] Counterposed to this catalogue of denunciations and expressions of scorn, noted Islamist and Ottomanist Bernard Lewis ventured to depict and highly praise Talaat in terms of his "swift and penetrating intelligence."[6] These denunciations of Talaat's duplicitous behavior are further highlighted by a remarkable disclosure made in Berlin. Following his assassination in Berlin by an Armenian "avenger," Talaat's personal belongings came into the possession of Weismann from Berlin's Public Security Office, which had been monitoring the activities of CUP's fugitive leaders in Berlin. Weismann informed the German Foreign Office that Dr. Bahaeddin Şakir had "screened" Talaat's memoirs before handing them over to the publisher.[7]

Talaat's elaborate web of deception and deflection with respect to the facts of the wartime Armenian deportations and massacres is in evidence at two other and separate levels involving Talaat's wartime claim of having investigated the crimes committed against the Armenians. Aziz Nedim, civil inspector in the Ottoman government and an old friend of Talaat's from the prewar Saloniki days, was sent in May 1916 to Boğazlıyan, a *kaza* (county) in Yozgat, in Ankara province, to investigate the abuses committed in the course of the Armenian deportations. In his pretrial written affidavit Nedim told the Turkish Military Tribunal investigating the wartime deportations and massacres that, based on the official order issued to him from "high office," he was to investigate only economic crimes and had "no authority to investigate the massacres." In commenting on the meaning of this statement, District Attorney Sami, prosecuting the crimes in the Yozgat area, stated at the eleventh sitting of the Yozgat trial series on 5 March 1919: "I infer from this statement that Inspector Nedim sought clarification on the scope of his mandate and was told that the matter of massacres was outside the purview of his investigative task."[8]

In his memoirs Talaat boasts of having sent four commissions of inquiry to the provinces to investigate the matter and punish the offenders. The tragicomic travesty of this highly deceptive ploy is revealed in the following account of a particular aspect of this series of investigations conducted by officials from the Justice Ministry and Civil Service Inspectorate; they were hand-picked by Talaat himself.[9] Hulusi Bey, the head of the first commission covering the provinces of Konya and Ankara, was likewise an ardent CUP man; he was first appointed president of the appeals court at Istanbul, and subsequently of the criminal court. He was also the father-in-law of Tahsin (Uzer), the famous *vali* of Van and later Erzurum. When in 1911 Zeki Bey, a pronounced anti-Ittihadist editor, was assassinated in broad daylight in Istanbul through Ittihadist plotting, it was Hulusi who, carrying out the will of CUP, helped engineer by way of an amnesty the release from prison of the two murderers, Çerkez Ahmet and Mustafa Nazım, the latter being the brother of the Serez deputy Derviş. The account below furnishes an example of the investigative and judicial methods of Hulusi, the president of that commission. The accounts are taken from the testimony of Mehmet Radi Bey, who was present at the investigative proceedings in Ankara, and who, as a notable of Ankara, was friendly with top CUP leaders as well as provincial governmental officials:

> Hulusi: What information do you have regarding gendarme Ahmet who is accused of terrorizing Armenian deportee Kevork, while appropriating his watch?
> Witness (Turk): Sir, I saw far more terrible things. I saw çetes and gendarmes massacring an Armenian deportee convoy with axes and spades.
> Hulusi: I didn't ask you that question. Answer my question only.
> Witness: I shall answer that question, sir. But for the sake of justice, do hear what I have to say. I saw people just like us, in a caravan, being savagely butchered with axes and spades.

Hulusi: Take him out, that dog [*köpek*]; bring in another witness.

The testimony that followed was more in tune with Hulusi's expectations. Some gendarmes who were relatively more benign toward the deportees but had engaged in petty robbery in the course of the deportation were charged. They were court-martialed and severely punished. Their cases served as the basis of embellished public reports about punishing the perpetrators who had victimized the Armenians. As was typical in this episode, in essence only those who chose to behave mildly, rather than viciously, against the Armenians were punished; massacres and massacrers were absolutely excluded from the jurisdiction of these inquiry commissions and independent inspectors.[10] When commenting on these four commissions and their investigations, Ahmet E. Yalman, mentioned above, expressed the following view:

> A commission of investigation composed of inspectors of the Ministries of the Interior and of Justice, was formed … to punish those guilty of excesses. Some minor offenders were really punished; but those favoring the deportations being very influential in the Government, the whole thing amounted more to a demonstration rather than a sincere attempt to fix complete responsibility.[11]

The following general critique may help to sum up the picture as far as Turkish appraisals are concerned:

> The memoirs of the responsible CUP men consist of odds and ends, reflecting an infantile simplicity and spirit of irresponsibility.… None of these touch on events that were pivotal or were turning points, or touch on culpabilities, on crimes, and on the kinds of ineptness that ruined the army and the country. Their memoirs convey the impression that they are dwelling in a dream world. What is evident in their writing in which a few details are revealed to conceal the substance, is indulgence in game playing—typical of guilty men.[12]

Even more compelling relative to the matter of Talaat's penchant for chronic lies are the judgments of German consuls on duty in the interior of Turkey, singular witnesses to the wartime massacres and deportations.[13]

The practice of deleting from official Ottoman documents passages confirming or attesting to evidence of a centrally organized mass murder against the Armenians appears to be standard practice by many Turkish historians adhering to the "official version" of state-imposed historiography. Examples abound in this respect, but one typical instance merits special attention here. When Interior Minister Talaat sent a cipher ordering the authorities of Diyarbekir province to refrain from new massacres against Christians—they already had killed some 2,000—he excluded the Christian Armenians, specifically identifying them as the actual target population. But when reproducing this cipher, Kamuran Gürün, a veteran Turkish diplomat and the author of a volume on this topic, studiously left out this critical instruction of the principal architect of the Armenian Genocide. Consistent with this pattern of omissions and deletions, in another part of his book, and again with utmost care, Gürün left out a very important cipher when reproducing a series of ciphers by jumping from references 854/54, 855/55, and 856/56 to 858/58, thus skipping 858/57. The issue involves an important cipher telegram sent to Talaat by Erzurum Governor-General Tahsin in an attempt to dissuade Talaat from ordering the deportations of his province's Armenian population, for whose reliability he vouched in that cipher.[14]

The Cabinet's Expedient Adaptation to Being Sidelined by the Central Committee of CUP

Acquiescing in the fact of being sidelined is certainly a form of adaptive behavior for which there are always both reasons and, equally important, consequences. The consequences in the present case involved the leeway of irresponsibility accruing to the CC of the CUP as a result of the more or less coercive transfer of executive power to it from the cabinet, the legitimate source of that power. With the resulting dissipation of legal restraints in the exercise of such power, however, it appears that the attendant ethical constraints dissipated even faster. How did this happen? This process was intimately connected to the CC's decision to intervene, unilaterally if necessary, in the war that had been raging for several months. Once more, the war-related aspect of the Armenian Genocide is here thrust into relief. Some of the specifics of this preemptive transfer of executive power therefore deserve attention.

As Bayur points out, it all started with the growing pressure that the CC—which, as far as official government business was concerned, "has no residual responsibility at all" (hiç bir bakımdan sorumlu olmıyan)—was exerting upon the cabinet. This became manifest on the day the combined Turko-German flotilla launched its preemptive attack against Russia in the Black Sea. There was a joint cabinet-CC meeting on that very day, and Talaat and Enver, both of whom had dual status (as both CC member and cabinet minister), were not only trying to "throw dust in the eyes" of the cabinet but were also bullying the cabinet's members.[15]

Grand Vizier Sait Halim's main complaint was that he was rendered "powerless" by the declaration of martial law,[16] which again in itself was illegal since it was not authorized by any imperial rescript, as required by law.[17] Notwithstanding, Halim ended up displaying remarkable aptitude for acquiescence and accommodation. He is criticized by Bayur for his equivocal attitudes, which often degenerated into what he called acts of "flattering" toward the top

CUP bosses. Tapping the shoulder of Cemal Paşa, the third member of the Itiihadist reigning triumvir, for example, Halim had called out, "May you live long, may you live long, Paşa" (Yaşa Paşa, yaşa) after the latter, in resignation, had joined the other two members of the triumvirate in welcoming Turkey's preemptive intervention in the war.[18] The same Cemal, however, had previously considered resigning in protest against Enver-Talaat machinations relative to an alliance with Germany.[19] Denouncing him as a "puppet" and, along with his other cabinet ministers, as "committee fanatics" prone to "pro-party legalism," Bayur explained these behavior patterns of Sait Halim as "typical of a man who is ignored but still wants to keep his job" (sözünü geçiremesse de makamında kalmak tercih eden…).[20]

The net result of all this was that the grand vizier and most of the cabinet ministers were not only inevitably sidelined but, beyond that, when required by the needs of the CC of the CUP, they became the latter's subservient tools. This fact was manifest in the initiation of a radically new anti-Armenian policy when the CUP saw fit to impose its will upon the cabinet by reducing it to a pliable instrument.

The Central Committee's Critical Role in the Unfolding of the Wartime Fate of the Armenians

The informal nature of the part played by the CC was such as to enable this committee, and especially the powerful Secretary-General Mithat Şükrü, to operate behind the scenes most effectively. The timing of its deliberations remarkably coincided with those of the cabinet when the issue of intervening in the war was paramount. CUP party boss Talaat had gone to Bucharest to assess the mood there relative to the same paramount issue—intervention in the war. Upon his return to the Ottoman capital, he convened the party's Central Committee to report to its members, as he had done to the cabinet. The two proponents of intervention, Talaat and Enver, were encountering opposition from the cabinet in this regard, which they tried to surmount with threats of resignation. Since such a resignation would lead to the collapse of the government and to its replacement, they eventually relented, however. Sait Halim was given a choice: either he would lose his job or "you do what we want" (istediklerimizi yaparsın).[21]

One of the first acts the CC performed in connection with these developments was the suspension of the Lower House of the Parliament, the Chamber of Deputies. The first such suspension had occurred on 2 August 1914, the day general mobilization was declared; the second suspension was undertaken on 1 March 1915.[22] With reference to the first, which involved no consultation, Bayur argued that the intent was to have complete freedom of action without any need of accountability, while another author, a legal expert and also a historian, described this act of suspension of the chamber as the CUP's "foremost mistake."[23]

With the progression of World War I, this act of suspending would prove consequential for the empire in general and for the Armenian minority population in particular. As happened in Nazi Germany some two decades later, the legislative branch of the government, for all practical purposes, was thereby shut down. Authority became concentrated not in the executive branch but rather in the CC of CUP, the party's actual source of power. On 16 March 1915, Cavit noted in his diary that the government's staying power had been in a steady process (*git gide*) of decline as it progressively became permeated by the exertions of CUP.[24]

The sequence of events leading to this predominance of the CC in state affairs, especially that of its Secretary-General Midhat Şükrü, reveals the latter's covert but decisive role in the shaping of the fate of the Armenians. This is how a British intelligence report described him: "Under a gentle and refined appearance, a most cold-blooded deviser of worst schemes … he turned all his hatred against the Armenians."[25] Two Turkish authors with rare access to the inner secrets of the CUP, perhaps inadvertently but independent of each other, confirm this role. We learn from one of them, for instance, that the suspension of the Chamber of Deputies at the time when the Armenian deportations were being launched came from the CC's Secretary-General, Midhat Şükrü. Equally significant, he also was identified as the architect of the Temporary Law of Deportation that Talaat then implemented.[26] Arif Cemil, Talaat's confidant, likewise reveals that the draft law for the deportation of the Armenians originated from CUP's CC unit,[27] thus once more underscoring M. Sükrü's key role. In line with this initiative, the latter proposed to the CC that the actual operations of the deportations take place under the terms of a projected temporary law (a law that insidiously authorized massive deportations on mere "suspicion" of evil intent), to be formally enacted by the cabinet.[28] As described above, the very same CUP party potentate had already succeeded in having the Chamber of Deputies, the proper venue to enact such legislation, temporarily suspended.

The conditions under which the subsequent Temporary Law of Deportation was introduced and enacted involved new encroachments on legality. First and foremost among these was the fact that, by his own admission, Talaat had started the deportations prior to the official enactment of the temporary law. When pointing out "this grave matter of responsibility," Bayur allows that Talaat did not recoil from assuming this responsibility to thusly act irresponsibly.[29] Moreover, Talaat "railroaded" the temporary law by disdainfully ignoring the need for a prior cabinet decision before it could be implemented. His deportation draft law was dated 13 (26) May but was submitted to the grand vizier on 14 (27) May 1915. Without waiting for the cabinet to consider, debate, and approve it, that very same day, 26 May 1915, Talaat proceeded to proclaim it as the Temporary Law of Deportation. Grand Vizier Sait Halim and the cabinet were then compelled to formally approve the bill, the former on 29 May and the latter on 30 May, thereby again subverting the normal sequence of official authorization.[30] Commenting on this instance of illegality, Tunaya declared that "this enactment, which should have been based on a decision reached by the government as such, was a procedure typical of the CUP."[31] Perhaps the most critical aspect of the illegality of the deportation law was its violation of Article 36 of the Constitution. That article stipulates that temporary laws enacted during periods when the Chamber of Deputies is not in session "should be submitted to the Assembly as soon as this may be convened," inasmuch as these laws "have [only] provisionally the force of law."[32] Finally, this catalogue of illegal acts most ominously manifested itself in the sudden arrest of two prominent Armenian deputies, whose parliamentary immunity was thereby insidiously violated.[33] As part of the overall scheme of the wholesale liquidation of the people whose interests they were trying to protect, they were ambushed and killed by specially tasked brigands while being deported.

This type of exercise of power by the CC and, more importantly, the operational secrecy of that power, is articulated by Zürcher:

> By 1918, the Ittihadists remained a still secret Committee … CUP exercised power without responsibility.… Real power remained with the control of committee and its secretary general.… After the January 1913 coup d'état, the CUP was in complete control of the internal political situation.… During the period 1913–1918, the inner councils of the CUP counted for much more in the conduct of policy than the cabinet which was quite often faced with accomplished facts.[34]

As may be observed in the text of the following statement, German Ambassador Wolff Metternich rather bluntly notified his government of the exterminatory thrust of this development:

> Nobody has any more the power to restrain the multiheaded hydra of the [CUP] committee, and the attendant chauvinism and fanaticism. The committee demands the extirpation of the last remnants of the Armenians, and the government must yield. The authority of the committee reaches into all the provinces. A committee representative is assigned to each of the provincial administrators, from vali down to kaymakam, for purposes of assistance and supervision.… Turkification means license to expel, to kill or destroy everything that is not Turkish, and to violently take possession of the goods of others.[35]

In fact Zürcher himself in the next breath confirmed the implication of his own diagnosis relative to the impending genocidal fate of the Armenians. As he stated:

> There are indications that, while the Ottoman government as such was not involved in genocide, an inner circle within the Committee of Union and Progress under the direction of Talât wanted to "solve" the Eastern Question by the extermination of the Armenians and that it used the relocation as a cloak for this policy. A number of provincial party chiefs assisted in this extermination, which was organized through the Teşkilât-ı Mahsusa under the direction of its political director (and CUP central committee member) Bahaeddin Şakir.[36]

In order to fully understand the pervasiveness of the CC's control of governmental affairs, one has to appreciate the uncommon extension of that pervasiveness to the military, and even to CUP's top leaders themselves—Enver and Talaat, for example. Bahaeddin Şakir set the stage for the CC's interventions in military affairs at the very start of the war. Unable to impose CUP's political designs on the military plans of the Ninth Army Corps of the Ottoman Third Army, which was bracing itself for an offensive against Russia's Caucasus Army, Şakir had Ahmet Fevzi Paşa, the commander of the Ninth Army Corps, replaced. His complaint and intercession with the CC in Istanbul evidently did the trick.[37] The following two examples further illustrate this point.

The German vice consul of Erzurum, together with party leader Ömer Naci, was organizing an expeditionary detachment that marched through Tabriz in Iran with the intent to wage guerilla war against the Russians in and around Baku in Azerbaijan. But the army refused to supply regular army combatants because of a shortage of reserves. Upon the prompt intervention of the CUP's Central Committee, the High Command reversed itself and complied with the request.[38] Six months later Enver, in consultation with the German and Swiss supervisors of the Baghdad Railway project, issued an order to the effect that the Armenians just then deported from their railway work station should, as an irreplaceable workforce, be immediately restored to their jobs; the order was issued to the Fourth Army commander and the *vali* of Adana, the nearest provincial and military authorities.[39] But ten days later, Gottlieb von Jagow, Germany's foreign minister, informed General Erich von Falkenhayn, at the time the chief of the General Staff in the German High Command, that after a series of conferences involving Talaat, Enver, and Foreign Minister Halil, the original order for deportation could not be rescinded despite Enver's intervention. Added Jagow, "The initial order for the deportation of the Armenian workers came from the [CUP] Committee. Even Enver and Talaat seem to be impotent [*machtlos*] against such fanatical decisions."[40] In explaining the mishap, Konstantin von Neurath, the senior counselor at the German embassy in Istanbul, informed Berlin that the *vali* of Adana, Tahirpaşazade Cevdet (Belbez), previously the omnipotent *vali* and "butcher" of Van, had denied having received such an order and declared that even should he ever receive it, he "would disobey it anyway."[41]

These cases once more dramatically demonstrate the superordinate power of informal authority, controlling and even directing the bearers of formal authority—including those who, though part of the informal authority setup, were caught in a situation where they were lawfully exercising their formal authority. Since the military played a prominent role in the organization of the liquidation of the Armenians, beyond the level of decision-making and authorization discussed in the preceding segments of this study, it is now necessary to examine the respective role of the military under the aegis of and in cooperation with the CC.

The Central Committee's Cooptation of the Military

When detailing the cumbersome prewar negotiations between Armenian political parties and the CUP leadership, Turkish historian Bayur points out their ultimate fruitlessness. According to him, the CUP, weary of negotiation, gradually drifted to the idea of eventually solving the conflict "through recourse to the army" (işi ordu ile görmek).[42] The radical resolution of the protracted Turko-Armenian conflict in the vortex of a raging global war was a very alluring prospect for the CUP. By any definition, wars in general afford optimum opportunity for powerful state entities disposed to seeking radical solutions to lingering intranational or international conflicts. The conditions of warfare in the past tended to allow a potential perpetrator the chance to target particularly a vulnerable victim group, often with maximum force at a minimum risk. The wartime concentration of optimal destructive power in the hands of the military does allow such a performance. Through the crucial intervention of the CUP's CC, the Ottoman Turkish military, especially the Third Army's High Command, proved instrumental for the effective organization of the main part of the Word War I Armenian Genocide. Equally significant is the fact that many high-ranking military officers involved were at the same time committed CUP partisans, and as such were highly politicized taskmasters.

The Third Army's commander in chief, General Mahmut Kâmil, was an ardent CUP ideologue and a close friend of the members of the radical wing of the Central Committee of the CU—that is, Şakir, Nazım, and Ziya Gökalp. He had been appointed to his post by the special intervention of these three men after Enver's original appointment of General Vehip, who as a result of their intervention, ended up being replaced. Kâmil's role was rendered especially important because the military but also civilian jurisdictions of the Third Army encompassed the largest concentration of Ottoman Armenians—that is, those in the provinces of Erzurum, Bitlis, Van, Sivas, Diyarbekir, Harput, and Trabzon. Ahmet Izzet Paşa, the Turkish army commander and later grand vizier, wrote in his postwar memoirs that it was Kâmil who "proposed and demanded" (*teklif ve talep*) the deportation of the Armenians.[43] Here is another scenario of informal authority interceding with the formal authority to effect a statutory change that would prove devastating for the targeted victim population. All three of them had no official position, and yet they prevailed upon a fellow CUP leader in terms of his official position as minister of war and defense. It would be quite implausible to suggest that the replacement of General Vehip with Mahmut Kâmil was normal military business as usual, with three civilians, and party chieftains at that, daring to intervene and ending up effecting the requested replacement.

As a matter of fact, the initiation of the Armenian deportations was directly linked to the seemingly preplanned role of General Mahmut Kâmil. It was he who dispatched a stream of reports from his headquarters at Erzerum alleging Armenian acts of disloyalty. Armed with these reports, Enver, the war minister and deputy commander-in-chief of the Ottoman armed forces, rushed to the CC of the CUP, demanding drastic counter-measures. As Talaat relates in his memoirs, "Enver, who normally has a quiet and calm temperament, came to us, armed with irrevocable proofs, intoning, 'What do we need external enemies for, aren't these ones enough?'"[44] In other words, the outlines of a prearranged and palpably sinister scenario are discernible here. As Pertev, acting commander of the Tenth Army Corps headquartered in Sıvas, reported, "Mahmut Kâmil Paşa has greatest responsibility for the Armenian massacres. He deliberately exaggerated small incidents, blamed the Armenians for the Turkish military debacles. I have in my possession telegrams from him ordering massacres" (Mahmut Kâmil Paşanın Ermenileri imha ediniz diye vermiş emri telegrafları bende mevcutdur).[45] Tahsin, Erzurum's wartime *vali*, provided a similar piece of information when he declared, "Dr. Şakir and IIId Army Commander Mahmut Kâmil are responsible for the Armenian massacres."[46]

Several official German reports confirm and corroborate Kâmil's critical role in the liquidation of the bulk of Turkey's Armenian population. Foremost among these are those of Vice-Consul of Erzurum Scheubner Richter. On 16 May 1915, he singled out Kâmil as the authority ordering the deportation of the region's Armenian population.[47] On 26 June and 28 June 1915 he repeated these accusations, arguing that Kâmil was thereby "sharply intervening" in the handling of this matter.[48] In his lengthy report of 5 August 1915, he underscored the combined exertions of General Kâmil and the CUP, whose "shady agents operating behind the scenes" (*dunkle Komite Hintermänner*) had the upper hand in the matter.[49] Colonel Stange, the only high-ranking German officer on duty in the epicenter of the massacre operations, similarly has identified General Kâmil as an avid organizer of these massacres.[50]

While General Kâmil was directing the field operations in a strategic framework, the tactical details of handling the killer bands were being directed by Colonel (and later, in the Turkish Republic, General) Şevket Seyfi (Düzgören), or Seyfeddin Bey Ben Riza. He was in charge of Department II in the Ottoman

General Headquarters, which was tasked with a whole array of clandestine operations. He too was a political appointee. A graduate of Harbiye's general-staff college and a classmate of War Minister Enver, Seyfi maintained close ties and a very close friendship with him throughout.[51] He actively helped Enver establish the CUP party organization in Rumelia and was consorting with lieutenant Atıf (Kamçıl) when the latter assassinated General Şemsi Paşa, (Birinci Ferik, Orgeneral) on 7 July 1908, thereby ushering in the CUP overthrow of Sultan Abdulhamit's regime. The notorious Special Organization, operating domestically, was under his supervision and control. Osman Bedri, Istanbul's police chief and a co-perpetrator, worked closely with Seyfi, who is reported to have substantially increased his own wealth at the expense of his Armenian victims.[52]

The paramilitary units formed under the name of the Special Organization, which comprised a large number of felons and former convicts, were mostly organized and administered by Seyfi. He was one of the five participants in a top secret decision-making meeting where the fate of the Armenians was reportedly decided.[53] The German military plenipotentiary at the German embassy at Istanbul, Colonel (later Major-General) Otto von Lossow, confirmed Seyfi's involvement in the matter. In a communication to the German General Headquarters dated 16 November 1916, Lossow indicated that Seyfi and his Department II at Ottoman General Headquarters were in charge of the Armenian deportations. As he stated: "He handles this matter and knows exactly about it" (der diese Sachen bearbeitet und genau orientiert ist).[54] Moreover, Colonel Fuat Balkan, one of the top leaders of the Special Organization operating in the Balkans, stated in his memoirs that Seyfi directed the operations of the Special Organization from his office at the General Headquarters.[55] Seyfi's CUP connections had already been exposed during the armistice, when the Turkish daily *Sabah* disclosed that he, in close cooperation with Şakir, mapped the strategy of the massacres to be enacted by the S.O.'s killer bands, the *çete*s, all "under the auspices of the CUP."[56] To the extent that these undertakings were a matter of "domestic policy," their execution devolved upon Department II of the General Headquarters, as stated by General Liman von Sanders, the head of the German Military Mission in Turkey.[57]

General Kâzım Karabekir, who knew Seyfi rather well (he had preceded Seyfi as chief of Department II at General Headquarters), acknowledged Seyfi's powerful position in terms of his close ties to Enver, Talaat, and the CUP's Central Committee, the principal authors of the mass murder under review here.[58]

A Final Comment

It is evident that a host of factors were involved in shaping the genocidal fate of the Armenians. They all deserve attention and analysis. But when it comes to discerning a predominant factor among them, one may argue without hesitation that it was the topic of the Armenian Reforms. This was an issue that had haunted the Abdulhamit monarchy for decades and, as a result, had provoked a sanguinary response entailing the 1894–1896 series of massacres against the Armenians, the intended beneficiaries of these projected reforms. Remarkably, that pattern obtained during the successor CUP regime. Renewed Armenian efforts in Europe—after abysmally repeated failures with reigning CUP authorities—had culminated in the 8 February 1914 Armenian Reform Act that CUP leaders were, one way or another, compelled to sign. Similar pressure exerted by the European powers had impelled Sultan Abdulhamit to finally sign the 11 May 1895 Armenian Reform scheme on 17 October 1895 (the date triggering the series of massacres noted above)—after he had first rebuffed the powers on 3 June 1895.[59]

The CUP's furious reaction to the 1914 Reform Act has already been discussed in another part of this work. That reaction is epitomized by Talaat's repudiation:

> Don't Armenians realize that the implementation of the reforms depends on us; we shall not respond to the proposals the European Inspectors may put forward … the Armenians are trying to create a new Bulgaria. They don't seem to have learned their lessons; all undertakings opposed by us are bound to fail. Let the Armenians wait, opportunities will certainly come our way too. Turkey belongs only to the Turks.[60]

Another member of the omnipotent triumvir, Cemal Paşa, was even more explicit, threatening the Armenians with actual massacres in the event they should succeed in getting the European powers to impose the reforms the Armenians were seeking:

> If you insist on European controls, we shall be obliged to accept them, but in consequence, the Muslim population of those six vilayets will rise in arms, and three hundred to four hundred thousand Armenians will be massacred. And it is likely that the Russians, taking advantage of the situation, will occupy these states.[61]

In his memoirs Cemal elaborated, saying:

> Our sole objective was, to completely free ourselves through this war from all shackles imposed on us … including the reforms projected for our eastern provinces that had resulted from Russia's pressures and coercion.… We entered the war to regain our self-respect.… This being the case, there is no longer a need for such reforms for which we signed the Agreement under the pressure of Russia, our eternal enemy, and which Agreement we wanted to tear up anyhow" (yırtmak istiyorduk).[62]

Enver, the third member of the triumvirate, likewise expressed his ire, when, in an exchange with Hans Humann, German wartime naval attaché in Turkey and "bosom friend" of Enver, he vowed to eliminate any and all grounds on which European powers could intervene for the benefit of the Armenians, the allusion being, of course, to the matter of Armenian Reforms.[63] A whole list of other Turkish authorities echo this overall virulent sentiment against the Armenian Reforms.[64]

The vehemence of the reaction to Armenian reform proposals by both the Sultan Abdulhamit and the CUP is particularly noteworthy because it reveals their reactions as issuing from parallel apprehensions regarding what they all believed to be a much-dreaded inevitable consequence. In other words, it was the projected results of these reforms that actually produced these apprehensions. As recounted by the German ambassador to Istanbul, Prince Von Radolin, Sultan Abdulhamit, during an audience, repeatedly and emphatically declared to him and "most solemnly swore that under no circumstances would he yield to Armenian pressure and grant them extensive reforms," which he was certain would pave the way for subsequent "autonomy." He "would rather die" than yield to such Armenian autonomy, the prospects of which proved to be the recurrent nightmare of Turkish authorities dealing with the "Armenian question."[65]

Moreover, the sultan reiterated this position in two separate memorandums, derogating the designation "reforms" as "phony" reforms, describing them instead as a way station to Armenian "independence." In another such memorandum, the sultan conveyed his fears that the Armenians were intent on establishing a principality (Ermenistan Prensligi), which would result, he wrote, in their "dominating the Muslims." The sultan's solution to all these problems was to play a game that, in Turkish, is called *oyalamak,* "to put off with trumped-up excuses."[66] The same kind of concern, if not apprehension, had gripped the CUP leadership, on whose behalf Talaat, in his memoirs, expressed himself as follows: "I repeatedly pleaded with the Armenians to refrain from seeking the intervention of the Europeans … but to no avail. I was fully cognizant of the fact that the Armenians were actually not seeking reforms but, through the help of the Russians, they were rather pursuing autonomy only to subsequently seek independence."[67]

There is no doubt that the enduring incubus of Turkish apprehension relative to the equally enduring pressure for Armenian reforms relentlessly being exerted by Europe and the leadership of Ottoman Armenians was, in the main, a product of a historical process. It was a process that was punctuated by the steady disintegration of the empire and its attendant dismemberment. Central to this process was again the issue of reforms, put forth and painfully pursued by a host of Balkan nationalities desperately seeking deliverance from the yoke of centuries-old Ottoman subjugation that at times degenerated into bloody oppression, including a series of episodic massacres. However, as Sultan Abdulhamit is reported to have argued, the various countries of the Balkan Peninsula that were under Ottoman dominion were, figuratively speaking, the arms and the legs of the empire, whereas the lands inhabited by the Ottoman Armenians were comparable to the digestive organs of Turkey. The inference intended here is that one can, if forced to, live without legs and arms, but not without one's digestive organs.

Even though the notion of Armenian Reforms denoted a claim to an array of rights denied the Armenians by virtue of the theocratic Islamic underpinnings of the Ottoman Empire, the overriding right that was pursued by them revolved around the principle of equality of rights. However, CUP's formal adoption of this principle in practice proved abortive. And a great deal of the abortiveness of Armenian efforts toward the goal of coming to an equitable understanding with CUP was due to the basic intractability of this problem. The Ottoman Empire, as it was constituted then, was not going to allow space for non-Muslim Armenians to coexist as equals with the overlord Muslim Turks, for the principles of domination and equality were mutually exclusive. While publicly pretending to be still pursuing an egalitarian system, Talaat delivered a speech to a top-secret conclave of CUP potentates gathered in Saloniki for a pre-Congress deliberation on 6 August 1910:

> You are aware that by the terms of the Constitution equality of Mussulman and gâvur [infidel, more often than not a derogatory label applied to non-Muslims] was affirmed but you one and all know and feel that this is an unrealizable ideal. The Sheriat [the religious laws of Islam], our whole past history and the sentiments of hundreds of thousands of Mussulmans and even the sentiments of the gâvurs themselves … present an impenetrable barrier to the establishment of real equality.… There can therefore be no question of equality until we have succeeded in our task of Ottomanizing the Empire.[68]

In commenting on the implied meaning of "Ottomanization," the then British ambassador to Turkey, Gerard Lowther, observed that "to them 'Ottoman' evidently, means 'Turk' and their present policy of 'Ottomanization' is one of pounding the non-Turkish elements in a Turkish mortar."[69]

That "Turkish mortar" was much in evidence when frenzied mobs, supported by military detachments, carried out the twin Adana massacres of 1909.[70] More important, these massacres proved to be the nexus connecting these two episodes of organized mass murder. The distinguished Ottoman-Turkish parliamentary leader and subsequently CUP's foreign minister, Halil Menteşe, did not hesitate to describe these atrocities as "eliminational" (*temizleme*) operations.[71]

As described in the preceding chapter, Talaat had formally announced, via the issuance of a memorandum, the start of empire-wide deportations of the

Armenians, even though some deportations had already been effected in some parts of the Empire. In the memorandum he tried to explain the reasons for this radical measure, namely that "A problem that is of vital importance for the Ottoman State will thereby be completely solved." The word he used was *külliyen*, which alternatively can mean "totally" or "radically."[72] As Tunaya observes, it being a comprehensive governmental decision, "this order for deportation should have been issued by the Cabinet as a whole. Instead, however, it was issued à la Ittihad, by a single Minister."[73] It is noteworthy that, barring one or two exceptions, this particular segment of Talaat's memo has been excised in the works of most other Turkish historians exploring that memo, noted Turkish historian Bayur included.[74] About one year after issuing this memo, when the eliminational operations were winding down, Talaat declared in a confidential yet revelatory cipher, "The Armenian question has been finally solved," using the Turkish words *surety kat'iye* to mean "finally."[75]

It is often believed that only the victims of a crime can, as a rule, feel the degree of the pain that is commensurate with the gravity of the crime. By the same token, one may maintain that the graver a crime is, the more intense the ensuing pain becomes. As they inevitably end up perishing, victims of genocide do not carry this pain into the future. However, the survivor-generations, generally speaking, cannot escape that experience—at several levels and in different degrees. Beyond all this, however, there are circumstances when exceptional people, total outsiders, may rise to such a level of commiseration that the animus of the powerful impulses of sympathy and empathy may propel them to extraordinary initiatives of vindication. Such was the case of world-renowned British statesman Winston Churchill with respect to the Armenian experience under review here. As he combined in his mind the Armenian experience with that of British combatants who were wantonly killed by their Turkish captors at the Dardanelles during the same war, he decided to embark on a drastically punitive initiative. His recognition of the gravity of the crime against the Armenians is framed as follows:

> In 1915 the Turkish Government began and ruthlessly carried out ... in accord with deliberate policy ... the infamous general massacre and deportation of Armenians ... the clearance of a race from Asia Minor was about as complete as such an act, on a scale so great, could well be.... There is no reasonable doubt that this crime was planned and executed for political reasons. The opportunity presented itself for clearing Turkish soil of a Christian race opposed to all Turkish ambitions ... and planted geographically between Turkish and Caucasian Moslems.[76]

Conceivably still under the spell of this decrial of the ongoing crime, which he characterized as "the infamous general massacre" and which today would be readily termed "genocide," Churchill ventured to make a bold and ominous proposal to the War Cabinet to punish the Turks. He proposed to use poison gas against them at the Dardanelles. As the eminent chronicler of these events Martin Gilbert narrates, on 20 October 1915 Churchill sent the War Cabinet "a proposal to use mustard gas in a final attempt to break through the Turkish defenses" in retaliation "for the massacre of Armenians as well as the killing of many British soldiers after they had tried to surrender." Churchill hoped "that the unreasonable prejudice against the use by us of gas upon the Turks will cease." Large installations of gas should be sent to Gallipoli "without delay."[77] But, Turkey being a Muslim country, Secretary of State for War Horatio Herbert Kitchener on the one hand, and Secretary of State for India First Marquess of Crewe, on the other, objected "in the interest of the Moslems in India and Egypt."[78]

Churchill's agility in combining political statesmanship with humanitarian impulses was evident even decades before the 1915 Armenian catastrophe when the Abdulhamit–era massacres (1894–1896) against the same victim population were raging throughout the Ottoman Empire. Newly arrived in India with his regiment, and mindful of the incidence of these massacres, he declared on 25 October 1896:

> We cannot continue to allow horrible outrages to be perpetrated under our nose … the only course open is to allow someone else to put a stop to an impossible state of things.[79]

Namely, he wanted Russia to protect the victim population, the Armenians.

Notes

1. *Talat Paşa'nın Hatıraları*, ed. Enver Bolayır (Istanbul: Güven, 1946).
2. Yusuf H. Bayur, *Türk Inkilâbı Tarihi* (Ankara: Türk Tarif, Kurumu, 1952). In vol. 2, part 4; examples are: "not corresponding to truth," p. 646; "concealed the truth," p. 647; "a fabricated claim," p. 652. In vol. 3, part 4 (1989), "unmitigated lie" (*pervasızca yalan*) p.776; "the very opposite of the truth," pp. 776–777.
3. Falih Rıfkı Atay, his prewar secretary, called him "a liar, a deceiver" (*yalan, aldatıcı*): *Zeytindağı*, pp. 24, 25; historian Ismail Hami Danişmend wrote, "his reputation as a liar has expanded" (yalancılık şöhreti … genişlemiştir), *Izahlı Osmanlı*, p. 448. A newspaper editor: "Talaat lied like a machine," *Sabah*, 2 (15) May 1919. In an editorial, the renowned public figure, writer, and *vali* of several provinces, Süleyman Nazıf, wrote, "Talaat had no other talent than just being tricky [*hile*]," *Hadisat*, 5 November 1918; Galip Vardar, *Ittihad ve Terakki Içinde Dönenler*, ed. S. N. Tansu (Istanbul: Inkilâp, 1960), pp. 122–123 refers to "Talaat's big lie."
4. *Peyami-Sabah*, 21 March 1921, written upon the news that Talaat was assassinated in Berlin.
5. In responding to Talaat's criticism of the "illegality" of the court-martial proceedings that had prosecuted him and the rest of the CUP clique, Velit retorted sharply. For someone whose clique "never abided by the law and, whenever annoyed, enacted a

new provisional law each and every day," observed Velit, it is unconscionable to speak of the need for law and lawful behavior. Arif Cemil, *Ittihatçı Şeflerin Gurbet Maceraları*, ed. Yücel Demirel (Istanbul: Arma, 1992), pp. 109–110. On pp. 117–118 the same author, in footnotes again, exposes the deceptions by virtue of which the CUP leadership plunged Turkey into the war, at the same time indicating their method of double-track, i.e., open and public vs. covert and secret, policies.

6. Bernard Lewis, *The Emergence of Modern Turkey* (London: Oxford University Press, 1962), p. 222.
7. A.A. Politische Abteilung III/ Türkei P.O. 11, no. 3, vol. 1, Chief of Public Security Weismann's 21 May 1921 report.
8. Istanbul's daily press, reporting in Turkish, Armenian, and French.
9. Talaat, *Talat Paşa'nın* [n. 1], p. 74; Osman S. Kocahanoğlu, *Ittihad Terakki'nin Sorgulanması ve Yargılanması* (Istanbul: Temel, 1998), pp. 104–105 for Sait Halim's, and p. 156 for Justice Minister Ibrahim's testimony on this investigation.
10. Armenian Patriarchate; Series 16, File H. nos. 37–38.
11. Ahmed E. Yalman, *Turkey in the World War* (New Haven: Yale University Press, 1930), p. 221.
12. Şevket Süreyya Aydemir, *Tek Adam Mustafa Kemal 1881–1919*, vol. 1 (Istanbul: Remzi, 1963), p. 211. Speaking of Talaat's memoirs, his widow Hayriye Hanım stated years later that her husband had "sold" his memoirs in Berlin. "Eşi Hayriye Hanım Talaat Paşayı Anlatıyor" *Yakın Tarihimiz* 2 (1962): 194.
13. The German consul in Adana branded Talaat's denials as "brazen-faced deception" (*dreiste Täuschung*) Türkei 183/38, A27578 or Botschaft Konstantinopel 170, no. 5263, 10 September 1915, Büge report. The German Mossul consul for his part condemned the denials as "blatant lies" (*krasse Lügen*). 170, No. 24 [4729], 14 August 1915, Holstein report. Finally, the German Aleppo consul, responding to the same denials, exclaimed, "Indeed, I could not trust my eyes as I read this declaration of denial, and I find no expression to characterize this abysmal untruth" (Fürwahr ich habe meinen Augen nicht getraut…) A.A. Türkei 183/38, A23991, or, R14087, K. no. 81/B, 1645, 27 July 1915, Rössler report.
14. For the details of governor Tahsin's futile intercession on behalf of the Armenians see note Chapter 2, note 116 in this volume; for the deletion in the cipher regarding Diyarbekir Armenians see p. 221 in Gürün's original Turkish text, and p. 212, in the English version of the same. The full text of the Diyarbekir cipher is in the Prime Minister's General Directorate for Archives.
15. Bayur, *Türk Inkilâbı* [n. 2], vol. 3, part 1 (1953), pp. 241, 248–249.
16. Ibid., vol. 3, part 2 (1955), p. 398.
17. Ibid., vol. 3, part 1 (1953), p. 63; vol. 3, part 2 (1955), p. 398; vol. 2, part 4 (1952), p. 647.
18. Ibid., vol. 3, part 1 (1953), pp. 244.
19. Ibid., p. 63. Cemal in this respect was joined by Cavit, both of them being somewhat pro-French.
20. Ibid., pp. 244–245, 247, 251. When rationalizing this obdurate clinging to his post, S. Halim averred that he was preventing incompetent people from replacing him and thereby sparing the country the risks of greater dangers. Kocahanoğlu, *Ittihad Terakki'nin*, 59–60. In the first volume of his memoirs, General Ali Ihsan Sabis likewise describes him as a vain weakling, acting cockily toward gentle people but meekly to-

ward CUP chieftains, always eager to be venerated but easily getting confused in face of emergencies. *Harp Hatıralarım* v. 1 (Istanbul: Inkilâb, 1943), p. 48.

21. Bayur [n. 18], pp. 159, 160, 205, 206.
22. Ibid., pp. 64, 376, 420.
23. Bayur [n. 2], p. 658; the legal expert is Professor Reşat Kaynar, *Türkiye'de Hukuk Devleti Kurma Yolundaki Hareketler* (Istanbul: Tan, 1960), p. 154.
24. Bayur, *Türk Inkilâbı* [n. 2], v. 3, part 2, p. 398.
25. FO 371/6500/E3557, 214-215, Turkey Desk at FO.
26. Cemal Kutay, *Talat Paşa'nın Gurbet Hatıraları,* vol 2 (Istanbul: Kültür, 1983), p. 907.
27. Arif Cemil, *Ittihatçı Şeflerin Gurbet Maceraları* (Istanbul: Arba, 1977), p. 142. Cemil uses the word *ihzar,* meaning "to prepare," to indicate the origin of the draft law. Humann, the German naval attaché and a close friend of Enver, personally confirmed this fact to US Ambassador Morgenthau, who recorded it in his book, *Ambassador Morgenthau's Story* (New York: Doubleday, 1918), p. 376.
28. Kutay, *Talat Paşa'nın* [n. 26], p. 907.
29. Bayur, *Türk Inkilâbı* [n. 2], part 3, p. 38.
30. The text of the formal Temporary Law of Deportation was published in the 19 May (1 June) 1915 issue of *Takvim-i Vekâyi,* no. 2189. Both the executive and legislative authorities of defeated Turkey decided during the armistice, however, to shelve (ref) this temporary law, with Tokat's deputy Tahsin Riza arguing that it was in any event in conflict with Article 36 of the Constitution. The proposal came from then Interior Minister Fethi (Okyar). *Meclisi Mebusan Zabıt Ceridesi,* 4 November 1918, 11th sitting, p. 114.
31. Tunaya, *Türkiye'de Siyasal Partiler,* v. 3 (Istanbul: Hürriyet, 1989), p. 579.
32. "The Ottoman Constitution," 372. During the interrogation conducted by the Fifth Department of Investigation of the Chamber of Deputies some members of the panel confirmed and others denied that the temporary law in question ever came up for consideration in the chamber itself. Kocahanoğlu, *Ittihad Terakki'nin* [n. 9], pp. 194–195. In fact it never was brought there.
33. Bayur, *Türk Inkilâbı* [n. 2], v. III, part 3, p. 47. According to the detailed account of this episode by a contemporary, Deputy Vartkes, who was still exempt from the general deportation due to his parliamentary immunity, sought from Talaat an explanation for his radical anti-Armenian measures. "During the Balkan war the Armenians acted against us while we were weak. As we are presently strong, we shall inflict upon the Armenians such a blow that they won't be able to recover for fifty years," Talaat reportedly retorted. On another occasion Talaat is said to have warned Vartkes "not to act so smug thinking that he is immune from trouble because of his parliamentary status." Dzeroug, "Dzerougee Housheru," *Djagadamard,* 2 March 1919, p. 1.
34. Erik J. Zürcher, *Turkey: A Modern History,* London, I.B. Tauris, 1998, pp. 10, 106, 115–116.
35. A.A., Türkei, 183/43, Botschaft Konstantinopel 172, no. 93, 30 June 1916.
36. Zürcher, *Turkey* [n. 34], p. 121
37. Arif Baytın, *Ilk Dünya Harbinde Kafkas Caphesi* (Istanbul: Vakıt, 1946), pp. 50–51. The author, who was the commander of the 29th Division of the Ninth Army Corps, bitterly complains about Şakir's meddling in military affairs but grants his "great influence" (*tesiri azimi*) in the Ottoman capital. Evidently Şakir was pushing for a precipitate initiation of an offensive against the Russians in the Caucasus.

38. A.A. *Der Weltkrieg,* no.11d secr. vol. 9, A37451. Germany's liaison officer for the Caucasus operation, Count Friedrich W. Schulenburg's 28 November 1915, no. 6 report, pp. 4–5, folio 116.
39. Ibid., Türkei 183/43, A16479. R14092, June 21, 1916.
40. Ibid., Grosses Hauptquartier 194, Türkei 41/1, 2 July 1916, no. 763.
41. Ibid., Türkei 183/43, A16607, R14092, no. 304, 22 June 1916.
42. Bayur, *Türk Inkilâbı* [n. 2], vol. 2, part 4 (1952), p. 13. In his 6 August 1910 top-secret speech in Saloniki, Talaat reassured the party potentates that "the army is solidly ranged in our support." See note 68 below.
43. Ahmet Izzet Paşa, *Feryadım,* v. 1 (Istanbul: Nehir, 1992), p. 201. In the second volume of his memoirs, General Ali Ihsan Sabis, World War I Turkish army commander, confirms the decisive role of the CUP leaders cited above in securing Kâmil's appointment as commander-in-chief of the Third Army. See chap. 10, n. 37.
44. Kutay, *Talat Paşa'nın* [n. 26], vol. 2, p. 907.
45. Armenian Partriarchate Archives, Series 22, File H, no. 149.
46. *Tasviri Efkâr,* 11 February 1919. In touching on the political nature of Kâmil's appointment, Major Rafael de Nogales, a South American volunteer enrolled in the wartime Turkish army, dismissed Kâmil as "a nullity of nullities" as far as military competence was concerned. *Four Years Beneath the Crescent,* trans. Muna Lee (New York: Scribner's, 1926), p. 46.
47. A.A., Botschaft Konstantinopel 168, no. 3007.
48. Ibid.,169, no. 47, folio 110; 170, J. no. 552.
49. Ibid., Türkei 183/39, A28584, R14088, J. no. 580, "Secret report."
50. Ibid., Türkei, Botschaft Konstantinopel 170, J. no. 3841, 23 August 1915, "secret" report in which Stange underscored Kâmil's "pushy and ruthless" campaign (*rücksichtslose Beschleunigung*) in this respect. German ambassador Metternich for his part confirmed Kâmil's role. Botschaft Konstantinopel 99, no. 2934, January 1916.
51. Şerket S. Aydemir, *Enver Paşa,* vol. 3 (Istanbul: Remzi, 1972), p. 613.
52. Armenian Patriarchate Archives, Series 10, File T., nos. 605–606.
53. Vahakn N. Dadrian, *History of the Armenian Genocide* (New York, Oxford: Berghahn, 2003), pp. 218, 220, 229, n. 5.
54. A.A., Botschaft Konstantinopel 174, no. 10105, A3351, A53.
55. *Yakın Tarihimiz,* vol. 2 (1962): 287.
56. Excerpting this news item from the Turkish newspaper, *Sabah. Ariamard* (namesake of Dashnak newspaper, *Djagadamard*) in its 13 December 1918 issue published that information).
57. Christoph Dinkel, "German Officers and the Armenian Genocide," *Armenian Review,* vol. 44 (Spring 1991): 91.
58. Kâzım Karabekir, *Birinci Cihan Harbine Nasıl Girdik?* vol. 2 (Istanbul: Emre Publications, 1994), p. 246. Seyfi's ties to CUP's CC are noted on p. 246. However, on p. 279 Karabekir indicates that this same CC of CUP was partly identified with the Special Organization. Seyfi was arrested late in January 1919 along with General Mahmut Kâmil Paşa and Istanbul's Military Commandant Colonel Cevat, both deeply implicated in the organization of the exterminatory campaign against the Armenians. FO 371/4174, folio 151; FO 608/247, folio 77. At one time during the war Colonel Cevat was reprimanded by War Minister Enver for allowing himself to be used as a tool by Talaat. In no uncertain terms, Enver told him, "The army must be free of politics. A

soldier is either a soldier or is a politician; in the latter case he must sever ties with the army." Sadi Borak, *Iktidar Koltuğundan Idam Sehpasına* (Istanbul: Yeni Matbaa, 1962), p. 59. Like Seyfi, Cevat eventually joined the Kemalists and occupied the post of director of the Legal Department of the National Defense Ministry (Milli Müdafaa Mahakim Şubesi Müdürü).

59. Dadrian, *History of the Armenian Genocide* [n. 53], p. 152.
60. Keğam Der Garabedian, "Kegham Der Garabetianee Vugayutiunu," in *Badmoutiun Daronee Achkharee,* ed. Garo Sassouni (Beirut: Sevan, 1956), pp. 838–839. Keğam was a deputy in the Ottoman Chamber of Deputies, representing Muş, the heartland of historical Armenia. He wrote these lines shortly before his death in 1918. His being sick in bed served to protect him from the fate befalling the other two Armenian deputies, i.e., Zohrab and Vartkes.
61. Armen Garo, *Bank Ottoman Memoirs,* trans. H. T. Partizian (Detroit: A.T. Publisher, 1990), p. 184 (the original book was titled *Abruadz Orer* [Boston, 1948]). The author was himself a one-time deputy in the Ottoman parliament. Cemal reportedly conveyed his threat to the Dashnak leadership.
62. Cemal Paşa, *Hatıralar* (Istanbul: Çağdaş, 1997), p. 438.
63. A.A., Botschaft Konstantinopel 170, folio 52, 6 August 1915.
64. See Dadrian, *History of the Armenian Genocide* [n. 53], pp. 207–209, 213–216.
65. *Die grosse Politik der Europäischen Kabinette 1871–1914,* vol. 9: *Der Nahe und Ferne Osten* (Berlin: 1927), doc. No. 2184, 16 November 1884 report, pp. 202–203.
66. Mehmet Hocaoğlu, *Abdülhamit Han'ın Muhtıraları: Belgeler* [Abdulhamit's memoranda: Documents] (Istanbul: Türkiyat, 1989), pp. 169, 170, 237.
67. *Talat Paşa'nın* [n. 1], pp. 49, 55. An identical view is found in the analysis of General Kâzım Karabekir. See his *Ittihat ve Terakki Cemiyeti 1896–1909* (Istanbul: Private publication, 1982), p. 468.
68. *British Documents on the Origins of the War 1897–1914,* ed. Gooch and Temperley (London, 1926), vol. 9, part 1, p. 208. Confirmation of the speech is in Austrian Vice Consul von Zitkovsky's No. 69 "secret" report of 14 October 1910, in A.A. Türkei, 159 No. 2 Bd. 12, A18643. French confirmation is in N.S. Turquie, 7:92–97. A particular additional phrase in this French version, not found in the British report, is Talaat's proposal to lull the potential victims of the Ottomanization program to complacency: "il faut que nous tranquillisions nos voisins." This report is stamped "received" by the Direction Politique et Commerciale of the French Foreign Ministry, bearing the symbols D, Carton 391, and the date 6 August 1910, thus indicating that it was wired the very same day on which the speech was delivered.
69. *British Documents on the Origins of the War 1889–1914* [n. 68], doc. No. 181, 6 September 1910.
70. When compared to the antecedent Abdulhamit–era massacres (in the 1894–1896 period) and the subsequent World War I genocide, the ghastliness and savagery of the Adana holocaust emerges as unmatched. Even though popular Armenian sources keep referring to 30,000 as the toll of these twin massacres, Hagop Babikyan, whom the Ottoman government had dispatched along with fellow Deputy Yusuf Kemal (Tengirşek) to investigate and prepare a report about these massacres, came up with the figure 21,000, specifying 19,479 as the actual number of Armenian victims. Though unable to speak or read Armenian, Babikyan was much respected by his Turkish colleagues as an upright and decent man. Prior to his service as a parliamentary deputy, he func-

tioned as an appeals court judge in Edirne. Before he was able to submit his report on his investigation in Adana, however, he died suddenly under mysterious circumstances. His report therefore could not be transmitted to the parliament as planned.

71. Halil Menteşe, *Halil Menteşe' nin Anıları* (Istanbul: Hürriyet Vakfı, 1986), pp. 236–237. Three times he served as president of the Chamber of Deputies, and from 24 October 1915 to 4 February 1917, he served as foreign minister. When Talaat was elevated to the rank of Sadrazam, Halil, his very close friend, was appointed chief of the Council of State. The term "eliminational," meaning radical cleansing or liquidation, was repeatedly used by US Ambassador Morgenthau as well. Morgenthau, in *Ambassador Morgenthau's Story* [n. 27], called it "The Murder of a Nation," p. 301; in file no. 867.4016/74, 16 July 1915 report, he called it a "campaign of race extermination"; and in file no. 867. 4016/117 on 3 September 1915 he told Washington, "Destruction of the Armenian race in Turkey is progressing rapidly."
72. *Ati (Ileri)*, 24 February 1920 issue, p. 5.
73. Tarık Zafer Tunaya, *Türkiye'de Siyasal Partiler,* v. 2, part 4 (Ankara: Turkish Historical Society, 1952), p. 658.
74. Bayur, *Türk Inkilâbı* [n. 2], vol. 3, part 3 (1957), pp. 40–41.
75. BOA (Başbakanlık Osmanlı Arşivi) Prime Ministry's Archive DH, ŞFR (Cipher Office), 54.426, 13 July 1915.
76. Winston S. Churchill, *The World Crisis: The Aftermath,* vol. 5 (London: T. Butterworth, 1929), p. 405.
77. Martin Gilbert, *Churchill: A Life* (New York: Henry Holt, 1991), p. 327.
78. Martin Gilbert, *Winston S. Churchill,* vol. 3: *1914–1916: The Challenge of War* (Boston: Houghton Mifflin, 1971), p. 195, and *Companion,* vol. 3, part 2, "May 1915–December 1916" (1973), pp. 1230–1231. In fact, some four months earlier, i.e., 26 May 1915, the last day he was officiating as Lord of the Admiralty, Churchill told Lord Kitchener, "You ought to send *at once* [italics in the original] to the Dardanelles the best helmets and the best gas-making outfit you have." Gilbert, *Winston S. Churchill,* vol. 3 (1971), p. 470. It is worth reiterating in this connection the very significant fact that, as noted in the latter part of the chapter's introduction, two days earlier on 24 May the Allies had issued an official and public warning to Ottoman Turkey, then a member of the opposing Entente, in which Turkey was threatened with retaliatory punishment for "again" committing massacres against the Armenians. Vahakn N. Dadrian, "Genocide as a Problem of National and International Law," 262.
79. Churchill Winston S. Autograph letter signed to Sir Algernon West, Bangalore (India), 25 October 1896. 5pp. folio. Provenance: L.C.R. Collection; Sotheby's 24 July 1987, Lot 300, Books and Manuscripts Depd.

CHAPTER 9

The Judicial Liquidation of Some of the Arch Perpetrators by Both CUP and Kemalist Authorities, and the Demise of Other Accomplices

Vahakn N. Dadrian

The existing literature on the Armenian Genocide makes but scant reference to the array of methods of retribution variously applied against many of the principal perpetrators of this wartime mass murder. One of the main reasons for this was the embarrassment and anxiety that the proceedings of the post-war Turkish courts-martial prosecuting the authors of the genocide produced throughout Turkey. Only grudgingly had the Turkish authorities agreed to institute these criminal proceedings. These trepidations were offset, however, by the expectation that in return for this prosecutorial effort, militarily defeated Turkey might be treated less harshly at the projected peace treaty negotiations. This was a stipulation the victors had repeatedly made when broaching the subject publicly.

In line with this consideration, the Military Tribunal did, in fact, decide to execute three middle level civil servants to accommodate the general public's clamor for punitive justice. Those executed for the mass murder of the Armenians were: (1) Mehmet Kemal, County Executive (kaymakam) of Boğazlıyan, and during the massacres, Deputy District Commissioner (mutasarrıf) of Yozgat. (*Takvim-i Vekâyi*, no. 3617, 7 August 1919); (2) Abdullah Avni, nicknamed Hayran Baba, who was in charge of the Erzincan gendarmerie. He was the brother of Abdülgani, a prominent Ittihadist and the Responsible Secretary of Edirne. (*Takvim-i Vekâyi*, no. 3917, 27 July 1920, pp. 5–6); and (3) Behramzade Nusret, Bayburt County Executive, later District Commissioner of Ergani, and subsequently of Urfa. (*Takvim-i Vekâyi*, no. 3924, 6 August 1920). After the debacle of the Damad Ferit regime and the ascendancy of Kemalism, the military appeals court overturned Nusret's 20 July 1920 Verdict on 7 January 1921. Both Kemal and Nusret were then declared "national martyrs" (*milli şehid*): Jaeschke and Pritsch, "Beiträge zur Geschichte des Kampfes der Türkei um ihre Unabhängigkeit," *Die Welt Des Islams* 5, no. 1–2 N.S. (1958): 16. On

25 December 1920, the Ankara regime allocated a pension for Nusret's family. For more details on this matter see Chapter 5, "Emergent Kemalism and the Courts-Martial, notes 23, 24, and 25."

Moreover, the brief postwar period, during which several fugitive CUP chieftains were tracked down, one by one, and assassinated by Armenian "avengers" is still shrouded in mystery and attendant secrecy. The Armenian Revolutionary Federation or ARF—otherwise known as the Dashnaks—which masterminded these "punitive" operations, offered only scant details about them. The circumstances under which these chieftains were assassinated are described in the individual memoirs of the assassins themselves. Among the victims were Interior Minister and subsequently Grand Vizier (Prime Minister) Mehmet Talaat, Trabzon province's Governor-General Cemal Azmi, Grand Vizier Sait Halim (Talaat's predecessor in that post), and other lesser perpetrators. These memoirs are, however, often embellished accounts in which the "heroic" saga of the assassin is counter posed to the characterization of the victim as "criminal." Common to the emotional world of all these targeted CUP leaders in the postwar period were pervasive fears resulting from their having become hunted and marked men, fears that haunted them until they died—whether on the scaffold or by bullets, heart failure, or stroke.

There was, however, another category of perpetrators whose elimination thus far escaped general attention. It included brigand chiefs—the so-called *çetebaşıs*—and their cohorts, who wrought havoc with the Armenian deportee convoys through resort to types of atrocities that were unprecedented in Ottoman-Turkish history. This was mainly due to the fact that a large proportion of these brigands were carefully selected bloodthirsty criminals. By specially arranged legal dispensations they were released from the various prisons of the Ottoman Empire for this particular task. Then there were the organizational taskmasters, the so-called CUP *comisars,* who streamlined the details of the murderous operations. Some of them were executed by the Kemalists during the 1926 trials, despite the fact that they had given impetus to and supported the 1920–1922 Kemalist liberation movement.

The Trial, Conviction, and Execution of Top CUP Leaders by the Kemalists

Without exception, all the defendants in question were prominent Ittihadist, i.e., CUP leaders, and almost all of them had played important roles in the organization of the genocide. The series of the trials were divided into various segments of court proceedings. The venue for the first series was Izmir, where the main charge was conspiracy to assassinate Mustafa Kemal; the winding up of the series took place, however, in Ankara, where the principal charge was conspiracy to subvert the constitution and overthrow the government, which by implication was the charge of scheming to install the now defunct CUP regime. The first series started in Izmir on 26 May 1926 and ended on the day of the verdict, 13 July 1926. On that day fifteen conspirators were condemned to death, and seven of them were hanged the same day at midnight. Of these, three had been involved in the organization of the Armenian Genocide, with two of them having played key roles, namely, Ahmet Şükrü and Ismail Canbolat; the other was Halis Turgut.

The second series, in continuation of the first, started at Ankara on 2 August 1926 and ended on 26 August 1926. It was set aside for the purpose of targeting a group of four top CUP leaders, three of whom had played rather principal roles in the organization of the genocide. They were Mehmet Nazım, Filibeli Mustafa Hilmi, and Yenibahçeli Nail. The fourth was ex–Finance Minister Mehmet Cavit, whose role in the overall scheme of the crime of genocide was negligible, if any. The four were executed on the gallows at 10:00 P.M. the same night the trials ended.

Halis Turgut was a leading CUP man. When volunteering his services to the Kemalists in the armistice period, he intoned: "First and foremost I am an Ittihadist [i.e., a CUP man]; only secondarily I am a Turkist. Before you enlist me for your cause, I would like you to know about my priorities." He then joined the Kemalist movement and was rewarded for the services he rendered with a deputyship in the Kemalist Grand National Assembly in 1923. During World War I he served in Erzincan's Reserve Officers Training Camp, where many Armenian cadets were murdered as part of the functions of the Special Organization, to whose command structure he belonged; he later served on the Caucasus front. As attested by several Turkish sources, he escaped after the war to the mountains in the area of Sivas in order to avoid prosecution by the Turkish Military Tribunal, which had issued an arrest warrant for him. He was accused of complicity in the Armenian deportations and massacres.[1]

Ahmet Şükrü, wartime minister of education and a fanatical Ittihadist who steadfastly denied his role as a key conspirator, was an arch foe of the Armenians. He was hanged twice, as the rope on his neck snapped at the first attempt at execution; he collapsed on the floor half-dead and later expired on the gallows, emitting death-rattle sounds. Having helped send tens of thousands of unoffending Armenian peasants to their gruesome deaths, he nevertheless could not help, upon seeing the gallows on his way to execution, being terrified enough to cry out in terror, "Vah! Vah!"[2]

Ismail Canbolat, a Circassian by ethnic origin and Talaat's right-hand man, was in charge of the empire's Public Security Office (Emniyeti Umumiye) and was the prefect of the Ottoman capital when the Armenian deportations and massacres were being organized. A graduate of the War Staff College, he emerged as one of the original cofounders of the CUP in Salonika and became implicated in a pro-CUP terrorist campaign. After the war he became a deputy in the Kemalist Grand National Assembly. He too protested his innocence, maintaining: "I am a man of law and justice. How can I be bloodthirsty?" When rejecting this claim of innocence, the attorney general stated that in nature and in purpose, Canbolat's crime could not be separated from that of Şükrü.[3]

Those executed in Ankara were:

1. Dr. Mehmet Nazım, a key figure in the supreme and all-powerful Central Committee of CUP, who along with his cohort Dr. Bahaeddin Şakir was in fact the brain trust in the overall scheme of the wartime mass murder. He studiously operated behind the scenes and exerted near-omnipotent influence in the councils of the party leadership, which included Talaat himself—particularly in the matter of the wartime handling of the Armenians. When trying to defend himself, he declared, "I was concerned only with supporting my family.... As a matter of principle I have always been against unlawful acts [*gayrı meşru*]." He approached the gallows in a state of shock, and he was shaking as he protested his innocence with the exclamation "I swear, yes I swear" (*vallahi, vallahi*).[4]
2. Yenibahçeli Nail was the CUP's responsible secretary for the province of Trabzon and as such the omnipotent executioner of that province's Armenian population; for that purpose he worked in tandem with the governor-general of the province, Cemal Azmi, another omnipotent and notorious executioner. Nail admitted that he was the station chief of Trabzon's Special Organization and a close friend of Abdulkadir, a fellow arch perpetrator of massacres in Trabzon province, especially in Gümüşhane, a district in that province. With inexorable zeal he destroyed that population by recourse to two methods: massacre and mass drowning in the Black Sea. But on the gallows, Nail pleaded with his son to take good care of his mother and siblings as he too protested his innocence. He asserted that he was "a man of conscience" and that he "cannot bequeath to his children and grandchildren a legacy of "stain."[5]
3. Filibeli Mustafa Hilmi had the title of the CUP's inspector, two degrees higher in rank than responsible secretary; interposed between the two ranks was that of delegate, in the hierarchy of the CUP's omnipotent *comisars*. Hilmi served as Dr. Bahaeddin Şakir's lieutenant and field commander of operations throughout the massacres in the eastern part of the empire. Like Nail, he had a military background and was an ardent Ittihadist with strong loyalties to Enver Paşa. As in the case of Ahmet Şükrü, Hilmi fell from the gallows as the rope snapped during the execution, and he too was hanged a second time.[6]
4. Abdülkadir Ayıntablı, one of the principal conspirators in the plot to assassinate Mustafa Kemal, whose friend he was from the days of their

> military duties in Saloniki, was able to remain a fugitive from justice until 22 August 1926. On that day he was apprehended as he was about to escape to Greece near the border, and after a brief appearance before the Independence Court that convened in Istanbul, he was retried, convicted, and sentenced to death by hanging. The verdict was carried out on the night of 1 September 1926. Approximately thirty people were arrested and charged with aiding and abetting his effort to remain a fugitive in hiding. Abdülkadir was known to have actively participated in the massacre of the Armenians of Trabzon province in his capacity as wartime governor of the district of Gümüşhane, located in the same province.[7] An Armenian survivor stated that Abdülkadir personally led the slaughter of the male members of the deportee convoys with a scythe in his hand.[8]

The summary liquidation of the opponents of Mustafa Kemal was not much different from the many purges the Ittihadists themselves had resorted to in order to deal with their own rivals and antagonists. The Independence Tribunal judges behaved like bullies, denying the defendants all standard procedures of legal defense such as access to defense counsel, the right to call witnesses, and the right of appeal. The prosecutor did not even try to sift, check, and ascertain the evidence. The defendants were presumed guilty unless they were able to prove themselves innocent. As Kılıç Ali, one of the judges, grudgingly acknowledged, the Independence Tribunal was decried by many people as the "Tribunal of Terror," with Kinross, the British biographer of Atatürk, declaring that the "reign of terror" was consummated and "Kemal's dirty work was done."[9]

The career of the Independence Court was intimately connected with an initial campaign against the sultan's "fifth column," against AWOLs among the soldiers of the emergent Kemalist army, and against "traitors." After considerable debate in the Grand National Assembly, it was decided to institute a special kind of tribunal that would be free from "the weaknesses" of regular as well as military tribunals—for the sake of swift, inexorable, and appeal-free punitive justice. The enactment in March 1925 of the Law for the Maintenance of Order (Takriri Sükûn kanunu) would serve this purpose. In other words, the tribunal to be constituted would be vested with inordinate and exceedingly broad powers. As one member of the tribunal's staff declared:

> The Independence Tribunal was, next to the Grand National Assembly and the army, the most important institution, for one can say without exaggeration that each one of these Tribunals acted like a Grand National Assembly itself, indeed, acted like a dictator. Operating simultaneously as a legislative, judicial and in many respects as an executive body, the judges, hand picked by Mustafa Kemal, nonchalantly issued orders to

> the military or civilian authorities of the State. In cases of disobedience they had the requisite competence to arrest and prosecute the offenders. Their verdicts were final and decisive and their execution could occur immediately without needing the approval of the Parliament.[10]

In brief, the trials enabled the cofounder of the modern Republic of Turkey to attain three principal objectives: to eliminate once and for all opposition that threatened his leadership and autocratic leanings, to settle old scores—especially with Dr. Nazım, who often tried to denigrate him with such puns as calling him "Gazoz [instead of Gazi] Paşa," meaning soda pop—and to administer summary justice to a handful of deadly conspirators. In doing so, however, he also ended up administering punitive justice against some of the most prominent authors of the Armenian Genocide. It is significant to note here that six years earlier, when denouncing the top Ittihadist leaders and commenting on their prosecution by the Turkish Military Tribunal, Mustafa Kemal was reported to have shouted angrily, "Why are the Allies putting off the act of having all these rascals hanged?"[11]

The Execution of Some Brigand Chiefs by CUP Authorities

Foremost among the brigand chiefs active in the Armenian Genocide were two *fedayi* ex-officers who, with uncommon ferocity, devastated large areas by inflicting wholesale massacres upon these areas' Armenian populations.

Serezli Çerkez Ahmet, a major and subsequently a colonel, was one of those CUP *fedayi*s who resigned from the military to carry out the CUP's secret criminal missions, which supposedly reflected unconditional party loyalty and patriotism. His pre-genocide record of political assassinations rendered him an invaluable CUP asset for the task of subsequent genocidal massacres against the targeted Armenians. He played a major role in the extermination of the bulk of the Armenian population of Van province. Subsequently he moved to the areas of Urfa, Diyarbekir, and Aleppo to continue—together with his cohorts, Halil and Mustafa Nazım—his murderous operations. Major Rafael de Nogales, who had volunteered his services to the Ottoman army during World War I, was an eyewitness to the carnage Ahmet unleashed against the victim population of Van province. In his memoirs, this Venezuelan officer relates that even the Kurds who had joined in the operations of massacres involving as victims "only women and children … were appalled by his fiendishness."[12] Following his murder of the two Armenian deputies of the Ottoman Parliament, Krikor Zohrab and Vartkes Serengulian, Ahmet was taken to task by Cemal Paşa, the military ruler of Syria and Lebanon. After a swift court-martial, he was convicted and hanged in Damascus on 17 (30) September 1915. When sanctioning this execution, Interior Minister Talaat sent this wire to Cemal: "His liquidation in any case is necessary. Otherwise he will prove very harmful at a later date. Talaat."[13] More revealing was the comment General Ali Fuat Erden, Cemal Paşa's chief of staff, made in his book: "Indebtedness to given executioners and murderers is bound to be heavy … those who are used for dirty jobs are needed in times of urgency [for the purpose of shifting] responsibility. It is likewise necessary, however, not to exalt but rather to dispose of them like toilet paper once they have done their job."[14]

Reserve Major Yakup Cemil, a very prominent *fedayi,* had played a decisive role in the overthrow of the last prewar Ottoman government in January 1913, thereby helping the CUP firmly entrench itself as a dictatorship. Cemil's decisiveness in that act of overthrow was afforded through his assassination of the war minister. This notoriety brought him instant fame and recognition, as well as commensurate influence in the councils of the CUP. During the war he assumed the command and control of a large regiment encompassing Special Organization cadres, and more particularly a large segment of convicts who had been released from the prisons by a special legal dispensation; their special tasks included large-scale massacres against the Armenians in Eastern Turkey.[15] When investigating the Armenian deportations and massacres, the Mazhar Inquiry Commission, in its request for information from the Ottoman War Ministry, specifically identified Major Yakup Cemil as having been implicated in the atrocities involved. The purpose was to gather pretrial evidentiary material, and of the eight questions the commission drafted, no. 7 dealt with the role of Cemil and of the Special Organization contingents he commanded.[16]

Kurdish Brigand Chief Şkaftanlı Amero, whose career was punctuated by brigandage and who was therefore always at odds with authorities, all of a sudden became a cohort of the authorities of Diyarbekir province. Pirinccizade Aziz Feyzi, that province's deputy, and Dr. Mehmet Reşit, the province's governor-general, consorted to recruit this brigand chief for massacre duty. He was entrusted with the task of executing the massacre of the province's most wealthy and prominent Armenians—636 of them, to be exact. They were placed on a number of rafts constructed of inflated skin, and were taken to the valley of Bezuan. In groups of six, naked, their arms tied together with heavy ropes, they were then butchered there by members of a Circassian Ramman tribe (*aşiret*)—after being robbed of all their money, jewelry, and other valuables. However, in less than two weeks, the same brigand chief, Amero, was lured back to Diyarbekir under the pretext of a plan to honor, decorate, and reward him on the part of both Feyzi and Reşit. Instead, by prior arrangement, he was pounced upon and killed by ten hired Circassians.[17]

Kurdish Murza Bey was likewise a brigand chief operating in the Erzincan area, and more particularly at Kemach defile, the ghastly graveyard of tens of thousands of Armenians from Erzurum province. He is on record as having assisted in the killing of 70,000 Armenians. "He was thought to be dangerous by the Turks, and was thrown into prison on the charge of having hit a gendarme"; however, like the other state-sponsored executioners, "he was eventually executed in secret."[18]

At his own discretion, Commander-in Chief of the Fourth Army Cemal Paşa "hanged several Kurds for participation in massacres against Armenians at Islayihe."[19] Yanyalı Mehmet Vehip Paşa hanged two gendarmerie officers for having carried out a large massacre against two thousand unarmed Armenian labor battalion soldiers in Suşehir, in Sivas province.[20]

The Liquidation of Brigand Chiefs by the Kemalists

Three prominent Special Organization chieftains exhibited legendary brutality against their Armenian victims in the macabre saga of the World War I Armenian Genocide. Yahya Kaptan (Ali Osman) was in charge of the massive drowning operations at the Trabzon harbor on the Black Sea littoral. Hundreds of Armenian children, women, and old men were loaded into lighters, taken to the high sea, and thrown overboard after being bayoneted by boatmen from other boats accompanying them. Yahya Kaptan later joined the Kemalist insurgents without completely severing his ties to the CUP and the Ittihadists, especially Enver. This suspected duplicity sealed his fate. It should be noted, however, that Yahya Kaptan, during inquiries into his loyalty, had threatened to reveal all he knew about state secrets in the event he was to be hard pressed by such inquiries and investigations.[21]

Feridunzade Topal Osman, a *milis* colonel and veteran guerilla from the days of the 1912–1913 twin Balkan wars, operated in the eastern border regions as a Special Organization brigand. He too had bragged repeatedly about his murder missions against the Armenians. After the war he also joined the Kemalist insurgents and in the process, as reprisal, organized extensive massacres against Greek populations in the Trabzon area, as well as against clusters of surviving Armenians. Mustafa Kemal eventually rewarded him with the position of Chief of the Personal Guard Contingent, with duties to protect Kemal. But he incurred the wrath of Kemalist deputies in the fledging parliament in Ankara when he lured an opposition deputy to his home and, out of spite, had his cohorts strangle him. He was killed during an exchange of gunfire with military units trying to capture him, and his decapitated corpse was subsequently hung on display at Ulus Meydan in front of the Parliament in March 1923.[22] His involvement in the carrying out of the Armenian massacres is indicated by Cemal Şener, especially in connection with the fall 1920 offensive against the nascent Republic of Armenia. For four months Topal Osman served in the ranks of the invading army that unleashed anti-Armenian bloodbaths in all the major cities captured in the process, especially Kars and Alexandropol.[23] Tevfik Bıyıklıoğlu[24] and Sina Akşin express a similar view.[25] It is important to note here that in one of his reflective moods, this arch perpetrator declared, during an exchange with the Turkish naval hero and postwar prime minister in the nascent Kemalist regime Rauf Orbay, "People like me should not be allowed to live."[26]

In terms of the operational execution of the scheme of the Armenian genocide, Eyuplu Deli (Mad) Halit Karsıalan stands out as one of the most effective executioners. That efficiency was largely due to the fact that not only was he a military officer equipped with streamlined command and control of resources, but also many of his charges were tasked for massacre duty. In the first stage of his involvement in organized mass murder he was indeed functioning not so much as a field commander but rather as a Special Organization (Teşkilât-ı Mahsusa) chieftain. That first stage comprised the invasion of Armenia in the spring and summer of 1918 and the ensuing months-long atrocities that were inflicted upon the Armenian population in the vast occupied territories. The second stage coincided with the second invasion of Armenia in the fall of 1920, entailing a new round of extensive massacres stretching all the way to Alexandropol in Armenia proper. In both instances he served under Colonel, subsequently General, Kâzım Karabekir.

Born in 1883 to a military family, Halit enrolled in Harbiye, the Ottoman military academy, from which he graduated in 1903 as a second lieutenant (*mülâzım sanisi*). From the very inception of his military career he got involved in the brigandage operations of his cohort and close friend Major Yakup Cemil, who is mentioned above. His notoriety as an arch massacrer is remarkably entwined with his fame as a military hero, as evidenced by his conquest of Ardahan in early winter of 1914, when he tenaciously fought and defeated a superior Russian army unit, thereby acquiring the title of "the hero of Ardahan." In the process, however, his brigands, led by the brigand chief Mehmet Sungur, carried out large-scale massacres in Ardahan and further to the south in Oltu.[27] His resumption of this pattern of massacres against the Armenians in the subsequent round of invasion of Armenia in the fall of 1920 is recorded in several authentic Turkish sources. Having since been promoted from lieutenant to captain to major, and later colonel, this time Halit had the Third Division fully under his command. What is most significant is that Mustafa Kemal, without any hesitation, availed himself of Halit's services, thereby knowingly protecting him from the acute danger of arrest and prosecution by the sultan's government in Istanbul on charges of massacring Armenians. The British in particular were pressuring that government to apprehend Halit for this purpose.

As several Turkish sources attest, Halit was deeply implicated in the Armenian massacres and had been consorting with other notorious massacrers, such as Ebuhintli Cafer from Erzurum and, to some extent, with Topal Osman;

Mustafa Kemal was thereby utilizing both of them for his campaign against the victorious Allies. Hunted intensively on account of his instigation of Armenian massacres, Halit went into hiding for a while in order to thwart his pursuers.[28] As Turkish historian Sina Akşin points out, Halit was a pronounced CUP partisan and was openly advocating the restoration of "a CUP spirit" as the only hope for Turkey's salvation, meanwhile acting as a "brutal committee man."[29] As indicated above, he embraced and implemented the ideology and genocidal designs of the Special Organization. He was a close friend of Dr. Nazım, one of the prime architects of the Armenian Genocide. With notable effusion, Dr. Bahaeddin Şakir, a cohort of Dr. Nazım, reassured Halit in a cipher telegram with the following words: "May God be my witness, my affection for you is so profound that you have to enter my heart to realize it."[30] A Turkish author even went so far as to assert that the 1920 victory against the nascent Republic of Armenia was not due to the leadership of Commander-in-Chief, Kâzım Karabekir, but to that of his subordinate commander, Halit.[31] However, if one is to believe Commander Karabekir, at the end of World War I, with Turkey suffering a crushing military defeat, Halit, in a state of despair and despondency, reportedly indicated to Karabekir that Turkey would have no choice but to make drastic territorial concessions in the East and accordingly be content with a few provinces in which to preserve its existence.[32]

But Kemalist Turkey, overcoming incredible odds, prevailed in the end and emerged victorious in 1922 after four years of dogged resistance to the consequences of defeat, occupation, and stiff peace terms—a resistance afforded through enduring stamina and ample military support from the incipient Bolshevik regime as well as the dissident postwar Italian and French Allies. As was the case with many other deputies of the fledgling Kemalist parliament, Halit was rewarded for his wartime services, including those at the western front against the Greeks, by being ushered in as a deputy, in his case from Kars. However, due to his cantankerous and bullying behavior, which a specialist had diagnosed as sign of a personality disorder, he began to quarrel and threaten other deputies in the course of parliamentary business. Inevitably, he soon became a worrisome problem for his colleagues and for Mustafa Kemal. On 9 February 1925, as a result of an altercation with some of his colleagues, he ended up being shot by one of them. For about five days he lay mortally wounded in one of the chambers of the Parliament, at times enduring excruciating pain.[33] Thus ended the life of a man whose martial aptitudes were sullied by an attendant murderous and even genocidal disposition.

After having used them for the liquidation of its Armenian population through a series of massacres, the authorities of Sivas province arranged for the trapping and the wholesale killing of the Circassian massacrers themselves. The Turkish sergeant Ahmed Şükrü who was involved in this operation is reported to have declared: "Arguing that without their knowledge they had massacred innocent Armenians, the authorities, who had instigated these massacres in the first place, got rid of them. Are you still unaware of the aptitude of the Turkish government to plot, and to set up traps [of this kind]?"[34]

The Suicides of Two Top Genocidists

Mehmet Reşit, MD, a veteran CUP partisan, became massively involved in the extermination of tens of thousands of Armenians of the province of Diyarbekir, of which he was governor-general, and of beyond. He is quoted as saying that he destroyed the Armenians by treating them as "microbes"; he then raised the rhetorical question, "Isn't the duty of a doctor to destroy such microbes?" In the same vein he retorted, "My Turkishness prevailed over my medical calling."[35] Dr. Reşit was arrested for prosecution and punishment by postwar Turkish authorities. With the help of CUP's clandestine agents he escaped from Bekirağa prison, only to be tracked down shortly thereafter by Istanbul police. Before he could be taken into custody again he committed suicide, in January 1919.[36]

General Mahmut Kâmil was commander-in-chief of the Ottoman Third Army from February 1915 to March 1916. An ardent CUP partisan and a close associate of Talaat and the two physicians Şakir and Nazım, all three of whom played a decisive role in securing his command appointment, General Kâmil had jurisdiction over the six eastern provinces of Turkey, plus that of Trabzon—thus, he had jurisdiction over the bulk of the Armenian population of the Ottoman Empire. He gave special orders not to spare the old, the infirm, or pregnant women from the perils of deportation. He also threatened that any Muslim who might dare to provide shelter to any Armenian would be hanged in front of his house. On 28 November 1922, he reportedly took his life through suicide.[37] General Kâmil was part of a group that escaped from Malta, where they were interned by the British for future court-martial on account of their complicity in Armenian massacres.

Death by Accident

Nuri Paşa Kıllıgil was a half-brother of War Minister and top CUP leader Enver Paşa, and was responsible for the perpetration of a series of massacres in Russian Armenia and Azerbaijan, especially the September 1918 Armenian massacre in Baku. After World War I, Nuri became a businessman, and by the end of World War II he had become an industrialist, operating a weapons and ammunition factory in Istanbul. On 2 March 1949, he perished along with others in the rubble of that factory, which was blown to pieces in a huge explosion that engulfed the entire complex in flames.[38]

Mehmet Memduh, district governor of Erzincan and subsequently governor-general of the provinces of Bitlis, Baghdad, and Musul, was the chief organizer of his district's massacres, in close cooperation with the local operatives of the Special Organization. He accumulated great wealth through the expropriation of his Armenian victims but died in an auto accident while trying to establish a business in Smyrna (Izmir) after the war. Not satisfied with local massacres, he also energetically organized a series of massacres of tens of thousands of deportees from Erzurum, Bayburt, and Tercan at the nearby Kemach defile, including the murder of Bishop Sumpad, the primate of Erzurum. He was Van Governor-General Cevdet's brother-in-law and thus related to War Minster Enver.[39]

Heart Attacks, Strokes, Fatal Sicknesses

Hassim Beg, deputy from Malatya in the parliament, was a fanatic Ittihadist and foe of the Armenians and sponsored his son Muhammed Beg's operations as a brigand chief of the area, carrying out a series of massacres and thereby annihilating Malatya's Armenian population. Following a quarrel with an old Kurd about a stolen horse, Muhammed Beg was shot by the Kurd's son. Deputy Hassim subsequently suffered a heart attack, and after much pain and anguish died in 1917.[40]

Sağırzade, mufti of Malatya, directed the strangulation of the Armenian Catholic primate of Malatya after subjecting him to manifold tortures and bodily mutilations for having refused to convert to Islam. Barely back home, the mufti suffered a stroke and died instantly.[41]

Servet Bey, district governor of Muş, Bitlis province, was a close friend of War Minister Enver. In November 1914, long before the April 1915 Armenian Van uprising, Servet explicitly foretold that the Armenians of his district would eventually be massacred. He indeed played a major role in the liquidation of the district's Armenian population, mostly through burning the victims alive in haylofts and stables, especially those living in Muş Plain. These atrocities were carried out primarily by an assortment of Kurdish tribes.[42]

Mahmut Nedim was Urfa's deputy to the parliament. He helped organize the Urfa massacre and also played a role in the trapping and murder of the two Armenian deputies mentioned above, when dealing with Çerkez Ahmet. Subsequently he went blind.[43]

The Punitive Act of a Righteous Turkish Military Officer

First Lieutenant (Mülazımievvel) Mehmet Izzet, the military commander of Çankırı, was in charge of the fourth section of Çankırı's Military Recruitment

Office (Ahzı Asker Şubesi), and temporarily Çankırı's deputy *mutasarrıf.* He had given his word of honor to Dr. Rupen Çilingiryan, one of the victims and a prominent writer-poet, that the safety of the group of five being deported to a new location was ensured. But the victims were ambushed en route by some ten brigands who were led by Alo, otherwise called Kurd Haci Ali oğlu, and were killed one by one after being subjected to excruciating methods of mutilation. Infuriated by this act of deception and savagery, Lieutenant Izzet went to work. He not only initiated protests to the governor-general of Kastamonu province, saying that "My military honor has been violated," but personally went to Tüney, the site of the crime, and following an on-the-spot investigation, had the perpetrators prosecuted and severely punished. Not satisfied with this act of retribution, he also tracked down and likewise prosecuted several other accomplices, all of whom would be released from prison a year later, however. (See also Ch. 6, note 16, p. 125 in the main body of this work). [44]

Notes

1. Ali Çankaya, *Yeni Mülkiye Tarihi ve Mülkiyeliler* [A new history of the civil service school and its graduates], vol. 4 (Ankara. Interior Ministry 1968-1969), p. 1522. Rauf Orbay, "Rauf Orbay' ın Hatıraları," 112, right- column; Doğan Avcıoğlu, *Milli Kurtuluş Tarihi,* vol. 3 (Istanbul: Istanbul, 1974), p. 1181.
2. Feridun Kandemir, *Izmir Suikasdının Iç Yüzü,* vols. 1 and 2 (Istanbul: Ekicigil, 1955), vol. 1, pp. 91, 93, 96, 119, 124, 128, 133, 139; Cemal Kutay, "Izmir ve Ankara Idamları," *Türkiye Istiklâl ve Hürriyet Mücadeleler Tarihi* 20 (January 1962): 11624.
3. Kandemir, *Izmir* [n. 2], vol. 1, pp. 99–101, 113–114, 119, 123, 124; Kutay, *Türkiye,* Ibid., p. 11629; A. N. Erman, *Izmir Suikastı ve Mahkemeleri* (Istanbul: Temel, 1971), p. 151.
4. Kandemir, *Izmir* [n. 2], vol. 2, pp. 50–67, 104, 107, 114, 123; Kutay, *Türkiye,* [n. 2], pp. 11631, 11632; Erman, *Izmir* [n. 2], pp. 186–187; Kılıç Ali, *Istiklal Mahkemesi Hatıraları* (Istanbul: Sel, 1955), pp. 31, 32–33 where Nazım is cited by his cover name of Dr. Rüstem; Lord Kinross, *Atatürk: A Biography* (New York: W. Morrow, 1965), pp. 487, 491, 492, 493.
5. Kandemir, *Izmir* [n. 2], vol. 2, pp. 81–85, 102–103, 114–115, 123; Kutay, *Türkiye* [n. 2], pp. 11631, 11632, 11633; Arif Cemil, *I. Dünya Savaşında Teşkilât-ı Mahsusa* (Istanbul: Arba, 1997), pp. 82–86, 101–102, 112, 114–115.
6. Ibid., pp. 45–49; Kandemir, *Izmir Suikasdının* [n. 2], vol. 2, pp. 81–85, 115; Kutay, *Türkiye* [n. 2], pp. 11631, 11633; Kinross, *Atatürk* [n. 6], p. 485.
7. Sadi Borak, *Iktidar Koltuğundan Idam Sehpasına,* (Istanbul: Yeni Matbaa , 1962), pp. 97–128; Erman, *Izmir Suikastleri* [n. 4], pp. 102–103; Andrew Mango, *Atatürk: The Biography of the Founder of Modern Turkey* (Woodstock: Overlook Press, 1999), pp. 444, 448, 450; Erik J. Zürcher, *The Unionist Factor: The Role of the Committee of Union and Progress in the Turkish National Movement 1905–1926* (Leiden: Brill, 1984), pp. 154, 156; Sadi Selçuk, *Esaretin Acı Hatıraları ve 37. Kafkas Tümeninin Trabzonu Düşmandan Istirdadı* (Konya: Ülkü, 1955), pp. 4–5; S. Zurlinden, *Der Weltkrieg,* vol. 2 (Zürich: Art. Institut Orell Füssli, 1918). On p. 686 the author portrays Abdülkadir as "a veritable Young Turk satan" who as military commandant of Gümüşhane had all the male members of deportee convoys in transit through that city separated and killed.

8. Hovagim Hovagimian, *Badmoutiun Haigagan Pontosee* (Beirut: Mushak, 1967), p. 268; no author, *Germany, Turkey and Armenia: A Selection of Documentary Evidence* (London: J. J. Keliher, 1917), Appendix, pp. 123–124.
9. Kinross, *Atatürk* [n. 4], p. 493.
10. Hıfzı Veldet Velidedeoğlu, *Anıların Izinde,* vol. 1 (Istanbul: Remzi 1977), p. 156. For the other references see Ali, *Istklal Mahkemsi* [n. 4], pp. 8–9; Kinross, *Atatürk* [n. 4], p. 493; Yalçın Küçük, *Türkiye Üzerine Tezler,* vol. 2 (Istanbul: Tekin, 1979), pp. 616–620.
11. "Qu'attendent les Alliés pour faire pendre toute cette canaille." This statement was reportedly made during an interview Kemal granted to Maurice Prax, correspondent of the French newspaper *Petit Parisien.* It appeared under the heading "Constantinople" in *Lectures pour tous,* March 1920. For the English translation of parts of the interview, see *Current History* 12 (May 1920): 334-336.
12. Rafael De Nogales, *Four Years Beneath the Crescent,* trans. Muna Lee (New York: Scribner's, 1926), p. 405.
13. Ziya Şakir, *Yakın Tarihte Üç Büyük Adam* (Istanbul: Ahmet Sait, 1946), p. 58.
14. Ali Fuad Erden, *Birinci Dünya Harbinde Suriye Hatıraları,* vol. 1 (Istanbul: Halk, 1954), p. 216. For extensive coverage of the episode relating to Ahmet's involvement in the implementation of the Armenian Genocide, see Vahakn N. Dadrian, "Documentation of the Armenian Genocide in Turkish Sources," in *Genocide: A Critical Bibliographic Review,* ed. Israel Charny, vol. 2 (London: Mansell, 1991), pp. 118–120.
15. Aziz Samih, *Büyük Harpte Kafkas Cephesi Hatıraları* (Ankara: Büyük Erkânıharbiye Matbaası, 1934). On p. 68 the author, a chief of staff of the Army Reserve Cavalry Corps, denounces Cemil as "crazy, reckless," heading a regiment comprised of "bloodthirsty criminals, convicts" (*kanlı katil mahkümlar*).
16. Armenian Patriarchate Archives Jerusalem, Series 21, File M, no. 555.
17. Thomas Mugurditchian, *Dikranagerdee Nahankeen Charteru* (Cairo: Djihanian, 1919), pp. 57–61.
18. The testimony of Muslim officer Lieutenant Sait Ahmet Muhtar in FO 371/2781/264888, report of 27 December 1916, no. 2, p. 7. See also *Current History,* vol. 5 (February 1917), excerpted from *The London Times.*
19. German Foreign Ministry Archives, Berlin. A.A. R14090 no. 16/K. no. 2, 3 January 1916, Aleppo Consul Dr. Walter Rössler's report.
20. Vahakn N. Dadrian, "The Naim-Andonian Documents on the World War I Destruction of Ottoman Armenians: The Anatomy of a Genocide," *International Journal of Middle East Studies* 18 (August 1986): 330.
21. Jaeschke and Pritsch, *Die Welt des Islams: Die Türkei seit dem Weltkriege, 1918–1928,* p. 25; Rasih Nuri Ileri, *Atatürk ve Komünizm* (Istanbul: Anadolu, 1970), p. 25; Avcıoğlu, *Milli Kurtuluş Tarihi* [n. 1], p. 1188, footnote.
22. Nurşen Mazıcı, *Belgelerle Atatürk Döneminde Muhalefet 1919–1926* (Istanbul: Dilmen, 1984), p. 132. While Atatürk biographer Kinross suggests that Atatürk arranged his liquidation, p. 413, Turkish army commander and subsequently Grand Vizier Ahmet Izzet maintains, likewise, that Mustafa Kemal Atatürk himself arranged Osman's execution under the guise of a police operation. *Feryadım,* vol. 2 (Istanbul: Nehir, 1993), pp. 235–236.
23. Cemal Şener, *Topal Osman Olayı* (Istanbul: Ant, 1992), p. 49 (citing Sabahattin Selek), 64 (citing Mahmut Goloğlu), 76 (citing Stefanos Yerasimos).
24. Tevfik Bıyıklıoğlu, *Atatürk Anadoluda: 1919–1921* (Ankara: n.p., 1959), p. 37.

25. Sina Akşin, *Istanbul Hükümetleri ve Milli Mücadele,* vol. 2 (Istanbul: Cem, 1992), p. 182.
26. Feridun Kandemir, *Hatıraları ve Söylemedikleri ile Rauf Orbay* (Istanbul: Ağbaba, 1965), p. 113.
27. Ihsan Birinci, "Kafirin Kurşunu Öldürmez," *Hayat ve Tarih* 2 (1 August 1967): 68; Cemal Kutay, *Sisli Tarihimiz* (Istanbul: Özkaya, 1976), pp. 100–101, 104–105; *Resimli Tarih Mecmuası* 2 (September 1951): 948; German Foreign Ministry Archives, Berlin. A.A., R14088, J. no. 580/secret report no. 23, 5, 1915 filed by Erzurum Vice-Consul Scheubner Richter; Ismail Kayabalı and Cemender Arslanoğlu, "Kuzey Dogu Anadolu Sınırlarının Tarihi" *Türk Kültürü,* vol XI (April 1973): 426, 438, 453.
28. Avcıoğlu, *Milli Kurtuluş* [n. 1], pp. 1184, 1185, 1186; Mazhar Müfit Kansu, *Erzurumdan Ölümüne Kadar Atatürk'le Beraber,* vol. 1 (Ankara: Türk Tarih Kurumu, 1986), pp. 301, 302.
29. Akşin, *Istanbul Hükümetleri* [n. 25], p. 205.
30. Cemil, *Ici Dünya* [n. 5], p. 234. For a biographical sketch of Halit see *Türk Istiklâl Harbine Katılan Tümen ve Daha Üst Kademelerdeki Komutanların Biyografileri,* 2nd ed. (Ankara: Turkish General Staff, 1989), pp. 214–215.
31. Nurşen Mazıcı, *Belgelerle Atatürk Dönümünde Muhalefet (1919–1926)* (Istanbul: Dilmen, 1984), pp. 49–50.
32. Kâzım Karabekir, *İstiklâl Harbimiz* (Istanbul: Türkiye, 1969), pp. 31, 38.
33. Ĉemal Kutay, *Sisli Tarihimiz* (Istanbul: Özkaya, 1976), pp. 57–114.
34. Fully convinced that an Armenian bishop whom he was escorting as a deportee was on his way to martyrdom, Sergeant Ahmed Şükrü opened up to him and made a whole series of other disclosures to him. Krikoris Balakian, *Hai Koghkota,* vol. 1 (Vienna: Mechitarist Publishers, 1922), p. 229. See the English version of this book, *Armenian Golgotha,* trans. P. Balakian and A. Sevag (New York: A. Knopf, 2009), p. 147.
35. Vahakn N. Dadrian, "The Role of Turkish Physicians in the World War I Genocide of Ottoman Armenians," *Holocaust and Genocide Studies* 1, no. 2 (1986): 175.
36. Mithat Şükrü Bleda, *Imparatorluğun Çöküşü* (Istanbul, Remzi, 1979), pp. 56–63; Feridun Kandemir, "Dr. Reşit'in Intiharı," *Yakın Tarihimiz* 2 (1962): 339–340; Feridun Kandemir, "Ittihat ve Terrakki Valilerinden Doktor Reşit Beyin Son Günleri," *Resimli Tarih Mecmuası* 2 (October 1951): 1052–1055.
37. Ali Ihsan Sabis, *Harp Hatıralarım* (Ankara: Güneş, 1951), vol. 2, pp. 165 and 179; Ahmed Izzet, *Feryadım,* vol. 1 (Istanbul: Nehir, 1992), p. 201; German Foreign Ministry Archives, Berlin. A.A. German Vice Consul Scheubner Richter's two reports, i.e., 2 and 26 June 1912 reports in K169 no. 1 and no. 47 respectively; see also his 28 July 1915 report K170, folio 63; FO 371/6500, folio 483/219 pp. The news of his suicide is recorded in the 28 November 1922 issue of *Tevhidi Efkâr.* According to Bilal Şimşir, however, in 1927 he was still alive. *Malta Sürgünleri* (Istanbul: Milliyet, 1976), 461.
38. Samet Ağaoğlu, *Babamın Arkadaşları* (Istanbul: Nebioğlu, 1959), pp. 30–34; "Patlayan Cephane Fabrikası" *Yıllarboyu Yakın Tarih Dergisi* 1 (April 1978): 21.
39. Zaven Badriark (Archbishop, Wartime Patriarch of Armenians of Turkey), *Badriarkagan Husherus* [Documents and witness testimonies] (Cairo: Nor Astgh, 1947), pp. 223–224. For the English version see his *My Patriarchal Memoirs,* trans. A. Misirliyan (Barrington, RI: Mayreni, 2002), p. 280.
40. Kevork Melidentzee, *Nakhjirner: 1915–1918* (Boston: Hairenik, 1929), p. 207.

41. Monsignor Jean Naslian, *Les Memoirs de Mgr. Jean Naslian,* vol. 1 (Vienna: Mechitarist Publishers, 1955), p. 255; the Mufti's death occurred in the second week of July 1915.
42. German Foreign Ministry Archives, Berlin, K171, German Embassy Councillor Mordtmann's 6 November 1915 Memo; Bryce and Toynbee, *The Treatment of the Armenians,* report no. 23, p. 127; FO 371/6501, folio 109.
43. See the third installment of a series of articles on the Armenian defensive uprising in Urfa: K. A. Urhayetzee, "Urfayee Herosamardu" *Hairenik* 5 (December 1926): 106. For the incident relating to the fate of the two Armenian parliamentarians mentioned above, see the second installment in *Hairenik* 5 (November 1926): 110–111.
44. Garo Kevorkian, ed., *Amenoun Darekirku* 7 (1960): p. 223; Garo Kevorkian, ed., *Amenoun Darekirku* 6 (1959): 134–137; Rev. Krikor Balakian, *Hai Koghkota* [Episodes from Armenian martyrdom], vol. 1: *1914–1920* (Vienna: Mechitarist, 1922), pp. 148–151 (for the English version of this volume see Balakian, *Armenian Golgotha,* pp. 98–102); Püzant Boyadjian, "Tebee Ayaş: Heen u Nor Husher," in *Hushartzan Abril Dasnemegee,* ed. Teotig (Istanbul: H. Arzuman, 1919), pp. 118–119.

PART II

The Trials and Beyond

CHAPTER 10

Death Sentences Handed Down by the Military Tribunal in Istanbul

Taner Akçam

Eighteen defendants in the Istanbul Number One Extraordinary Court-Martial were condemned to death for crimes against the Armenians. Additional death sentences were meted out during the genocide and during the Republic Period. Of these eighteen persons, fifteen were condemned in absentia, leaving the number of defendants ultimately executed at three. The British commissioner in Istanbul, Mr. Webb, made the following observation on the matter: "It is interesting to see … the manner in which the sentences have been apportioned among the absent and present so as to effect a minimum of real bloodshed.[1]

Those Sentenced to Death

1) Mehmet Kemal, the district head of Boğazlıyan, and during the massacres the lieutenant governor of Yozgat, was sentenced to death on 8 April during the Yozgat trials (see Chapter 6, "The Yozgat Verdict") and hanged on 10 April 1919 (*Takvim-i Vekâyi,* no. 3520).

2) The officer in charge of the Erzincan gendarmerie units, Hafız "Hayran Baba" Abdullah Avni, was sentenced to death during the Erzincan trials (see Chapter 6, "The Erzincan Verdict") along with three other defendants. Avni was hanged on 22 July 1920.[2]

3) The district head of Bayburt (later Ergani, and subsequently the lieutenant governor of Urfa), Behramzade Nusret, was sentenced to death during the Bayburt trials. The decision was handed down on 20 July, and the execution by hanging was carried out on 5 August 1920. The decision was published in *Takvim-i Vekayi*, no. 3924, 8 August 1920.[3]

Those Sentenced to Death in absentia

The Trial of the CUP Leaders

4) Talaat Paşa fled to Berlin, but was assassinated on 15 March 1921 by an Armenian youth named Soghomon Tehlirian, who had survived massacre by a coincidental turn of events.[4]

5) Enver Paşa fled to Russia in an adventure-filled journey and was killed during an armed clash with Bolshevik forces on 4 August 1922.[5]

6) Cemal Paşa first fled to Berlin, and later to Russia. He was assassinated in Tiflis (Tblisi) on 21 July 1922.[6]

7) Dr. Nazım was among those who fled to Berlin. He was later arrested, tried, convicted, and hanged by the Ankara Independence Tribunal (İstiklal Mahkemesi) in 1926 for his alleged involvement in a plot to assassinate Mustafa Kemal.[7]

The Trabzon Trial

8) Cemal Azmi, governor-general of Trabzon, fled to Berlin alone three months before Talaat and Enver Paşas. He was assassinated there along with Dr. Bahaeddin Şakir by members of an Armenian revenge organization on 17 April 1922.

9) Yenibahçeli Nail, CUP responsible secretary for Trabzon, also fled. He was later sentenced to death and executed by the Ankara Independence Tribunal in 1926 for his alleged involvement in the Izmir plot.

Death sentences in the Trabzon trial were published in *Takvim-i Vekâyi*, no. 3616.

The Harput Trial

10) Dr. Bahaeddin Şakir fled to Berlin. He was assassinated by an Armenian revenge organization on 17 April 1922.

Death sentences in the Harput Trial were published in *Takvim-i Vekâyi*, no. 3771.

The Erzincan Trial

11) Sağırzade Halit Efendi

12) Kırmo Yusuf (bandit)

13) Sergeant Aslan (gendarmerie)

14) The district head of Kako (a Kurdish chieftain)

The verdict was published in *İkdam*, *Vakit*, and *Tercüman-ı Hakikat*, 29 July 1920. The sultan's ratification of their death sentences was published in *Takvim-i Vekayi*, no. 3917, 31 July 1920.

The Bayburt Trial

15) Lieutenant Mehmet Necati's death sentence was delivered on 20 July 1920, ratified on 4 August 1920, and published in *Takvim-i Vekayi*, no. 3924, 8 August 1920.

The Deir Zor Trial

16) Zor eski Mutasarrıfı Zeki Bey's death sentenced was delivered on 28 April 1920. The verdict was published in *Alemdar* on 30 April and in *Vakit* on 2 May 1920.

Other Trials

17) Dr. Ahmet Midhat, CUP responsible secretary for Bolu[8]

18) Dr. Bosnalı İsmail Efendi

Both of the defendants were convicted and sentenced to death in the first Extraordinary Court-Martial, in a decision read on 28 August 1920. The decision was ratified on 1 September 1920 and published in *Takvim-i Vekâyi*, no. 3944, 1 September 1920). In the court's decision it was stated that both defendants had since fled and joined the National Forces (Kuvva-yı Milliye) in Anatolia.

Death Sentences for Nationalists

In the same court-martial, the representatives of the Turkish nationalist movement were also sentenced to death. The court tried Mustafa Kemal in absentia, along with more than one hundred leading members of the nationalist movement, and sentenced them to death.[9] Sixteen people with links to the National Forces were sentenced to death, and four were eventually executed on 12 June 1920 for attempting to assassinate Damad Ferit Paşa.[10]

Notes

1. FO 371/4174/18392, No. 267, 7 July 1919, cited in V. N. Dadrian, "The Documentation of the World War I Armenian Massacres in the Proceedings of the Turkish Military Tribunal," *International Journal of Middle Eastern Studies* 23, no. 4 (November 1991): 562.
2. Ratification by sultan published in *Takvim-i Vekâyi,* no. 3917, 31 July 1920.
3. Nusret had previously been given a life sentence of hard labor, the decision being written and signed by the panel of judges. But later, trial judge Nemrut Mustafa ordered a second decision written up for Nusret's execution, as a result of which Nusret was hanged. The first decision was destroyed and hidden among the trial documents. According to Ebubekir Hazım Tepeyran, "The panel of judges was tried, because, since there had been two rulings issued from one court on the same question, and the first one of these was valid and the second one was not, then the execution of Nusret Bey was a crime like killing a prisoner sentenced to hard labor … the murderous president and other members of the Extraordinary Court-Martial number 1 were sentenced to seven months … and put in military prison." *Zalimane Bir İdam Hükmü* (Istanbul: Milli Mecmua, 1946), p. 226. Nemrut Mustafa, the court president, was pardoned by the sultan three months later.
4. Tehlirian was acquitted on 23 June 1921. For details, see Tessa Hofmann, ed., *Der Völkermord an den Armeniern vor Gericht: Der Prozess Talaat Pascha* (Göttingen, 1985); *The Case of Soghomon Tehlirian.* Translated by Vartkes Yeghiayan (Los Angeles: A. R. F. Varantian Gomideh, 1985).
5. Şevket Süreyya Aydemir, *Makedonya'dan Ortaasya'ya Enver Paşa,* vol. 3 (Istanbul: Remzi, 1985), p. 648.
6. In addition to the claim that he was killed by an Armenian revenge organization (Wolfgang Gust, *Der Völkermord an den Armenien: Die Tragödie des ältesten Christenvolkes der Welt,* (München, 1993), p. 299), there is the competing claim that the Bolsheviks killed him (İsmet Karadoğan, "Cemal Paşa'yı Ruslar öldürtmüştü" and Firuz Kesim, "Cemal Paşa Nasıl Katledildi," both in *Yakın Tarihimiz* 2 [1962]: 36–38 and 131–132, respectively). Additionally, in the memoirs of Enver Paşa's uncle, Halil Paşa, the latter relates that a functionary from the Soviet Foreign Ministry told him privately that the decision was taken by his government that Cemal Paşa be killed. Halil Paşa, *İttihat ve Terakki'den Cumhuriyet'e Bitmeyen Savaş,* ed. M. Taylan Sorgun (Istanbul: Yedigün, 1972), p. 9. Gust, however, claims that he derived his information from the memoirs of the Armenian guerilla fighter (*çeteci*) who organized the action, whereas the information contained in the Turkish sources relies more on gossip and hearsay. For more information see, Jacques Derogy, *Resistance and Revenge: The Armenian Assassination of the Turkish Leaders Responsible for the 1915 Massacres and Deportations* (New Brunswick, NJ, and London: Transaction, 1986).
7. Whatever Dr. Nazım's personal involvement in the so-called Izmir Conspiracy, his death sentence was ultimately a settling of accounts between Kemal and the surviving leadership of the Committee of Union and Progress. Feridun Kandemir, *İzmir Suikastının İç Yüzü,* 2 vols. (Istanbul: Ekicigil, 1955).
8. Dr. Ahmet Midhat, a defendant in the Trial of the CUP Responsible Secretaries and Delegates, had been found guilty of participating in the massacres of Armenians and sentenced to ten years' hard labor in exile. He was retried (see number 17, above), but

while the case was being investigated he fled. He was again sentenced—to death, this time in absentia.

9. The death sentence against Mustafa Kemal was published in *Takvim-i Vekâyi,* no. 3864 (27 Mayıs 1336 / 27 May 1920). For the other verdicts, see *Takvim-i Vekâyi,* no. 3866 (30 Mayıs 1336 / 30 May 1920); and no. 3883 (21 Haziran, 1336 / 21 June, 1920).
10. The death sentence was handed down on 9 Haziran 1336 (9 June 1920), approved on 11 Haziran and published in *Takvim-i Vekâyi,* no. 3878 (13 Haziran 1336 / 13 June 1920).

CHAPTER 11

Coverage of the Trials by the Istanbul Turkish Press

Taner Akçam

In the aftermath of World War I, the newly established Ottoman government began its term with the prosecution of war criminals, those accused of misappropriation of government funds, and the perpetrators of massacres against the Armenians. The trials of the military tribunal, or Divan-ı Harbi Örfi, were conducted between 1919 and 1922, mainly in Istanbul, though some were carried out in various provinces of Turkey. The following is an attempt to compile a comprehensive list of those trials that pertain to the massacres and deportation of the Armenians. Other cases investigated by the same court involving other crimes will generally not be included, except for some selected examples.

The first step toward establishing these tribunals was the publication of the sultan's edict on 14 December 1918. Later, the cabinet pronounced its decision to conduct tribunals not only in Istanbul but also in the various provinces.[1] The first Extraordinary Military Tribunal was formed on 16 December 1918 in Istanbul.[2] As analyzed elsewhere in this book, there were numerous changes in both the structure and the procedures of the tribunals. As the months rolled on, further changes would be made.

Most of the extant documents were produced by the Istanbul tribunal. We are not in possession of much material in connection with the activities, prosecution, and judgments of the military tribunals that were active in other parts of Anatolia. Still, we have learned from data available in the Istanbul press that the courts elsewhere were in fact active. From this newspaper coverage one can see that some of the defendants were transferred to other jurisdictions in Anatolia. For example, the *Kaymakam* (county executive) of Ömerli, Ali Haydar Bey, was arrested in Istanbul and on the eve of his prosecution transferred to Kastamonu.[3] There are other examples; in the Yalova case, defendant Mehmet Cemal, a retired lieutenant with the military police, was sentenced in absentia to six months of imprisonment. In the case of the Bolu Military Tribunal, the pending bill of charges was moved to Istanbul for actual prosecution.[4] Similarly, after the Samsun Military Tribunal was shut down, the Istanbul newspapers reported that there was some discussion as to where the incomplete cases should be transferred.[5]

Up to this point, for various reasons, a comprehensive list could not be compiled with respect to these trials, in either Istanbul or other regions of Anatolia. We can begin to make such a list using the information available in the contemporary Istanbul press. Until the present study, scholars have only been aware of the limited number of cases presented in the *Takvîm-i Vekâyi.* We have combed virtually all of the available press accounts from that period in Istanbul. Nevertheless, we have to admit that even this approach is incomplete because of the impossibility of finding complete sets of these newspapers in any location. In addition, since there was no standard naming practice with respect to accounts, scholars must assess whether separate press accounts discuss the same trial or not. As a result, gaps exist. It is entirely possible that some court news escaped our attention, or even more likely that some of the prosecutions failed to make the news at all.

Interest in these cases waned after the initial intense scrutiny of the early months. With the passage of time (particularly after the resignation of Grand Vizier Damad Ferit Paşa, forced by the Kemalist Nationalists in September 1919), the newspapers started to allot less space to the tribunal cases; eventually they were covered by a weekly "tribunal activity column." Over time the cases would even be classified as "unimportant."[6] News of the hearings was often reduced to two or three sentences, often with several cases being discussed together in a single sentence. For example, in the 16 December 1920 edition of *İkdam*, it was briefly reported that ten defendants had had their cases heard. Three of them related to the Armenian deportations, but their cases had been postponed due to lack of time.[7]

There is a direct correlation between the Turkish Nationalist movement in Anatolia and the way that these cases were conducted and then reported in the press. As the Nationalist movement gained strength, decisions to acquit or to end investigations altogether increased, and the trials gradually lost their significance.

With the exception of the initial trials, a general pattern can be observed in the press coverage. In most cases, testimony given against the defendants is not reported in either essence or detail. Most newspapers give a general statement to the effect that witnesses "gave testimony on behalf of [or against] the defendant." It is impossible to know what was actually said.

The following accounting of these trials includes our summaries of the information found in all of the various press accounts available. When summarizing, generally no extra information or commentary is provided. If it is, it is given in brackets and noted as such. Each summary includes the sources used so that readers can easily access the original accounts.

We were able to confirm sixty-three different court cases directly involving crimes against the Armenians. Of these sixty-three cases, twelve are documented in the *Takvîm-i Vekâyi.* The trials were variously reported upon. The first category of documentation consists of complete accounts of the trials, including the indictments, minutes, and verdicts (such as the accounts of the trials of cabinet members and the members of the Central Committee of the Union and Progress Party). The second category consists of partially complete accounts, such as the trial against the party secretaries. The indictment, verdict, and minutes of three of thirteen sittings of these were published in *Takvîm-i Vekâyi.* The third category includes those trials that were documented only by their verdicts, such as the Yozgat and Trabzon cases. The fourth category includes only the sultan's official confirmation of the sentences rendered by the court. This category includes the Bayburt and Erzincan cases. Information about the other fifty-one cases was gleaned from the daily newspapers.[8]

Of the fifty-one cases, twenty-two came to a judicial conclusion (seventeen of them ending in acquittals). The results of twenty-one out of the remaining twenty-nine cases remain unknown; eight were dismissed due to lack of sufficient evidence with which to prosecute. In the first Mosul case, the defendant was deported to Malta and the case was dropped. In another trial (Mosul-2), one defendant was acquitted while it was decided that the other cases should be held over for further investigation.

The long process of compiling this list from scattered sources over great time and distance has revealed a considerable wealth of previously unknown information about the last years of the Ottoman Empire. It is therefore of immeasurable value and unique in its scope, despite the methodological challenges.

Cases Registered in Respective *Takvîm-i Vekâyi* Issues Whose Minutes Were Completely or Partially Recorded

1) *Trial of Central Committee Members of the Union and Progress Party (Main Trial)*

This complaint was brought against the former wartime cabinet members and Central Committee members of the Union and Progress Party and responsible officials of the Special Organization (Teşkilât-ı Mahsusa).

In the second session, cabinet members were separated from the main case and a second trial (discussed below) was initiated. After the separation, the remaining defendants were Midhat Şükrü, Ziya Gökalp Bey, Talaat Bey (Küçük, i.e., "little"), Riza Bey, Atıf Bey, and Cevat Bey. The following defendants were charged in absentia: Dr. Nazım, Dr. Bahaeddin Şakir, Dr. Rüsuhi Efendi, and Aziz Efendi.

Despite the fact that the case was separated into two, the verdict was presented as a unitary, single case.

The press coverage of this trial was very intense. Much space was allotted to coverage of the trial, and hearings were printed verbatim, although unlike in other trials no witnesses were called to testify. Once the trials were underway, headlines in the Turkish press included such terms as "Historical Day," "Historical Judgment," and "Incredible Indictment."

The sessions lasted from 28 April to 17 May 1919. No immediate judgment followed the seven sessions because the process was temporarily interrupted. All seven sessions were documented verbatim in the *Takvîm-i Vekâyi.*

Takvîm-i Vekâyi numbers: 3540, 3543, 3547, 3549, 3554, 3557, 3561.

2) *Trial of the Cabinet Members (Continuation of the Main Trial)*

A new supplementary indictment was added to the bill of charges, and new government officials were added to the list of defendants from the Main Trial (see above).

Defendants: Sait Halim Paşa, Hayri Efendi, Musa Kâzım Efendi, Halil Bey, Ahmet Nesimi Bey, İsmail Canbolat Bey, Abbas Halim Paşa, Ibrahim Bey, Ali Münif Bey, Şükrü Bey, Mustafa Şeref Bey, Kemal Bey, Haşim Bey, Rifat Bey.

Defendants tried in absentia: Talaat Paşa, Enver Paşa, Cemal Paşa, Dr. Nazım.

Date: 3 June–25 June 1919. Seven hearings in total. The court records were printed verbatim.

Takvîm-i Vekâyi numbers: 3571, 3573, 3575, 3577, 3593, 3594, 3595.

A single judgment was entered for both cases on 5 July 1919 and printed in *Takvîm-i Vekâyi,* no. 3604.

3) *Trial of the Union and Progress Party Secretaries* (Katib-i Mesul)

Although this case began with seven defendants, by the final session there were twelve individuals included in the indictment. The judgment was against all twelve defendants. The trial started on 21 June 1919 and the proceedings of the first three sittings were published verbatim in *Takvîm-i Vekâyi.*

Defendants: Mafenya Secretary Avni Bey, Beyoğlu Secretary Hasan Salahaddin Bey, Eskişehir Secretary Dr. Besim Zühdi Bey, Bursa Secretary Dr. Midhat Bey, Mirgün Secretary agent Cevdet Bey, Aleppo Secretary Cemal Bey, Edirne Inspector Abdülgani Bey, Konya Secretary Abdülkadir Efendi, Kastamonu Secretary Münir Bey, Kastamonu Secretary Hasan Fehmi Efendi, Karahisar former Chief of the Liquidation Commission Agah Bey, Karahisar former civil servant of the Liquidation Department Hayreddin Bey.

The sessions that were *not* included in *Takvîm-i Vekâyi,* are summarized below based on newspaper accounts, since they have previously been unavailable for study.

At the first hearing, the identity of the defendants was established, the indictment was read out, and the formal demand for their punishment was made, based upon their "having been made the tools of the illicit purposes of the Union and Progress Party (CUP) and having violated internal security."[9] The case was postponed to allow the defendants to consult with attorneys.

At the second hearing on 23 June, the defendants all denied the charges. Some claimed to have "not heard about the deportations," or that deportations "had not taken place in their regions," though they had heard about them later.[10] After the third hearing, dated 28 June, a continuance was given while procedural changes by the military tribunal went into effect. What we consider as being the fourth hearing, it began on 6 October 1919, after a break. Since the papers did not number the sessions, we cannot tell if there were other hearings between those dates. At that hearing the legal representatives moved to have the case dismissed for lack of jurisdiction; however the motion was denied.[11]

The fifth hearing took place on 27 October 1919. At this time the case of Çankırı Secretary Cemal Oğuz Bey was merged with the present case. Cemal Oğuz had been accused of murdering the Armenians who were deported from Istanbul to Çankırı. The written statement of Armenian priest Karabetyan, claiming that Cemal Oğuz had been behind the murder of five Armenians who were sent from Ankara to Ayaş, was read into the record. A written statement of the governor-general of Kastamonu, Reşit Paşa, was also read into the record. This statement was in connection with the actions of the region's party (CUP) secretary, Hasan Fehmi Bey. The governor claimed that he had received an official signed memo from Bahaeddin Şakir, the head of the Special Organization of the Union and Progress Party (Teşkilât-ı Mahsusa), stating that the deportation of Armenians from Kastamonu was deemed necessary. He, the *vali,* claimed that he had been discharged from his post for having refused to obey the order. He also stated that the party secretary, Hasan Fehmi, had slandered him in Kastamonu by stating that Reşit Paşa was the "Governor of the Armenians, not the Turks." While Hasan Fehmi put up no defense, nor gave any explanation to these accusations, Cemal Oğuz would object to the accusations against him by stating that "the claim that I'd caused the Armenians pain and suffering is a lie."[12]

The sixth hearing took place on 3 November 1919. It consisted of the reading of written statements and the taking of testimony against defendant Cemal Oğuz. Besides the Armenian witnesses there were two Turks, Hacı Tevfik and Ziya Efendi, whose statements, taken in Çankırı, were read into the record. The defendant objected to all of the claims.[13]

During the seventh hearing, which took place on 12 November 1919, several of the Armenians who had been deported from Istanbul to Çankırı gave testimony. From the testimony of pharmacist Krikor Efendi, we learn that there were as many as one hundred households within Çankırı that had been thrown into the deportation group—virtually all of them. He testified that "of the 180 sent to Kengırı, there are today thirty of them who are alive." The murder of the Armenians was under the direction of Cemal Oğuz from the Special Organization (Teşkilât-ı Mahsusa). Çankırı's deputy mutasarrıf, Izzet Bey, was so upset by the events he apparently wept in front of the Armenians who came to visit him. According to Krikor Efendi, five Armenians had remained in the custody of the local officials. After the officials asked for instructions from Istanbul regarding what was to be done with them, they were taken out of the city by carriage, left with a gang, and ordered killed. When the driver returned with his carriage empty, he stated, "I came back after the police handed over the Armenians to the gang." According to the testimony of the witness, the driver became sick over it. The witness added: "I was supposed to be sent too on the day those five people were killed. They couldn't get a carriage for us, so we stayed. Those people died in our place."

In the same hearing, damaging testimony against Hasan Fehmi was read aloud. According to the record, Hasan Fehmi was assigned to the Commission on Abandoned Armenian Properties, which was responsible for the sale of Armenian properties (Emval-i Metruke). Before actually putting them up for sale by auction, he embezzled various items of property for his own use.[14]

During the eighth hearing, which took place on 22 November, the Armenian witnesses gave further testimony pertaining to the murders of five Armenians under Cemal Oğuz's direction. According to architect Simon Efendi, who was among those deported to Çankırı, the Armenians numbered about 200. The witness recounted that the local gendarmerie commander had stated that the murders were "state matters" and that he had not bothered to investigate them.

One of the witnesses in the trial of defendant Abdülgani Bey, the CUP inspector of Edirne, also testified. Abdülgani Bey later repeated that he had had nothing to do with the events in question. The defendant testified that there were seventy to eighty Armenian households in Edirne and that the state had had them all removed in one night: "I woke up one morning, and they were all deported."[15]

The ninth hearing took place on 23 December 1919. Accompanied by a doctor's report, Cemal Oğuz asked to be transferred due to illness. He was furious when the court administrators rejected the request. Later, written testimony from various regions was read into the court record. The most damaging testimony was reportedly directed against Hasan Fehmi. Kastamonu Governor-General Reşit Paşa had this to say: "He had acted cruelly toward the Armenians." Similar statements were made by the mayor of Kastamonu; unfortunately the newspapers did not publish the statements in detail. Hasan Fehmi claimed that all of the damaging statements were made by members of the opposition party, Hürriyet ve İtilaf, and denied all of the allegations.[16]

The tenth hearing took place on 29 December 1919. The prosecutors stated the recommendations of the prosecuting office, demanding a ruling of guilty for the crimes charged against the Bursa, Eskişehir, Edirne, Manisa, and Kastamonu party secretaries. The charges were formation of gangs, murder of Armenians, forced deportation, and other similar charges. As for the Beyoğlu secretary and the Karahisar Emval-i Metruke commission secretaries, the prosecutors recommended a verdict of guilty on misdemeanor charges; they chose acquittal for the Halep and Kastamonu party secretaries, the Konya delegate, and the local national defense chief. The Cemal Oğuz file was removed from the trial for health-related reasons.[17]

In the eleventh hearing, which took place on 1 January 1920, the defendants' attorneys and those appearing pro se were given the opportunity to present their statements of defense. The defendants and their attorneys stated that the claims were all baseless slander, with the latter demanding that the former be acquitted.[18]

In the twelfth hearing, on 3 January 1920, the defendants were asked to make their final statements, and they in turn demanded their acquittals.[19]

The thirteenth hearing took place on 8 January 1920. The public prosecutor read his closing statement and recommended that the charges against the Edirne inspector be merged with those against Edirne Governor Vali Adil Bey, who was being charged with the same crime in a different case. The judgments that were issued later provided that Kastamonu and Bolu Party Secretaries Hasan Fehmi and Dr. Mithat Bey would each get ten years prison time; the others were meted out various punishments. Some were acquitted; others had their files merged with other trials, had their cases separated, or were made subject to further investigation.[20]

The verdict was formally appealed on 13 February 1920 and was overturned by the Appellate Court (Divan-ı Temyiz), which remanded the case to the First Military Tribunal for retrial.[21] There is no information available regarding the outcome. However, a news report dated 30 December 1920 states that the documents surrounding the Hasan Fehmi Bey case were being evaluated.[22] Meanwhile, newspapers dated 10 March reported that Edirne CUP Inspector Abdülgani Bey would be receiving his sentencing with the other defendants from Edirne accused of the crime of forced deportations, and that the matter had been remanded to that court.[23] The *Takvîm-i Vekâyi* published the verbatim court minutes from the first three hearings in *Takvîm-i Vekâyi* issues 3586–3589, 3596, and 3772. The judgment that had been rendered on 8 January 1920 was also published in *Takvîm-i Vekâyi,* no. 3772.

Verdicts or Padishah Approvals of Verdicts, as Recorded in the *Takvîm-i Vekâyi*

4) *Bayburt*

The Bayburt case related to the massacres and acts of looting that took place in and around Bayburt and Ergani; former Urfa District Governor Nusret and Pire Mehmet from Erzurum (Mehmet Necati Efendi) were prosecuted. Nusret had been arrested; Mehmet remained a fugitive from prosecution. The case started on 15 March 1920. In the first session, Nusret testified that the deportations were carried out "on the orders of Mahmut Kâmil Paşa" (Third Army commander in charge of the eastern provinces of Anatolia). Some of the witnesses' testimonies were read into the record. The testimony of Ömer and Ali Efendi was inculpatory against Nusret. At the initial questioning, Nusret had stated: "We were getting intense orders from the military command.… In fact, at one point, [from Mahmut Kâmil Paşa] I got the order that no matter what, Armenians who had not been deported were to be moved out immediately. Anyone not obeying this order would be hanged."[24]

The 20 March session was postponed because documents ordered from Bayburt had not yet arrived. On 1 May 1920, witness testimony was taken. On 5 July 1920 *Tercüman-ı Hakikat* published a report that the case had concluded and stated that it had been sent for the "padishah's approval." The verdict was published on 20 July 1920 and its full court record was laid out in the daily newspapers on 5–6 August 1920. Two of the defendants were sentenced to death. Additionally, the court ordered the investigation of twenty-six individuals in connection with the murders and deportations of Erzurum, Bayburt, and the Ergani mine. Nusret was executed on 5 August 1920.

The testimony of Turkish witnesses was crucial. The witnesses identified in the court record are: then–Lieutenant Commander of the Bayburt Gendarmerie Salih Efendi; businessmen Ömer and Ali Efendis from Sürmene; former Bayburt Mayor (and Beyazid Deputy Governor) Ziya Bey; Erzurum Gendarmerie Regiment Commander Adil Bey; and mine engineer Abdullah Hüsrev from Ergani.

The testimony reveals the abrupt nature of the execution of the Armenian deportations. Within one night residents were expected to leave their homes, without any time to prepare. Mehmet Necati Efendi came from Erzurum with a force of thirty to forty men to implement the deportations. Over the course of fifteen days, the Armenians who were sent group by group to Erzincan were murdered. Nusret gathered about 150 Armenian children, packed them into an inn, and allowed everyone to take whomever they wanted. In his conclusion, following an investigation, Gendarmarie Regiment Commander Adil Bey stated that the Armenians "had been murdered by … those connected with the Special Organization [Teşkilât-ı Mahsusa] … based upon my investigation and the written statement from the Bayburt Gendarmerie commander." Turkish witnesses testified that they had made complaints regarding the murders at the time, but that their demands for investigation were ignored. Further, Nusret had been rewarded for his actions by being promoted first to the rank of deputy governor of Erzincan and then later to governor of Ergani district.

Sources: *Ati*, 14, 15, 16, and 21 March 1920; *Alemdar*, 14, 16, and 21 March, 2 May, 6 August 1920; *Peyam-i Sabah*, 16 March 1920; *Tercüman-ı Hakikat*, 5 July; *Vakit*, 6 August 1920. For the verdict see *Tercüman-ı Hakikat*, 5 August 1920. For the Sultan's confirmation see *Takvîm-i Vekâyi*, 8 August 1920.

5) *Bosnalı (Bosnian) Ismail, His Friends, and Ahmet Midhat*

This case involved eleven individuals accused in connection with the escape of Dr. Ahmet Midhat from the Gümüşsuyu Hospital in Istanbul, where he was undergoing treatment. He was one of the defendants in the trial involving the CUP party secretaries. During the trial he was accused of deporting and murdering Armenians as well as inciting the public to "get rid of the Armenians" while he was CUP secretary in Bolu. When Bolu Deputy Governor Ali Hilmi protested the deportations, Midhat had him removed from his position. Not limiting himself to Bolu alone, Midhat was involved with the deportations in Düzce, Çankırı, and Ankara as well. As a result of these crimes, in the trial of the party secretaries he was sentenced to ten years of hard labor. His case was overturned on appeal and remanded for new trial when he escaped from the hospital to which he had been sent for treatment.

The ringleader behind the escape was Bosnian Ismail, who with Midhat subsequently joined the Turkish nationalist forces from Bursa (Kuvay-ı Milliye). Ismail, a doctor in the hospital at the time, ended up helping Cemal Oğuz and Ahmet Midhat, who were both patients there, escape. With Ismail's help, Oğuz received a six-day pass out of the hospital, and Midhat followed suit. The court record states that Bosnian Ismail "fled at a stage where the investigation and trial had recessed for further work" and joined the nationalist forces (Kuvay-ı Milliye) with Ahmet Midhat. Both Bosnian Ismail and Midhat, while fugitives, were sentenced to death on 19 July 1920 for joining the nationalist forces. Four of the defendants received various punishments for assisting in the escape, while six of them were acquitted. The record of the trial was published in the 22 July 1920 edition of *Vakit* and the 22 and 23 July 1920 editions of *Alemdar*. The decision was approved by the Sultan on 28 August 1920, and was published in *Takvîm-i Vekâyi*, no. 3944, 1 September 1920.

6) *Büyükdere or Boğaziçi*

In the press, the cases of Büyükdere or Boğaziçi were also referred to as the "Yeniköy" or "Tarabya Deportation Case." This trial started on 23 April 1919.

Because the case was given various names by the contemporary press and the defendants were given different nicknames in the papers (for example, Celal is referred to variously as "the baker," "laz," and "Muhtar [Elder] Celal"), the information we have on the case is confusing. It is therefore difficult to know, for example, how many sessions were actually held. The case was about the looting of the property of Greeks and Armenians deported from Büyükdere, specifically Boğaz-Yeniköy and Tarabya in the Bosporus. The defendants were Büyükdere Central Police employee (Abdul) Kerim, Hıfzı Bey-zade Refik Bey from Saloniki, and Laz (Muhtar) Celal Efendi. During a hearing on 6 May 1919, Hafız Mahmûd was arrested and added to the list of the defendants, making the number of defendants four in total.

During the first hearing on 23 April 1919, Abdulkerim testified that Boğaziçi had been declared a military zone and that there were orders to have the entire population there evacuated. Apparently everything was going smoothly until the military arrived. A witness testified that "what actually happened [was] that the soldiers and police arrived and started to act out of order. They even assaulted some of the civilians and beat up a couple of the gentlemen." Also, "there were some soldiers who acted like thieves." The defendant testified a second time at the same sitting and stated that "the soldiers were breaking down the doors and going in."[25]

The second session took place the next day, on 24 April 1919. Turkish witnesses like Samih Bey from the Büyükdere Council of Elders and Büyükdere notable Kemaleddin Bey testified. Kemaleddin Bey testified about the state employees. "Sir," he said, "those aren't civil servants; they're nothing more than despots or tyrants." The witness stated that Kerim Bey had threatened people and that if he had wanted to, he could have stopped the crimes. Lieutenant commander Ali Bey testified that there had indeed been many acts of malfeasance during the deportation and that he had considered lodging a complaint, but that he had been warned to "not intervene in acts of state." Further, he reported that stolen goods were placed in copper kettles and buried. Asked why the local population feared Refik Bey, the witness answered: "His excellency Talaat Paşa would visit Refik Bey's villa once a week and pay his respects to the man's father by kissing his hand. At the time, who wouldn't be afraid of anyone Talaat Paşa said 'hello' to?"[26] In his testimony Halid Efendi, the director of the Second Precinct police department, had this to say: "Many of the homes were ruined, and you can't even tell where they were now." Witness Raşid Efendi (in the second sitting) also stated that goods had been stolen and buried.[27]

During the third sitting, which took place on April 27, 1919, the Armenian witnesses' testimony was taken. They testified that they had been given twenty-four hours notice, that they had not been allowed the opportunity to take anything with them, and that when they returned, their homes and personal property had been looted.[28]

During the fourth hearing on 1 May 1919, more witnesses testified. Besides the inculpatory testimony given by the Armenian witnesses, police officer Raşid Bey and Osman Bey from the Second Division of the Army Corps also testified against the defendants. According to *Yeni Gazete,* goods were stolen, "homes with 3–4 floors were sold for 10 lira," and Osman Bey had provided some exculpatory testimony for some of the defendants.[29]

The fifth sitting took place on 6 May 1919, and the court continued to listen to witness testimony. Nuri Efendi, the director of the police department, testified that stolen goods had been found in the home of Celal Efendi. The file of Hafız Mahmud from Rize was merged with the present trial, and he was arrested. Other Turkish witnesses also gave their testimony.[30]

During the sixth sitting on 7 May 1919, more witnesses testified.[31] The seventh sitting, on 10 May 1919, also continued with witness testimony.[32] During the eighth sitting on 13 May 1919 Turkish witnesses continued to testify, giving evidence that Armenian property had been looted. Exculpatory testimony was also taken. After hearing this testimony, the court decided that the questioning was complete and that the time had come for a decision to be made.[33] The court handed down its decision on 24 May, but no news of it was published in the papers. *Takvîm-i Vekâyi,* no. 3618, reports that defendant Kerim was sentenced to one year, and Refik two years of prison. The other defendants were acquitted. On 18 January 1920, *Ati* reported that "Kerim, the Büyükdere central police office employee, and Refik Hıfzı Bey who had been sentenced to one and two years hard labor respectively as a result of the Büyükdere deportation trial, had been released after having their remaining prison time commuted."

The transcript of the final court decision was published only in *Takvîm-i Vekâyi,* no. 3618, 9 August 1919.

7) *Cemal Oğuz and Nureddin Bey*

Tried for charges arising from the murders of Armenians deported from Istanbul to Çankırı, Çankırı Party Secretary Cemal Oğuz was initially under a separate investigation, but his file was merged with the "Secretaries" trial during the fifth hearing on 27 October 1919. Later still, his case was again separated from that trial during the tenth sitting, as a result of his personal health issues. Cemal Oğuz's individual trial began on 27 October 1920. During the first hearing the written testimonies of some of the Turkish witnesses were read into the record. The witnesses' statements indicated that Oğuz had misused the provisions and funds belonging to the Army Corps. The defendant denied all the claims.

The witnesses continued to give testimony during the second hearing on 3 February 1920. Kasbar, one of the Armenians who had survived the deportation to Çankırı, testified against Cemal Oğuz. He stated that a convoy of 160

Armenians had been sent to Çankırı initially, but then they had been dispersed to other areas. "We left [Çankırı] as a convoy of fifty-one people. Of this group only nineteen returned. Later twenty-four people left and of these only 4 returned." According to the witness, any Armenian who survived the deportation was charged a fee of 800 lira.[34]

The final sitting took place on 5 February 1920, and more witness testimony was taken. Another survivor of the deportation, Mihail Ohannes, testified. Ohannes related a story of how five Armenians deported from Ayaş had been killed, and how the assistant district governor, Izzet Bey, had opened an investigation and as a result "two scoundrels were caught and stuffed into the jail. The guards aided their escape."[35] Ohannes described Cemal Oğuz as an influential person at the time. After Oğuz again denied the accusations against him, the prosecutor made a closing statement and finished with a demand that the defendant be found guilty. The defendant, with his attorney's help, made his final statement in defense and pleaded for acquittal.

The court's decision was announced during a session held on 8 February 1920. Cemal Oğuz was found guilty of murdering Dr. Çilingiryan and four friends in the "Tüney" area of Çankırı. The finding stated that Cemal Oğuz had brought Kurd Ali,[36] the man who murdered the Armenians, to Çankırı and directed his actions. Cemal Oğuz got five years and four months of hard labor, while Captain Nureddin Bey, who had fled prosecution, got six years and eight months of the same. The case was appealed to the Military Tribunal Appellate Division on 5 March 1920, and the final decision was approved by the sultan on 27 May 1920 (for more details see Chapter 6, "*Cemal Oğuz and Major Nurettin*").

Sources: *Ati*, 27 and 28 January, 4, 6, and 8 February, 5 March 1920; *Alemdar*, 4, 6, and 9 February, 5 March 1920; *Peyam-i Sabah*, 9 February, 2 May 1920; *Vakit*, 2 May 1920.

The sultan's approval was published in *Takvîm-i Vekâyi*, no. 3867, 31 May 1920.

8) *Erzincan*

The trial of former Erzincan District Governor Memduh Bey, former Erzincan Assembly Representative Halid, Hafız Abdullah Avni, Haci Vahidzade Rıza Efendi from Erzincan, Dersim Tribal Leader Karmo (Kırma?) Yusuf, Gendarmerie Sergeant Arslan from Erzincan, the Danezbey (?) Township Director (of the city of Pülümür) and Tribal Leader Kagü (Kako?) Semakon (?).

Defendant Memduh Bey was exiled to Malta at the start of the trial, and Halid Bey fled prosecution. The trial was supposed to start in January 1920 but was delayed; its start was published on 18 May 1920, and there is news of it continuing on 23 June 1920. Having proceeded with haste, the trial came to a conclusion on 28 July 1920. In the court decision that was published on 29 July 1920, the papers *Vakit, Alemdar, and Ikdam* state that the defendants were all active members of the Special Organization (Teşkilât-ı Mahsusa) and go on to describe how the Armenians had been killed. The trial resulted in five judgments for death by execution. The testimony of Erkân-ı-Harbiye Mayor Rıza Bey is mentioned as having played an important role in the decision for capital punishment. Of the defendants in the trial, only Hafız Abdullah Avni was actually present to hear his sentence. The others were prosecuted in absentia as they had taken flight. The sentence against Avni was officially approved by the sultan on 27 July, and Avni was executed on 29 July 1920.

Sources: *Ati,* January 1920; *Peyam-i Sabah,* 17 May 1920; *Alemdar,* 23 June, 29 July 1920; *Ikdam, Vakit, Tercüman-ı Hakikat,* 29 July 1920.

The sultan's approval was published in *Takvîm-i Vekâyi,* no. 3917, 31 July 1920.

9) *Harput (Mamuretülaziz, aka Elazığ)*

This trial was for the crimes of looting and murder in the city of Elazığ and the surrounding areas. The defendants were former Elazığ Governor Sabit; Bahaeddin Şakir, member of the Party Central Committee; CUP Responsible Secretary Resneli Nazım; former Harput Mayor Asım; Safvet, former Assembly representative from Harput; former Assembly Representative Hace Said; Mehmet Nuri, Assembly representative from Dersim; and Elazığ Education Director Ferid Bey.

On 13 June 1919 the papers wrote that the administrative office of the courts had found the file inadequate and had returned it to the prosecutor's office for completion. It was reported in *Alemdar* that "the trial [would] start during the following week." The trial started on 28 July 1919, and it is not clear how many sessions took place.

On 2 August 1919 there was extensive coverage about the session and the facts it revealed about the Special Organization (Teşkilât-ı Mahsusa). Halil Paşa had this to say: "I had nothing to do with the region of Elazığ." His testimony confirmed the claims made by witnesses in the main trial, referred to above as the Main Trial of Members of the Central Committee. Further, Halil Paşa stated that the "Teşkilat-ı Mahsusa set up a tent and lived in Beyazıd [Istanbul]." Later during his testimony, former Governor of Erzurum and Damascus Tahsin Bey had this to say:

> During the Armenian deportations, I was in Erzurum. The deportations were carried out in accordance with the order of the Minister of the Interior. The order came down on May 12.... Later, the army requested that the deportations start forthwith. We called in some of the more

> prominent Armenians. We never had an explicit directive. I conveyed [to the Armenians] every order that I received [from Istanbul]. The convoys that got attacked and destroyed were comprised of groups that were put together by the Teşkilat-ı Mahsusa. There were two different Teşkilat-ı Mahsusas. When I came from Erzurum it was a single strong unit and they had been involved in the war. The Army knew about it. Later another Teşkilat-ı Mahsusa group got started that had Bahaeddin Şakir Bey's name written all over it. He would send telegrams with the title "Teşkilat-ı Mahsusa Chief" written on them. This was not the one involved in fighting the war. That Teşkilat-ı Mahsusa was the one which had captured Artvin and Ardahan. Bahaeddin Şakir Bey had a code with which he reported to the Bab-ı Ali and the Ministry of War. During the deportations he was reporting to the army also.[37]

In the testimony of another witness, Colonel Tosun Paşa, we read: "I saw some tents around the Ministry of War that might have belonged to the Teşkilat-ı Mahsusa … when I went to Uzunköprü I saw some men, irregulars, there. Later I wrote that they should get rid of those guys."[38]

Another sitting (perhaps the third) took place on 5 August. Mayor Hüsameddin Bey (most likely Hüsameddin Ertürk), as a member of the Teşkilat-ı Mahsusa, was required to testify. He stated that "[He] was a member of the Teşkilat-ı Mahsusa and after it was decided to dissolve it [he] was involved in its liquidation." The purpose of the organization was to establish Islamic unity, according to Hüsameddin Bey, and about the founding members he had this to say: "Despite the fact that Atıf, Nazım, Bahaeddin Şakir and Rıza Bey were civilians, they were part of the Teşkilat-ı Mahsusa. Nevertheless they weren't involved in military matters;" instead they were assigned work in a supportive role. He added that at the start of the war, Bahaeddin Şakir "had been in the command of the sector which comprised volunteers and who had attacked Ardahan."[39]

Witness Miralay Nasuhi Bey gave many "stories and accounts" of the deportations at Bitlis. According to him the killings that took place in the region had been carried out under the direction of Gendarmarie Commander Major Faik Bey (unfortunately there is no account given of this accusatory claim, in the newspapers). The witness also stated that he had heard that Major Faik had been prosecuted and acquitted by the Elazığ Military Tribunal.

The sitting that was supposed to take place on 7 August was postponed, and on 20 August, at what was probably the fourth sitting, the court continued to hear witness testimony.

We do not know of any other hearing until 20 September. At that hearing (possibly the fifth), witness testimony continued to be taken. From witness Fuad Paşazade Ali Bey came the testimony that he was in Istanbul during the deportations, but that he learned from Deputy Mustafa Efendi that "many of his acquaintances had been deported and that some had been murdered." He had also heard from Mustafa Efendi that "the transfer and deportation order had not come down from Governor Sabit Bey, but rather that the local Committee of Union and Progress Party apparatus had executed it." Among the stories recounted by Mustafa Efendi is the claim that "Deputy Mehmet Nuri Bey had caused four villages to be deported."[40]

During the next hearing (probably the sixth), which took place on 22 October, the court heard testimony from the Izmit Postal and Telegraph Director, Asaf Bey. Asaf Bey, who had been the mayor of Harput during the deportation, stated that the Armenians who had been [Armenian political] committee members were arrested, while the others were deported. The witness, who was a member of CUP, testified on behalf of fellow witness Mehmet Nuri, who was his brother-in-law. He stated that not only was Nuri innocent of any crimes against the Armenians, but that Nuri had even sheltered several hundred Armenians on his farm. Another witness, by the name of Mehmet Ali Bey, testified that Asaf had promised to reveal an important document in connection with the deportations. "He [Asaf] was going to apply for a civil position and when he saw me there he stated 'For God's sake, don't tell anyone I'm a Unionist. If we keep it a secret, I'll get you the document that I promised you.' And I never told a soul." However, Asaf Bey ended up getting arrested and never produced the document.[41] The document referred to concerned the deportation and the killing of Armenians and bore the signature of Party Secretary Ferid Bey.

At the same session Mazhar Bey testified that during the deportations he was assigned to the commission to investigate misdemeanors and minor abuses by civil servants for the regions of Elazığ, Bitlis, and Diyarbakır. The commission had the authority to take into custody and turn over any individuals who were found to have committed any abuses of the system. While he had not been able to go to Bitlis, he had been to both of the other cities. "I turned in hundreds of people to the Military Tribunal. Whatever information could be had, I investigated it. I even sent the [district] governor of Malatya to the Tribunal and I know that he got a two year sentence." (The investigation which Mazhar Bey was referring to had to do with minor irregularities.)[42] The trial was continued to another date for further testimony by more witnesses.

During the hearing on 29 October, County Executive Muhiddin Bey, who had been appointed the director of military affairs in Harput during the war years, testified for the defense: "During the deportation, nothing was going on in the center of the province. Still, I heard that there were killings going on in the outskirts." Additionally, he stated that "[a]nyone sheltering the Armenians was going to be executed" and that not all of the Armenian property that was confiscated got into the hands of the state, because "the locals had looted some of it." After hearing the testimony of another witness for the defense, a memo from the Ministry of the Interior was read in court demanding that the trial be moved to Elazığ, where apparently another, similar trial was taking place. The motion was rejected. Defense attorneys also presented a document from an American Mr. Riggs stating that Nuri Bey and Ferid Bey had nothing to do with the deportations, as well as a written statement "from the families which Nuri and Ferid Bey had protected."

The hearing on 17 November (most likely the eighth hearing) yielded the testimony of Süleyman Faik Paşa, who stated that Mayor Asım Bey had taken some of the carpets owned by Armenians and sent them to Nuri Bey's house. He further stated that Asım Bey "had tried to help [the Armenians] with what ever he has in his hand" and that he "reported to the regional authorities about the irregularities that had occurred." The witness testified that "one by one, property had been appropriated from Armenian houses." Even though Mazhar Bey's investigation into the charge that Asım Bey had confiscated Armenian property for his own benefit resulted in Asım being sent for prosecution to the military tribunal, he would ultimately be acquitted of the charges.

Faik further testified that he did not know that Nuri Bey had confiscated Armenian property. In response, the court read Faik his own telegram, complaining to the higher authorities of Nuri Bey's confiscation of Armenian property; whereupon he confirmed in court that he had in fact sent the telegram. Additionally, Faik stated that even though there had been an order to "keep the Assyrian Christians out of the deportation," both Nazım and Nuri Bey had engaged in extortion by threatening the Assyrians with deportation if they didn't pay up.[43] Other witnesses' testimony was taken during this hearing as well.

Another hearing was scheduled for 20 November 1919 (probably the ninth hearing). However, at that hearing it was determined that the trial needed to be postponed pending the receipt of answers to the questions asked in a telegram from Elazığ. Also, witnesses failed to appear for the hearing.

During the tenth session on 4 December 1919, the answers from Elazığ were considered inadequate, and it was decided that further inquiries be made. Additionally, an Armenian who had been put to work on Nuri Bey's farm testified on his behalf.

Three more sessions took place on 4, 8, and 10 January 1920. The case came to a close after the prosecution's closing statement and the defense's concluding remarks. During that session the secret telegram sent by Bahaeddin Şakir to Harput was read aloud. In this telegram Şakir asks what happened to the deported Armenians and whether they were liquidated or merely exiled. The court's decision was announced on 13 January 1920. Of the defendants who had fled, Bahaeddin Şakir received the death penalty, while Elazığ Party Secretary Resneli Nazım was sentenced to fifteen years of hard labor. Defendants who were in custody (Party Secretary Ferid Bey and former Dersim Deputy Mehmet Nuri Bey) were acquitted and released.

Sources: *Alemdar,* 13 June, 3, 6, and 7 August, 21 September, 30 October, 18 and 21 November, 5 and 30 December 1919, 5, 11, and 14 January 1920; *Ati,* 23 and 30 October, 18 November 1919, 11 and 14 December 1920; *Ikdam,* 4 and 5 December 1919; *Tercüman-ı Hakikat,* 28 July, 18 and 30 October 1919; *Yeni Gazete,* 3 and 21 August 1919.

Only the record of the court decision is published in *Takvîm-i Vekâyi,* no. 3771, 9 February 1920.

10) *Township Directors Trial, Sometimes Called the İzmit or Bahçecik or Derbend Trial*

This trial against six defendants—including the Derbend Township Director Vecihi, Bahçecik Township Director Ali Şuuri Bey, former Prison Director İbrahim Bey, and companions—was for the crimes of "pillage, deportation and bribery." The trial started on 27 November 1919. During the first hearing, the testimony of defendant Ali Şuuri Bey was taken. He was charged with raping an Armenian girl and wrongfully seizing Armenian property. The defendant denied all charges. During the second hearing on 29 November another defendant, Sergeant Ahmed, testified against Vecihi Bey. He stated that Vecihi Bey had seized Armenian properties with the help of a Circassian group. He also added that "nearly 20 Armenian soldiers from the village had been deported along with their families." Another defendant who gave damaging testimony against Vecihi Bey was the commander of the Arslanbey village police, Gendarmerie Sergeant Süleyman. According to this sergeant, Vecihi Bey took close to thirteen truckloads of Armenian goods without paying a single cent for them. He stated, "I objected but no one listened to me."

During the third hearing on 3 December, defendant and former Bahçecik Township Director Ali Şuuri Bey testified against Prison Director Ibrahim Bey. According to Ali Şuuri Bey, Ibrahim had beaten and tortured the Armenians. Vecihi Bey had testified that Ibrahim had "deported all the Catholics and Protestants" from his region. The testimony of the sergeants Ahmed and Süleyman included the statement that Ibrahim "beat many of the Armenians with a *falaka.*"[44] The testimony of Sergeant Süleyman was quite detailed. "We gathered up the Armenians. We put them into the school. Ibrahim Bey asked them 'How many are you?' They answered 'six hundred' and then he said 'well, then if there are six hundred of you I expect six hundred weapons.' Anyone who didn't have one got beaten up. He even beat up a priest. He used a *falaka* to beat them with." The sergeant also added to his prior testimony about Vecihi Bey's seizing of Armenian property: "When Vecihi Bey started taking the property away, I tried to stop him. Vecihi Bey said, 'Stop getting involved, it's none of your business, I'm the township director and I'm your superior.' I then put that into a written memo which I sent straight to the Major."[45] Later the written statements of witnesses, many of which verified the statement given by

Sergeant Süleyman regarding the charges of torture and beatings, were read into the record.

The fourth hearing took place on 7 December 1919, and the written testimonies that had not been read in the prior hearing were read. The testimonies of both Armenians and Turks (Sergeant Murat and Izmit police headquarters employee Süleyman Fehmi Bey) were damaging to the defense. The witnesses stated that Prison Director Ibrahim Bey and Ali Şuuri Bey had tortured the Armenians and looted their properties. In all of the testimonies read out in court, one of the common assertions was that Ibrahim Bey had "beaten and tortured people on the excuse of collecting weapons from them."

During the fifth session, which occurred on 10 December 1919, more witnesses were heard; they continued to give testimony about the torture meted out by Ibrahim Bey. Two more hearings took place on 13 and 18 December, during which some of the witnesses wished to recant their prior testimony, while others continued to provide damaging testimony. One of the latter was Istanbul Patriarchate Custodian Kirkor Efendi, who had been tortured. Kirkor, who had had the *falaka* administered while he was lying down, had this to say, "I…was laid on the ground before Ibrahim Bey, when they gave me the *falaka*. At that point I fainted. When I came to, I noticed that the money in my belt had been taken."[46] One of the Armenians who had been deported from Istanbul stated that there were about 200 people who had been deported along with him. From his testimony, one can surmise that the Armenians deported from Istanbul had left around July-August 1915.

The eighth session took place on 4 January 1920, and the written testimony of witnesses taken in Iznik, most of it of a damaging nature, was read into the record. During the two hearings that followed on 20 and 22 January, witness testimony continued. During the hearing on 30 January, the minutes of a record showing that Vecihi Bey had "entered the homes and taken the abandoned property" of Armenians was read, thereby providing evidential proof of that charge. Vecihi Bey had been charged with this crime earlier (probably around 1915), but the investigation had been deemed incomplete and the matter had been dropped. After the hearings that took place on 7 and 14 February, the court determined that enough evidence had been presented. The hearing on 17 February was postponed because a witness failed to appear. On 19 February, a brief from the Armenian Patriarchate was read into the record. This brief requested that more Armenian witnesses be permitted to testify. The testimony taken on 24 February was damaging to Ibrahim Bey but exculpatory for Ali Şuuri Bey. At the 25 February hearing the witnesses, some of whom were Turks, gave damaging testimony against Vecihi Bey, and in closing the prosecutor gave his statement of recommendation.

The court's decision came down on 29 February 1920 and was published in the newspapers on 1 March 1920. Among the fugitive defendants was former Prison Director Ibrahim Bey, who was sentenced to fifteen years. Military Police Sergeant Faik received three years in prison. Vecihi Bey was sentenced to two years, while Ali Şuuri Bey received one year of hard labor. Sergeant Ahmet and Hasan Efendi each received four months of prison along with fourteen blows with a stick as their punishment. Meanwhile Haji Halid Efendi and Sergeant Süleyman were both acquitted. Both Ali Şuuri Bey and Vecihi Bey were released on the same day as those who had been acquitted, the former for having his punishment satisfied with time served and the latter for having had the good fortune to have his case dismissed under the prevailing rule of statute of limitations. The decision received the required sultan's formal approval on 6 July 1920. On 12 July 1920 *Alemdar* republished the court decision (or the sultan's approval, it is not quite clear from the report).

Sources: *Alemdar,* 25, 28, and 30 November, 4, 8, 11, 14, and 19 December 1919, 5 January, 1 and 8 February, 1 March, and 12 July 1920; *Ati,* 28 and 30 November 1919, 4, 8, and 19 December 1919, 19, 20, and 23 January, 1, 6, 15, 17, 18, 19, 20, 25, and 26 February, 1 March 1920; *Ikdam,* 4, 8, 11, and 19 December 1919; *Tercüman-ı Hakikat,* 18 December 1919; *Peyam-i Sabah,* 15, 20, and 29 February, 1 March 1920.

The sultan's approval was published in *Takvîm-i Vekâyi,* no. 3900, 11 July 1920.

11) *Trabzon*

This trial was for charges of murder and looting in Trabzon. The defendants, from the Trabzon region, were Customs Director Mehmet Ali Bey, Police Director Nuri Bey, Agent Mustafa Efendi, Gendarmerie Assistant Talat Bey, Hotelier Niyazi Efendi, Health Director Ali Saib Bey, Yusuf Riza, and Party Secretary Nail Bey. Trabzon Governor Cemal Azmi Bey was prosecuted in absentia. The case against Yusuf Riza was separated from the others by his own motion after the sixteenth hearing. He was in the process of being prosecuted concurrently in the main trial. The case against Ali Saib was also taken out and tried separately.

This trial was held between 26 March and 20 May 1919. The verdict was read out in the twentieth session on 22 May 1919. Defendants Cemal Azmi and Nail both received death sentences, while the others received various lesser sentences. The verdict was published in *Takvîm-ı Vekâyi,* no. 3616, 6 August 1919. Because this is one of the earliest trials it was widely reported in the Ottoman press, and the testimony of Turkish witnesses was crucial for the verdict.[47]

12) *Yozgat*

This trial concerned murder and looting in the area surrounding Yozgat. The defendants were the Yozgat Deputy Governor and Boğazlayan County Executive (*Kaymakam*) Kemal Bey, Gendarmerie Commander Major Tevfik Bey, and Feyyaz Ali Bey, an employee of Religious Foundations (Evkaf). At the seventeenth session, the case against Feyyaz Bey was removed from the trial and ordered to be processed separately. Kemal Bey received a death sentence and was executed on 10 April 1919. Tevfik Bey received a sentence of fifteen years' hard labor.

The trial ran from 5 February to 7 April 1919. There were eighteen sessions in total. The final verdict was reached on 8 April 1919. The court decision alone was published in *Takvîm-i Vekâyi*, no. 3617, 7 August 1919. It is an important trial due to the fact that it was the first to be heard, and also because it produced the first execution. Kemal Bey's execution resulted in an enormous nationalist demonstration.

Trials Covered in the Press Only That Came to a Judicial Conclusion

Each of the following twenty-two cases, with one exception, ended in a decision by the court and was published in the press. Only Mosul 1 (Case #28) did not end in a decision because the defendant was exiled to Malta. This case is included here because it contains information pertaining to the subsequent Mosul 2 (Case #29).

Three of the trials presented here concluded with the defendants receiving various punishments. An interesting point is that capital punishment was doled out only to those defendants who were fugitives and were, therefore, tried in absentia. Seventeen of the cases ended with acquittals. One of the cases ended with a partial acquittal and a remand for further investigation. As mentioned above, another one was not prosecuted because the defendant had been exiled to Malta.

13) *Adapazar*

This trial was against the party secretary from Adapazar, Hamid Bey. He was charged with beating and threatening Armenian merchant Murâdyân Ohânis, causing the death of a person named Yorgi, who had been a victim of the deportation, looting, and beating. A report implicating Hamid Bey had been prepared by the county executive (*kaymakam*) of Adapazar, Recai Nüzhet Bey, and submitted on 31 March 1919 to the district governor of Izmit. This report, along with the statements of others, proved to be especially damaging to the defendant. County Executive Recai Nüzhet Bey appeared in court and repeated the allegations in the report. It came out in the trial that Hamid Bey had threatened the locals by reporting them to CUP and had used the party in carrying out his designs in the area. He was one of the prime perpetrators in the matter of the deportation of Armenians and the looting of their property. According to one of the testimonies, Hamid Bey, who had been a "'400 lira' man before the deportation, turned into a '50,000 lira' man afterwards." During the hearing on 6 November 1919, Hamid Bey denied being the party secretary, and at the last hearing on 16 February 1920 the prosecutor recommended acquittal. On 17 February 1920 the court formally acquitted the defendant.

Sources: *Alemdar,* 1, 5, 7, 12, and 15 August, 8 November 1919, 11 February 1920; *Ati,* 7 November 1919, 19 January, 11, 13, 17, and 18 February 1920; *Peyam-i Sabah,* 13, 17, and 18 February 1920.

14) *Ali Saib*

Ali Saib had previously been a defendant in the Trabzon trial, but his case had been separated. This case relates to the charge that Armenians had been murdered through the use of gas and poison in Trabzon's municipal hospital. The trial started on 8 July 1919. Several witnesses testified, including Dr. Ziya Bey, who had prepared a written report implicating the defendant in the crime. According Dr. Ziya's report, Saib Bey, using poison, had injected children by syringe and later removed the bodies by stuffing them in baskets (*küfe*). During the second session on 20 August, more witness testimony was taken. In the papers, the only news was that Dr. Vahab Bey had had no knowledge of the events that had taken place. The third and fourth hearings took place on 16 and 21 December, respectively, and more witness testimony was taken. According to the press coverage given at the time, witnesses had heard that children had been poisoned with morphine and stuffed into "*küfe.*" Even though there were testimonies regarding these events, the court dismissed them as untrustworthy.

There were four hearings in total. During the final hearing on 21 December 1919, the prosecuting authorities requested that the defendant be acquitted, and at the same hearing the defendant was in fact acquitted, the court deciding that "Ali Saib Bey had not had the ascribed Armenians murdered, extinguished lives and thrown the corpses into the sea." He was released. The final decision was published in *Alemdar,* 22 December 1919.

Sources: *Alemdar,* 9 July, 16 and 22 December 1919; *Yeni Gazete,* 9 July, 21 August 1919; *Ikdam,* 17 December 1919; *Ati,* 17 and 22 December 1919.

15) *Amasya*

It is extremely difficult to understand how many trials involving the deportations in Amasya actually took place because of the variety of accounts in the press. In one case, Muammer, the former governor-general of Sivas, former Deputy from Izmit, Süleyman Sırrı, and Amasya Deputy Nafız Ismail Bey, along with nineteen other individuals, were charged with crimes related to the deportations from Amasya.[48] We have not been able to ascertain the date this trial actually began or how it ended. We do, however, have information that another trial involving Amasya Governor Sırrı, Gendarmarie Battalion Commander Tevfik Bey, and Amasya notable Hasan Efendi took place. We do not yet know if these defendants were among the nineteen defendants mentioned above.

We do not know when the trial of this second group actually commenced. It was reported on 10 March 1919 that Hüseyin Efendi had been arrested ten months previously and taken to Bekirağa prison on charges related to the Amasya deportations and murders. On 19 January 1920 it was reported that the trial had yet to start. On 28 July 1920, it was reported that judicial questioning in the matter of one of the defendants, "tin tin" Hasan, was continuing. Similar news was reported on 9 August. On 17 August the papers reported that the case was continuing and that "it appears likely that the case will conclude this week." Many witnesses were heard during the session that took place on 24 August 1920, and the papers reported that many defendants were being tried in absentia. On 31 August, the press reported that the case had come to a conclusion and that the decision regarding Governor Sırrı Bey had been submitted to the sultan for formal approval. Nevertheless, reports on 3 September 1920 claimed that the case was continuing and that more witnesses had been subpoenaed for testimony. An article published on 6 November 1920 reported that the trial docket for the First Military Tribunal had been reorganized and that the trial of former Gendarmarie Battalion Commander Tevfik Bey and Amasya notable Hasan Bey, arising from the Amasya deportations, would be the first on the list. Just as the trial was about to conclude, a reorganization of the military tribunal resulted in the opening of a new investigation and a delay in the prosecution of the case.

A newspaper reported on 13 November 1920: "Yesterday, former Amasya governor Sırrı, former Amasya gendarmerie commander Major Tevfik Bey and Amasya notable Hasan Efendi, who have been … for the past two years detained by military officials in connection with the Amasya deportation charges, were transferred to the 'First' Military Tribunal. Despite having had their case come to a judicial conclusion forty days ago by the Amasya Court administration, the court's decision was not officially confirmed after being formally presented before the High authority." According to news reported on 21 November, the case was being reexamined. On 6 December 1920, a newspaper reported that this case was listed as a high priority among the cases that had not been prosecuted to their final conclusion. The defendants had been under arrest for well over a year at that point. When the case was reopened, the court decided that the defendants should be acquitted, and they were released that same day.

Sources: *Alemdar,* 10 March 1919, 25 and 28 July, 25 August, 3 September 1920; *Ati,* 19 January 1920; *Ikdam,* 9 August and 10 December 1920; *Vakit,* 17, 25, and 31 August, 21 November, 3 and 6 December 1920.

16) *Bayburt Trial*

This was the case against Yusuf Ziya Bey. The trial began around 26 January 1921 but was postponed until 9 February 1921 (*Vakit,* 27 January 1921). According to news reported in *Ikdam* on 18 February 1921, because of the prosecuting authorities' inability to make the connection between the indicted felony and the defendant, Yusuf Ziya Bey was acquitted and released. The same news appeared in *Vakit,* 18 February 1921.

Sources: *Vakit,* 27 January, 18 February 1921; *Ikdam,* 18 February 1921.

17) *Deir-Zor Deportation 1*

This trial, against the defendant former Deir-Zor Police Director Mustafa Ökkeş Efendi, which was based upon charges related to the deportation in the Deir-Zor region, began on 20 January 1921. The indictment was read into the court record, and the testimony of witnesses was taken on that date. There were two sessions, one on 23 January and the other on 27 January, in which the trial record against Deir-Zor District Governor Zeki Bey was immediately ordered from the appellate division. That trial, which had been concluded earlier, had made mention of Mustafa Ökkeş. According to the news reported on 10 March 1921, in the last session the fact that the court could not establish the crimes of "cruelty" with which the defendant had been charged resulted in his acquittal and release.

Sources: *Alemdar, Vakit,* 21 January 1921; *Ikdam,* 24 January 1921; *Peyam-i Sabah,* 4 and 10 March 1921.

18) *Deir-Zor Deportation 2*

This second Deir-Zor trial was against former Deir-Zor Governor Zeki Bey, who was a fugitive at the time of the trial. As reported in the papers on 23 March 1920, the decision to indict had been made against "former Deir-Zor district governor Zeki Bey … who was suspected of the crimes of murder, annihilation and seizure of property of deported Armenians from the region of Zor." The trial was quite short and resulted in the issuance of a death sentence on 28 April 1920. The court's decision was published in the papers on 30 April and 2 May 1920. According to this decision, former Deir-Zor Governor Zeki Bey was accused of murder and annihilation, looting, and seizure of property of the Armenians deported to the province of Zor from the various regions of the empire. It was decided that he had participated in attacks and organized gangs to attack Armenians who were being deported while they were en route, and seized their cash, jewelry, and property. Those who were murdered were dumped along the canals of the Habur River basin. This decision was based on the testimony of both Muslims and non-Muslims under oath. Zeki Bey's guilt was secured after the court considered that he had taken flight from prosecution. He was sentenced to death. Additionally, the local prosecutor's office determined that in order to examine the activities of the former Deir-Zor Deputy Nuri Efendi on claims of his having participated in and been a witness to the events mentioned, an investigation would be opened along with that of the commanders of the gendarmerie, military, and the police commissioner's office at the time.

Sources: *Alemdar,* 23 March, 30 April 1920; *Ati,* 23 March 1920; *Vakit,* 30 April and 2 May 1920.

19) *Dolapdere*

The Dolapdere trial centered on accusations of the deportation of Armenians and the sale of their property in and around Dolapdere by a former employee of the governmental administrative office, Mehmet Ali Efendi, and Refiki Salih Efendi. It is not clear when the trial began, but according to the news reported on 31 March 1921, after listening to witness testimony, the court decided that the defendants were not guilty and ordered that they be acquitted.

Source: *Ikdam,* 31 March 1921.

20) *Edirne*

This case relates to the deportation of Armenians from Edirne. Defendants were Edirne Party Inspector (Abdul) Gani Bey, Director of Religious Foundations (*Evkaf*) Sadreddin, Director of Agriculture Avni Bey, Rıfat Bey, and Gani's servant Hayrullah Ağa. When another defendant, Servet Bey, died during the trial, his case was removed from prosecution. One of the defendants (Avni) was tried without being arrested. It is very difficult to give the exact number of defendants because the press covering the trial referred to them by a variety of names and professions.

According to the newspapers, Gani Bey had been prosecuted in the Party Secretaries Trial and found guilty, but his sentencing was postponed pending the result of the Edirne trial. Therefore his trial was merged with this one; according to press coverage on 10 March 1920 his file was transferred to the present case. On 15 October 1920 the trial was reported to be proceeding, and on 18 October it was reported that some witnesses' testimony had been heard in court. On 9 December 1920, in a statement given to *Ikdam* by the chief of the military tribunal, Hurşit Paşa, it was reported that "the case will start today." The restructuring of the court in the fall might have caused the delay of this case.

It was reported on 6 December 1920 that this trial was the second important trial that would be resumed shortly. News from 23 December 1920 shows that the trial was in fact in progress, and it was reported to have resumed under Chief Judge Hurşit Bey. The last hearing took place on 1 January 1921: "The court's decision was in favor of acquittal for detainees Gani and Rıfat along with lieutenant Kasım Efendi, for failure to establish a case for the crimes at hand." There was no report about the other defendants; however, one can gather from the acquittal of the three top defendants that the others may have been acquitted also. Gani Bey was acquitted the next day of the crimes he had been charged with in the Union and Progress Party Secretaries Trial.

According to the *Tercüman-ı Hakikat,* there had been a case in the Edirne Military Tribunal; however, when this tribunal was disbanded, that case was heard by the First Military Tribunal in Istanbul. It is unclear whether the trial reported here had anything to do with the other trial above.[49]

Sources: *Ikdam,* 9 December 1920; *Vakit,* 24 September, 4, 6, 15, and 18 October, 6 and 23 December 1920, 6 January 1921.

21) *Eğin 1*

This trial relates to the deportations in Eğin. The charges were brought against Abdullah, the son of Mehmet. It is not clear when the trial started, but news reports indicate that it continued on 16 February and 4 March 1921. According to the news reported on 21 March 1921, the trial ended with the conclusion that Abdullah's alibi, which apparently put him in Malatya at the time of the events occurring, required that the court rule in favor of acquittal.

Sources: *Vakit,* 18 February 1921; *Ikdam,* 18 February, 20 March 1920; *Peyam-i Sabah,* 4 and 20 March 1921.

22) *Eğin 2*

This trial was against the defendant Butcher Mustafa Efendi. It is not clear when the trial started, and it is possible it may have been part of the Eğin 1 trial described above, for both trials seem to have taken place on the same dates. It was reported on 6 February 1921 that the trial had started, but no information was provided about the exact date. The trial was postponed to 21 February 1921. On 5 March 1921 it was reported that the trial had been postponed because of the failure of witnesses to appear. News items dated 24 March and 31 March state that the case was continuing and that the final hearing was near its conclusion. On 17 May 1921 it was reported that the trial had ended and that the defendant had been acquitted.

Sources: *Alemdar,* 6 February 1921; *Vakit,* 6, 11, and 18 February 1921; *Ikdam,* 6 February, 20 and 31 March 1921; *Peyam-i Sabah,* 10, 20, and 24 March, 17 May 1921.

23) *Giritli (Kiraathaneci) Necati Efendi*

Necati Efendi was charged as a member of Teşkilit-ı Mahsusa in the region of Diyarbakır. The newspapers labeled the trial "the most important to arise from the activities of the Committee of Union and Progress." It began on 13 July 1919. The indictment stated that the defendant should be punished for having been the "*fedai*" (person who is willing to sacrifice his life for a cause) of the Union and Progress Party (from the Bab- ı Ali raid in 1913), for having been involved in the murder of Nazım Paşa. In the hearing on 21 September 1919, the defendant was questioned under oath; in his testimony he claimed that he had joined the army of Halil Paşa in Van to fight as a soldier and that he had had nothing to do with the deportation or murders in Diyarbakır.

Witness testimony was taken during the hearing of 24 October, in which the defendant admitted to having met with the mayor of Beşiri in a hotel. He claimed to not know anything about the relations between the mayor and the governor-general of Diyarbakır, and he repeated his claim that he "absolutely didn't have anything to do with the deportations and killings" (the mayor of Beşiri was among those who were killed by the order of Diyarbakır Governor-General Reşit).

There was more witness testimony given during the session of 27 October. Glassmaker Naci Efendi read aloud his written statement that Necati Efendi had gone to Arabia with Dr. Nazım. The witness then recanted his statement and claimed that he did not know Necati. It is apparent from the defendant's testimony at this hearing that he had been a part of Eşref Bey's gang in Diyarbakır. He gave the following testimony: "I didn't know that our battalion was thought of as a gang. Our dress, our numbers, everything about us said we were soldiers." The judge asked, "There are coded messages, telegrams from the Interior Ministry stating 'Eşref Bey's gang of 170 in number have gone to Diyarbakır' or 'Eşref Bey's gang of 200 have arrived in Urfa,' what say you to that?" To which the defendant answered: "We never did any of the damage referred to in that message.... We never destroyed or massacred. Whether it's Siverek or Diyarbakır or whether it's the Şitan stream. I never saw any Armenians deported or killed."

In the session on 3 November 1919, a coded telegram written by the Interior Ministry and sent to Diyarbakır on 30 June 1915 was read into the record. Based upon this telegram, the judge repeated that it was clear that Eşref Bey's battalion was a gang and asked again what the defendant thought about the telegram. Necati again denied everything. At this hearing the prosecution brought up the opinion that the court lacked jurisdiction to be hearing a case involving the deportation at Diyarbakır and moved that the matter be transferred to the military tribunal situated there. The defendant's attorney objected on the basis that the case was near conclusion.

On 12 December 1919 the prosecution's motion was denied and the trial continued. At the hearing, certain telegrams from Siverek and Diyarbakır responding to questions that had been sent by the court were read aloud. Based upon the information in the telegrams, the judge asked: "The telegrams from the Interior Ministry announce that you were part of Eşref's gang and that you took part in much of the criminal activity and illegal seizures in the region of Urfa. What say you to that?" The defendant continued to deny involvement. The panel of judges declared the questioning over, and the prosecution's closing statement and recommendation was read into the court record. It stated that Eşref Bey's gang was formed for the purpose of deporting, killing, and looting; that Necati had been a member of that gang. However, because they could not establish that he had been directly involved in killing or looting, it was recommended that he be acquitted.

The final hearing took place on 15 December 1919. The defense attorney stated that the Teşkilat-ı Mahsusa had been formed eighteen months before the deportation, that it had engaged in very important activities, particularly in Russia, that its founders were patriots, that his client's activities in the organization had not been of the kind to "arouse suspicion," and that for these reasons he should be acquitted. The court decided that it had not been able to establish that the Eşref Bey gang had had anything to do with the deportation and killing, and that the thievery that had taken place around Urfa was not military in nature and therefore was not within the jurisdiction of the military tribunal, and that therefore Necati Efendi should be acquitted. He was released the same day.

Sources: *Alemdar,* 9, 14, and 21 July, 21 September, 27 October, 3 November, 12, 14, and 16 December 1919; *Ati,* 24 and 27 October, 3 November, 16 December 1919; *Ikdam,* 12 December 1919; *Yeni Gazete,* 22 July 1919.

24) *Harput Mayor Asım Bey*

The trial of Asım Bey began on 30 December 1920 and continued, after interruptions, for some time. On 17 February 1921 it was reported to be ongoing, and on 23 February the press reported that Harput American College President Mr. Riggs had testified as a witness. On 20 March 1921 it was reported that the file had been given back to the prosecutor in order to prepare his closing statements. According to the news on 24 March 1921, the prosecutor read his statement and Asım Bey made his defense. In the end the court ruled that the defendant be acquitted for failure to establish a link with the crime.

Sources: *Vakit*, 6, 14, 18, and 21 January, 18 and 24 February 1921; *Ikdam*, 24 January, 6 and 18 February, 20 March 1921; *Peyam-i Sabah*, 14 January, 24 February, 20 and 24 March 1921; *Alemdar, Ikdam*, 6 and 18 February 1921.

25) *Karamürsel*

Charges related to the looting in Karamürsel were brought against the defendants Rıfat, Ibrahim, Karamürselli Ali Bey, the agent İsmail, and Imam Selahaddin Efendi. The trial started on 15 January 1920. Rıfat Efendi was among those who had been arrested and exiled to Malta, so his file was separated. Except for Ibrahim Bey, the other defendants were detainees during the trial. During the first session the indictment was read aloud and the defendants were charged with the crimes.

It is not clear how many hearings were held in total. During the 18 January sitting, the complaint of Mümeyyiz Nahid Efendi against the defendants was read into the record. According to him, the defendants were involved in the deportation and had wrongfully seized Armenian properties. Additionally, they had "liquidated" a Turkish opponent of the war. During the 25 January hearing, former Mayor of Karamürsel Sezai Bey testified as a witness and gave information about the investigation into the irregularities indulged in by Imam Selahaddin. On 1 February a Turkish eyewitness, Ali Ulvi Efendi, testified against the defendant Ali Bey. During the 3 February hearing there were more witnesses, all of whom were Turkish, "some of whom gave testimony for and some against the suspects." On 1 March the prosecutor read the final closing statement, and on 3 March the final court decision was announced. In conclusion, it was determined that former Prison Director Ibrahim Bey should not be punished since he had already been sentenced to fifteen years prison in another trial (the Izmit or Nahiye Township Directors Trial). Rıfat Efendi's case had been separated due to his exile to Malta, and Ali, Ismail, and Imam Selahaddin Efendi were all acquitted. Any of the defendants who had been detained were released.

Sources: *Alemdar*, 15 January, 1 February, 2 and 5 March 1920; *Ati*, 16, 19 and 26 January, 2, 3, and 11 February, 4 March 1920.

26) *Kiği 1*

The Kiği 1 trial related to the murder of an Armenian named Agop. The defendant was Timur Bin Ismail (referred to as Timur Efendi), and the start date is not clear. It was reported that the trial was underway on 6 February 1921, but no exact date is given for when it began. During the first session witness testimony was taken, and the trial continued on 16 February. After more witness testimony was heard, the case was put off until 28 February; during this last hearing the court ruled that the defendant be acquitted based upon conflicting testimony from witnesses and insufficiency of evidence. There was a second trial against two people, Demir Ağa and Zileli Dursun Ağa, who were also tried for the murder of Agop. However, from what we can gather from the press coverage, we will assume that these are two separate trials.

Sources: *Ikdam,* 6 and 17 February 1921; *Peyam-i Sabah,* 4 March 1921.

27) *Kiği 2*

The Kiği 2 trial, arising out of the charge of deportations, was brought against Demir Ağa and Zileli Dursun Ağa. The first press coverage of it was on 18 October 1920, but the exact starting date of the trial is not clear. Even though, according to some of the newspapers, both were defendants in the same trial, others allot separate coverage for each of the trials.[50] On 19 January 1921, the trial was postponed until 19 February because the defendant Dursun Ağa had not been brought to court from the prison where he was being held. In the way of complaint, the court decided to send a memo to the Interior Ministry to make note of "the degree of laziness and ignorance of duty that is evident at the Detention Center." The trial continued on 24 February 1921, and it is reported that the court had decided to question several witnesses. On 2 March, several witnesses testified, and the case was scheduled to reconvene on March 6. It was reported on 10 March 1921 that during the session on 6 March 1921 the prosecutor had recommended acquittal for Zileli Dursun Ağa due to an inability to connect the defendant with the crime. He was thereby acquitted. At that hearing the testimony of Miralay Şahabeddin Bey played an important role in securing the acquittal of the defendant. Şahabeddin had been arrested during the Yozgat trial and remained in custody while Esat Paşa was the president of the military tribunals. Later (22 October 1919), when the military Tribunal was reorganized, he was released (information about his trial follows below). We cannot find any record about Demir Ağa's sentencing. He might have been acquitted as well.

Sources: *Alemdar,* 18 October 1920, 6 February 1921; *Ikdam,* 6 February 1921; *Vakit,* 18 October 1920, 6 and 24 February 1921; *Peyam-i Sabah,* 4 and 10 March 1921.

28) *Mosul 1*

It is not clear when the Mosul 1 trial against former Mosul Military Commandant Nevzad Bey actually started. The first news of it concerns the session that took place on 10 April 1919. When the subpoenaed witness failed to appear, the defendant Nevzad Bey was questioned about the Yakup Cemil matter.[51] The defendant's counsel objected to the questioning, stating that the matter had nothing to do with the trial at hand, and that his client had been prosecuted and had already served his sentence. However, his objections were overruled. According to the official claim, Nevzat Bey had complained to Enver Paşa over Yakup Cemil's attempt to engage in separate peace negotiations with the Allied powers. Nevzad's appointment as the Mosul military commandant was directly related to his sentence of exile issuing from that trial. Later the defendant gave his testimony in connection with the charges that were being brought in the present trial. In his testimony he reiterated that he had not killed anyone, nor had he intervened to have any of the dead quickly buried, and that in fact, all of the crimes attributed to him were a lie and the witnesses were all lying.

During the session of 12 April, Şerif Efendi, an employee of the police department, testified that he "was a witness to many abuses by Nevzad Bey." According to Şerif Efendi, during that time Nevzad Bey would take money from the Armenians who were being deported before having them actually exiled to far-off places. At the same time, the witness testified that Nevzad had had the children of many notables arrested on the pretext that they were fugitives from military duty, had them tortured while in custody, and then extorted money from their families in exchange for their release. The witness testified that he had seen "an Arab soldier beaten to death." Additionally, Nevzad Bey had, with the help of Military Army Commander Halil Paşa, "sold the soldiers' provisions" and "caused the army to be without provisions."

The second witness, Mosul Municipal Counselor Circassian Bekir Efendi, gave similar testimony. According to him, Nevzad Bey's every action was "contaminated with abuse and was illegal." There was not a family around who had not been hurt by him, according to the witness. Five soldiers who had been caught stealing were tortured to death on his orders. Thousands of Kurds who had migrated from Bitlis and Erzurum had had their provisions cut by Nevzad Bey, who left them to starve. He had had all the Armenian stores closed and sent the Armenians into the desert to their death. He had had several Arab soldiers killed in front of the door of the Central Command. The defendant Nevzad Bey's response was that the witnesses were lying.

On 14 April, defense witnesses continued to be questioned. However, their testimony neither helped nor harmed him. Most of them had not been in Mosul long enough to be able to provide compelling testimony. The testimony of one of these witnesses, former Mosul Deputy Fazıl Efendi, could even be argued to have worked against the defendant. He stated that with the start of the war, the situation in Mosul had begun to deteriorate badly. According to Fazıl Efendi, torture, irregularity in operations, and similar assertions were all true, but he could not honestly state that they were all caused by Nevzad Bey. "That's what everyone was saying," he stated:

> They were taking food and provisions out of the hands of the locals, beating and torturing them if necessary to get it. They would go to the outer regions and beat women for the handful of food they'd managed to scrounge up from somewhere. There was so much starvation in Mosul that they were losing 250–300 people a day from it. To make matters worse they would round up the men, under the nose of a gun, on the excuse that they were needed for the army and throw them in jail. There were many abuses taking place and under these circumstances, I couldn't stay in Mosul long.

When questioned by the judge as to how, as a member of the Assembly, he could stay silent under these tragic circumstances, the witness replied that he was hated by the Union and Progress Party, that he was saved at the last minute from a death sentence, and that as an Arab member of the Assembly he had lived in constant fear and under threat. He ended with the statement that he had left politics.

At the hearing on 19 April the witnesses continued to be questioned. Gendarmerie Officer Namık Bey confirmed the claims of torture and additionally recounted an event that was an example of the abuses committed by Nevzad Bey. "One soldier had killed someone while drunk. He was court-martialed, but before we [the court] ruled on his sentence he was already executed, and approval for the execution was sent to us [the court]. If we had objected to it, there would have been two bullets with our name on it." (The matter referred to here had to do with Gendarmerie Sergeant Tahir, who had been assigned to kill Armenians. Before the military tribunal could rule on his case, he was executed. The matter would be the subject of questioning throughout the hearing.)

Based on Namık Bey's own testimony, the prosecutor called for his arrest, but the court denied his request. Later in his testimony, Namık Bey stated that Nevzad, in accordance with the wishes of Halil Paşa, had executed five Jews and, after putting their corpses into a big sack, had them transported to the Tigris River and thrown in. He also stated that Armenians between the ages of fifteen and fifty had been sent to perform forced labor, but that he had no idea if they had arrived where they were supposed to have gone. Another witness, former Mosul Director of Refugees Celal Bey, stated that Bedirhani Abdürrezzak Bey had been a guest at the Central Command and that he had looked perfectly fine when Celal had seen him the day before his death (later Bedirhani's family was told that he had died from dysentery).

During the session on 22 April, Aksaraylı Cemal Efendi, who was an employee of the Mosul Central Command, testified that he had worked closely with Nevzad Bey and that the defendant was cruel to people and had even personally tortured others: "One of the soldiers died from the torture." Elderly people had been used to build roads along with Armenian deportees. At this session the testimony of Halil Paşa was also taken, and when he began to engage in a long speech praising the character of Nevzad Bey, the judge stopped to read back the testimony of Director of Refugees Celal Bey. The judge asked; "have you no idea of the tragic circumstances described herein?" to which Halil Paşa replied, "I received no complaints from anybody."

More witness testimony was taken during the hearing of 26 April. A second written statement of Cemal Efendi was read into the record. This statement describes acts of torture, death by torture, embezzlement, and similar offenses. The statement also recounts that "all night long Armenian women were assaulted." From another witness, Şekerci Ali Efendizade Said Efendi, the court learned that Nevzad Bey "would torture every man that walked in and take bribes from him." On 28 May 1919, Nevzad Bey became one of the many convicts exiled to Malta. He arrived there on 2 June but would be among the sixteen defendants who escaped and became fugitives.[52] For this reason his trial was postponed and never resumed.

Sources: *Alemdar,* 11, 13, 20, 23, and 27 April, 3 June 1919; *Tercüman-ı Hakikat,* 12, 14, 19, 22, and 26 April 1919; *Yeni Gazete,* 11, 13, 20, and 27 April 1919.

29) *Mosul 2*

The Mosul 2 trial against Captain Ferid Bey was based upon "the cruelties which took place in Mosul." The trial started on 2 June 1919. Among the other defendants in the case was Captain Zekeriye Bey, who had fled prosecution. The defendants were accused of having been accomplices to Nevzad Bey, of the Mosul 1 trial. At this session it was decided that Nevzad Bey's case would be tried separately since he had been exiled to Malta. The accusations against Nevzad Bey were again repeated in court during this trial. During the first hearing, the District Treasurer for Edirne, Kazım Bey, testified about Abdürrezzak Bey's poisoning and the fact that Nevzat Bey had caused 60,000 soldiers to die by embezzling their wages. "Nevzad was the army's executioner. And the governor's executioner was the Gendarmerie Commander." Another witness, the former Criminal Court Judge, Hasan Bey, testified that the people of Mosul were extremely unhappy with Nevzad Bey. In response to another question, the witness stated, "When it comes to Tahir, who was executed, he was a man behind a lot of killings. He was tried and sentenced to death" (Again, the issue of the execution of the officer without a court decision arose in this trial, as in Mosul 1).

During the hearing of 14 June 1919, more witness testimony was taken. The written statement of Director of Security Halid Bey was read into the court record. Halid testified that Nevzad and Ferid Bey killed Abdürrezzak by poisoning his tea.

During the hearing of 28 July 1919, the former Mosul Police Chief, Halid Bey, confirmed a previously submitted written statement and added that "Nevzad Bey was the cause of a lot of cruel acts in Mosul, but he, Halid, had remained silent about it out of fear."

After another session on 19 August, there was no other until 24 December 1919. Because of the changes made to the organization of the military tribunals, the trial was recessed for four months. At the 24 December session the new court, "having not had enough time to review the file," requested the findings of the prosecutor's office. The prosecution responded with the statement that Ferid Bey, like Nevzad Bey, was suspected of cruelties toward the Armenians who had been deported to Mosul, of wrongfully seizing the money of individuals, of threatening to send anyone who voiced an objection to the front, and of destroying homes and killing Abdürrezzak Bey. Still, the prosecution was of the opinion that the crimes against Armenians could not properly be considered to have been committed during the deportation because once the Armenians arrived in Mosul, they became Mosul residents and therefore would come under the laws of that region. For this reason, it was the prosecution's opinion that the file should be transferred to Mosul. The court recessed and ordered the trial reconvened at a later date in order to have time to consider the issues.

On 27 December 1919, the court rejected the prosecution's motion and opined that it had jurisdiction to hear the case because the Armenians had been tortured during the deportation and not after their arrival in Mosul.

In the newspapers dated 19, 25, 27, and 30 January 1920, there was news that the case was progressing. On 14 March 1920 a newspaper reported that the final sitting had taken place. Once the court had concluded that the investigation had come to an end, the prosecution declared that of the charges brought against the defendant, only those related to the death of Abdürrezzak Bey's murder had been established with the requisite level of judiciousness. It was the prosecution's opinion that not enough evidence had been presented to establish the other charges; hence they should be dismissed. The court ordered a recess for time to make a decision.

The decision, which was announced on 18 March 1920, stated that Ferid Bey and Zekai Efendi should be acquitted of the charges of "causing the death of Armenians who had been deported to Mosul." These charges asserted that "by creating the pretext of conscripting them into road construction service and instead having them sent to the outskirts of Zaho village, where they were murdered," Ferid Bey and Zekai Efendi played some role in the murders; but, the court concluded, there was not sufficient evidence to convict. As to the other charges, which were listed one by one (torture, death by torture, execution of a gendarmerie sergeant without following proper judicial procedure, the murder of Abdürrezzak Bey, and looting) the court decided that it lacked jurisdiction to try any charges outside of those related to crimes occurring during the deportation of Armenians. The court had the file sent back to the Interior Ministry.

Sources: *Alemdar,* 3 and 15 June, 29 July, 28 December 1919, 14, 18, 19, and 22 March 1920; *Ati,* 25, 27, and 28 December 1919, 19, 25, 27, and 30 January, 14 March 1920; *Peyam-i Sabah,* 14 March 1920; *Tercüman-ı Hakikat,* 29 July 1919; *Yeni Gazete,* 3 and 15 June 1919.

30) *Mosul 3*

The Mosul 3 trial was against the Mosul Deputy Fevzi Bey for crimes related to the deportation. It is not clear when the trial began, but on 30 January 1920 the newspapers reported that "Fevzi Bey was acquitted of charges related to the deportations, it being determined that he had had nothing to do with the crimes alleged."

Source: *Vakit,* 30 December 1920.

31) *Sivas and Koçhisar*

The Sivas and Koçhisar trial was against the defendants Nabi Bey, former Koçhisar Mayor Ali Şefik, and the businessman and Sivas Gendarmerie Commander, Balıkzade Rauf Bey. The trial started on 20 January 1921, with the testimony of witnesses being taken. The questioning of witnesses continued during the second hearing on 27 January 1921. At the final hearing on 30 January 1921, the prosecution gave its closing statement and the defense presented its case. On 1 February 1921, the court made its decision that it was of the opinion that the defendants were not guilty.

Source: *Vakit,* 30 January, 6 February 1921; *Ikdam,* 24 January, 6 February 1921.

32) *Syrian Deputy Governor Tevfik Bey*

The trial of Tevfik Bey was related to crimes connected with the deportation that occurred while the defendant was deputy governor of Syria. It is not clear when the hearings started. In a newspaper article of 6 January 1921, it was reported that "in order to conduct an investigation the trial has been put off to a later date." On 27 January 1921 it was reported that the trial was continuing and that two witnesses, one of them a woman, had been questioned in court. More hearings were scheduled, according to the newspapers of 2 and 12 February, while on 6 and 18 February it was reported that the trial was progressing. On 18 February 1921 the paper reported that the prosecutor had charged the defendant with four separate crimes, that some of the crimes "are beyond the jurisdiction of the Military Tribunal," and that therefore a judicial decision should be made on this issue first. The court decided that the crimes were within its jurisdiction and it reached its conclusion on 24 February with a ruling against the defendant, finding him guilty and sentencing him to six months prison followed by a six-month suspension from his official duties.

Sources: *Vakit,* 6, 14, and 27 January, 18 and 24 February 1921; *Ikdam,* 18 February 1921; *Alemdar,* 6 February 1921.

33) *Trabzon Yomra*

The Trabzon Yomra trial was directed against Major Tevfik, former First Lieutenant (*Mülazım-ı Evvel*) "Manastırlı" Salim, and Muhlis Efendi from Istanbul. There is no information as to when the trial actually started, but there is a news report of its conclusion, which appeared on 20 October 1920. On 22 October there was news of the sentencing. Tevfik received a sentence of ten years' hard labor. For the other two defendants it was determined that further investigation was required, and the files were sent to the prosecutor's office. The transcript of the court decision appeared in *Ikdam* in installments, 23–25 October 1920. In the transcript of the court decision one sees that on 6 June 1915, Tevfik had received a written order from Trabzon Governor-General Cemal Azmi containing nineteen separate items related to the Yomra deportation. It is interesting to note that many Turkish-Muslim witnesses from among both civil and military ranks testified against the defendants. Several testified that Armenians had been put on boats and sent to their deaths by drowning on the Black Sea.[53]

Sources: *Vakit,* 20 and 22 October 1920; *Ikdam,* 23 and 25 October 1920.

34) *Yusuf Ziya Bey*

Mayor Yusuf Ziya Bey was accused of crimes related to the deportation in Bayburt and the surrounding area. A news report dated 27 January 1921 states that "Yusuf Ziya Bey's trial has started," but there is no mention of the actual date. Three witnesses were questioned, and the matter was ordered continued on 9 February.

On 18 February 1922 it was reported that "Yusuf Ziya Bey was acquitted of the crime for lack of sufficient evidence."

Sources: *Peyam-i Sabah,* 4 February 1921; *Vakit,* 27 January 1921, 18 February 1921; *Ikdam,* 18 February 1921.

Trials Covered in the Press Only, Whose Outcomes Are Unknown

35) *Abulahad Nuri Bey*

Abulahad Nuri Bey was charged with crimes related to the deportation. There is no further information about the trial except a report dated 27 January 1921 stating that the trial had been postponed because of the defendant's illness.

Source: *Vakit*, 27 January 1921.

36) *Ali Şevket Efendi*

The trial that was opened against the Bahçecik Township Director Ali Şefket Efendi was remanded for further investigation pending the reorganization of the military tribunals that took place in September 1919.

On 29 February 1920 it was reported that the trial had finished and that its outcome would be published. We have not yet located this outcome. (This trial appears to be distinct from the İzmit Township Directors or Bahçecik trials [Case #10] because the defendant's name did not appear in connection with the aforementioned trials.).

Sources: *Alemdar*, 22 October 1919, *Peyam-i Sabah*, 29 February 1920.

37) *Bilecik Trial*

A clear starting date was not found for the trial of the Bilecik Gendarmerie Battalion Commander Captain Rıfat Bey. According to news reported on 5 March 1920, the defendant was released from Bekir Ağa prison by paying an 800 lira bond. There are no reports at all of how the trial concluded.

Source: *Ati*, 5 March 1920.

38) *Çanakkale 1*

The Çanakkale 1 trial of Edip Efendi and his friends was related to the deportations. It is not clear how many defendants were being prosecuted, but the trial ended with Edip's acquittal in December. There is no information on how the trial ended for the other defendants.

Source: *Peyam-i Sabah*, 4 February, 9 April 1921; *Vakit*, 23 December 1920.

39) *Çanakkale 2*

Çanakkale 2 was a trial of "seventeen individuals suspected of stealing from the homes and stores of Çanakkale." It is not clear when the trial started, and there is a chance that it was part of the Çanakkale 1 trial mentioned above (#38). The news media reported only that the trial was ongoing.

Source: *Peyam-i Sabah*, 9 April, 23 May 1921.

40) *Deir Zor Deportations 3*

The start date of the trial of Commissioner Ibrahim Efendi is not clear. On 27 February 1921 the file was sent to the Appellate Division and the case was postponed because the defendant's name appeared in the trial slated for Deir Zor Governor Zeki Bey, which was under review in the Appellate Division at that point.

Source: *Peyam-i Sabah,* 4, 7 February, 4 March 1921.

41) *Diyarbakir*

The Diyarbakir trial was brought against "boat steward [*sandalcı kahyası*] Rizeli Ali Osman on charges of deportation and murder, and of violating domestic security." Due to the reorganization of the military tribunals that took place in autumn 1919, the defendant's trial was recessed pending further review of his file, and it was reported that it was expected to start soon. On 28 January 1920, a news item appeared that stated that the trial had started again. However, there is no further news of how it concluded.

Source: *Alemdar,* 22 October 1919; *Ati,* 28 January 1920.

42) *Erenköy and Surrounding Areas*

This was a deportation trial with eight defendants. Other than the fact that the trial was proceeding, no information can be gleaned from the press.

Source: *Peyam-i Sabah,* 4 February, 23 May 1921.

43) *Giresun*

The trial of the Giresun notable Hasan and his brother, Eşref Efendi, and former Giresun Gendarmerie Commander Hasan Sabri Efendi concerned charges related to the deportations. It started on 1 May 1921, but on 2 May 1921 it was reported that it had been decided that the trial should be postponed pending an investigation as to whether Hasan Sabri Efendi was or was not assigned to the Giresun region during the deportations. Later the trial was continued with the same defendants on 15–16 May and 20 June 1921. Some of the defendants were called to appear for the 20 June hearing. There is no information, however, as to how the trial concluded.

Source: *Peyam-i Sabah,* 2 and 16 May 1921; *Vakit,* 17 June 1921.

44) *Hidayet Efendi*

Charges having to do with the deportation of Armenians from Istanbul were brought against Hidayet Efendi, a former political policeman and detective from Istanbul's Main Police Headquarters. The trial started on 16 June 1919.

Hidayet Efendi was an Ottoman citizen of Armenian Catholic heritage who had converted to Islam in 1899. After the Balkan wars, he became a police officer. He was charged with the deportation of unmarried Armenians in Istanbul, particularly from the area of Üsküdar, and with going into their homes and seizing their possessions. It was claimed that he had taken bribes in exchange for not deporting individuals, but then had turned around and had them deported anyway. In his statement he claimed that he had "received orders to have Armenians in Istanbul detained but not to have them deported." He also claimed that in fact he had detained them. "Since the [Armenian] political committee members who had records with the police were already known to us, an order came down to have them detained." The order covered all those "unmarried individuals mainly whose birthplace was in the provinces, those without families or children, those without businesses." The witnesses gave damaging testimony. One young single man, about to be deported, was apparently given a twenty-four-hour grace period within which to marry because he was told that would save him from deportation. Having done so, he testified to this interesting turn of events. When questioned in court, Hidayet Efendi answered that his knowledge of the Armenian language made him useful for these kinds of operations. The charge involved the deportation of up to 350 Armenians.

On 18 June 1919 some of the Armenians who had been victims of his threats to extort money or commit torture testified in court. As an example, Ermenak Efendi declared: "He tortured me quite a bit. Hidayet is a man with no conscience." During the third and fourth sessions on 23 and 26 June there was more damaging testimony. Again, the claims were that Hidayet had inflicted "cruelties" and that he had forced people to pay him money. The examination of witnesses ended on 8 July, and at that point the prosecution moved that the defendant be acquitted because the statute of limitations had passed on the alleged crimes. His own attorney made the same motion on 15 July. We have no knowledge of how the court ruled.[54]

Sources: *Alemdar,* 17 and 19 June, 9 July 1919; *Yeni Gazete,* 24 June, 16 July 1919.

45) *Izmit 1*

The Izmit 1 trial was against Izmitli Otçu Hakkı Efendi. There is no information about the trial except that it was to begin on 18 February 1920, and that due to the defendant's illness it had been postponed to a future date. There is no information on how the trial concluded.

Source: *Ati,* 18, 19 February 1920.

46) *Izmit 2*

In the Izmit 2 trial of the former Chief of the Izmit Recruiting Office Major Rüşdü Bey, it was alleged that he had "violated his responsibilities" during the Izmit deportation. We do not know the start date of the trial or how many defendants there actually were. There was a report that trial had been postponed, but nothing on how it concluded.

Source: *Peyam-i Sabah,* 22 April 1921.

47) *Karamürsel*

This Karamürsel trial was against defendant Sergeant Emin. We have no information about whether this trial is related to the Karamürsel trial (#25) above. The name "Sergeant Emin" was not among the defendants in the trial above. A report dated 25 November 1919 states that "Sergeant Emin from Karamürsel's Gendarmerie corps, who had been detained for the charges of being involved in deporting, killing and bribing, was released from Bekir Ağa prison yesterday." It is not clear when the trial started, but in the same paper it was reported that the defendant had been previously sentenced by the Number One Military Tribunal. On 19 January 1920 it was reported that the case was continuing and that "Circassian Bekir Bey who had been released two days ago was arrested and detained again."

Sources: *Alemdar,* 25 November 1919; *Ati,* 19 January 1920.

48) *Kastamonu*

The press referred to this trial as both the "Kastamonu" trial and the "Hasan Fehmi" trial. It was against defendant, CUP Party Secretary Hasan Fehmi from Kastamonu, who had already been detained for quite some time. The first news of it appeared on 9 December 1920, when it was reported that the trial would begin soon. On 30 December it was reported that "the documents related to the matter of Hasan Fehmi Bey, Party Secretary for the Kastamonu region, who was previously imprisoned by the Military Tribunal, but whose case was overturned and remanded on appeal," would appear in his new trial, starting soon. From 6 January 1921 comes the news that the case that ranked third in importance after the Amasya and Edirne trials, that of "suspect Hasan Fehmi Efendi on the Kastamonu deportation," had been heard on 3 and 4 January, that witness testimony had been taken, and that the matter would continue to be heard. The case was then postponed. There is no further information on how this separate case against Hasan Fehmi concluded. However, on 8 January 1920 Fehmi was convicted and sentenced to ten years' hard labor in the Responsible Secretaries Trial.

Sources: *Ikdam*, 9 December 1920; *Vakit*, 16 and 30 December 1920, 6 and 30 January 1921, *T.V.*, no. 3772.

49) *Kırkkilise*

The Kırkkilise trial concerned charges against Kasım Efendi. According to a news item dated 19 January 1920, the defendant had been arrested but the trial had not yet begun.

Source: *Ati*, 19 January 1920.

50) *Konya*

The Konya trial was of Party Deputy Abdülkadir Efendi. On 7 July 1919 it was reported that his file was complete. According to *Ati*, as of 19 January 1920 the case had not started yet.

Sources: *Ati*, 19 January 1920.

51) *Muş: Trial against former Muş deputy İlyas Sami.*

Sources: *Ati*, 19 January 1920.

52) *Yalova*

In the Yalova trial of retired Gendarmerie Captain Mehmet Cemal Efendi, the defendant was sentenced in absentia to six months in prison by the Bolu Military Tribunal, but when the tribunal was disbanded, the case was forwarded to the tribunal in Istanbul and reviewed. The charges had to do with bribery, corruption, and deportation. There was no news indicating when the trial started. At the first hearing in Istanbul the defendant denied the charges and claimed that he "had nothing to do with the deportation." At the hearing on 14 March 1920, witness testimony was heard and a future hearing date was set for more questioning of witnesses. There is no information as to how the trial concluded.

Sources: *Ati*, 10 and 15 March 1920; *Peyam-i Sabah*, 10 March 1920.

53) *Süleymaniyeli Mustafa Kemal Paşa*

For the case against Süleymaniyeli Mustafa Kemal Paşa, neither the starting date nor the date of the trial's conclusion is available from the press sources. On 27 January 1920 a telegram belonging to Haji Şükrü Bey, the commander of the National Independence Army of Aydın and the surrounding area, was read into the court record. In this telegram, Haji Şükrü Bey stated that the claim that "Armenian girls are being placed in brothels" was a lie. According to him, the brothels of Bitlis were filled with Turkish and Kurdish women and girls who were escaping the cruelties of the Armenians in Erzurum, Van, Bitlis, Bayezid, and Muş. There is no further information about this trial.

Source: *Ati,* 27 January 1920.

54) *Abdülahad Nuri Bey*

According to news dated 27 January 1921, the trial of the defendant Abdülahad Nuri Bey was postponed due to illness.

Source: *Vakit,* 27 January 1921.

55) *Dr. Avni Bey*

Concerning the "trial dealing with one stage of the deportation in Trabzon," a 21 January 1921 report stated that a recommendation by the prosecutor's office that an investigation be made into Dr. Avni Bey was accepted by a court order. However, there is no further information as to how and when the trial was ever commenced.

Source: *Vakit,* 21 January 1921.

Cases that Were Dismissed or Transferred

56) *Akhisar*

This case was against Corporal Arif from the gendarmerie corps of Geyve township. The investigation was based on charges that Arif had "assaulted" individuals who had been deported from the township of Akhisar, but the case was dismissed by the prosecutor, Artin, on 7 January 1919. In this decision it is stated that "despite having shown that Armenians had been subjected to cruelties, there was not enough evidence to prove anything in this particular matter," which resulted in the case's dismissal.

Source: *Ikdam,* 21 October 1920.

57) *Ankara*

The Ankara investigation was opened against two prominent citizens of Balatlı, Kör Riza and Yağcı Haim. The charges were for wrongful seizure of the property of Armenians deported from Ankara and profiteering in its sale. In addition, the defendants were charged with complicity in the murder of two Armenians who were alleged to be army deserters. Prosecutor Osman Remzi Bey decided on 15 October 1919 to dismiss the charges.

Source: *Ikdam,* 21 October 1920.

58) *Astanköylu Şükrü and Talat Bey*

The trial of Şükrü Bey, a former employee of the Directorate of Refugees, and Talat Bey, the "Director of Scribes" (Müdiriyet-i mezhure ihsasiyat), was opened on charges that the two had been involved in the murder of Armenians deported from around the Aleppo and Deir Zor regions. It was reported on 21 October 1920 that prosecutor Osman Remzi Bey had decided to dismiss the case because further investigation was required in the locations where the crimes were committed. It is likely that the prosecutor's decision was made in October 1920.

Source: *Ikdam,* 21 October 1920.

59) *Emanuel Karasu*

Upon the conclusion of an investigation into the actions of Istanbul Deputy Emanuel Karasu in connection with charges of deportation and murder, the case was dismissed on 8 October 1919.

Source: *Ikdam,* 20 October 1920.

60) *Iznik 1*

The Iznik 1 case was opened on charges of "wrongful seizure and looting of homes" during the deportation of Armenians from Iznik. The accused were Iznik Township Deputy Mayor Abdurrahman; Cemil, clerk from the Commissions of Abandoned Properties; Ismail Hakkı, employee of the Register of Revenues; and notable Ahmed Bin Ali. According to news reported on 21 October 1920, the prosecutor Osman Remzi Bey decided to dismiss the case.

Sources: *Ikdam,* 21 October 1920; *Vakit,* 22 October 1920.

61) *Iznik 2*

The Iznik 2 case, which arose out of the deportation from Iznik, was brought against Halil Ibrahim Bey and his accomplices. The trial was set to start on 9 February 1920, but when the defendant became ill, the matter was postponed for fifteen days. In news reports from 29 February 1920, it appears that the matter was then determined to be within the jurisdiction of the civil courts, and therefore it was transferred.

Sources: *Alemdar,* 9 February 1920; *Ati,* 9 and 10 February 1920; *Peyam-i Sabah,* 10 February 1920.

62) *Miralay Şahabeddin Bey*

The suspect Miralay Şahabeddin Bey was charged with crimes related to the deportation and murder of Armenians from the Kayseri region, but the prosecutor, Artin Efendi, dismissed the charges on 25 March 1920. Şahabeddin Bey testified during the Yozgat trial, wherein it became apparent that he had been involved in the crimes of "deportation and murder" himself, for which he was subsequently arrested. Telegrams of his had been read into the record during the Yozgat trial series. He remained in detention while Esat Paşa served as the president of the military tribunals, but when the tribunals were reorganized in autumn 1919, Şahabeddin Bey was released. The press regarded this decision as disturbing.

Sources: *Alemdar,* 22 October 1919; 26 March 1920; *Ati,* 26 March 1920; *Ikdam,* 21 October 1920.

63) *Sami Sabur*

In the course of investigating crimes that occurred during the deportation from Kayseri, a case was opened against the former Governor of Antalya Sami Sabur. The court later dismissed the matter.

Sources: *Alemdar, Ati,* 26 March 1920.

Trials That Arose from Crimes Indirectly Related to the Deportation and Mass Murder of Armenians

A series of other trials were held by the First Military Tribunal in Istanbul. The following is a set of examples. Some were cases that were indirectly related to the deportations. Some were cases that arose out of unlawful economic activity, such as embezzlement, which was particularly prevalent during the First World War. Other crimes, connected with the Turkish National Independence Army (Kuvay-ı Milliye), were related to disturbing the peace and public order. Finally, some were trials of the leaders of the Nationalist movement in Ankara, such as Mustafa Kemal. There were also two other military tribunals in Istanbul at the time, and some of the cases unrelated to the Armenian deportation were later transferred to these courts. For example, in October 1920 ninety-six cases were transferred to the Second Military Tribunal, and they continued to be transferred.[55]

Below are some very limited examples of these cases that were taken from the First Military Tribunal.

Examples of Cases Indirectly Related to the Deportations

1) Trial of Celil Bey and His Accomplices, Sometimes Referred to as Arslan Bey's Gang

This case was brought against Muallim Mehmet Celil, Selanikli Hüseyin, and Kandıralı Çoban Mehmet, who were accused of aiding the escape of Halil Paşa.

They were members of the Arslan Bey gang. The trial started on 15 November 1919. The indictment stated that the defendants had joined the Arslan Bey gang after Halil Paşa's escape. The defendants gave their testimony during the first hearing; according to this testimony, the gang consisted of twenty people. The case was postponed, but there were later reports that it was progressing. Celil Bey requested that the case be moved to Bursa, but the motion was denied. The last hearing took place on 9 December 1919, and after the closing statement of the prosecution the defendants received a variety of punishments.

Sources: *Alemdar,* 25 and 28 November, 5 and 10 December 1919; *Ati,* 16 and 28 November 1919; *Ikdam,* 5 December 1919.

2) Şadi Efendi Trial

The trial of Şadi Efendi, who was a military police lieutenant in a detention center, arose out of the support he provided to the escape of Halil Paşa. The trial proceeded in his absence, and he received a sentence of three years' prison time and discharge from the army. Sergeant Ismail, who was under his command, received one year in prison and the removal of his rank.

Source: *Ikdam,* 12, 1919.

3) Cevdet and Mahmud Beys

In the trial of Beyşehri Property Director Cevdet Bey and Refik Mahmud Bey, defendants, only Cevdet Bey had been detained. The trial started on 2 November 1919, but after the execution of the Boğazlıyan Mayor Kemal, the charges were changed to "disturbing the public order"; later the court would decide that it lacked jurisdiction to try the defendants, and therefore they were released.

Sources: *Ati, Alemdar,* 2 and 3 November 1919.

4) Mustafa Paşa

The prosecution of the former Chief of the Military Tribunals charged Mustafa Paşa with giving a slanderous brief to an Armenian newspaper. The trial started on 20 October 1920. During the first hearing the defendant tried to explain what had occurred to the Armenians, but the judge quashed his testimony, declaring it irrelevant to the matter at hand. Mustafa Paşa claimed that those who had brought the charges that were before the court were the very people who were guilty of these crimes that he had tried to describe. He attempted to describe a litany of crimes and abuses:

> Those who have presented a terrible picture of the Ottoman nation to the public opinion of Europe, America, Australia and Asia by their depraved crimes which they committed without regard to anyone, those who organized with such great cruelty and lack of conscience the crimes of forced deportations and killing, who burned innocent children, who

> cut off their hands and feet in front of their elderly fathers, who violated girls before their brothers and sisters, who took away the wives from their husbands, the girls from their parents, who seized the property and lands of these families sending them to the hills like sheep…

While he proceeded to elaborate further, the judge cut him off and stated he had "gone outside the scope of the testimony requested." When the defendant continued by saying that the "Paşas who support me, those who are close to me will reveal the names of those who have tried to malign me," the judge decided to call a recess and then upon return decided to let the defendant continue. The papers did not report what was said after the recess. The trial was continued to a future date (*Ati*, 21 January 1920). Mustafa Paşa was also charged with being a member of the Kurdish Sublime Society (Kurt Teali Cemiyeti), which, for a member of the armed forces, was a violation of the rule against membership in political organizations. Even if the court was obligated to find the defendant guilty of that violation, it nevertheless refrained from prosecuting him, reasoning that this was an infraction that was beyond its jurisdiction. According to the news in *Ati* on 26 January 1920, the Greek newspaper *Perüeüdüs* praised Mustafa Paşa's testimony and held it up as an example of great personal integrity and courage.

Sources: *Ati,* 21, 25, and 26 January 1920; *Alemdar,* 15 January 1920.

5) Boğazliyan County Executive Kemal

Thirty individuals were tried on charges of having disturbed the public order during Boğazlıyan Mayor Kemal's funeral procession. It is not possible to know when this trial actually started. The defendants had been arrested for causing disorder on the day of Kemal's funeral. On 4 July 1920, the news media reported that the trial was underway. According to news on 20 and 22 October the trial had come to an end, but it is not clear what the final decision was.

Source: *Vakit,* 4 July, 15 September, 20 and 22 October 1920.

6) Müştak Lütfi Bey

The trial against former Ertuğrul Governor Lütfi Bey started on 14 July 1919. The defendant had been detained for four months. According to the press coverage, a series of abuses had occurred during his service in the Refugees Commission in Samsun when Armenian property started being distributed to refugees. The defendant, who had been unhappy with the way the aftermath of deportation was being handled in Samsun, wrote letters to the Union and Progress Party headquarters criticizing Vehip Paşa, the military authority in the region. The defendant supported harsher measures toward the Armenians, who could return to their homes, than Military Commander Vehip Paşa was implementing. The defendant believed these Armenians represented a threat to the security of the region. Additionally, he had threatened those who opposed the Union and Progress Party. Also, according to the defendant, after his arrest, his wife had wanted to remove documents from the house, but they had fallen into the hands of the police. These documents were letters written to Midhat Şükrü, the general secretary of the Union and Progress Party and one of the defendants in the Main Trial. The prosecutor's original indictment, dated 7 October 1919, charged that the documents contained orders that the Unionists should use violence if necessary to get their own men elected. According to the prosecutor, the defendant had used violence during the election period and was being tried for those acts.

After the hearing on 28 July 1919, the trial was postponed for two months to take into account the reorganization of the military tribunals. On 7 October 1919 the prosecutor's final closing statement was read into the record. The prosecutor stated that based upon the evidence presented, the defendant had used force and had misused the authority bestowed on his position. However, the matter fell beyond the jurisdiction of the military tribunal, and therefore it was decided that the file should be removed and returned to the civil courts. On 8 October 1919 the defendant made his defense and the court made its final decision. The defendant was acquitted of violating security, but he was found guilty of using force in Sinop during the elections in order to get Union and Progress candidates elected, and of threatening people and misusing his authority. He was sentenced to one year in prison and three years' suspension from employment with the state. He was released after being given credit for time served.

The verdict would later be appealed, as a result of which the case was remanded for retrial. There is no information as to how this trial was concluded in its second turn with the military tribunal.

Sources: *Alemdar,* 15, 27, and 29 July; 10 October 1919; *Ati,* 8 and 9 October 1919, 10 March, 2 January 1920; *Peyam-i Sabah,* 10 March 1920; *Tercüman-ı Hakikat,* 29 July 1919; *Yeni Gazete,* 27 July 1919.

7) Osman Nuri Efendi

The defendant in this trial, the former Çatalca Postal and Telegraph Deputy Director, Osman Nuri Efendi, was charged with burning documents. The trial started on 4 August 1919. The defendant testified: "I'm a civil servant.... I burned documents on orders given to me. My superiors told me to take certain documents from this year to that year and to burn them, so I did. I couldn't tell them that I wouldn't do what they asked me to, or that I wouldn't burn the documents. Because the orders sent to the General Edirne Headquarters on special post were obeyed and the documents were destroyed, I burned them too." The order had come from the Edirne Headquarters. The trial came to a conclusion at the second session, and the judge told the defendant that he would have to wait for the decision. We cannot know what that ruling was because it is not available in the newspapers researched, but the trial was mentioned in the Armenian newspapers *Jhogovourt* and *Moniteur Oriental* on 6 June 1919; according to these newspapers the defendant acknowledged that the documents were burned because of their connection with the deportation and killings.[56]

Source: *Alemdar*, 5 and 6 August 1919.

Examples of Trials Related to Disturbing the Peace and Economic Transgressions

1) Onnik Efendi Davası

The trial of Onnik Efendi, who was an employee of the Office of Public Debts, concerned the charge of violating public security. The defendant, who was actually Armenian in origin, had been serving in the army during the deportations; he had avoided the fate of so many of his fellow Armenians by converting to Islam. The trial started on 10 November 1919 and ended on 10 January 1920. Its subject was an incident in which Onnik Efendi had sent letters to an Armenian newspaper in Istanbul for publication. These letters, which were intercepted, called the Turks "murderers" and "barbarians." At the first hearing, Onnik claimed to have written one of these letters during a drunken episode. Another charge was "disturbing the peace or public order" (in his case, encouraging villagers to steal sheep and firing upon the gendarmerie, among other offenses).

The defendant claimed that he was being targeted because others resented that he worked on behalf of Armenian orphans. In fact, during the second hearing on 19 November, some Turks testified that Onnik Efendi had lodged complaints against them in an attempt to lure their Armenian daughters-in-law and wives away from them. At the hearing Onnik Efendi denied the claims and defended himself by saying: "Dear Sirs, I wrote a letter. But in the letter I didn't write against all Turks, just against those who've done bad things. I lost a brother during the Balkan War. I didn't run away from the War the way my friends did. In the face of this I also lost almost forty of my relatives. I was born an Armenian; I'd like to die an Armenian. Am I a criminal for having used harsh language when describing the Union and Progress party and those who follow it?" In one of his letters, which was read out in court, Onnik stated that "as long as I can remember, Turks have been wild and cruel." When the judge reminded the defendant that he had said something about "all Turks" not just the bad ones, the defendant described the family members he had lost in the deportation and also how he had written the letter while drunk. Some of the witnesses confirmed that Onnik Efendi walked around drunk a lot.

In the other sessions there were questions about Onnik Efendi's involvement in an incident where Greek villagers raided the police headquarters and fired on the gendarmerie. Significantly, this trial occurred during a period when interest in the deportations and killings had waned. Nevertheless, it received a great deal of press. The most likely reason was probably related to the fact that an Armenian was being charged with insulting the Turks and was accused of resisting the gendarmerie. Every hearing was given a great deal of press coverage. At the last hearing, on 10 January 1920, the defendant Onnik Efendi was found not guilty and acquitted.

Sources: *Alemdar,* 11 and 20 November, 2, 12, 14, 15, 16, 22, 23, and 26 December 1919, 4 and 11 January 1920; *Ati,* 11 and 20 November, 12, 15, 16, 23, and 26 December 1919; 1 and 9 January 1920; *Ikdam,* 2, 12, and 14 December 1919.

2) Vehip Paşa

In this trial against Third Army Commander Vehip Paşa, the defendant was charged with misusing his authority. Right after the war, the press had started publishing critical pieces against Vehip Paşa resulting from rumors that the starvation that was prevalent in the region where he was from was a direct result of the Paşa's abusive actions. It is not clear when the trial started, but there was news from time to time of the fact that Vehip Paşa remained in custody. On 1 September 1921 there was news of various indictments against Vehip Paşa. The punishment meted out to him was related to some of the expenses he had incurred during his term of duty, and it was relatively minor.

Sources: *Ati,* 19 January 1920; *Tevhid-i Efkâr,* 1 September 1921; *Vakit,* 5 December 1918.

3) Sapancalı Hakkı

The trial of defendant Sapancalı Hakkı arose out of charges that he had taken advantage of his authority to engage in unlawful economic activities. The trial started on 9 August 1919 and ended on 15 September 1919. There were five hearings in all, and their minutes were recorded and published in the *Takvîm-i Vekâyi.* The final ruling of the court, however, did not appear in the *Takvîm-i Vekâyi* but was published on 29 November 1919 in the daily newspapers. The trial ended with the acquittal of the defendant.

Sources: *Takvîm-i Vekâyi,* nos. 3623, 3632, 3634, 3637, 3656; *Alemdar,* 7, 9, 10, and 12 August, 10, 11, 26, and 29 October 1919; *Ati,* 10, 26, and 29 October 1919; *Yeni Gazete,* 13 and 17 August 1919.

4) Bribery and Corruption

Commander Refet Paşa from Samsun and its surrounding areas (a fugitive from prosecution), retired Gendarmerie Captain from Yalova Cemal Efendi,

Deputy Ferhad Bey from Karesi (also absent from prosecution), businessman Dehhani Zade Ibrahim Naji, and Hüsnü Efendi all faced charges of profiteering and were accordingly prosecuted.

Source: *Ati,* 9, 15 and 16 March 1920.

Examples of Trials of Members of the Kuvay-ı Milliye (National Independence Army)

For having established communications with the Kuvay-ı Milliye between Istanbul and Bursa while serving as the second aide-de-camp of Mustafa Kemal, Cavalryman and former Lieutenant Hulisi Efendi was prosecuted but acquitted (*Vakit,* 2 August 1920).

For having joined the Kuvay-ı Milliye, six members of the army were punished with expulsion from the army, removal of their rank, and execution (*Vakit,* 17 August 1920).

For having joined the *Kuvay-ı Milliye,* seven individuals were acquitted and later released. On the same day, there was news of others being acquitted of similar crimes (*Vakit,* 16 December 1920).

Notes

1. Prime Ministry. General Directorate of State Archives. *Osmanlı Belgelerinde Ermeniler, 1915-1920* (Ankara: Başbakanlık Devlet Arşivleri Genel Müdürlüğü, 1994), Record No. 220, pp. 189–190; Ali Fuad Türkgeldi, *Görüp İşittiklerim* (Ankara: Türk Tarih Kurumu, 1951), p. 173.
2. *Takvîm-i Vekâyi,* no. 3424, 21 December 1334 (1918).
3. *Yeni Gazete* (translation: New Newspaper), 6 April 1919.
4. *Peyam-i Sabah,* 10 March 1920.
5. *Tercuman-ı Hakikat,* 31 March 1920.
6. *Vakit,* 18 February 1921.
7. *İkdam,* 16 December 1920. The same pattern was followed in other Istanbul papers of the time. For example, see *Peyam-i Sabah,* 4 February 1921.
8. Because of the abovementioned methodological considerations, this number must necessarily be used with caution.
9. *Alemdar,* 22 June 1919.
10. *Alemdar, Yeni Gazete,* 24 June 1919.
11. *Alemdar,* 7 October 1919.
12. *Ati, Alemdar,* 28 October 1919.
13. *Alemdar, Ati,* 4 November 1919.
14. *Ati,* 13 November 1919.
15. *Alemdar, İkdam, Ati,* 23 November 1919.
16. *Alemdar, Ati,* 24 December 1919.
17. *Ati, Alemdar,* 30 December 1919.

18. *Ati,* 2 January 1920.
19. *Alemdar,* 4 January 1920.
20. For the full list of the names, see *Takvîm-i Vekâyi,* no. 3772.
21. *Alemdar, Ati,* 26 March 1920.
22. *Vakit,* 30 December 1920.
23. *Ati,* 10 March 1920.
24. *Alemdar,* 16 March 1920.
25. *Yeni Gazete,* 24 April 1919.
26. *Alemdar,* 25 April 1919.
27. *Alemdar,* 25 April 1919.
28. *Tercüman-ı Hakikat,* 27 April 1919.
29. *Alemdar, Yeni Gazete,* 2 May 1919.
30. *Tercüman-ı Hakikat,* 6 May 6, *Yeni Gazete,* 7 May 1919.
31. *Alemdar, Yeni Gazete,* 8 May 1919.
32. *Tercüman-ı Hakikat,* 10 May, *Yeni Gazete, Alemdar,* 11 May 1919.
33. *Yeni Gazete, Alemdar,* 14 May 1919.
34. *Alemdar,* 4 February 1920.
35. *Alemdar,* 6 February 1920.
36. In some documents Kurd Ali is called Kurd brigand Alo; Alo is a Kurdish version of the name Ali.
37. *Yeni Gazete,* 3 August 1919.
38. *Yeni Gazete,* 3 August 1919.
39. *Alemdar,* 6 August 1919.
40. *Alemdar,* 21 September 1919.
41. *Ati,* 23 October 1919.
42. *Ati,* 23 October 23 1919.
43. The newspapers *Renaissance,* 20 May 1919, and *Djagadmarad,* 18 May 1919, both reported that Faik Paşa testified before the military tribunal that he possessed a telegram from Mahmut Kâmil Paşa giving the order to annihilate the Armenians. This testimony was not repeated in court. Dadrian, "Documentation of the Armenian Genocide in Turkish Sources," pp. 117–118.
44. Bastinado, a punishment inflicted by beating the soles of the feet.
45. *Ikdam,* 4 December 1919.
46. *Alemdar,* 19 December 1919.
47. Because of their importance, this trial and the Yozgat trial will be the subjects of a separate study.
48. *Vakit,* 23 April 1920.
49. *Tercüman-ı Hakikat,* 18 February 1919.
50. *Vakit, Alemdar,* 6 February 1921.
51. Yakup Cemil, an infamous *fedai* of the CUP (the Union and Progress Party) and a member of Teskilât-ı Mahsusa, tried to arrange a coup in 1916. As a result of this attempt he was sentenced to death and executed by a firing squad.
52. For more information see Bilal N. Şimşir, *The Malta Exiles and the Armenian Question* (Ankara: Foreign Policy Institute 1985), pp. 109, 218, 545, and Vartkes Yeghiayan, *British Foreign Office Dossiers on Turkish War Criminals* (La Verne, CA: American Armenian International College, 1991), pp. 57–60.
53. We will deal with this trial in a forthcoming book on the Trabzon and Yozgat trials.

54. There is additional information about Hidayet Efendi in Armenian sources. For example, Arshavir Shiragian's *The Legacy: Memoirs of an Armenian Patriot* (Boston: Hairenik Press, 1976), p. 8. This author alleges that he tried to kill Hidayet Efendi during the armistice period in Istanbul but that Hidayet managed to escape to Anatolia (pp. 42–44). Hidayet was also the police officer who accompanied Armenian Patriarch Zaven der Yeghiayan on his deportation to Deir-Zor in 1916. Zaven Der Yeghiayan, *My Patriarchal Memoirs,* trans. Ared Misirliyan (Barrington, R.I.: Mayreni, 2002), p. 129.
55. *Vakit* 8 December 1920; *Ikdam,* 9 December 1920.
56. Dadrian, "Documentation of the Armenian Genocide in Turkish Sources," pp. 91, 107.

CHAPTER 12

The Formation and Operation of the Ottoman Military Tribunals

Taner Akçam

The initial impetus to form special military tribunals (Divan-ı Harbi Örfi) in order to prosecute those who were suspected of crimes in connection with the deportation and massacres of Armenians appeared in November 1919.[1] It is important to point out, however, that both during this period and in the years preceding there were already military tribunals in operation. The reason they were in existence at all had to do with the fact that starting in April 1909 (with the exception of the period from 15 July to 7 August 1912), the Ottoman Empire had been under martial law.[2]

It was determined that the existing military tribunals of the time would be inadequate to investigate the crimes that occurred during the Armenian deportations, so by official decree an Extraordinary Military Tribunal was ordered established. However, the fact that there were other, similar courts in operation during this period of martial law creates a great deal of confusion over the names. On 20 December 1918 in the newspaper *Vakit,* there are references to three separate military tribunals in operation in Istanbul. By 16 April 1920, the Turkish daily *Tercüman-ı Hakikat* would refer to twelve different military tribunals operating in Istanbul alone.

In February 1919 (about two months after the establishment of the Special Military Tribunal), name changes were made to bring some order to the confusion. "In order to distinguish among and to remove the resemblance between the military tribunals entrusted with the investigation of deportation cases and the original military tribunals, it is befitting that the latter shall from now on be known as the *Dersaadet* [Istanbul] Military Administration Tribunal."[3] As will be discussed below, the changes made on 8 March 1919 by a special decree of the padishah (i.e., the sultan) included not only changes to the name, but also the structure and functioning of the courts. From this time forward in public discourse, the *Dersaadet* Military Tribunal would be known as the "First Military Tribunal," thereby ending the confusion. On the other hand, the establishment of special military tribunals assigned to hear special cases opened up a well of criticism in the public. When the 1920 election results were in, the newly elected members of the Chamber of Deputies lost no time in demanding that the tribunals be disbanded as violating the Constitution.[4]

The initial effort to start examining the crimes, transgressions, and irregularities that had occurred during the deportation and ultimately the massacres of the Armenians started around November 1918. Further detailed analysis of this process of examination is provided in chapters 3 and 4. It is useful here to provide a general overview of the chronology.

We can divide these events into two categories. The first revolved around the efforts made in the Ottoman Parliament. The members of the Chamber of Deputies took some definite steps by proposing various investigations and posing inquiries to the state. Of all the proposals made, only one actually resulted in something concrete—the proposal of Deputy Fuad Bey, whose proposal for an investigation, dated 28 October 1918, resulted in the formation of an Investigating Commission on 4 November 1918.[5] The second category resulted from a variety of actions taken by the new government upon the departure of the Committee for Union and Progress. This can be divided into two groups, one having to do with the formation of investigating commissions charged with examining the deportation and killings, and another with the formation of the military tribunals.

Investigating Committees

With the removal of the Union and Progress Party from power, a new government was formed on 14 October 1918 with the new cabinet of Ahmet Izzet Paşa. Still, no proposals were made at the time to investigate these matters.[6] In fact, this government even took certain actions, such as destroying certain important documents, to prevent an investigation from taking place.[7] The first real effort to investigate these events was made on 11 November 1918 with the formation of the Tevfik Paşa cabinet and the establishment of the Commission for Investigation of Misdeeds (Tedkik-i Seyyiyat). The first news reports on the subject revealed that the new commission had been announced to the Chamber of Deputies by the minister of interior. According to the same newspaper, "former governor of Bitlis, Ohrili Mazhar Bey" had been appointed president of the commission; the other commission members were "Emin Hüsnü Bey from the state inspectors, Avramaki from the Judicial Appellate Board, Artin from the Court of Appeals, Ömer from the Ministry of Justice, [and] Haralamabos Efendi, assistant legal director."[8] The commission would "work out of an office assigned to it from the Directorate of Security."[9] The newspaper *Sabah* would dub the commission the "Tedkik-i fecâyî" (Investigation of Calamity).[10]

At the start of December, the cabinet members decided they needed to assign joint commissions from among members of the Justice and Interior Ministries, which would travel to the various regions with the aim of executing the operations of the Commission for Investigation of Misdeeds.[11] According to the news of 8 December 1918, "these committees [were] going to travel to the various regions, listen to the complaints of the locals, investigate them, and when necessary send the complaints to the local prosecutor's offices for prosecution."[12] These committees who would be traveling throughout the regions "had been given the fullest authority to treat severely all those who were found, as a result of investigation, to have committed crimes and abuses."[13] Also in the news was the information that the commission would be made up of ten individuals, and that they would have the authority to detain and punish at their discretion.[14]

The president of the Mazhar Inquiry Commission (Tedkik-i Seyyiyat), Mazhar Bey, was part of the first commission to travel out into the provinces. While it is not clear what the legal relationship was between the Tedkik-i Seyyiyat and the various commissions that went out on investigations, a decision was made to allow each commission to act independently of the other. *Ikdam*, in describing these commissions, stated that in the event of the movement of individuals under investigation, the regional and central bodies of the commission would share information and jurisdiction. These commissions, which would act independently of one another, would nevertheless be directly tied with one another through the Justice Ministry.[15] Whether it was the Tedkik-i Seyyiyat or the commissions sent out into the provinces, they would all be operating in service of the military tribunals, which were about to be established.[16]

Later, the list of different provinces where the commissions had been sent was published in the newspapers.[17] Once the commissions had identified the individuals they felt needed to be prosecuted, those individuals were sent to the military tribunal in Istanbul for prosecution.[18] Over the course of two months, the commission would find, in the twenty-eight different provinces it was investigating, numerous documents connected with the deportations and murders.[19] After a preliminary investigation, 130 files were opened on 130 people whose prosecution was demanded.[20] When the cases had not yet started in January, there was a lot of finger pointing in the press, by both the Ministry of the Interior and the military tribunals. Each institution accused the other of letting matters drag on.[21]

The Special Military Tribunal investigating the Armenian massacres would end up finding the work of the commissions to be lacking and would engage its own commissions to investigate matters. According to an announcement made by the Special Military Tribunal president, there were five investigating commissions connected with the tribunal and assigned to the task of investigating the deportations and violations of rules that occurred during the war.[22] These commissions had managed to obtain additional information, but the time needed to perform the investigations resulted in delays in prosecution, which was attracting negative press.[23] As we shall see below, in August 1919 the commissions that had been appointed to investigate the deportations were disbanded for causing delays in the prosecution of cases. Investigating judges were to take their place.[24] Only the Commission to Investigate Profiteering (Tedkik-i Ihtika) continued to operate, but not for long; on 10 September 1919 it was disbanded as well.[25]

We must add that there is one other investigating commission of note: the Parliament Commission (Beşinci Şube) was formed for the purpose of investigating the unlawful acts of government officials during the war. The investigation process was interrupted by the sultan's proroguing of parliament, and the commission's documents were transferred to the prosecutor's office of the military tribunal on 17 May 1919.[26]

A military tribunal was formed within the Ministry of War on 26 November 1918 for the purpose of investigating war crimes. This tribunal was focused only on the prosecution of Enver and Cemal Paşas. Kâzım Paşa served as the tribunal's president.[27] This military tribunal demanded the surrender of Enver and Cemal Paşas on 12 December 1918, and it announced that if they failed to surrender, they would be prosecuted immediately, their property seized, and their civil rights taken away.[28]

The Formation of the Military Tribunal

The first military tribunal aimed specifically at furthering the investigation of crimes related to the Armenian massacres was established on 14 December 1918 by a special decree of the sultan.[29] There were two major influences on the formation of this decree. The first was pressure from public opinion, and the second was pressure from the former Allied powers.[30]

The government, furthering the sultan's will, formally decided on 14 December 1918 to establish tribunals around the nation for the purpose of prosecuting those accused of deportation crimes.[31] These tribunals would be formed in accordance with the Regulations on Martial Law of 20 September 1877.[32] Also, as mentioned above, investigating commissions that would work under the military tribunals in furtherance of their objectives were formed, and the scope of their authority and their method of investigation were set out by official decree.[33]

The first military tribunal was established in Istanbul on 16 December 1918, and Mahmut Hayret Paşa became its president.[34] Three of the seven civil members of the court panel were Christian. One of these was a judge. However, there would be frequent resignations and new appointments to this panel. Changes made on 8 March 1919 eventually put an end to any civil or Christian members serving on the board.

It was not simply enough to establish the military tribunals to investigate and prosecute. Because of a law, in force since in 1913, that prohibited investigation of civil servants without the permission of higher authorities, an inquiry required special permission to proceed.[35] According to the law, permission for an employee to be detained had to be obtained first from the provincial administration, then from the Council of State. This not only slowed down the investigative process but also made it virtually impossible to investigate and question witnesses. Despite the words of Interior Minister Fethi Bey, published in the contemporary press in October, that "in furtherance of the law, the investigation and examination of all employees would be made, regardless of rank or grade, and in fairness and justice," it was simply not enough.[36]

As was to be expected, on 20 December the newspapers reported that an official bill would be introduced to overcome the difficulties presented by the earlier law.[37] On 22 December 1918, the minister of the interior stated that "War Cabinet members would be prosecutable by the Military Tribunals."[38] By executive decision on 25 December 1918, officers and state civil servants became subject to the jurisdiction of these criminal courts without the need for official permission.[39] The news reported that a new law, comprised of five sections, had been issued by the state.[40] On the same day another executive decision was published stating that the prosecution of deportation-related crimes would be transferred to regular criminal courts in places where martial law was not in force, in order to not violate Article 88 of the Constitution.[41]

On 8 January 1919, appointments were made "for the military tribunals in Izmir, Bursa, Tekirdağ, Edirne, Samsun and Ayıntab," as authorized by the decision of 14 December.[42] On 21 January, the tribunals' scope of duties would be reevaluated and restated. The tribunals in Istanbul, Izmir, Van, Tekirdağ, Antep, Samsun, Bursa, and Beyazit were authorized to hear cases in the provinces and provincial subdivisions. Information about the jurisdiction, authorization, and area of responsibility of these tribunals was published in the papers.[43] This did not quell the confusion, however, as to what these courts would be doing, so yet another commission was formed to clarify the jurisdictions of each of the commissions and tribunals.[44] In February this issue was clarified again.[45] The Edirne and Bandırma tribunals were disbanded for lack of necessity.[46]

The First Damad Ferit Paşa Cabinet and the Re-formation of the Military Tribunals

The most important change to the structure of the military tribunals was made by Grand Vizier Damad Ferit Paşa on 8 March 1919. On that date a decision was taken to remove all civil members of the court's panel and to have them replaced with strictly military personnel. By Article 1 of the aforementioned decision, the right to appeal tribunal rulings was taken away as well. Article 3 of the decision officially dissolved the first tribunal as of 16 December 1918. The trials that had already started with the former tribunal (like the Yozgat trial) would be transferred to the competence of the new tribunal.[47] In a parallel decision taken by the government on 8 March, the jurisdiction of the military tribunals would be expanded. According to the decision, the new tribunal would have the expanded authority to investigate any individuals who pushed the country into war, who organized massacres against Greeks, Armenians, and Muslims, or who incited hatred between groups.[48]

Under the new system the investigations, trials, and number of arrests increased quickly. The Yozgat trial came to a conclusion. Boğazlıyan County Executive Kemal was executed on 10 April 1919.[49] Similarly, the Trabzon trial, the Union and Progress party leaders' trial, and the wartime cabinet members trial all quickly came to their conclusions during the spring and summer months.

The changes on 8 March 1919 were not the only ones made. From time to time there would be other changes to the jurisdictional scope and rules of procedure. Besides these, there were frequent changes in the personnel of the court. Along with resignations, changes in the government often brought changes in the panel of judges. The first significant change following 8 March 1919 occurred on 27 August 1919. During the two months preceding this change there had been highly critical pieces in the press complaining of the slow tempo of justice in the proceedings. In answer to these criticisms, the military tribunals felt obliged to give an explanation. That explanation appeared on 7 July. It clarified that the slowness was due to there being no new material forwarded to the tribunal from the investigative bodies. In July 1919 there were five trials, two of which had come to a conclusion. Other matters were still being investigated. The blame was placed on the investigating commissions who had been assigned the task of researching, investigating, and preparing cases for prosecution.[50]

As the criticisms intensified, it was decided on 27 August 1919 to dissolve the investigating commissions; matters would now proceed through "examining magistrates." In addition, the court administration was changed. As much as the government was criticized for intervening in this process, the slow movement of cases through the system was an important consideration.[51] Not only did the state intervene to change the structure of the investigations, it went as far as changing the location of the court itself. In September 1919, it was moved to a building closer to the Ministry of War. However, since the new building was still under repair, all hearings were stopped pending its completion. Additionally, the press reported that rumors that the hearings were to be conducted in secret were false, and that they would continue to be open to the public.[52]

In addition to the change announced on 27 August 1919, a fundamental change was made on 18 September 1919. All decisions previously taken regarding the tribunals, including the one enacted on 8 March 1919, were canceled, and the sultan approved this decision on 23 September 1919. This act completely reworked the rules of court procedure for the military tribunals. Among the changes were the requirements that there be a two-thirds majority vote for all death sentences, and that cases in which a death sentence had been issued would have the right of appeal.[53]

Despite the changes in procedure, cases did not start in September, and the press continued to criticize the slow tempo at which the tribunals were operating. "There is not a person among us who doesn't want those who've caused our tragic state of affairs to be subject to punishment," stated the *Tercüman-ı Hakikat*. "The trials that were postponed because of the hairsplitting of the panel of judges are now stuck on issues of venue and transferal. As if these weren't enough, for the past 4–5 days the prosecutor's office has been without an examining magistrate. The prosecutors' office can't continue to work."[54] In fact, there was general criticism in the press that the government had followed a conscious policy of leaving trials hanging for a protracted period.

It was not mere coincidence that caused the trial docket to come to a complete stop in September 1919. The Nationalist congress in Sivas under the leadership of Mustafa Kemal met between 4 and 11 September. At this time the Nationalists organized an action to boycott the Anatolia-Istanbul communication lines, and they also launched the "telegram war" against the government of Damad Ferit Paşa. When the crisis between Istanbul and Anatolia intensified, the padishah finally intervened on 20 September 1919 with the publication of an edict in favor of the Istanbul government,[55] but it could not stop the resignation of Damad Ferit Paşa on 30 September 1919.[56] This situation illustrates how the progress of the courts was directly influenced by political developments of the time, especially those involving Turkish nationalist insurgency.

The Ali Rıza Paşa Cabinet and the Military Tribunal

One of the first issues to be tackled by the new Grand Vizier Ali Rıza Paşa, who came to power on 2 October 1919, was that of the military tribunals. He and his cabinet were pro–Ankara Nationalist Movement and even saw themselves as their representatives in Istanbul. Thus they were disposed to hinder the entire process of conducting the trials and, if possible, help reach decisions in favor of Union and Progress party members who were in custody. The newspapers of 10 October reported: "In accordance with the official decree of September 18, 1919, the Military Tribunals of Bursa, Edirne, Tekfur Dağ" were merged. Even though the necessary administrative appointments had been made to the tribunals, trials and hearings had not yet begun because of the renovations and repairs that were occurring in the newly assigned building that was to house the tribunal.[57] In the press there was news that the panel members of the military tribunal would change yet again, and that the hearings had not started for this reason.[58] This did in fact occur. The newly formed tribunal's administrative board of late September would be subject to yet more changes on 19 October.[59] The news that the new panel of the judges had started operating again was reported on 22 October.[60]

Another measure taken by the new cabinet was to form a new committee on 30 October 1919, with members from the War, Justice, and Public Works ministries along with the president of the Council of State, who would "review the decisions already taken and try to speed up the process of prosecution" in the military tribunals.[61] This committee came to the decision that all deportation trials should take place in the tribunals that had jurisdiction over the location where the related crimes had occurred. The trials would be seen "in the local Tribunals, and barring that, then before the Courts Martial." This decision was sent to the various regions by way of coded messages on 9 November 1919.[62]

As a result of the cabinet's pro-Nationalist disposition, the military tribunal started to issue rulings one after the other, favoring the release of the CUP defendants and "dismissal of pending cases." The press was full of critical reports accusing the tribunal of "being completely inactive and letting the trials drag on interminably." In an attempt to assuage the press, the court president held a press conference to explain why the hearings had not continued and also to explain the releases and dismissals. According to the court president, they were not politically motivated. "There were some releases on bail and some dismissals," he said, but they had been issued according to the dictates of the law, in a just manner. "The guidepost for our actions was the law and conscience."[63]

In point of fact, Court President Esat Paşa was being less than truthful. The tribunal was not simply operating at a snail's pace during the Ali Rıza Paşa government; judicial decisions were being sent down that sided not only with the accused, but also with those who had already been convicted. The rulings favoring the defendants, which had started with the second term of Damad Ferit Paşa on 5 April 1920, began to reach the surface during the period of Ali Rıza Paşa's cabinet. The newspaper *Tercüman-ı Hakikat* shed light on this phenomenon with an article published on 22 April 1920, titled "What's Happened at the Military Tribunal?" According to the newspapers, two defendants accused of crimes in the Giresun deportation and jailed pending prosecution for their crimes had been released.[64] The papers reported that they had begun investigating this and other similar instances involving methods of "bending of the rules" that had already taken place.[65]

On 9 August 1920, the newspapers published an interview with Court President Mustafa Paşa, who had been in charge since April of that year. In reference to the former court administration he had this to say: "A number of documents which relate to persons who were ordered arrested have been destroyed." Moving on to comment on the prior court president, Esat Paşa, he said that the defendant Feyyaz Ali in the Yozgat trial, who had been found guilty and sentenced, was "released on probation, for reasons which are incomprehensible, illogical, and which he could not justify." According to Mustafa Paşa, "the release of someone who has been involved in many felonies and crimes is not something that can be forgiven." The documents related to Feyyaz Ali "had been either completely destroyed or misplaced." Esat Paşa would eventually be arrested for his role in the release of Feyyaz Ali. Feyyaz Ali, for his part, headed straight for Ankara after his release and became a member of the newly formed Turkish National Assembly.[66] His first important act, once he joined the Assembly, would be to introduce a bill on 12 August pardoning all those who had been prosecuted by the military tribunals.[67]

By mutual understanding between the Ankara and Istanbul governments, an election had been held in October 1919, and on 12 January 1920 the last Ottoman Chamber of Deputies began its term. This newly elected pro-Nationalist Chamber made several attempts to stop the activities of the military tribunals. One of the driving forces behind this, without a doubt, was the presence of many of the members of the Assembly who were then under investigation. According to the newspaper *Peyam-i Sabah*, in the news published on 17 February 1920 at least ten of the deputies had open files with the military tribunal for crimes related to their involvement in the Armenian deportations, and they were the subject of a request from the tribunal to the Interior Ministry to investigate. The newspaper asked, "Let us wait and see if the Interior Ministry is going to report their names to the Senate and if so, whether the Senate will be willing to part ways with these comrades."[68]

Süleyman Sırrı was one of these deputies, and during the three months that the Chamber was in session, he struggled to have the military tribunal disbanded.[69] His first effort was on 12 February, when he presented a memo stating that the "formation of a special Military Tribunal for deportation and killing-related crimes is against the Constitution," and that the matter should more properly be handled by the War and Justice Ministries.[70] This is the same argument made by the attorneys of the CUP cabinet member defendants before the military tribunal. Based on this claim, Süleyman Sırrı demanded that the hearings immediately cease and desist. In response to his memorandum, the government responded in writing on 23 February with the opinion that the tribunals were not in violation of the Constitution. The government's response was read in parliament; however, during the ensuing discussion, in which it continued to be argued that the tribunals were against the Constitution, cries of "bravo" and applause from members of the Assembly could be heard.[71]

In the same parliament there were other attempts to disavow the anti-Unionist actions of the previous government. One bill, for example, proposed that "Ferid Paşa and his cabinet shall be sent for prosecution to Divan-i Ali [the High Court established by parliament] for allowing the Greeks to occupy Izmir and for having formed the military tribunal and its courts contrary to the principles of the Constitution." Without even submitting it to a formal vote, the bill was treated as having passed and sent to the responsible Chamber committee.[72] To go from debating the prosecution of those suspected of crimes in the massacres of the Armenians to pushing for the prosecution of Ferit Paşa for having prosecuted those very same individuals makes clear just how much the country had changed in one year.

After the British occupation of Istanbul, and after the Chamber of Deputies went into recess, an investigation was initiated into ten Assembly members, Süleyman Sırrı being at the top of the list. *Alemdar* newspaper published the names of the Assembly members; however, there was another list, of thirteen members, that was also mentioned.[73] In the days that followed, the press would publish varying reports on which and how many deputies were being investigated.[74] Following the investigation of Süleyman Sırrı, the decision came down as "prosecution is recommended," and his file was transferred to the military tribunal.[75]

The Second Term of Damad Ferit Paşa's Cabinet

With the occupation of Istanbul and the disbanding of the Chamber, the second term of Damad Ferit Paşa's government started on 5 April 1920 and continued until 17 October of the same year. During this period an extensive revision of the operation and jurisdiction of the military tribunals was made, and in turn the disposition of trials continued apace. The first action taken by the government was the publication on 23 April 1920 of the Decree on the Organization and Jurisdiction of the Military Tribunals.[76] The decree was comprised of thirteen articles, the first two of which were devoted to the composition of the panels of the tribunals. Some of the most important changes proposed were: Article 3, "The Military Tribunals will issue judicial decisions on matters of deportation, murder, profiteering, open and violent seizure of goods, and pillage [*tahribi bilad cürümlerini irtikâb etmiş*], prosecuting all those who have violated the domestic and foreign security of the Ottoman State, without right of appeal"; Article 4, "The trials shall not be public, nor will a proxy or attorney be present"; Article 8, "The aforementioned sentenced individuals shall not be granted waiver or exception as a result of either formal or special characteristics or position of honor."[77]

During Damad Ferit Paşa's second term there was an observable increase in the prosecution of crimes by the military tribunals, and some of the trials concluded with death sentences for the defendants. From the Erzincan trial, defendant Abdullah Avni was hanged on 29 July 1920,[78] and the defendant Nusret from the Bayburt trial was hanged on 5 August 1920.[79] It should be added that during this period, the military tribunal was not limited to prosecuting crimes related to the Armenian deportation. During the period between April and June in particular, the trials related to the Kuvay-ı Milli (National Independence Army) movement, and those directed against the Ankara government took a prominent place in the tribunal docket. In fact, at one point, a moratorium was declared on "deportation and murder" trials in order to prosecute the members of the Kuvay-ı Milliye.[80]

In the trials against the Kuvay-ı Milliye, the death sentence against Mustafa Kemal and his friends garnered a great deal of attention. Almost a hundred defendants were sentenced to death.[81] Additionally, there was a trial against a large group of individuals accused of attempting to assassinate Damad Ferit; in total, sixteen of them were sentenced to death. Four of the defendants who were in custody were executed on 12 June 1920.[82] The Istanbul police chief stated in a press conference that the order to assassinate Damad Ferit Paşa had come from Ankara (Mustafa Kemal).[83] In this way the prosecution of crimes related to the Armenian deportations and those related to the Ankara movement occurred simultaneously. This would ultimately prove to have been the death knell of the military tribunals.

Another temporary law was issued on 2 September 1920. Using the state of martial law as a justification, the sultan's approval was made a necessary procedural requirement for high-ranking officers or civil servants to be prosecuted by the tribunals.[84] It was claimed that Damad Ferit Paşa had this law issued in anticipation of the prosecution that would be lodged against him later.[85]

The number of executions that took place during the summer, combined with the increased strength of the Turkish Nationalist movement in Anatolia, created an atmosphere that was hostile to the military tribunals. The tribunal president, Mustafa Paşa, would make a public announcement in an attempt to defend the prosecutions: "There have been some criticisms that I have acted harshly, but you should be sure that those who have attacked me and maligned my character are either CUP men or nationalists or men whose interest lies in covering up the crimes of these two groups of people." The most important detail of the court president's speech is that he made a connection between the crimes against Armenians and the nationalist movement in Anatolia: "Those who dress themselves up as patriots have pinned their hopes on the gangs who have been caught in the claws of justice and support the murderers who took part in deportations and killings."[86]

The final change to the organization of the military tribunals would be made on 5 October 1920. This decree, like the one made on 23 April of that year that had changed much of the procedural rules and organization of the military tribunal, would change the processing of trials. The most important feature of this reorganization was that the right of appeal was to be restored.[87]

The Term of Tevfik Paşa's Cabinet

Damad Ferit Paşa's cabinet resigned on 17 October 1920, and Tevfik Paşa's began its term on 21 October 1920. Tevfik Paşa, who would remain in power throughout the Second Government's term up until November 1922, would move in lockstep with the increasingly strong Ankara Nationalist movement. The first real influence their policy had over the government concerned the activities of the military tribunals and involved yet more re-organizational changes.

As soon as the new government was established, the press started issuing reports that the military tribunals would be changing. The newspaper *Vakit* stated that the only way the current government would be able to come to an agreement with the Nationalist movement in Ankara would be to stop the unjust prosecutions and close the tribunals. It called for "the recess of the administrative machinery which is operating upon the incitement of personal ambitions and cruelty rather than the aims of justice."[88] The same newspaper, while noting that there were protests against the closing of the military tribunals and expressing the view that it did not consider the release of those responsible for the wartime events as a prerequisite to establishing peace, nevertheless did also note that there were many voices expressing the view that the machinery of justice was operating unjustly. According to this newspaper, too many people were getting thrown into jail and prosecuted by the military tribunals without regard for their culpability.[89] The desire on the part of the Tevfik Paşa cabinet to make peace with the Nationalist movement led to an effort to invalidate the prosecutions that had taken place during the Damad Ferit Paşa regime.

The first step taken was to review all the judicial files of the military tribunals of the Damad Ferit Paşa period and to have them sent to the Court of Appeals. This set of wide-ranging changes would be published first in *Takvim-i Vekâyi* on 1 November 1920,[90] then later in the daily papers. According to the decree, all of the cases that had resulted in the most serious penalties—death, life in prison, and hard labor—would be reviewed. Of the lighter sentences, the right to appeal would be upon the defendant's application. For this purpose a Board of Appeals (Heyet-i Temyiziyye) was formed.[91] The newspapers were saying, "While it is not clear what the final opinion of the Appellate Court will be after examining the files, it is clear that many of the judicial decisions will be annulled."[92] The newspapers reported that the reorganization would be complete in a few days, and that prosecutions would continue soon after.[93] Possibly the greatest change of all would be the replacement of the entire panel of judges.[94]

The new judges immediately started to review the files from the previous period. Additionally, administrative employees visited the Bekirağa Bölügü prison and "noted the presence of 15 persons who had been detained without the issuance of a warrant of detention," and a report was prepared.[95] *Vakit* stated that the hearings would not be reconvened until the investigations were complete.[96] It reported on 10 November 1920 that the trials were to begin again.[97]

The president of the military tribunals, Hurşit Paşa, visited the detainees in prison. One of the complaints he heard was that some of the detainees had been tortured. An investigation into torture and mistreatment was opened, and arrests were made.[98] According to the news reported on 16 December 1920, the First Military Tribunal confirmed that "during their detention, many detainees had been victims of illegal treatment, assaults and verbal insults."[99]

The investigation of the acts of previous military tribunals was not limited to their judicial decisions; members of past tribunals were also subjected to investigation.[100] The most significant example of this was the arrest of past Tribunal President Nemrud the Kurd, Mustafa Paşa, and four members of the tribunal. The basis given for the arrest was the court's failure to follow proper procedure during the Bayburt trial, in which the defendant Nusret was found guilty and executed.[101] Although there were judges who had voted for execution during the initial deliberation, by majority vote the defendant had been sentenced to fifteen years of hard labor. Despite the fact that there was a written record of this vote, on 20 July 1920 the sentencing was taken up *again* and this time the decision was for execution of the defendant, which was immediately carried out.[102]

The trial against Mustafa and the four panel members moved quickly, concluding on 8 December 1920.[103] The defendants got three to seven months in their sentencing.[104] However, the Military Tribunal Appellate Division overturned the decision and remanded the case for a retrial. The motion to release, made by the defendants, was rejected.[105] The court firmly defended its initial decision, but the Ministry of War ruled that the time served by the defendants fulfilled the sentencing requirements, and the sultan formally commuted the defendants' sentences.[106]

Another complaint against the previous military tribunals was that despite being held for over two years, many detainees had yet to see the inside of a courtroom.[107] First their files were taken for review and then, based upon the start dates of their investigations, trial dates were set.[108] Later, based upon the review of these files, the defendants were released one by one for failure to prosecute and/or acquittal. Most of these acquittals and releases were given to defendants who had been arrested for their connection to the National Independence Army (Kuvay-ı Milliye).

With the appointment of the new tribunal judicial panel and the renewal of the prosecutions, the press started to release the list of trials to be heard.[109] One by one, most of the trials involving the Armenian deportations and related crimes ended with the acquittal of the defendants and their subsequent release. The first acquittal occurred in the Amasya trial.[110] This was followed by the acquittal of Beypazarlı Fahri Bey. The number of defendants who would receive acquittals, including some related to deportation crimes, reached thirty-six in a short period of time.[111] A significant number of the acquittals were in trials involving defendants who had connections to the National Independence Army (Kuvay-ı Milliye).[112]

The Demise of the Military Tribunals

All of these developments could be interpreted to mean that the prosecutions of the military tribunals were reaching their conclusion. Whether one looks at it from the perspective of the newly formed government in Ankara or the government in Istanbul at the time, the military tribunals had outlived their usefulness. Over time there would develop a movement, in both Istanbul and Ankara, to minimize the influence of, and eventually to end, the trials. The signing of the Sèvres Agreement on 10 August 1920 revealed to both the Ankara and Istanbul governments that there would be no favors forthcoming from the Allied powers for the prosecution of those responsible for the war crimes, deportations, and massacres.

On 9 December 1920 the Military Appellate office asked the Military Appellate Assembly in Istanbul if involvement in the Kuvay-ı Milliye did or did not constitute a crime. The position of the Ministry of War on this question was made quite clear on 21 April 1921: "One should applaud involvement in the Kuvay-ı Milliye. Dismiss all of these trials."[113] In fact, even before the Ministry of War's decision, starting on 15 February 1921 all of the judicial rulings involving the Kuvay-ı Milliye that had been tried in the defendants' absence were dismissed one by one.[114]

The Military Tribunal handed down a decision on 24 April 1921 in which it affirmed that "involvement with the Kuvay-ı Milliye cannot be considered a crime." The tribunal asserted further that the property of defendants that had been taken as part of their punishment for this crime, be returned to them. According to the memo, "considering a person guilty of association with the Kuvay-ı Milliye conflicts with the honor of defending one's country."[115] As a result, trials that had started on 1 May 1920 against close to a hundred defendants involved in the Nationalist movement who had been sentenced to death were terminated. On 24 April 1922, the last Istanbul government would be forced to state that it had no jurisdiction to prosecute members of the Kuvay-ı Milliye.

The conclusion of the trials related to the Armenian deportations and massacres was no different. Ruling after ruling favored acquittal or dismissal for failure to prosecute. According to an article in *Peyam-i Sabah* on 11 April 1922, "Based on the examination which we have conducted, there are no further trials related to the deportation at the First Military Tribunal." One can therefore conclude there were no further trials on the deportations after this date. On 11 July 1922 the newspapers reported that the military tribunals were in the process of being disbanded.[116] With the taking of Istanbul by the Ankara Nationalist movement on 6 November 1922, the laws issued by the Grand National Assembly of Ankara canceling the military tribunals would extend to Istanbul as well, thereby ending the tribunals entirely.

In Ankara, there had been a variety of moves to have the tribunals' activities in connection with the Armenian deportations come to an end. For example, on 11 May 1920, the new Assembly considered a bill to have a general amnesty; however, the defendants of crimes against the Armenians were excluded from this amnesty. The amnesty was never approved. In the same session Mustafa Kemal made a statement on behalf of the government, which had decided that "the prosecution of those detained because of the deportations would be performed in a manner not requiring their detainment."[117] The decision to try the defendants of deportation crimes without their detainment was made by the government on 8 May 1920. This decision has a certain symbolic significance, as most of the defendants were in Istanbul's jurisdiction and we do not know which military tribunals were under the control of the Ankara government. In the decision there was language acknowledging that the deportation of Armenians had been abused by certain individuals for their own opportunistic reasons and that these same individuals should not escape punishment for their actions; however, the decision was taken to prevent the further punishment of people who were not guilty of crimes.[118]

The Ankara National Assembly took some direct actions toward disbanding the military tribunals. For example, on 13 May 1920 there was a proposal to disband the military tribunal of Çine.[119] On 31 July, a similar proposal was made for the Samsun Military Tribunal.[120] In a bill dated 21 July 1920 the Assembly proposed that all of the decisions of the Istanbul Military Tribunal be considered null and void. The proposal was rejected, but the necessity of bringing it is significant. A previous assembly had already ruled that the Istanbul government and all of its decisions were null and void. For this reason there was no need to have a separate bill submitted for vote on the issue of the military tribunal.[121] The last step was taken on 11 August 1920. "The Ankara government with one decision ruled to disband all tribunals covering the deportation-related matters."[122] After the decision of 11 August, the Assembly reviewed each of the proposals related to the Çine and Samsun Military Tribunals and decided ultimately to disband each of them. Finally, on 31 March 1923, all those imprisoned by decisions from both civil and military courts were granted a general amnesty.

Notes

1. We will be giving here only technical information regarding the establishment of commissions and courts during the 1919–1922 period to prosecute crimes that took place during the Armenian deportations and massacres. For more detailed information see the analysis by V. N. Dadrian elsewhere in this book. See also V. N. Dadrian, "The Documentation of the World War I Armenian Massacres in the Proceedings of the Turkish Military Tribunal," *International Journal of Middle East Studies* 23, no. 4 (November 1991); V. N. Dadrian, "A Textual Analysis of the Key Indictment of the Turkish Military Tribunal Investigating the Armenian Genocide" *Armenian Review* 44, 1–173 (Spring 1991); V. N. Dadrian, "Genocide as a Problem of National and International Law: The World War I Armenian Case and Its Contemporary Legal Ramifications," *Yale Journal of International Law* 14, 2 (1989). For information regarding the general history of the prosecutions in Istanbul and the judicial outcome during the armistice period, see Taner Akçam, *A Shameful Act: The Armenian Genocide and the Question of Turkish Responsibility* (New York: Metropolitan, 2006).
2. For the suspension of martial law, see *Takvim-i Vekâyi,* no. 1186, 24 July 1912. On the reestablishment of martial law, see *Takvim-i Vekâyi,* no. 1249, 7 October 1912. For further information, see Tunaya, *Türkiye'de Siyasal Partiler,* vol. 3, p. 268.
3. *Tercüman-ı Hakikat,* 14 February 1919; *Yeni Gazete,* 15 February 1919.
4. Arguments on the subject were made on 26 February in the 14th Assembly. M.M.Z.C., 4th Period, Assembly Year 1, vol. 1 (Ankara: Turkish Grand National Assembly, 1992), pp. 213–218.
5. Ottoman Parliament. Chamber of Notables. *Meclis-i Ayan Zabıt Ceridesi* [Minutes of the Chamber of Notables]. Ankara: TBMM Basımevi, 1990, p. 103.
6. Seven cabinets in total were formed during the armistice period (1918–1922). For a list of them see Tunaya, *Türkiye'de Siyasal Partiler,* vol. 2: *Armistice Period* (1986), p. 37.
7. For example, Hüsamettin Ertürk would state that Ahmet Izzet Paşa gave him orders to destroy the archives of the Teşkilât-ı Mahsusa. Hüsamettin Ertürk, "Milli Mücadele Senelerinde Teşkilât-ı Mahsusa" (typed text), p. 14, Ankara Stratejik Araştırmalar ve Askerlik Tarihi Enstitüsü, Tarihsiz. In Bilge Criss, ed., *Işgal Altinda Istanbul* (Istanbul: İletişim 1983), p. 147.
8. *Vakit,* 24 November 1918.
9. *Vakit, Ikdam,* 24 November 1918.
10. *Sabah,* 25 November 1918.
11. For the record of communication of the decision from the cabinet to the Ministries of Justice and the Interior see Prime Ministry. General Directorate of State Archives. *Osmanıı Belgelerinde Ermeniler, 1915-1920* (Ankara: Başbakanlık Devlet Arşivleri Genel Müdürlüğü, 1994), Record No. 219 and 220, pp. 188-191.
12. *Ikdam,* 8 December 1918.
13. Ibid.
14. *Ikdam,* 9 December 1918.
15. *Ikdam,* 12 December 1918.
16. *Ati,* 15 December 1918.
17. *Ikdam,* 15 December 1918.
18. *Ikdam,* 15 December 1918.

19. For information about the activities of the commissions, see Dadrian, "The Documentation of the World War I Armenian Massacres," pp. 552–553.
20. United States National Archives, Record Group 256, 867.00/59, p. 3 (U.S. Commissioner at Istanbul, Lewis Hecks' 20 January 1919 report to the State Department) transcribed by V. N. Dadrian, "Genocide as a Problem of National and International Law," p. 295.
21. *Alemdar,* 4 January 1919.
22. *Ileri, Yeni Gazete,* 7 July 1919.
23. *Yeni Gazete,* 7 July 1919, "Muhakeme İsleri Neden Ağır Gidiyormuş?"
24. *Tercüman-ı Hakikat,* 27 and 29 August 1919.
25. *Tercüman-ı Hakikat,* 10 September 1919.
26. For the full text of this writing see Tunaya, *Türkiye'de Siyasi Partiler,* vol. 3, p. 627.
27. *Vakit,* 26 November 1919, the decision was published in *Takvim-i Vekâyi,* no. 3407, 30 November 1918.
28. The court's decision was published in *Takvim-i Vekâyi,* no. 3416, 12 December 1918.
29. Cabinet Board news, appeared in *Ati,* 15 December 1918, and *Hadisat,* 16 December 1918.
30. For the opinion of the padishah on the subject, see Ali Fuad Türkgeldi, *Görüp İşitiklerim,* (Ankara: Türk Tarih Kurumu, 1987), p. 173.
31. *Osmanli Belgelerinde Ermeniler,* Record No. 220, pp. 189–190.
32. Ibid,, p. 190.
33. Ibid., p. 190.
34. The 16 December decision of the government was published in *Takvim-i Vekâyi,* no. 3424, 21 December 1918.
35. This law, which was enacted on 4 February 1913, was published in *Takvim-i Vekâyi,* no. 1751, 24 February 1913.
36. *Hadisat,* 22 October 1918.
37. *Ati,* 20 December 1918.
38. *Istiklal,* 21 December 1918.
39. *Takvim-i Vekâyi,* 28 December 1918; *Ati,* 26 December 1918.
40. *Ati,* 26 December 1918.
41. The decision was published in *Takvim-i Vekâyi,* no. 3430, 28 December 1918. There is information about this decision in the daily newspapers of the time. *Yeni Gazete,* 1 January 1919.
42. This decision dated 8 January 1919 was published in *Takvim-i Vekâyi,* no. 3445, 14 January 1919.
43. *Tercüman-ı Hakikat,* 25 January 1919; *Yeni Gazete,* 1 January 1919.
44. The decisions taken by the commission were published in the daily papers. *Alemdar,* 26 January 1919; *Tercüman-ı Hakikat,* 25 January 1919.
45. *Yeni Gazete,* 25 February 1919.
46. *Takvim-i Vekâyi,* no. 3452, 21 January 1918.
47. The decision dated 8 March 1919 was published in *Takvim-i Vekâyi,* 11 March 1919.
48. Transcribed from *Alemdar,* 9 March 1919, in Bilgi, *Ermeni Tehciri ve Boğazlayan Kaymakamı Mehmed Kemal Bey'in Yargılanması,* p. 59.
49. *Tercüman-ı Hakikat, Yeni Gazete,* 11 April 1919.
50. *Yeni Gazete,* 7 July 1919.
51. *Tercüman-ı Hakikat,* 29 August 1919.

52. *Tercüman-ı Hakikat,* 10 September 1919.
53. *Takvim-i Vekâyi,* no. 3653, 23 September 1919.
54. *Tercüman-ı Hakikat,* 26 September 1919.
55. *Takvim-i Vekâyi,* no. 3651, 21 September 1919.
56. For more detailed information see Akşin, *Istanbul Hükümetleri ve Milli Mücadele,* vol. 1, pp. 534–589.
57. *Alemdar,* 10 October 1919; *Tercüman-ı Hakikat,* 13 and 20 October 1919.
58. *Tercüman-ı Hakikat,* 13 October 1919.
59. *Alemdar,* 30 October 1919; press conference given by President of the Military Tribunal Esat Paşa on reasons for the delay in prosecutions.
60. *Alemdar,* 22 October 1919.
61. Zeki Sarıhan, *Kurtuluş Savaşı Günlüğü,* vol. 2: *Erzurum Kongresi'nden TBMM'ye* (Ankara: Öğretmen Dünyası Yayınları, 1984), pp. 184–185.
62. *Osmanli Belgelerinde Ermeniler,* Record No. 265, pp. 249–250. We were unable to obtain any information regarding the courts that were formed or their activities.
63. *Alemdar,* 30 October 1919.
64. *Tercüman-ı Hakikat,* 22 April 1920.
65. *Tercüman-ı Hakikat,* 24 April 1920. On 26 April this paper reported on other irregularities discovered in its investigation.
66. *Tercüman-ı Hakikat,* 9 August 1920.
67. *The Transcripts of the Grand National Assembly (TBMM Zabit Ceridesi),* Period 1, Assembly Year 1, Vol. 3 (Ankara: TBMM Press, 1941), pp. 172–497. On 20 September 1920, the subject was taken up again, only this time it was transferred to another committee. *Transcripts of the Grand National Assembly,* vol. 4, pp. 199–200.
68. *Peyam-i Sabah,* 17 February 1920.
69. For the debates on the subject of the military tribunals in the last Ottoman Assembly, see Akçam, *A Shameful Act,* chap. 3.
70. *Meclisi Mebusan Zabit Ceridesi* (Ottoman Chamber of Deputies Record), Period 4, Assembly Year 1, vol. 1, p. 98.
71. Ibid., pp. 214–218; these debates were also covered by the press; see *Ati,* 29 February 1920.
72. Ibid, p. 105.
73. *Alemdar,* 15 April 1920.
74. *Alemdar,* in its 19 April 1920 edition, states that the list consisted of ten members with an additional three being added on later. *Peyam-i Sabah* of the same date published the number as eleven with an additional three.
75. *Tercüman-ı Hakikat,* 22 April 1920.
76. It was published in *Takvim-i Vekâyi,* no. 3837, 26 April 1920.
77. *Takvim-i Vekâyi,* no. 3837, 26 April 1920.
78. *Tercüman-ı Hakikat,* 29 July 1920. The sultan's formal approval of the death sentence was published in *Takvim-i Vekâyi,* no. 3917, 31 July 1920.
79. *Tercüman-ı Hakikat,* 5 August 1920; *Vakit,* 6 August 1920. The sultan's formal approval of the death sentence was published in *Takvim-i Vekâyi,* no. 3924, 8 August 1920.
80. *Tercüman-ı Hakikat,* 29 April 1920.
81. Mustafa Kemal's death sentence was published in *Takvim-i Vekâyi,* no. 3864, 27 May 1920. For the other rulings see *Takvim-i Vekâyi,* no. 3866, 30 May 1920; *Takvim-i Vekâyi,* no. 3883, 21 June 1920.

82. The sentence of death, which was given on 9 June 1920, was approved on 11 June and published in *Takvim-i Vekâyi*, no. 3878, 13 June 1920. For information about the trial, see İbnülemin Mahmut Kemal İnal, *Son Sadrazamlar*, vol. 4, p. 2058, 4th print (Istanbul, Dergâh, 1982).
83. *Vakit*, 3 June 1920; additionally see Sarıhan, *Kurtuluş Savaşı Günlüğü*, vol. 3, p. 71.
84. *Takvim-i Vekâyi*, no. 3946, 4 September 1920.
85. Tepeyran, *Zalimane Bir İdam Hükmü*, p. 219.
86. *Vakit*, 15 September 1920.
87. The decision regarding the changes was published in *Takvim-i Vekâyi*, no. 3977, 10 October 1920.
88. *Vakit*, 24 October 1920.
89. Ibid.
90. This decision, dated 30 October 1920, was published in *Takvim-i Vekâyi*, no. 3996, 1 November 1920.
91. *Vakit*, 2 November 1920.
92. Ibid.
93. *Vakit*, 1 November 1920.
94. *Vakit*, 31 October 1920.
95. *Alemdar*, 4 November 1920.
96. *Vakit*, 7 November 1920.
97. *Vakit*, 10 November 1920.
98. *Vakit*, 8 November 1920.
99. *Vakit*, 16 December 1920.
100. *Vakit*, 3 December 1920.
101. *Vakit*, 16 December 1920.
102. The affair was described in detail in *Vakit*, 17 December 1920.
103. *Vakit*, 8 December 1920.
104. Tarık Zafer Tunaya, *Türkiyede Siyasal partiler*, Vol. II, *Ibid*, p. 299–300.
105. *Vakit*, 19 December 1921.
106. Tunaya, *Türkiye'de Siyasal Partiler*, vol. 2 (1986), p. 299–300.
107. *Vakit*, 25 November 1920.
108. *Vakit*, 6 December 1920.
109. *Vakit*, 8 December 1920.
110. *Ikdam*, 9 December 1920.
111. *Vakit*, 10 December 1920. For some additional examples of acquittals related to massacres see *Vakit*, 16 and 23 December 1920.
112. For example, in the 10 December 1920 edition of the newspaper *Ikdam*, it is reported that seven individuals who had been prosecuted for being involved with the Kuvay-ı Milliye were acquitted.
113. Sarıhan, *Kurtuluş Savaşı Günlüğü*, vol. 3, p. 313.
114. Ibid., p. 399.
115. Sarıhan, *Kurtuluş Savaşı Günlüğü*, vol. 3, pp. 449 and 493.
116. *Tercüman-ı Hakikat*, 11 July 1922.
117. *Transcripts of the Grand National Assembly (TBMM Zabit Ceridesi)*, vol. 1 (1940), p. 272.
118. *Düstur*, 3rd series, vol. 1, p. 8 (Istanbul, 1928).
119. *Transcripts of the Grand National Assembly (TBMM Zabit Ceridesi)*, vol. 1, p. 281.

120. *Transcripts of the Grand National Assembly (TBMM Zabit Ceridesi),* Ibid., vol. 3, pp. 268–269.
121. The proposal of 21 July appears in *Transcripts of the Grand National Assembly (TBMM Zabit Ceridesi),* Ibid., vol. 2, p. 341. The rejection of the proposal, ibid., vol. 3, p. 52.
122. Sarıhan, *Kurtuluş Savaşı Günlüğü,* vol. 3, p. 167; Gotthard Jaeschke, *Türk Kurtuluş Savaşı Kronolojisi* (Ankara: Türk Tarihi Kurumu, 1970), p. 116.

CHAPTER 13

The Full Texts in English of the Indictments and Verdicts[1]

Unlike the other chapters of the present volume, this one differs in that it comprises a verbatim translation of every document. As indicated in the chapter's title, presented here are the texts of the twin indictments as well as those of the seven verdicts, almost all of which were issued following a series of court-martial trials run by a military tribunal. The original source in Ottoman Turkish for each document is described above the title of that document. In some cases, the translators have added explanatory phrases and clarifications between square brackets.

Takvîm-i Vekâyi' # *3540 (27 Nisan, 1335) s. 4–14 (Karârnâme)*

The Key Indictment

The Extraordinary Military Tribunal's Key Indictment in the trial against the leading CUP (Committee of Union and Progress) members and wartime cabinet ministers. 27 Nisan above is a misprint for 28 Nisan.

The above-mentioned indictment [submitted by] the Office of the Prosecutor of the Extraordinary Military Tribunal has been studied and examined along with the records and details of the [pretrial] interrogations, which, including the investigations, were carried out in regard to the President of the now disbanded Committee of Union and Progress, Sa'îd Halim Paşa, ordinary members of the [Committee's] General Assembly Talaat, Enver, Cemal, İbrahim, Şükrü, Halil and Ahmed Nesimi, Secretary-General Midhat Şükrü, Central Commmittee members Ziya Gökalp, the [party's] Istanbul delegate Kemal, Dr. Rüsûhi, Küçük Talaat, and the following Central Committee members who were appointed to the Special Organization, Dr. Bahaeddin Şakir, Dr. Nazım, Atıf, Rıza, former General Director of Security Aziz and former Military Governor of Istanbul Cevad, who were also members of the Administrative Council of the above-mentioned organizations.

In the above-mentioned indictment, it is evident that two contradictory natures secretly exist [within] the Committee of Union and Progress [hereafter CUP, or Unionist]: the first, based on the [party] program and by-laws, is open and public; [and] the second [involves reliance] on oral and confidential instructions, and whose moral personality is accused, on the basis of the existing evidence and testimony, of [having carried out] a series of massacres, plundering and [other] abuses. Among the important heads and influential members of the aforementioned Committee, which was formed in accordance with the provisions of the Law of Associations, are Enver and Cemal Beys, who were among the influential members of the Committee at the time of the general mobilization that was declared in [20] Temmuz, [1]330 (2 August 1914) in consultation with the [other] Committee leaders, and who were [subsequently] dismissed from military service for fleeing [the country at the end of the war], and who, along with Talaat Bey and his friends, who likewise fled, carried out the base crimes with which they are charged and which are detailed in their indictments. These [individuals] bear the legal responsibility for the events that transpired.

By taking advantage of the World War in which Europe was then engaged, they became imbued with the desire to solve the [yet] unresolved problems that needed solutions through understanding and ability, through justice, wisdom, and mercy. Instead, they resorted to violence, and, by sowing terror on all sides, visited calamity and disaster upon everyone. They ventured to [undertake fearful] actions and grave deeds that would bring immense transformations and endless upheaval upon the fate of the nation, and, by exploiting this opportunity, they amassed wealth through acts of tyranny and oppression.

After having brought about [the Ottoman Empire's] participation in the World War by employing a number of ruses and deceptions, they quickly set about implementing their secret aims. With the intention of carrying out their hidden agenda during the course of military actions, former General Director of Security Aziz and [CUP] Central Committee members Dr. Nazım and Atıf created a committee with the name "Special Organization" (Teşkilât-ı Mahsûsa); [while] [Istanbul] Military Governor Cevad Bey saw through the ratification and implementation of the decisions that they took. [This was done with the aim of] entrusting their secret and confidential committee with [various] actions and deeds, preparing the groundwork for the criminal actions of the gangs of convicts that they had ordered released from the prisons, and allowing them to give the latter orders and instructions and to employ them in Istanbul in all manner of actions such as these. They [then] distributed large amounts of money to the persons who served them and sent these persons to the various provinces. They gave the code keys to leaders such as Dr. Bahaeddin Şakir and assigned to them automobiles, invested them with great authority and provided them with large quantities of explosives, and it is evident that in this way the leaders of the CUP were able to secretly carry out their plans as prescribed.

Some of the functionaries who were sent to the provinces by this committee [the Special Organization] carried out abominable deeds, such as the looting of money and property, the burning of houses and corpses, the massacre of the population, rape, torture, and oppression—all without regard to sex, religion, or nationality—in accordance with the instructions and signals of its leaders, the CUP delegates in the provinces and certain obedient officials who complied in the aim of assisting the Committee [CUP], and through the guidance and assistance of a small number of individuals who joined them out of naiveté or ignorance. While it is indeed the case that a sizeable portion of those victimized were Armenian, the prosecution maintains that a great part of the total number of claims of victimization were from other communities, in particular, always and in all places, Turks.

The material of concern determined to be the subject of this inquiry consists not only of the matter of the calamities that occurred at various times and places during the course of the deportation of the Armenians, or in isolated events, but rather encompasses the execution and overseeing, through the transmission of oral and secret orders and instructions, of actions planned by the forces identified with a centr[-al body] composed of the persons mentioned above. The evidences and testimonies, along with depositions and reliable documents which emerged as a result of the inquiry shall be presented. Whereby:

The document addressed to Bahaeddin Şakir and including decision number 150 contains the sentences "It is demanded that Galatalı Halil be punished by the committee. [This is] to notify that security shall be taken back from the post office and given to the people," and below this it contains the personal signatures "Aziz," "Atıf," and "Nazım." Below that [are] the act of ratification and signature "Approved: Cevad." Further down is the "reason for treachery: monetary gain." This proves that the CUP leaders first created [the committee] under the name "Special Organization" with the intention of involving it in the war, and that, as was explained at length in the indictment, the administrative council of the secret network which they kept occupied with criminal actions and operations consisted of the following members of its [the CUP's] Central Committee: Dr. Nazım, Bahâeddîn Şakir, Atıf, Rızâ, and former Director-General of Security Aziz. [It also shows] that, among these, Bahâeddîn Şakir assumed the command of the forces in the Eastern Provinces, whose [administrative] center was Erzurum, and that, while Riza Bey was circulating in the environs of Trabzon, Aziz, Atıf, and [Dr.] Nazım were carrying out activities in Istanbul, and that [Istanbul] Military Governor Cevad Bey was responsible for the ratification and execution of the jointly-reached decisions. ***(File: 10, Document: 1)*** [Furthermore,] attached to this decision is the document that shows that the state of affairs was ordered and communicated through a coded telegraph signed "1. Cevad" and bearing the instruction "The same is to be deciphered for Bahaeddin Şakir in Artvin."

The written communication to Midhat Şükrü Bey, numbered 59 and bearing the signatures "Halil, Nazım, Atıf, Aziz" proves that Halil Paşa, the paternal uncle of the fugitive Enver Paşa, was a member of the Special Organization during the period that he served as Istanbul's Military Governor, and that said organizations were in communication with the CUP ***(File: 10, Document: 4)***; and the telegraph numbered 67 from the above-mentioned Halil Bey to the Office of the District Governor of İzmit is proof that they gathered and trained bandit leaders and released prisoners for the sake of th[ese actions].

The memorandum numbered 68 and dated 16 Teşrinisâni, [13]30 (29 November 1914), which was written by the above-mentioned Halil Bey (Paşa) to the Directorate of the War Ministry, as well as similar documents were discovered among the various papers of the Special Organization, show that explosive materials were given to the Special Organization. Additionally, it was established that, during the course of the investigation into these events, an important portion of the papers belonging to this ministry as well as all of the registries and papers of the Central Committee had been whisked away [*aşırıldığı*]. It is further confirmed by the evidence [contained in] the written testimonies and by the contents of the written communications of the Interior Ministry, that former Director of General Security Aziz Bey took the dossiers concerning important information and communications from the [Interior] Ministry before the resignation of the fugitive Talaat Bey, and did not return them after he left office. ***(File: 31)***

From a message signed by [CUP] General Secretary Midhat Şükrü Bey on 17 Ağustos, 1330 (30 August 1914) and passed on to Bahaeddin Şakir Bey by means of the Governor-General of [the province of] Erzurum, it is understood that [the CUP] was resolved to [undertake] military action long before the [declaration of] war, and that this had been both the intent and desire of the Committee [of Union and Progress].

The cancellation of the coded telegraph bearing the stamp "save," which the aforementioned Talaat Bey sent to the District Governor of [*Zor*] Syria, 'Ali Su'ad Bey, and whose text enjoined that the governor-general [*vâlî*], along with his assistant and the Police Commissioner, Memdûh, be punished with death, confirms that the fugitive Talaat Bey continued to allow and instigate the murders and calamities carried out in Diyarbakır. ***(File: 8, Document: 1)***

The Director of the Special Secretariat of the Interior Ministry, İhsan Bey, reports that while he was County Executive of Kilis, Abdulahad Nuri Bey, who had been sent from Istanbul to Aleppo, attempted to convince him that the deportation had been set up with the goal of annihilation, saying "I was in contact with Talaat himself, and I received the order for annihilation from him personally. The well-being of the country depends on it." (pretrial ***Interrogation Papers, page 15)***

In the coded telegram dated 11 Eylül, [13]31 (24 September 1915) to the Interior Ministry from District Governor Müfid Bey, which was sent from Kangırı (Çankırı) to the Office of the District Governor of Bolu and received by the Party Secretary for Bursa, Dr. Midhat Bey, during the time he served in this same function in Bolu, it is written that the total number of Armenians deported from Ankara Province reached 61,000; and that, in regard to this [action] the Muslim inhabitants of the province admired the CUP and the government, which was its true child, and adds that the effect of this [deportation] would last for years. ***(File: 8, Document: 2)*** Consequently, he proposed that similar actions be repeated [in Bolu] in order to secure the region's future well-being. Thus, it becomes clear that, in an area such as Bolu, which was neither a war zone nor considered as such, the deportation was [undertaken] neither [as] a military action nor a [as] disciplinary measure. Rather [it was] the result of the Committee [for Union and Progress]'s objectives and desires, with which Midhat Şükrü Bey was imbued.

It is clear that this individual, who was in Çankırı but a short time, would not be able to [fully] gauge from afar the sentiments of the population of Ankara Province, and that it was easier and more natural for him to know the mood of the province in which he was located. In any case, it is corroborated through the written declarations on the 15th page of the second Annex that the Muslims of [the Province of] Kastamonu, to which Çankırı belongs, recalled and viewed the events outside of their region with loathing. [So much so] that one day the government *mufti*, along with a large group of sheikhs and notables, spoke the following words to Governor-General Reşid Paşa: "We heard that they are driving the Armenians, along with their women and children, from the surrounding provinces into the high mountains and slaughtering them [there] like sheep in a slaughterhouse. We do not want such a thing [to occur] in our country. We fear Divine punishment. The government [can] endure blasphemy. It cannot endure oppression. [*Küfr ile hükümet pâyedâr olur. Zulm ile pâyedâr olmaz.*] We ask that such actions not be committed in our province." Upon receiving the declaration and assurance from Governor-General Reşid Paşa, that such a situation would never be allowed [to occur there], they left, weeping tears of joy.

The coded telegram from the Governor-General of the Province of Erzurum, Tahsin Bey, dated 15 Temmuz, 1331 (28 July 1915), which gives a detailed account of the forays and assaults against the Armenians of the province by the Special Organization and by the gendarmes attached to them, contains the following passage: "A lieutenant by the name of Faik seized the four daughters of Arabyan, and a lieutenant called Kemal Efendi stole 1,863 lira, 35 loads of goods and a large quantity of jewelry; the vile deeds concerning women and money are exceedingly shameful and cowardly. We must put an end to these conditions and especially to the armed brigands which are multiplying under the name of 'Special Organization'. The Governor-General of Mamuretülaziz (Elazığ) says: 'All of the roads are so full of the corpses of women and children that we are unable to bury them all. We must preserve our honor and national history.'" ***(File: 8, Document: 4)*** [The fact that] this telegram was found among the papers belonging to the fugitive Talaat Bey that were compiled by the 5th [Investigative] Department of the Chamber of Deputies corroborates the nature of the important coded telegram of Ali Su'ad Bey mentioned above and his intention of saving and keeping it to himself and canceling it.

The contents of a coded telegram, a copy of which is found in the ninth [document] file, bearing the signature of the head of the Erzurum Special Organization, Bahaeddin Şakir Bey, and sent to the Governor-General of Mamuretülaziz, Sabit Bey, and addressed to Nazım Bey, are as follows: "Are the Armenians driven from there being liquidated? Are the troublemakers, whom you reported as being driven forth and banished, being destroyed or are they merely being driven out and sent away? Please give an honest report, my brother." The fact that the above-mentioned Resneli Nazım Bey was the CUP Inspector for [the Province of] Mamuretülaziz (Elazığ) at the time, and [the ancillary fact of] his having fled, reinforce the [other] evidence concerning the connection between the CUP and the Special Organization with respect to its task of liquidating [the Armenian population].

A telegram bearing the signature of Rüştü, the [CUP] Secretary for Samsun, and sent to the Central Committee of the CUP and delivered on 16 Kanunuevvel, 1330 (19 December 1914) to Dr. Nazım, of the Special Organization states that "a [-n armed] band of 55 persons under the command of Tufan Ağa has been sent by motor[-ized] transport as the fifth such group." This suggests the connection and relationship between the CUP and the Special Organization, and that the branches of the CUP had, among other things, concerned themselves with the organizing of [armed] bands.

The contents of a letter bearing the signature: "Musa, Union and Progress Inspector for Balıkesir," which was sent to Midhat Şükrü Bey on 20 Teşreni sâni, 1330 (3 December 1915) and [later] passed on to Dr. Nazım, show that the Committee [of Union and Progress] along with the Interior Ministry dealt with these [armed] bands separately. Likewise, the written correspondence between the office of the delegate of Bursa and the Central Committee dated 19 Kanunuevvel, 1330 (1 January 1915) shows that the murderers and brigands were enlisted into the Special Organization.

Although attempts [had already been] made at the start of the General Mobilization to persuade the naïve and well-intentioned that these bands would be incorporated into the war [effort], it is clear from the overall body of evidence, testimonies and documents on this matter that have been partially mentioned and cited above, that these gangs were afterward brought into service with the purpose of massacre and destruction of those groups subjected to deportation.

That these massacres were carried out under the [express] orders and with the knowledge of Talaat, Enver and Cemal Beys ***(File: 11)*** [is attested to] by the following coded messages: 1) In Talaat Bey's coded telegram dated 21 Temmuz, 1331 (3 August 1915) to the Governors-General of [the Provinces of] Diyârbakır and Mamuretülaziz (Elazığ), and to the District Governors of [the Districts of] Urfa and Zor (Syria), ordering that the bodies of the dead remaining on the roads not be thrown into ravines, rivers or lakes, and instead be interred and their remaining possessions burnt; 2) The telegram, dated 1 Temmuz, 1331 (14 July 1915) and marked "urgent" and "for your eyes only," from Fourth Army Commander Cemal Bey to the Governor-General of Diyarbakir. [In it Cemal Bey] declares that the bodies carried downstream by the Euphrates should not be left exposed, but should be [pulled from the river and] buried in the districts in which they are found, while making mention that they are, in all probability, the bodies of Armenians killed during acts of rebellion. ***(File: 11, Document: 3)***

In the coded telegram dated 3 Temmuz, 1331 (16 July 1915) and marked "for your eyes only," which was sent [by the Governor-General of Diyarbakır] in response to the above-mentioned [communication of] Cemal Bey, the text reads: "The Euphrates has very little contact with our province. It is likely that the bodies being carried [downstream] are coming from Erzurum and Mamuretülaziz. The bodies of those killed during acts of rebellion are being dealt with either by casting them into abandoned and deep ravines or, as has been done in most cases, by burning, burial being the rare exception."

The former District Governor of Zor (Syria), Ali Su'âd Bey, [at one point] provides information regarding the fate of the Armenians deported to that district, and claims that, according to Ağah Bey, who was still reporting for the paper *Tasvîr-i Efkâr* and printing out news agency dispatches in Aleppo, that he [Agâh] once remarked to Salih Zeki Bey, the [subsequent] district governor of Zor, "The word going around is that you killed 10,000 Armenians," whereupon Zeki Bey replied, "I have my honor. I disdain the figure of 10,000; you'll have to go higher." ***(Files: 6 and 14, Document: 4; File: 11, Document: 1)***

In the coded order given by the Governor-General of [the province of] Mamuretülaziz (Elazığ) to the District Governor of Malatya, it is stated that, despite clear and definitive communiqués [having been sent], there was still a great number of corpses [left] on the roads. Just as there is no need to explain the [potential] problems [inherent in such a situation], notice is given of the need to quickly assign a sufficient number of gendarmes and several leading officials to this task in every place, in order that care be taken to bury all of the bodies found within the borders of their territory. Accompanying this is the unambiguous notice from the Interior Ministry that those officials found to be remiss in this task shall be severely punished.

The coded message dated 15 Eylül, 1331 (28 September 1915) and sent by [Governor-General] Reşid [Paşa] to the Interior Ministry, which says that the number of Armenians deported from Diyarbakır comes to 120,000, is sufficient to confirm the scope and significance of the events. ***(File: 12, Document: 1)***

The telegram signed by Mahmûd Kâmil, Commander of the Third Army, threatens any Muslim who provides shelter to an Armenian with hanging in front of his house and the burning down of that house, while government officials will be removed from their posts and military men shall be expelled from the army. In either case the offenders are to be brought before the Military Tribunal for trial. ***(File: 13, Document: 1)*** It makes clear to anyone of sound mind and satisfies one's sense of justice that neither could the Muslims present there have succeeded [in helping the Armenians] during this tragedy, and given [the presence of] all manner of threat and intimidation, and [the mandate to] obey the Islamic commandment to refrain from those things not allowed, nor can the local Muslim population or petty officials be held responsible for this tragic event.

Among the corroborating elements proving Talaat Bey's criminal liability is the account of the former Deputy for Trabzon, Hafız Mehmet Bey, in which he describes the manner in which the Armenians were placed on caiques on the coast and [then] drowned [at sea], and adds that, although he informed Talaat Bey of these calamities, [the latter] took no action in regard to the Governor-General Cemal Azmi. ***(File: 15)***

The coded telegram dated 14 Kanunuevvel, 1334 (14 December 1918) ***(File: 16)*** from the Governor-General of [the Province of] Erzurum, Münir Bey, suggests that the processions of wealthy [Armenians] sent by way of the Erzurum-Kığı road, in opposition to the request of the former Governor-General, Tahsin Bey, were subjected to murder and plundering at the hands of the residents of Dersim and the members of the armed band organized by Central Committee member Bahaeddin Şakir Bey, and corroborates the [other] evidence of a crime having been committed.

The transcribed account of Cemal Asaf Bey ***(File: 18)*** concerning the manner in which some of the deportees and even merchants were killed by the Kurd Alo's brigands, which were formed by Cemal Oğuz Bey, who is the former [CUP] Party Secretary for Kangırı (Çankırı) [and] presently a merchant, is but one part of the total actions and deeds of the Committee [of Union and Progress]'s representatives which must be attributed to a centrally-governed design.

The lengthy accounts of Colonel Halil Recayi Bey ***(File: 2, page 1)*** describe in detail that, during the Ankara deportations, the local CUP club sent someone by the name of Tayyip Efendi to the [Army] Commander proposing the dismissal and separation [from the military] of Armenian health officials serving at the front for the purpose of [their] deportation. It also describes the manner in which Central Committee member Memdûh Şevket and his brother Ref'et Bey came to Ankara and grew wealthy,[2] the details of the Ankara deportation, the degree of involvement of Necati Bey, the CUP Party Secretary [for Ankara], and the deeds and actions of the province's former police chief, Manastirli Bahâeddîn Bey, who played an important role in this regard. These accounts contain the names of [a number of] witnesses whose declarations are considered to merit special attention, and who are capable of providing information.

Although the aforementioned Bahâeddîn Bey was [arrested and] handed over to the Military Tribunal there [Ankara] and an attempt was made to put him on trial in this matter, he was recalled to Istanbul, and subsequently escaped prosecution when the documents from the investigation were, in accordance with the Interior Ministry's request, not sent [to Ankara] and were later procured and taken back by the Ministry of War.

According to the findings of the investigation, the greatest degree of protection and support was bestowed upon active agents like Bahâeddîn Bey, while those who had chosen the path of vehemently rejecting these calamit[-ous deeds] and refusing to participate [in them], for whatever reason, were considered as traitors to the homeland. It is known that former Interior Minister Talaat Bey sent this Bahâeddîn Bey especially to Eastern Army Group Commander Vehîb Paşa so that he might engage in service under the commander, and that serving for a period within the personnel of the Samsun Military Tribunal, he sneaked off to an unknown location. ***(Vehîb Paşa's transcribed testimony, [found] in the "for your eyes only" dossier)***

[Listed below is the series of] proofs [along with] thorough documentation [supporting] the accusations against the Central Committee of the CUP and the [government] ministers who were among its obedient members: 1) The declarations of Governor-General [of Kastamonu] Reşid Paşa ***(File: 2, page 13)*** [stating] that, although he had written to the [Interior] Ministry describing the Kastamonu deportations and the crimes and evil deeds of the Party Secretary there, Hasan Fehmi Efendi, his complaints were not heard, and also statements concerning the coded telegram [he received] from Dr. Bahaeddin Şakir Bey regarding the need for [him to carry out] the deportation, along with the attached telegram; 2) the statement of Izmir Deputy İhsan Ohnik ***(File: 3)***, who says that he had demanded, in a proposal that he gave to Talaat Bey during a session of the Union and Progress Party explaining the various calamities and oppression visited upon the Armenians, that investigations be undertaken in regard to [the actions of Diyarbakir Province Governor-General] Dr. Reşid, Cemal Azmi, Sabit, Mu'ammer, Atıf, Director General of Prisons İbrahim and all of the Secretaries, but that Talaat Bey had the proposal tabled with the words "save for later." He also claims that Talaat Bey said to him at the Sporting Club in Izmir, "I would have subjected the ones here [i.e., the Armenians of Izmir] to the same fate as the ones there [in Anatolia]," and that Dr. Nazım and every one of his accomplices were active participants [in the deportations]; 3) Vehib Paşa's written statement ***(File: 7, page 3)*** [claiming that] the killing and liquidation of the Armenians, as well as the plundering and seizure of their property was the result of the decisions of the CUP Central Committee, and that the person who outfitted, commanded, and brought into service these butchers of humanity within the Third Army's zone [of operation] was Bahaeddin Şakir Bey. Vehib Paşa added [that] the government heads submitted to the orders and instructions of Dr. Bahaeddin Şakir Bey, [and that] the entirety of the human tragedy within the Third Army['s zone], and all of the crimes and evil deeds came about and were manifested under the direction of Bahaeddin Şakir Bey, who in one place would summon friends freed from prison sentences, in another, gendarmes with bloodstained hands and bloodshot eyes … and so on. This written testimony is but an indictment and is evidence of the complicity of CUP's Central Committee and of the General Assembly.

Among the main points of evidence and sufficient inferences for proving the current assertions, are: 1) Süleyman Nâzıf Bey's testimony ***(Interrogation Records, page 6)*** that upon arrival from Baghdad to the border of Diyarbakır, they held their noses from the stench of [dead] bodies; 2) the testimony of former Konya Governor-General Celal Bey ***(Pretrial Interrogation Records, page 7)***, claiming that, when Fourth Army Commander Cemal Pasha asked Talaat Bey [the reasons for] his [Celal Bey's] removal from Aleppo, he was told in reply that it had come to light that there was divergence between his viewpoint and that of the central government in regard to the Armenian question, and, as he (Celal) had protected the Armenians of Konya, [Parliamentary] Deputy Ali Riza Efendi was sent by Dr. Nazım to make a proposal, with all good intent, along the lines that he (Celal Bey) should not insist on a question on which the CUP Central Committee had decided after long and thorough deliberations, and that, ultimately, it was for this reason that he had been dismissed from his post. When he (Celal) was in Istanbul and explained to Talaat and Nazım the pitfalls of pursuing this policy, they said that they believed it to be [both] necessary and beneficial, and, going even further, Dr. Nazım said that "this effort will solve the Eastern Question." And as for Hayri Efendi, despite his tremendous efforts, he did not have the [political] power to block [these deeds]; 3) the statement of the former Governor-General of [the Province of] Ankara, Mazhar Bey, ***(Pretrial Interrogation Records, page 17)*** saying that he was dismissed for refraining from carrying out their requests in regard to the deportation and annihilation; and 4) from the former Director-General of the Civil Service School's Inspection Committee, Hamit Bey, a statement regarding the death sentences carried out against the Arabs, and the two district officials who were eliminated for opposing the deportations carried out by the Governor-General of Diyarbakir; 5) the declarations of the former Finance Ministry's Director-General of Revenues, Lütfi Bey ***(Pretrial Interrogation Records, pages 34, 38, 43)*** regarding the Party Secretary for Trabzon, Nâil Bey and the tragic events in Trabzon and their perpetrators; 6) the testimony of the former Lieutenant Governor of [the] Antalya [District], Sabur Sami Bey, mentioning the coded telegraph sent [to him] by Bahaeddin Şakir Bey from Erzurum, asking in effect "what was he doing in Antalya" after the Armenian deportees were sent to Mosul and Syria (*Zor*) from there so [as to ensure] that not a single Armenian is left in the regions of "Erzurum, Van, Bitlis, Diyarbekir, Sivas and Trabzon" ***(Pretrial Interrogation Records, page 44)***. Sami then claims that, although he sent a copy of this [telegram] to Talaat Bey, he never received a reply; and finally, 7) the information [provided by] Ra'di Bey concerning the Ankara deportation and the [CUP] Party Secretary there, Necâtî Bey.

In the written reply numbered 69, which was written on the back of a document appearing in the Special Organization Dossier, a decoded message, sent by Bahaeddin Şakir Bey [to the Central Committee] via Interior Minister Talaat Bey, reads: "... seeing that you have no more business there, proceed immediately to Trabzon, in order to take up a task more important than the Artvin problem. Yakub Cemîl Bey, who will depart from here, will bring you the necessary explanations and instructions." This [evidence] further elucidates the correspondence and relationship between them [Bahaeddin Şakir and Talaat].

In their statements [made during] questioning those among the accused who were found in ministerial positions have in their defense denied [their guilt], and have invoked the issue of official duty and argued that their trials belong not to the Extraordinary Military Tribunal, but rather to the High Court, in line with the statutes of the Constitution. But as has been adequately explained, the [relevance of the] 92nd Article of the Constitution to which they have referred is limited to the criminal acts and offenses which result from the political acts falling within the framework of their official duties as [government] ministers and those participating in the Council of Ministers. [Furthermore,] according to the terms of the 33rd Article of the aforementioned Constitution, [government] ministers possess no legal immunity for common offenses which they either carry out personally or in which they are accessories. For such crimes, jurisdiction devolves upon the ordinary courts, while in places where martial law is in effect, civil and judicial laws are entirely mute, as provided for in the relevant decree on this matter. Accordingly, the Military Tribunals would become the competent recourse for criminal proceedings. After the rejection of the [defense] argument concerning official duty, it has been determined that the investigation of matters such as massacres and profiteering also constitutes the entire task of this Tribunal in accordance with the last decision concerning the formation and duties of this Extraordinary Military Tribunal.

On the basis of substantive evidence and proofs obtained to a sufficient degree, and with reference to the aforementioned offenses, Dr. Bahaeddin Şakir, Dr. Nazım, Atıf, Riza, Cevad, Aziz, Enver, Cemal, and Talaat Beys are considered to be perpetrators of the crimes of massacres and their respective actions are deemed subject to punishment under the provisions of paragraph 1 of the 45th Article, as well as the 170th Article of the Penal Code. Dr. Rüsûhî, Midhat Şükrü, "Küçük" Talaat, Ziya Gökalp, Kemal, Şükrü, İbrahim, Halil Bey, and Said Halim Paşa were found to be subject to the provisions of paragraph 2 of the 45th Article of the aforementioned [Penal] Code, because although they were, by their own admissions, not involved [in the massacres] but knew [of them]; they are thus determined to have acted as accessories in the crimes of the accused.

Consistent with the indictment, it has been decided that the documents pertaining to the investigation and all [accompanying] details be sent without delay to the Office of the Procuror General of the aforementioned Military Tribunal so that the accused might be tried in the Istanbul Extraordinary Tribunal in accordance with the articles mentioned above.

10 Receb 1337 / 12 Nisan 1335 (12 April 1919)

Takvîm-i Vekâyi' *Nr. 3571, s. 127–140 (İddi'ânâme ve Karârnâme)*

The Supplementary Key Indictment

The supplementary Key Indictment against the top CUP leaders and wartime cabinet ministers. From the first trial of the military tribunal, dated 3 June 1335.

These investigation documents and enclosed papers have been studied and examined.

Due to its desire for distinction and domination, which were its true aims, the Committee for Union and Progress (CUP) found itself, after the proclamation of the Constitutional Regime, utterly unable to transform [itself] into a political party that would, by relying on the nation's mandate, take matters of state and the nation's affairs into its sound hands as were entrusted to it and administer them. Instead, the Committee always preserved its secret political nature, which had been its true state, and, as the life of a [-n open and public] political party was incompatible with those goals [of] tyranny and domination, it remained necessary to continue and maintain th[-e Committee's] original secretive character.

Violence and wicked deeds were now seen [by the CUP] as acceptable on the [assumption] that the sole means and way to ensure the people's compliance with every order and obedience to every law consisted of instilling fear and terror [in the hearts of the populace]. As for those who dared to speak out against and to criticize, in reliance upon the rights of liberty and speech which had been envisioned in the Constitution, these persons quickly found themselves the targets for attacks and hostility by a secret network, and were thereby eliminated. Likewise, through the government's acts of repression and [its] inauguration of a period of subjugation and destruction the people were denied and forbidden the right to use and exercise even the most fundamental of those human rights mentioned and guaranteed by the Constitution.

After successfully seizing sole and independent control of the administration of the state, which had been their ultimate goal, through the coercive means and restrictive measures that they did not hesitate from employing and imposing, they began to spiritually destroy and eliminate the nation's laws by stripping them of all force and authority even though there no longer remained any material obstacle or hindrance whatsoever to the[-ir] use [of the laws] for whatever purpose they desired. [Through all these measures] they [eventually] attained a state of absolutism.

As for the structure of the political party, although it is true that there existed both a Central Committee and a General Assembly that were subject to a [party] program and to [its] internal regulations, and that they would hold a congress at an appointed time each year, this consisted [largely] of an [exercise for] external effect. This court rejects and denies the account [claiming] that the Central Committee was actually entrusted with the task of attempting [to procure] the ways and means to enable [them] to provide and ensure the party's ability to secure a majority during the elections, as well as the claim that this committee was entrusted with the sorting out of matters which would occasionally arrive from the [party's] branches and that they were entrusted with the preparing and raising of issues that needed to be discussed in the General Assembly. Also denied and rejected is the claim that the Central Committee was the place where matters and issues relating to the party were studied and resolved and that their involvement and influence in ministerial affairs and state policies were ongoing.

Apart from [the fact] that neither the secretary, the delegates nor the [other] members composing the Central Committee held any sort of official title, it is clear from the one-page document we have obtained, which contains the decision that was reached to execute someone by the name of Galatalı Halil, that they (the Central Committee members) were also among the leaders of the secret committee.

As for the General Assembly, it is composed of and formed by the Central Committee, the [CUP government] ministers and some members of the Chamber of Deputies. The fact that an important member of any assembly was found among the leaders of the secret committee is sufficient to prove the committee's true character. Not only can the extent of the Central Committee's involvement and influence in the state administration be deduced and ascertained from the testimony of the defendant Ismail Canbolat, [who claimed] that he had long opposed the discussion in the Central Committee of matters and questions that [consisted] of government matters and issues, but the fact that the lists and registries that would help to prove the type and nature of the discussions held and the decisions reached were hidden and concealed [after] removal clearly indicate the [suspicious] manner of business and issues with which the Central Committee and General Assembly concerned themselves.

The country was plunged into confusion and panic when, in accordance with the dictates of the special law, convoys [of Armenians] which were dispatched in order to relocate them elsewhere became the targets of attack by wicked bands specially formed and organized [for this purpose]. They [the Armenians] were annihilated and their goods and possessions looted and plundered, and although some parts of the populace attempted to protect them from that dreadful fate, the government [itself] displayed no interest in preventing instances of killing and looting or in punishing the perpetrators. On the contrary, it assumed responsibility [for this state of affairs] by removing from office certain governors-general and district governors who declared that there was no need for the deportation [in the first place].

It is also evident from the deciphering of the coded telegram which was obtained that the massacres and destruction of this group and the plundering of their goods in this manner may be [considered to have been] among the despicable acts organized by a secret committee whose ringleaders were the committee heads Bahâeddin Şâkir, Dr. Nazım, Rızâ, and Atıf. It is likewise clear and manifest that the evil cabal was in a position to dominate the ruling governmental body while using this body as an instrument for the fulfillment of the aforementioned committee's base aspirations and objectives.

During wartime, some of the most important duties devolving upon a government are the orderly procuring and appropriating of the basic commodities needed by the population, the preventing of price increases due to profiteering or hoarding, and the general provisioning of the population. Nevertheless, this task was entrusted to Kemal Bey, one of the defendants [in this trial] who held no official position whatsoever [that would authorize him to undertake] the aforementioned tasks. [Yet,] instead of procuring the stores of basic foodstuffs and other provisions and clothing on which the population depended at below-market prices and distributing to everyone in accordance to their need, [and] in a manner [designed] to protect and shield their lives and well-being, the Committee [CUP] instead allowed the ruination of the lives and property of [these] travelers [the Armenian deportees] by distributing these to the Committee members and their families for the sole purpose of enabling them to line their pockets. This is yet one more definitive proof of the extent to which the Committee was the driving force in the administering of the business and affairs of the state, and of its [pattern of] activity, and its influence and sway over the decision-making process.

Preserving the overall balance of power [within] the state is only possible when the government, whose form has been established in the Ottoman State in accordance with the Constitution, and [its] ministers, under the exclusive control of the legislative branch, direct and administer state policy and order the affairs of each ministry according to their own opinions and counsel with his Excellency the Sultan acting as the mediator between the legislative and executive branches. It is therefore obvious that the interference and involvement of some influential agent [who acts] above these powers [could] modify and transform the lawful form of government.

The former Grand Vizier, Said Halim Paşa, recounts that, upon the occurrence of the ill-omened Black Sea affair, there had been a call to remedy this wicked act and prevent [or] remove its harmful results. Furthermore, though in his opinion it was generally necessary to choose a course of action in a manner wherein a decision would be reached in consultation with the [other] cabinet heads, the account of the incident shows that instead he summoned the members of the Central Committee to his mansion on the Bosporus for discussion and consultation. From this account, it [can be] deduced that in his opinion and interpretation, there was a force which prevented him from independently using the right to his own opinion and authority that the law had bestowed upon his office.

The testimony of former Grand Vizier İzzet Paşa concerning the circumstances surrounding his resignation from the Ministry of War is among the total evidence confirming that a secret power had been an effective and influential factor in the administration of the affairs of state.

After seizing total control of the country's land and sea forces by bringing Enver and Cemal Efendis to the Ministries of War and the Navy [respectively] and by [their acquiring, thereby, the] ability to use and employ the[-se forces] according to their whim this peculiar form of government, which runs contrary to the edicts of the Constitution, [the CUP] attained control of the legitimate power of government through displays of overwhelming power and fury.

As persons relied upon by the CUP Committee, former Grand Vizier Talaat, Enver and Cemal Beys had adopted the evil aims and heinous purposes of the Committee as their own and dedicated themselves to putting the[-se plans] into action, with the cooperation and support of the following individuals who served both spiritually and physically: former Grand Vizier Said Halim Paşa, former Sheikh ul-Islam Hayri Efendi, former Minister of Education Şükrü, former Minister of Justice Halil, former President of the Council of State İbrahim, former Foreign Minister Ahmed Nesimi, and former Minister of Provisioning

Kemal. With their combined efforts, the CUP managed to establish [itself] as a force [which was] above the legitimate power of government.

Because th[-e CUP's] power derived from having changed the government by force and compulsion and by sowing fear and terror among the population, as has been described in detail above, and [because] those actions of which the [defendants] are accused consist of criminal acts subject to the provisions of paragraph 5 of the amended 55th Article and the 45th Article of the Imperial Penal Code, there is no inference that would confirm the suspicions [necessary] to justify their being referred and sent to the Extraordinary Military Tribunal for trial. Nor does there exist such an inference in regard to the alleged collaboration on the part of former Sheikh ul-Islam Musa Kâzım and former Minister of Public Works Abbâs Halim Paşa. Furthermore [in regard to the others], former Post and Telegraph Minister Hüseyin Haşim, Ali Münif and Mustafa Şeref Beys having obtained their ministerial positions in the last days [of the war], and İsmail Canbolat having resigned from the provincial and ministerial posts to which he had been appointed in protest of the evils that were taking place, it is requested that a decision be made to dismiss the prosecutions of the aforementioned persons and to release them from custody in view of the fact that there is no further reason for detaining them.

22 Mayıs [1]335 [1919]

VERDICT (Decision to proceed with the prosecution)

Along with the indictment contained above, the court has examined and carefully considered the [written] record of testimony pertaining to the investigations and examinations that were carried out and in response to the following findings:

The members and leaders of the CUP who are accused of having carried out the crimes of massacring the population, plundering of property, burning of buildings and bodies, dishonoring and rape of women and torture, by means of organizations [specially] created [for this purpose] in both the capital and the provinces, shall be [charged and tried] in accordance with the degree of culpability.

During the course of the trial[s] of the fugitives Talaat Paşa and Cemal and Enver Efendis and their companions whose names are mentioned in the verdict, who were sent to the Extraordinary Military Tribunal by the [court's] decision dated 12 Nisan [1]335 (12 April 1919), new evidence of additional crimes was obtained by the above-mentioned court. Therefore in accordance with the 311th Article of the Code of Criminal Procedure it was decided the former Grand Vizier Sa'îd Halim Paşa and Halil, İbrahim, Kemal, Ahmed Nesimi, and Ahmed Şükrü Beys be tried separately from the aforementioned defendants who are now fugitives, and that extensive investigations be undertaken against all their accomplices, who had not previously been separately prosecuted.

This manner [of action] had been requested and called for by the Office of the Procuror-General in the indictment dated 3 Mayıs, [1]335 (3 May 1919).

While the CUP was set up to externally resemble a political party, and a code of internal [party] regulations was actually created for this purpose, it (the CUP) never abandoned its other organizations and institutions, both covert and overt, which were outside [the realm] of the institutions of political parties. Both the Special Organization Commission, which was comprised of Dr. Nazım, Atıf, and Bahaeddin Şakir among the CUP's most eloquent and persuasive speakers, as well as others like the Commission in Charge of Provisioning formed by Kemal and his companions, who were likewise members of the Central Committee, were examples of this sort [of organization].

From the extensive explanations and communications regarding the activities and actions of the aforementioned committee and commissions, which were laid out in the aforementioned decision and which there appears no need to repeat here, the following findings were made:

1) In order to attain their secret and particular aims, and to trample the aspirations of all members of the nation without exception, the CUP resorted to all manner of forceful and violent measures.
2) They decreed that persons such as Galatalı Halil and others like him, whom they [the CUP] viewed as opposed to their goals and ideas, be executed, and commissioned some of its own members and others to carry out [these decisions].
3) The provisioning of Istanbul was [likewise] unilaterally taken over by the Committee with the purpose of amassing and storing the immense wealth of the Committee and its members. These individuals took advantage of the extraordinary circumstances resulting from extraordinary wartime conditions to enrich themselves at the cost of the obvious impoverishment and at the expense of the wretchedness of the nation's members. Within just one year a profit of 700,000 lira was amassed and appropriated by the Committee congress. This was openly admitted and confessed in the manifesto published in issue number 2809 of *Tanin*, dated 24 Eylül 1332 (7 October 1916) which had been read and adopted at the [party] congress.

That the calamities which took place were organized and prepared by the CUP is proven by the following evidence:

1) One of the Committee's many activities was the organizing of the [illegal] actions [which were carried out] during the implementation of the Deportation Law.
2) It has been [generally] admitted and accepted that Bahaeddin Şâkir Bey was appointed by the Special Organization Commission, formed from [the pool of the] leaders of the CUP, to head this organization in the Eastern Provinces, which comprised the main zones of deportation and which

were presided over by the CUP's delegates and responsible secretaries. The events that transpired in every corner of the Ottoman Realms during that period, and [in particular] the series of actions in the aforementioned [Eastern Provinces] were directed by him, and he recruited into his service the [CUP] responsible [secretaries and] delegates for this purpose.

This claim is [further] corroborated by the following facts:

1) Just as the CUP had actively undertaken and carried out the destructive aims and objectives on which they had agreed in this manner, at times upon one section of the nation, at others, upon the entire Ottoman nation without exception, they [also] took great pains and [placed] the utmost importance on [the aim of] consistently maintaining the official power of government within their control considering as they did that the power of government would be the sole power that could compete with their own immense power. The extraordinary events that occurred in the country in unending succession since [1]324 (1908)—and in particular, the calamitous events during the Balkan War[s]—are but a few of the total [examples] of this determination and [inordinate] ambition;
2) The Committee's decision to appoint the [now-]fugitive Enver to the Ministry of War;
3) The repeated calling on former Grand Vizier Ahmed İzzet Paşa to resign from [his] ministerial position [for] promoting his [own] ideas and decisions, and his being threatened and intimidated to this end;
4) the summary dismissal of those devoid of a disposition to serve the particular aims of certain Committee members and which members likewise had the audacity to issue confidential instructions to the governors-general of the various provinces during the deportation—among them, the District Governor of Yozgad, Cemal Bey, the Governor-General of [the Province of] Kastamonu, Reşid Paşa, and the Governor-General of [the Province of] Ankara, Mazhar Bey;
5) the testimonies of Tahsin, Governor-General of Erzurum.

The Committee, which had taken control of the reins of government in the provinces by this type of threat and compulsion, naturally did not stop [there]. On the contrary, [it continued] up to the very center of government, [and] by placing state ministers, whom it had selected from among its most influential members, into the General Assembly, [and] even though [this body] had no [official] title or legal authority, it did not refrain from holding discussions over the administrative affairs of state. Among others, there are reports that there were political discussions in the General Assembly regarding the Treaty of Brest-Litovsk, that the problems relative to provisioning were routinely discussed and even decided in this assembly, and that [its members] engaged in an exchange of ideas in regard to the military situation.

It has been admitted and confirmed by some of the defendants that the Committee [actually] took part in [governmental] decisions during meetings at the Premier's [Sa'îd Halim Paşa's] mansion on the shores of the Bosporus with the aim of ensuring that its own point of view prevailed in vital questions, such as whether or not to enter the General War [WWI].

[When viewed as a whole,] the actions and decisions of the [CUP] delegates and party secretaries and of central committees subject to them, along with the testimonies of all the members of the nation who had reached a general degree of concern, help to confirm that the different elements of the population were [intentionally] alienated from one another through various means of intimidation unseen and unheard of in this country before the appearance of the Committee. Sadly, ground was paved for the engendering of hatred and enmity among the peoples of Anatolia, peoples who for centuries had dwelt [among one another] in complete peace and prosperity, through the organizing of boycotts and the forced displacement of Muslim and non-Muslim in diverse places. Those [responsible for] the creation, implementation, and spread of this situation were members of the Committee.

As is understood from the previous discussion, the Committee firmly resolved to implement and realize its own private ideas and agenda within the country by resorting to the most extreme means. Then, [after] succeeding in directing the powers of government toward its own ends and adopting an isolated and tyrannical attitude within the government, it [finally] took on the status of a government within a government.

Naturally, this very same Committee, which, by its persistent and unilateral oppression brought about the appearance of a secret and unaccountable force within the government, was composed of the individuals who had formed it. The aforementioned individuals were, of course, jointly responsible, according to the special edicts of the Law of Associations, for the crimes and offenses carried out by members of its [CUP's] committees and performed in its name and on its behalf.

[Therefore,] in view of this and in response to this and pursuant to this charge under the guidance of the 45th Article of the Penal Code and in line with the stipulations of the last paragraph of the 55th Article, and as there is sufficient evidence for trying the following individuals for the crimes of which they are accused, the unanimous decision has been rendered that they are to be tried for the crimes of establishing, through [their] cooperative effort, a power above and beyond the legitimate authority of government, and in this way, altering the form of government by force and compulsion, by sowing fear and terror among the populace:

the fugitive Talaat Paşa, who was the acting [party] Chairman of the aforementioned Committee, Enver and Cemal Efendis, who were members of the General Assembly; former [party] Chairman Sa'îd Halim Paşa, whose examination was conducted and completed while [he was] in custody; as well as General Assembly members the honorable Hayri and Musa Kâzım Efendis and Kemal, Şükrü, and İbrahim Beys and Abbâs Halim Paşa.

Furthermore, in regard to [the other defendants] it is decided that:

1) Mitigating circumstances be taken into consideration by the court in regard to İbrahim Bey, in light of his having possessed a lesser degree of influence [within the CUP community].
2) Ali Münif Bey should be tried on the [basis of the] same legal articles in light of the telegram that was sent from the Interior Ministry and found among his papers, and which was [subsequently] brought to our attention, concerning the deporting of Armenians [who had been previously] exempted from deportation in the Province of Adana. Apparently, though he was under no official duty to do so, Ali Münif carried out these deportations while he was traveling through Adana, purely out of Unionist partisanship.
3) Concerning the defendants Halil and Ahmed Nesimi, it is necessary that they be tried on [the basis of] the same [legal] articles, on the condition that these circumstances be taken into consideration as mitigating factors: the former was a member of the General Assembly at the time of the deportations, and cannot have been involved in the calamities of that era because he was in Europe at that time, and was not part of the General Assembly during the start of the war but instead was appointed the President of the [Ottoman] Chamber of Deputies. As for the latter [Ahmed Nesimi Bey], he was in Europe during this period.
4) İsmâ'il Canbolat, Hüseyin Haşim, and Mustafa Şeref, who [only] received their ministerial posts in the last days [of the war] and who from their positions as [government] ministers and provincial [authorities] had always argued against and opposed the interventions and evil acts that occurred, shall have the charges dismissed against them.
5) As for Rif'at, of whom the [Court] President's Office has decided to merge the documents [concerning him], it is determined here that although a prior decision had been made to dismiss the charges against him, he shall be sent to the Military Tribunal for prosecution.

25 Şaban [1]337 26 Mayıs, [1]335 (26 May 1919)

Takvîm-i Vekâyi' *#3617, s. 1–2: Yozgad Tehcir ve Taktili Muhakemesi (Karar Sureti)*

Yozgad Verdict

The assertions, explanations and defenses of both sides in the current trial have been heard and all of the documents in the case have been thoroughly studied and examined. Additionally, while the underlying circumstances were discussed and both the defendants and their attorneys have denied the accusations and demanded [their] acquittals, the persuasive testimonies of witnesses, who were heard one by one, and the presentation of evidence which left no doubt in our minds compel us to conclude that the defenses put forth by the defendants and their attorneys are completely baseless and therefore void.

According to the Sublime Ordinances of Islam and the commands and customs of the assembled laws of the Ottomans, the ensuring of the preservation of the honor, life, and property [of the entire populace] without differentiating between [its] various [constituent] elements, and the protection of their civil rights from all manner of loss or damage are among the foremost duties of all state officials. The deportation of all of the Armenians, even their helpless wives and children, thereby discounting the officially allowed exceptions, was ordered through the auspices of Boğazlıyan County Executive and Acting District Governor of Yozgad, Kemal Bey, and Gendarmerie Commander for the provincial district of Yozgad, Major Tevfik Bey, whose convictions are being demanded [here].

Driven by their own personal ambition and greed, and [after] accepting the secret, illegal communications and instructions of a few evil individuals, [they undertook the deportations] after [first] taking all of the money and valuable possessions from these persons who made up the departing convoys, in complete disregard for the[-ir] individual rights. Not only did they fail to adopt the necessary measures to ensure the protection of the aforementioned [deportees], so that they might reach their destination point in comfort and ease, they bound the hands of the men, thus allowing these premeditated tragic events to take place, causing all manner of slaughter, looting, and pillaging, such as are entirely unacceptable to human and civilized sensibilities and which, in Islam's view [of the severity of crimes] are considered among the greatest of offenses. The defendants even blocked [attempts at] preventing their occurrence by concealing the truth from their superiors, who have testified how they repeatedly asked for reports [concerning] the aforementioned tragedies. What is more, they supported and facilitated the realization of the[-ir] accursed aims by dispatching irresponsible persons without any official authority as supervisors over the officials and guards responsible [for the deportations].

[This has been established] from the persuasive testimonies heard as well as from the following evidence:

1) the contents of official telegraphic communications that were exchanged between certain military officials;
2) the examination of the admissions by the aforementioned defendants which do not deny or refute [the events];
3) their separating the minors and women in the deportation convoys from their guardians and close relatives which revealed [malicious] intents and aims in the[-ir] extensive actions.

Finally in response to the defense [arguments] of the defendants and their attorneys, [this court] makes the following observation:

Although some weak-minded persons were inclined toward sympathy with the enemy after they were gripped by the incitements and encouragements of the members of revolutionary groups, and although [many of] these persons participated in revolutionary movements and revolts in the areas of military operations, and especially in the lands of the enemy and in the areas under his occupation, this [does not and] cannot prove that the other members of their community in other parts of the Ottoman Realms were involved in the harboring of the[-se aforementioned] vile ideas. It is true that a segment of the Armenian nation did indeed participate in seditious actions such as these, which materialized from time to time, but the rest of the populace, contrariwise, proved their loyalty and devotion [to the Ottoman state] in numerous ways.

As was recorded above it is an absolute command for [all] government officials, regardless of their position, to devote themselves to the defense of the lives and legal rights of the population, which were entrusted to their protective hands as unto a benevolent father, without prejudice to national sentiment or personal rancor.

Therefore, there existed no legal or moral justification, such as Kemal Bey has suggested in his defense, for the laying the responsibility for the atrocities which occurred in the areas of Van, Erzurum, and Bitlis by the Armenians against Muslims, upon the Armenian inhabitants of Yozgad who had not been involved in any significant revolutionary activity. This conclusion and the aforementioned [Kemal Bey]'s displays of feelings of revenge and of a personal vendetta regarding the aforementioned [Armenians], and his viewing it as natural and even necessary that not only the Muslim population of the provincial district under his administration, but all Muslims should harbor the sick idea of [carrying out] a retaliatory massacre against the aforementioned [Armenian] nation, supported by proof and from a handwritten document found among the papers in our possession as evidence, which shows that the three persons acting without authority nevertheless exerted power over officials who were treated as subordinate to them, and [these three] demanded obedience from the convoy escorts, [allow us] to conclude that their true aim was the massacre of the people in the convoy.

In light of the aforementioned decisive proofs, the arguments offered by the defendants and their attorneys in their defense would appear to have no validity.

Thus, although the Procuror-General's Office demand for the application of the 56th Article of the Imperial Penal Code for Officials is rejected, it has been decided that the aforementioned Kemal and Tevfik Beys are guilty according to the 45th Article of the [aforementioned] Code. Furthermore, as a result of the deliberation held in regard to the determination of their punishments, each one of the aforementioned convicts, having been determined to have been a principal co-perpetrator in accordance with the aforementioned 45th Article, is also to be treated as a sole perpetrator in the crimes he committed.

Based on the following findings the opinion has been formed [by this panel] that Kemal Bey was indeed the principal perpetrator [of these actions]:

1) he was the highest official of the aforementioned provincial district;
2) he planned the manner in which the criminal acts of massacre, looting, and pillaging were to be carried out;
3) he ordered a group of individuals without official title or authority to accompany the convoys;
4) seeing no need to even observe the chain of command, he encouraged Sergeant Şükrü, the official [legally] in charge of the convoys, to directly obey the commands of the aforementioned unauthorized individuals.

The panel has also unanimously concluded that Tevfik Bey was an accessory [to the crimes]. Furthermore, according to the [terms of] the aforementioned 45th Article they were both principal co-perpetrators in those aforementioned actions which consisted of killing, looting, and plundering.

Pursuant to the [terms of the] 171st Article of the Imperial Penal Code for the Military and the 170th Article of the Imperial Penal Code for Officials, [and especially in consideration of] the aforementioned 171st Article which states that "[someone who] loots and damages the collective stores, provisions and wares, or possessions by open attack whether armed or unarmed, or whether by breaking down doors or walls or by applying undue pressure upon individuals … [shall be] sentenced to death by execution," [as well as in consideration of] the existing 170th Article of the Imperial Penal Code for Officials which also states that "The person who premeditatedly kills an individual or willfully kills a father or grandfather or mother or grandmother even though without premeditation is put to death," the aforementioned convict Kemal [is hereby] sentenced to death by execution.

On the basis of what is written in paragraph 2 of the aforementioned 45th Article, namely that "those who are accessories in the commission of a felony [*Jinayet*] or misdemeanor [*Junha*] become subject to punishment in the following manner where there is no explicitness in the law: There is awarded with regard to those who are accessories the punishment of temporary hard labor [*kyurek*] for not less than ten years."

Tevfik is sentenced to a finite period of 15 years of hard labor in exile.

6 Receb [1]337 8 Nisan [1]335 (8 April 1919)

Receb Ferdi *Ali Nazım* *Mustafa* *Zeki* *Nazım*

Chief of the Officers of Extraordinary Military Tribunal
Abidin Daver

Takvîm-i Vekâyi' *#3616, s. 1–3: Trabzon Tehcîr ve Taktîli Muhâkemesi (Karar Sureti)*

Trabzon Verdict

As is customary for the current court proceedings, the assertions, explanations, and defenses of both sides have been heard and all of the documents in the case have been thoroughly studied and examined, after which the necessary circumstances were discussed, and although both the defendants and their attorneys have denied the accusations and demanded [their] acquittals, [a contrary picture] has been demonstrated at every stage of the trial and the [following] opinion has thus been formed by our entire panel [of judges]:

According to the sublime ordinances of Islam and the commands and customs of the assembled laws of the Ottomans, the ensuring of the preservation of [the population's] honor, life, and property and the guarding of their rights against [all] dangers, with no distinction made between the various Ottoman peoples, are among the foremost duties of all state officials. Nevertheless, CUP Party Secretary Nail Bey acquired power by complying with the orders secretly sent by the former Governor-General of [the province of] Trabzon, Cemal Azmi Bey, who is [also] among those whose conviction is demanded. Through their collaboration, and in conformity with the secret orders that Nail had received, [the two of them then] decided, in accordance with these secret orders, [to implement] the plans necessary for the actual massacre and annihilation of the Armenians under the guise of implementing the Law of Deportation.

They ordered the defenseless Armenians sent off for the [ostensible] purpose of deportation by means of convoy guard details which they had formed from certain persons of corrupt morals and recidivist criminals and from gendarmes who would collaborate with them. Then, after putting some distance between [the convoys] and the city [of Trabzon], and reaching an out-of-the-way and concealed place, the men and women were separated from one another, after which the possessions that were found [on their persons] were looted and plundered by the robber brigands composed of those persons mentioned. The killing and annihilation [of the men] by all manner of atrocious and cruel means was ordered, after which the helpless women were brought to another place and, after being likewise stripped of their jewelry and money and clothing and such, a good number of them were then raped.

Although they [the women] were then sent on treks on foot lasting for months on roads and on what amounted to a forced march (*sürüklenme derecesinde*), they [subsequently] ordered them sent to [yet] another place by way of Erzincan, even though they were exhausted and lacked strength and a good number of them died of hunger and thirst [and] the hardships of the journey. Then, a portion of the women who had been ordered to remain in Trabzon, along with the male and female children who had been sent to the houses of religious sheikhs and hospitals for the ostensible purpose of protecting [them], were [now] ordered placed in small groups on barges and caiques for the supposed purpose of transporting them by sea to another location. After setting off and [traveling out far enough from the coast] to be lost from sight, they were drowned and annihilated by being thrown overboard. The acts of massacre and looting and plunder were not carried out within the city of Trabzon, [but were] carried out almost entirely outside [of the city] and in a pre-planned fashion.

As the above-mentioned defendant, Director of Customs (Rüsumat Müdiri) Mehmet Alî Efendi, had, upon the orders of Governor-General [of the Trabzon Province] Cemal Azmi Bey (with whom he had been in previous contact), been involved in the commission on abandoned property, jewelry, [extraordinary] war tax[-es], military construction, and war production, the Military Telephone Bureau, the Customs Bureau for checking the passports of those entering and leaving, and the agency representing the women's issues at the Red Crescent hospital, [one can conclude that] he therefore aided [in the commission of] the abuses and offenses that occurred as a result the of self-seeking, ambitious aims of the aforementioned Governor-General.

Furthermore, as the Armenian women and young girls were ordered assembled in the aforementioned hospital, which had been established for humanitarian purposes and in the abodes of religious sheikhs for the [ostensible] purpose of protecting them, as though it were a patriotic duty, he [Mehmet Alî Efendi] was responsible for violating their womanly honor by delivering and surrendering the aforementioned women to those men desiring to take them into their houses, some with the intent of marrying [them], others with the aim of reducing them to servitude or [in some cases] for subjecting them to poverty and ruin through other forms [of abuse]. The fact that those [women] who entered the aforementioned abodes were quickly taken away and those in the aforementioned hospital were violated was established by way of eyewitness accounts.

By attaching absolutely no importance to the warnings, which had been given both verbally and in writing by the Customs Inspector, who was an official superior to him in rank, that getting involved in illegal matters outside the confines of his orders and duties would have grave consequences, [Mehmet Alî Efendi] knowingly assisted in almost all of those actions, so replete with suffering, that were ordered carried out within the city [of Trabzon].

Likewise, although Police Chief Nuri Efendi was among those entrusted with maintaining order within the city, and he was an official appointed to the Commissions for the Discharge and Inquiry into Property and Jewelry, he showed himself incapable of adopting any serious disciplinary or administrative measures for the preservation of good order and protection from loss of the possessions [found] within the houses that remained unoccupied due to their owners having been deported. He made no effort for the [protection of the] property, which had been [taken] from the aforementioned residences and sent to the places that were used as depots, by first ordering it separately recorded in registries and [then] transported by means of trustworthy individuals. Thus, he failed to properly carry out his duty, [instead] allowing the abandoned properties of the deportees to be stolen and subject to loss.

Although he [did] order some gendarmerie officials sent to the military tribunal for having stolen items from amongst the abandoned property, he made absolutely no attempt, either officially or unofficially, to prevent [such acts], even though he witnessed them with his very own eyes. He knew that the possessions, which Governor-General Cemal Azmi Bey and those in his service had seized by exploiting the martial law curfew prohibition on wandering the streets at night, had been smuggled [out] with the knowledge of the police and the gendarmes. [He was likewise aware] that the women and children who remained in the city were being transported by police, gendarmes, and other persons onto caiques in order to be drowned at sea. In his testimony he claimed that he had been exceedingly grieved on several occasions by the distressing events that he had witnessed, and that he had locked himself in his office; however, he did not make a single outward expression of helplessness or grief. [From this one can conclude that] by shutting his eyes to the deeds of the Governor-General, he was incapable of even displaying the patriotism to resign his position so that a successor might perhaps have been able to prevent the occurrence and perpetration of shameful acts such as these.

As for Agent Mustafa Bey, although he was [merely] a soldier with the rank of private, due to his having won the favor of Governor-General Cemal Azmi Bey and his frequent contact with him, important military duties, such as the responsibility for the harbor and for shipping were entrusted to him, and he maintained his official duties by virtue of the power he derived from the aforementioned Cemal Azmi Bey, who in turn was sustained by the [Third] army and by the central government. Yet, he abused his official position by employing naval transport vessels belonging to the soldiers under his control for the [private] purposes of transporting the abandoned and personal belongings seized by both the Governor-General and by those whom the latter had commissioned [with this task].

[On the other hand, he did [indeed] save some Armenians from deportation, through his contacts with the Governor-General and through his own influential standing, As the owner of a personal fortune [and] a member of the city's notables, and supported by the accounts of those who testified in his favor, it does not seem plausible that he would have conceivably sacrificed his honor for the sake of personal gain.

Nevertheless, it has been understood from the convincing accounts of witnesses which were heard, and from his own previous confessions, that he [nevertheless] allowed the jewelry and money, which was unmistakably found in a chest of drawers and that had been delivered to him, to be lost by leaving it in the greedy hands of Cemal Azmi Bey without [first] counting it.

Thus, the defense [arguments] offered by the attorneys for the above-mentioned Nuri, Mehmet Alî, and Acenta Mustafa Efendis appear, in the face of the ample evidence and definitive proofs in our possession, to be entirely non-valid in this matter, and a unanimous decision was thus reached to convict [Trabzon] Governor-General Cemal Azmi Bey, [CUP] Party Secretary Nail Bey, and Mehmet Alî Efendi in accordance with the provisions of the 45th Article of the Imperial Ottoman Penal Code and [to convict] Police Chief Nuri Efendi and Agent Mustafa Efendi for having perpetrated the crime of misusing their official positions.

Whereupon, and as a result of the deliberation held regarding the determination of [their] punishments, the aforementioned criminals Cemal Azmi and Nail must be considered as principal co-perpetrators and therefore as the sole perpetrators, in accordance with paragraph 1 of the aforementioned 45th Article, which explicitly states that "If several persons unitedly commit a felony [*jinayet*] or misdemeanor [*junha*] or if a jinayet or junha is composed of several acts and each of a gang of persons perpetrates one or some of such acts with a view to the accomplishment of the offence, such persons are styled accomplices and all of them are punished as sole perpetrators."

According to the reasoning found within paragraph 3 of the aforementioned [45th] Article, which explicitly states that "Those who by way of giving presents or money or making threats or using fraud or device or exercising influence or abusing the authority of office incite another person to commit a felony [*jinayet*] or misdemeanor [*junha*], or who being aware that a jinayet or junha is to be committed, give information serving the accomplishment thereof, or who knowingly procure arms or instruments or other means which will help the commission of a jinayet or junha, or who knowingly assist the principal perpetrator in acts which are the means of preparing, facilitating, or completing a jinayet or junha are deemed accessories in the commission of such jinayet or junha. Those who, being aware of the deeds and acts of criminal persons who practice brigandage or use force or violence against the safety of the Government or public tranquility or the safety of life and property, willingly provide them with eatables or a place to sleep, hide, or assemble in are deemed accessories." Therefore Mehmet Alî must be considered an accessory.

Furthermore, because the actions of the aforementioned Cemal Azmi and Nail correspond to the 171st Article of the Imperial Penal Code for the Military and the 170th Article of the Imperial Penal Code for Officials, and as it states in the passages from the aforementioned 171st Article that "[someone who] loots and damages the collective stores, provisions and wares, or possessions by open attack, whether armed or unarmed, or whether by damaging an edifice or by applying pressure upon individuals shall be sentenced to death by execution," and in the 170th Article that "The person who premeditatedly kills an individual or willfully kills a father or grandfather or mother or grandmother even though without premeditation is put to death." Cemal Azmi and Nail are sentenced to death by execution in accordance with the terms of the two articles mentioned above. Their seized property, being outside of the reach of civil law, is to be administered in accordance with the processing office.

In accordance with paragraph 2 of the aforementioned 45th Article, in which it is written that "those who are accessories in the commission of a felony [*jinayet*] or misdemeanor [*junha*] become subject to punishment in the following manner where there is no explicitness in the law: There is awarded with regard to those who are accessories the punishment of temporary hard labor [*kyurek*] for not less than ten years." Mehmet Alî is sentenced to hard labor for a period of 10 years, [to be counted as having] commenced from the day of his arrest.

As the actions of Acente Mustafa and Nuri Efendis correspond to the first addendum of the 172nd Article of the Imperial Penal Code for Officials, and as it is expressed in the aforementioned addendum that "[in cases] other than those specified in the law, the official who misuses his official office in any manner whatsoever, is to be sentenced to prison for a period of three months to three years, according to his rank, [and] in cases [where there exist] mitigating circumstances, [the offending official] is to be imprisoned [for a period of] no less than 15 days, or to be punished with a monetary fine of between five and 100 lira, and in both cases he shall be permanently or temporarily stripped of his official title," the two [defendants] are, in accordance with [the precepts of] this article, each sentenced to one year in prison and both are to be stripped of their titles of office for a period of two years.

As for the defendant Niyazi Efendi, it has been understood from official documents that his traveling to Istanbul by motorboat twice in order to transport to the capital the free-floating [naval] mines which he had ordered gathered from the ocean and that his return to Trabzon after repairing his craft did not correspond to the period of deportations. Likewise, it has not been verified that he participated in the massacre actions, nor has it been proven that he was involved in the instances of looting and the seizing of property. Although it is clear that [such goods] were [indeed] awarded to the aforementioned [defendant] at favorable prices through the intervention of Cemal Azmi Bey, [Niyazi] did not allow himself to be corrupted by [Cemal Azmi] through bribery or the attainment of personal advantage. Rather by relying upon the esteem that Governor-General Cemal Azmi had shown him as a result of his having displayed the courage to repeatedly bring [the aforementioned] free-floating mines to the capital, he [was able to] stop the auctions in question and purchase the property by way of public offer. In view of the fact that only a small portion of the properties purchased correspond to the period of the bombardment and the most dangerous period of the war, [the deed] cannot [be seen to] form a legal offense [and the defendant] is acquitted of the acts of massacre, plundering, and looting, and is [ruled] not responsible for the other matters.

As for District Official Talaat Bey, although it is clear that he did not participate in the actions and crimes under discussion, and as the testimonies of certain witnesses have not [adequately] demonstrated whether or not he carried out his duties in the War Taxes Commission honorably because the aforementioned actions and crimes are outside of [the purview of] this case, he is acquitted and the aforementioned matter shall be examined by the relevant department.

Furthermore, in the event that Niyazi Efendi and Talaat Bey are not [being] detained on any further cause, they are to be released.

As for the other defendant, Chief Health Official Ali Sa'ib Bey, a separate trial shall be held for him for [the purpose of] the deeper investigation and elucidation of certain matters which appear to demand clarification.

This decision was given unanimously in the presence of all of the defendants other than Cemal Azmi and Nail, [who are] in absentia.

Sâ 21 Şaban [1]337 and Sâ 22 Mayıs [1]335 (22 May 1919)

Receb Ferdi *Ali Nazım* *Mustafa* *Zeki* *Nazım*

Official Chief of Transcripts of the Military Tribunal
Abidin Daver

Takvîm-i Vekâyi' *#3771, s. 1–2: Ma'muretü'l'aziz Taktil Muhâkemeleri (Karar Sureti)*

The Harput (Mamuretülaziz) Verdict

The assertions, explanations, and defenses of both sides have been heard in the current trial; all of the related court proceedings in the case have been thoroughly studied and examined. Additionally, the circumstances in question were discussed and both the defendants and their attorneys have denied the accusations and demanded [their] acquittals. Afterward, [and] upon the required deliberations having taken place, the following ruling has been made:

The defendant [and] CUP Central Committee member Dr. Bahaeddin Şakir Bey set out from Istanbul for the Provinces of Trabzon, Erzurum, and other regions, bearing the title "Head of the Special Organization." [He then] assumed the leadership of the ensemble of convicts who were set up and formed out of a group of criminals released from prison [for just this purpose] and of various other wicked persons. He sent them into action, [there-]by executing and delivering secret orders and instructions, some verbal, others written in code, to certain persons and [government] officials, who either out of naiveté and ignorance or because of greed and [personal] advantage joined the aforementioned Committee [of Union and Progress]. [In furtherance of the aim of] the atrocities and evil deeds of massacring the population and plundering their possessions, which were committed and perpetrated at various times and places during the deportation of the Armenians, he took into his service individuals from this section of the Special Organizations, which had been formed for the purpose of destroying and annihilating the Armenians.

In view of the ample [existing] proofs and inference issuing from the reports of other testimonies that have been heard, which are recorded in detail in the official proceedings, the [charges] are confirmed and strengthened by the following evidence:

1) the communication [contained] in the coded telegraph dated 21-4-31 (21 June 1915), which the aforementioned Bahaeddin Şakir Bey sent from Erzurum, by means of the Governor-General of [the Province of] Mamuretülaziz (Elazığ), Sabit Bey, to the Party Secretary for Mamuretülaziz [Province], the defendant and [currently] fugitive Resneli Nazım Bey, and which reads "Are the Armenians who have been deported from there being liquidated? Are the harmful persons whom you reported having been exiled and banished being annihilated? Or are they merely being sent off and deported? [Please] report openly [on this matter]";
2) the contents of the coded telegram of Erzurum [Province] Governor-General Münir Bey, which is one of the documents found in the dossier concerning the members of the CUP Central Committee, reporting that the members of the convoy of rich [Armenians], which was sent out from Erzurum by way of the Kığı road, had been killed and subjected to pillaging by the inhabitants of Dersim and by persons from the armed brigands that had been organized by Bahaeddin Şakir Bey;
3) the [following] abundant utterances:
   a) of the former governor-general of [the Province of] Kastomonu, Reşid Paşa, declaring that he received a coded telegram from Bahaeddin Şakir Bey concerning the deportation;
   b) of Vehîb Paşa, suggesting that the killing and annihilation of Armenians and the looting and seizing of their property were the result of decisions [made by] the CUP Central Committee, and that the person who equipped, directed, and brought into service the[-se] butchers of people in the zone of the Third Army was Bahaeddin Şakir;
   c) of the former lieutenant governor of [the provincial district of] Antalya, Sabûr Sami Bey, [stating] that in the coded telegram that Bahaeddin Şakir Bey sent [him] from Erzurum it was written: "Having sent [the Armenians of Erzurum, Van Bitlis, Diyârbekir, Sivas and Trabzon] toward

> Mosul and Zor (Syria) in such a way as to ensure that not a single Armenian remained in the region, what was he [now] doing in Antalya?"

[From the preceding evidence], a high degree of certainty having been attained [regarding the defendants' involvement in the crimes of which they are accused], it has been unanimously decided to convict the aforementioned Bahaeddin Şakir Bey as a principal co-perpetrator among [other] active participants in the atrocities under discussion.

As for the second defendant, the [now] fugitive Resneli Nazım Bey, the three members of the judicial panel have decided [to convict him] as a principal co-perpetrator in the aforementioned atrocities on the basis of the following facts:

1) his having been in communication with Bahaeddin Şakir at the time of the deportation, as was proven by the contents of the telegram dated 21-4-31 (21 June 1915) and recorded above;
2) the recorded declarations of the governor general of [the Province of] Mamuretülaziz (Elazığ) Sabit and the secretary-general of the [CUP] Central Committee, Midhat Şükrü Bey;
3) the witnesses who[-se testimonies] have been heard;
4) [the defendant] having fled following the start of the [legal] investigation into his person and his remaining a fugitive [until] today;
5) the evidence such as the contents of the other documents of correspondence found among the trial documents.

As to the other person, Resneli Nazım, [the following evidence was weighed]:

1) the failure to obtain a single [piece of] admissible proof or evidence in regard to the aforementioned [defendant] having joined those who were the main perpetrators, or his having ventured to undertake any actions or deeds with the intent of bringing about the aforementioned crimes, [was balanced against]
2) [the defendant's] having nevertheless undertaken the aforementioned communication with Bahaeddin Şakir and the manner of testimony of the witnesses who were heard.

After weighing these facts, it has been decided that, as [the court] is of the opinion that he was an accomplice in the actions which prepared [the groundwork for] and facilitated [the carrying out of] the aforementioned atrocities by knowingly assisting the main perpetrators, and in accordance with the rules of procedure in such cases, the minority opinion shall prevail and as a two-thirds majority could not be produced in regard to his having been a principal co-perpetrator (*hem-fi'il*), he is convicted of having been an accessory in the crimes under discussion.

As a result of the deliberations over sentencing, it was decided that: of the aforementioned, convict Bahaeddin Şakir be sentenced to death by execution pursuant to the terms of the 181st and 170th Articles of the Penal Code under which his actions fall. Resneli Nazım is sentenced to 15 years of hard labor in exile in accordance with paragraph 2 of the 45th Article of the aforementioned Penal Code, and to the aforementioned articles. [Furthermore,] the confiscated properties of both shall be administered by the processing office, and Nazım is to be stripped of his civil rights.

As for the other defendants, the former [Parliamentary] Deputy for Dersim, Mehmet Nuri Bey, and the current Director of Education for Konya, formerly for Mamuretülaziz (Elazığ), Ferid Bey, the following testimony was taken into consideration:

A woman named Margrit, who, when [summoned] to the Military Tribunal, was heard as a complainant during the trials that were held, accused [Nuri] of having incited the gendarmes to carry out killings during the expulsion from their villages of the Armenians, who are understood to have been expelled and banished to his farm from the nearby village of Hulvenek. The defendant, she claimed, had uttered before the gendarmes entrusted with the deportation such words as "I will send you to the village of bones. I will have barley sown here."

She also declared that Mehmet Nuri Bey came to the village of Hulvenek during the period of the deportation and, refusing to accept their entreaties, said: "You are going to the same place that your husband went. I will have barley sown here." Then, nailing a piece of paper reading "Whoever puts his possessions here shall return and get them three months from now" on the house of Karabet, he mounted his horse and left.

As for the complainant Kasbar Movsesyan, who was in Istanbul at the time of the deportation and who gave reports based on the testimonies of the woman Margrit, he has also claimed that he had heard from the aforementioned Margrit that Mehmet Nuri Bey collected money from a good number [of persons], and that he [Mehmet Nuri Bey] made a soldier sign a red sheet [of paper] in the house of Karabet. Furthermore, when some of the women, veiling themselves with their skirts, begged for his intervention, he (Mehmet Nurî Bey) replied: "I will have barley sown [over] this village," then mounted his horse and left, after which the armed gangs who were poised for assault entered the village.

[Movsesyan] also claimed that Mehmet Nuri Bey did not have any information about Karabet having the paper stuck on his house, despite the fact that their testimonies contradict one another and that the aforementioned [Karabet] stated under oath, in rejection and refutation of his previous testimony under oath, [that he] was saved from the deportation by hiding on the farm of Mehmet Nuri Bey and that though he remained in the house of Mehmet Nuri

Bey throughout the deportation, from beginning to end, he did not see his (Mehmet Nuri Bey's) brother-in-law [wife's sister's husband, *bacınâh*], Asım, bring the plundered goods into the house of Mehmet Nuri Bey. [Furthermore,] his efforts to demand money from Mehmet Nuri Bey in jail appear worthy of attention in their own right.

Whereby, [in light of this evidence] the following findings are made:

1) Despite [the fact] that those who hid persons subject to deportation were threatened with execution by the government, the testimony of more than 30 persons from a previous hearing evince that the defendant saved the lives of a good number of the inhabitants of the village of Hulvenek by hiding and protecting [them] and thereby enabling them to escape.
2) the American, Mister Riggs, whose impartiality—on this matter, in particular—there can be no occasion to doubt, has confirmed the matter of Mehmet Nuri Bey having protected a great many Armenians during the deportation;
3) the fact that the reports of Mehmet Alî Bey, one of the witnesses who has been heard [in this trial] and whose utterances are recorded in detail in the official transcripts [of the trial], diverge from and cast doubt on the aforementioned reports. It is revealing that following his testimony on this matter to the investigative committee, when he encountered Mustafa Safvet Efendi, he provided his address after mentioning his testimony and expressing a willingness to change it [in order to be truthful];
4) The failure to unearth even a single piece of proof or report [that would indicate that] the other defendant, Education Director Ferid Bey, had facilitated the commission of the crimes which occurred by the participation in the forming and dispatching of the convoys [of deportees] or that would raise the suspicion that the atrocities carried out against the populace were performed with the government's approval.

[Based upon these findings] it has been unanimously decided that those [defendants] who are present for the trial shall be acquitted: [specifically] Mehmet Nuri Bey, of [the crimes of] the massacring and plundering the property of the Armenians of the village of [Hu]lvenek which is in the area of his farm; his brother-in-law, the defendant Asım, of the crime of transporting and hiding seized goods in his house; and Ferid Bey, of the aforementioned acts of which he was accused. Furthermore, in the event that they are not being detained for any other cause, they are to be released.
[These rulings were given] in the presence of [the defendants] Mehmet Nuri and Ferid Beys, and with [the defendants] Bahaeddin Şakir and Resneli Nazım Beys in absentia.

21 Rebî'ül-ahir [1]338 and 13 Kânûn-u Sânî [1]336 (13 January 1920)
Mustafa Kerimi İhsan

Although we participate in this decision, we are of the opinion that the aforementioned Bahaeddin Şakir and Resneli Nazım are equally guilty of having been principal co-perpetrators.
Süleyman Şakir Ismail Hakkı Es'ad

(Not published in* Takvim-i Vekâyi*)

Bayburt Verdict

Tercümân-ı Hakikat, 5 August 1920, p. 3

Death Sentence

Judgment from the Military Tribunal on the Bayburt Deportation

From the Presidency of the First Military Tribunal

A decision has been reached after extensive investigations and examinations and a series of prosecutions regarding the following defendants and charges:

Yanyali Nusret Bey, son of Behram Efendi, former district governor of Urfa, age 44, a resident of Erenköy, on Baghdad Street prior to being detained on charges of (1) causing the suicide, by hanging, of Hovâkim Efendi, Director of Finance in Bayburt, and the suicides of his wife and daughters by poisoning as a result of the exercise of excessive force while taking part in the murders and plundering of property which took place during the deportation of Armenians from the Township of Bayburt, during the period the aforementioned defendant was serving in the office of the Bayburt District Governor, and of (2) raping Filomen Toryan, daughter of Alku, age 24, and her sister, Na'ime, age 12, thereby deflowering the latter, both of whom had been deported from Trabzon, while the defendant was serving in the Ergani District Governor's office.

Mehmet Necati Efendi son of Haci Bekir, also known as "Erzurumlu Pire Mehmet," age 35, discharged from the rank of lieutenant, and a resident of Erenköy, the Old Station area, operating a business in the Karakaş Inn (*Han*), Room #10 in Eminönü, prior to facing charges of having taken part in the Bayburt deportation and massacres before fleeing prosecution.

In his defense, the defendant Nusret Bey denied the charges that were brought against him, and in explanation stated that because the township gendarmerie forces had been transferred to the mobile gendarmerie unit, there was insufficient military manpower to manage the movement of the convoys of deportees. He further claimed that in consultation with the gendarmerie commander from the garrison, he had requested and been given control over three complete squadrons along with military police, and with the addition of more gendarmes to the existing military detachments, had succeeded in moving two convoys of Armenians comprising 6–7 thousand people, safely and soundly to Erzincan. In addition, he claimed that there had been no incidents of massacre within the boundaries of Bayburt and that the abandoned properties of the deportees had been gathered up by a special commission, recorded in a ledger, and transferred to the church.

In contrast to the defendant's statement of defense, we were presented with the following statement given at another trial, of Lieutenant Salih Efendi, who was the Bayburt Gendermarie Squadron Commander at the time of the events in question and who is now employed with the Hart Team Command which is attached to the aforementioned squadron. Salih Efendi described the situation in Bayburt by stating that since the majority of the gendarmerie squadrons had been transferred to the mobile units in order to support the war effort, the numbers of soldiers that remained were barely enough to handle the capture and return of deserters and absentee conscripts to their units. Therefore, according to Salih Efendi, the gendarmerie had very little to do with the deportations but rather it was the work of Mehmet Necati Efendi and his retinue of approximately 30–40 people who had arrived from Erzurum. It was he and that group who were responsible for sending the Armenians to Erzincan; according to Salih Efendi, however, he had no information as to what actually happened to the Armenians. He observed that the following individuals were involved in driving off the Armenians of Bayburt, convoy after convoy, in a miserable state, and that they returned approximately two hours later to Bayburt: (1) Őmer, son of Hasan, from the village of Zevâlı in Sürmene, who was employed at the Menzil flour mill during the mobilization for war and who is presently running a business. Őmer's testimony was taken in another hearing. (2) Second Lieutenant Kaşıf, son of Kefeli, from the Koçere village of Sürmene, who was employed at the time in the Labor battalion of the Honorary Officers; (3) his brother Mahmud, and (4) Sabit, son of Ilyas who is one of the sons of Kerim, from the aforementioned village of Zevâlı, and many others whose identity is unknown to the witness. Salih Efendi even recognized the faces of children as young as one year old in Bayburt, whom he had seen among the throngs transported by convoy and also [stated] that he had witnessed the murder of Armenians, after their property and money had been taken from them. Likewise, from the sworn testimony of Ali Efendi, son of Es'ad from the village of Baş Tüccar of Sürmene, which was taken at a separate hearing, we learn that under the orders of Mayor Nusret Bey, without forewarning, one night the police and gendarmes, with a great deal of noise and trouble, gathered all the Armenians and transported them through the night under inhumane conditions and that under Nusret Bey's orders, again, their properties which had been left behind were sold. Ali Efendi testified that despite having been appointed to the office only two days earlier, he could not tolerate the injustice and abuse which was occurring and therefore resigned. He testified that Nusret Bey acted with complete disregard of the law as he relied upon the latter's friendship with the Governor of Erzurum, Tahsin Bey. Ali Efendi testified that he had witnessed the murder of Armenians, who were transported over the course of 15–20 days, by groups of gendarmes, soldiers, and irregulars who had joined up, and that it was his opinion that the majority of the Armenians had been murdered during the journey. He further testified that Nusret Bey had taken around 150 Armenian boys and girls to a place called Binbaşı Hanı and that others went there and took whomever they wanted, though later Nusret Bey had had some of the children who had been residing with Muslims taken away and transported elsewhere.

From the courtroom testimony of Ziya Bey, former Mayor of Bayburt, and Deputy governor of Bayazid we learned that Sa'di Bey, reserve lieutenant, Senate secretary, and fellow countryman of Ahmet Riza Bey, and Mehmet Necati Efendi, a.k.a. Pire Mehmet, had organized the deportation and massacres which took place in Bayburt. From Regiment Commander of the Erzurum gendarmerie, Adil Bey, we heard that his understanding of what occurred is that the Bayburt Armenians were attacked and murdered, in a place called "the Mill" which was about two hours distant from Bayburt, by members of the Special Organization (Teşkilat-ı Mahsusa) after being removed from Bayburt within a 24-hour period by Mehmet Necati Bey, who moves about Erenköy today freely by car [i.e., in luxury]. Based upon a written response from the Bayburt gendarmerie command, and an investigation, it was Adil Bey's belief that the actions were performed in furtherance of government necessity. He gave this information to Governor Tahsin Bey. He believed that the Teşkilat-ı Mahsusa's contingent was comprised of Dr. Bahaettin Şakır, who was from the Central Committee of the Committee for Union and Progress and who happened to be in Erzurum at the time, along with Hilmi Bey, the Delegate from Erzurum for the aforementioned Committee, and reserve lieutenant Sa'di, nephew of Ahmed Riza Bey, as well as the aforementioned Necati and others whose identity is known to us. His testimony that Nusret Bey had had the aforementioned Mehmet Necati removed from the group, and that the convoy had been safely and soundly delivered to Erzincan by the gendarmerie and police, flies in the face of reality, as that same convoy was annihilated in Pülümür. Even Mayor Mehmet Ali Bey, the Deputy Division Commander and Secretary of Army recruitment and Chief of Construction at the time in Bayburt, had heard that the Armenians of Bayburt had been removed by the aforementioned Mehmet Necati, something he had in time given notice of and informed others of. Likewise, the following witnesses from the population in Bayburt, women named Şaynisik, Ağavni, Varsenik, Araksiya, and Armanouhi and men named Haçatur, Seferyân Efendi, and child of Hampartsum, testified before the Military Tribunal in person, that Nusret Bey was the gang leader and that he had, with the aid of the gang members, by force of whip demanded money from the convoys around the areas of Binbaşı Han and Hindi Han, had been present at the massacres, and taken by force the prettier girls in the group with the help of gendarmes.

Let us now address the assignment and appropriation, and assignment of internal defense that was made in connection with the aforementioned event. According to the prosecutions which have taken place thus far before the Military Tribunals, the massacres which occurred in various places were firstly organized and documented under the auspices of the Central Committee of the Committee for Union and Progress, specifically under the bloodthirsty presidency of Dr. Bahaettin Şakir and gangs comprised of vile and miserable human beings, working on behalf of the Special Organization (Teşkilat-ı Mahsusa). This policy was disseminated to the various provincial directors by way of specially appointed officials. While most of these directors approved of the policy, individuals such as Cemal Bey, the district governer of Yozgad, and Reşid Bey, the governor-general of Kastamonu, and many other officials of good will whom we can identify, were dismissed for opposing this violence. Kemal, the governor of Yozgad County, who was [subsequently] hanged and who became a victim of their [Dr. Şakır and others] rapacious acts and wishes, and Atif, the governor-general of Ankara, just like other cruel inhumane individuals, were [then] appointed to posts.

The Military Tribunal, establishing a case by way of evidence and definitive proofs against the individuals subpoenaed to this court for having initiated the deportation and massacres, makes the following findings. It is clearly manifest that the testimony of the aforementioned defendant, Nusret Bey—to the effect that he had executed the deportation in Bayburt from the office of the garrison command with regular soldiers and the gendarmes that were present, that he had rejected the services of bandit Mehmet Necati, not recognizing the latter's apparent official status as a civil servant assigned to Bayburt, and finally that no acts of massacre had occurred in the region—is absolutely against the body of evidence as established by the witnesses and their testimony. Nor did the defendant resort to any manner of legal means or precautions to prevent the reoccurrence of the calamities described, despite being aware of their existence. The defendant failed to report the calamitous events to his superior and remained silent knowing that no news had been forwarded regarding the transport of people to Erzincan. His explanation in his testimony was that he had sent the first convoy to Erzincan with an official written notice. However, having not received a response, he had, by his own testimony, failed to follow through with an inquiry about it on the excuse that by then it was too late.

Despite the fact that it was obvious, during the period of the rule of the Committee for Union and Progress, that all civil servants from the very lowest of rank to the directors of offices were appointed based upon no other qualification other than loyalty, from among the witness testimonies we heard the testimony of Abdullah Hüsrev Bey, metallurgical engineer from Ergani, that Nusret Bey, known on the street by the nickname "Iron Fist Governor," was promoted to the Bayburt Mayor's office, then later appointed an agent for the Erzincan governor's office, and further on to the Ergani Governor's office, after the Bayburt deportation had ended. It was found that he has taken Armenians, who had been rendered weak and helpless by the difficulties of being transported from faraway places, to Ergani on the pretext of false orders and forced them to labor on the building of roads with the excuse that they were going to stay at the Inn for 2–3 days and had bread to eat. According to the testimony of the aforementioned Abdullah Hüsrev Bey, this was done in order to get a road built for nothing, since those whose labor was used were never given the wages that were due to them. During the period he served as Ergani's district governor (*mutasarrıf*), Nusret, on the excuse of sending to Diyarbekir several young [Armenian] boys who had not yet been deported and were left behind, delivered them into the cruel hands of Reşid, the governor-general of Diyarbekir who [later, during the armistice] committed suicide. We find that there is more than enough evidence to prove that even in Ergani, 15–20 thousand Armenians, as was confessed to, had been sent from various provinces and gathered there after being treated with kindness at the refugee crossroads known as the Urfa Independent district, and that the defendant was the accomplice of those who had organized and executed the criminal deeds that have been referred to here.

Though the defendant denies any blame for the suicides of Hovakim Efendi, the Director of Finance for Bayburt, and his family, specifically denying that he had sent a notice declaring that after the deportation not a single Armenian should be left behind and the issuing of threats that there would be executions if any were found and force being exerted, and information being given that Hovakim would not be exempt from the deportation, nevertheless we find that Hovakim Efendi and his family had been initially exempt from the deportation for having converted to Islam. However, later Nusret Bey visited the victim's home and demanded that his daughters be handed over to him, which the victim opposed. At that point, the defendant began to threaten the victim with deportation. We heard from all of the witnesses' testimony that rumors circulated that Hovakim Efendi was going to be deported also. Believing that they would be murdered and destroyed if they surrendered to the calamity around them, Hovakim Efendi and his two sons committed suicide by hanging themselves while his wife and daughters poisoned themselves.

The fact that Nusret Bey declared that he had not visited the site of this tragic event, that he obtained information about it from the police and evaluated it from a hostile standpoint, pleading ignorance of the last written words of the victim, which had been left near the window of the victim's home, gives strength to the aforementioned charges which have been directed at the defendant.

We find that the aforementioned Nusret Bey, despite being a bachelor during the time in which he was with the Governor's office of Ergani, did take the aforementioned young girl, Na'ime, to his house and deflower her by raping her, and find as well that he is guilty of raping her sister Filomen. This is based upon the sworn testimony of Filomen, which was taken in the course of the prosecutions regarding the Trabzon deportations, whereby the victim described the sad event in her own words, in the defendant's absence.

Nor do we believe the defendant's defense claim that the charges are a fraud being brought for the sole purpose of taking revenge upon a nation. Neither an entire nation, nor all state officials or civil servants can be held accountable for the inappropriate or criminal acts of a single individual. Proof of the reliability of the testimonies of Armenian witnesses and those with complaints, taken by the Military Tribunal, may be gleaned from the many accounts, by these same individuals, of having their honor and their lives protected by others, and by the way they recounted these compassionate acts with deeply felt thanks and gratitude. This belies the defendant's claim of ulterior motive by the victims. It is obvious that the efforts expended by the victims to lodge their complaints and issue reports immediately after the event would have had no effect other than risk of an escalation of the violence itself. The fact is that the elimination of the aforementioned matter would not constitute proof enough to render invalid the underlying cause of action for this trial and therefore the entire defense argument made by the defendant Nusret Bey is of no consequence.

Therefore, based upon the proofs presented, it is the court's opinion that the defendants Nusret Bey and the abovementioned Necati Efendi, also known as "Pire Mehmet," are guilty of organizing and executing the killings and shameless plundering that resulted during the deportation of Armenians from Bayburt, and that Nusret Bey is guilty of causing the suicides of the abovementioned Hovakim Efendi and his family and of raping Filomen and deflowering the young girl, Na'ime.

In light of the seriousness of Nusret Bey's crime, both defendants' actions violated the 170th Article of the Imperial State Criminal Code as guided by paragraph 1 of the Code's 45th article and the 171st Article of the Military Criminal Code. Namely, under the terms of both articles, if two or more individuals together engage in an act which comprises a felony or misdemeanor or if two or more individuals engage in one or more acts, either individually or jointly, which together in combination are responsible for causing a felony or misdemeanor, then the aforementioned individuals are accomplices to the crime and are punishable as if they had committed the criminal act alone. [Anyone who kills another with premeditation, or those who are responsible for the deaths of a father, mother, grandparent, or older ancestor with or without premeditation, shall be executed.] [An open attack with or without the use of weaponry, and the plundering or destruction of granaries, or provision stocks or wares or property, by a mob, through the breaking down of walls, or doors or by force upon persons, (shall be punishable) by execution.]

Upon declaration of these sentences, in accordance with the statutes identified it is unanimously decided that both defendants shall be executed and that the prosecution of Mehmet Necati be dismissed and their properties confiscated and processed by the Procedure office, and that the identified 26 individuals, whose culpability in both the deportation of 20,000 Armenians from Erzurum in a single day and the deportations which took place in Bayburt and Ergani M'adeni was established, be prosecuted in the presence of the defendant Nusret and the absence of Mehmet Necati.

20 July year 1920

(Not published in **Takvim-i Vekâyi***)*

Erzincan Verdict

Vakit, 29 July 1920

Erzincan Deportation and Murders: Judgments by the Military Tribunal

From the First Military Tribunal (Court-Martial): The following defendants, who have been accused of taking part in the murder, annihilation, and plundering of properties of the Armenians of Erzincan, were investigated and prosecuted: (1) Former District Governor of Erzincan, Memduh Bey, 44 years of age and born in Muğla, transferred to Malta by the Allied Powers while detained by Istanbul's Military House of Detention; (2) 45-year-old Hafız Abdullah Avni Efendi son of Haci Hüseyin, detained in the aforementioned Military House of Detention, a hotelier from Erzincan who was living with his brother-in-law Fevzi Efendi, the Sheikh of Hüsrev Pasha Dergah in Eyüp; (3) Former Deputy of Erzincan Halit; (4) Haci Vahid-zade Efendi from Erzincan; (5) Tribal leader from Dersim, the infamous bandit Karmo Yusuf; (6) gendarme sergeant from Erzincan, Arslan; (7) tribal leader Kagü, director of the Daniz Bey village connected to the Township of Pülümür.

Of these individuals, Hafız Abdullah Avni Efendi, who at the start of the mobilization for war was taken into the employ of the Erzincan Gendarmerie as a so-called clerk instead of being armed for combat, and who, two months prior to the deportation, with the aid of friends whose identity is unknown, under a policy of disarming the populace, did go to the villages and torture and cause injury and pain to the Armenians, causing the death of small children by beating them with bats after demanding that they reveal the whereabouts of weaponry. The aforementioned Hafız Abdullah Avni and former deputy Halit Efendi, Karmo Yusuf, Arslan, and Kagü did with the aid of a specially organized heinous group of unknown individuals, comprising a gang, together at various times around the area of the Zenberek bridge, Tebelli stream, and Kemâh strait within close range of Erzincan, engage in an armed attack of the thousands of Armenians in convoys who had gathered or been sent there for purposes of deportation, including small children and the elderly, and did cause the murder, annihilation, plundering, and seizure of goods of most who had gathered there.

The aforementioned Hafız Abdullah Avni and Riza Efendi likewise, with the aid of their retinue of brigands, did abandon around 70 Armenians in the river and did proceed to fire at those who struggled in the water. Again the aforementioned Hafız Abdullah Avni, with two other friends, did mount horses [and] force themselves into the home of someone by the name of Haçık Efendi within the borders of the Town of Erzincan. Upon hearing the cries of distress from within the house, which brought forth neighbors who ran for help and the aid of several public-spirited officers, he (Haçik Efendi) was saved, thereafter assigning two private guards to stand watch (over his home) until morning.

From the recorded testimonies of many live witnesses who were present it is established that the defendant Hafız Abdullah Avni Efendi did subject Armenians, who had been gathered from villages and brought to Erzincan, to a variety of acts of torture, and that shortly before the end of the deportation, with ID papers and a car which was procured and delivered, was sent in comfort by way of the Sivas road to Edirne to the side of his brother Gani Bey, the inspector for the Committee for Union and Progress.

Based on the sworn testimony of Riza Bey, one of the public officials of the general staff, who at times confessed and other times completely denied responsibility, and factual information which is available and the obvious catastrophe that has occurred, we have come to the conclusion by majority vote and in the presence of the defendant Hafız Abdullah Avni and in the absence of the others who are *in absentio* that the aforementioned Hafız Abdullah Avni and Halit Efendi, Karmo Yusuf, Arslan, and Kagü were the organizing perpetrators of the aforementioned crimes, and that their acts (violate) the 170th article of the Imperial State Criminal Code as guided by paragraph 1 of the 45th article of the aforementioned Code ("If several persons unitedly commit a felony [*jinayet*] or misdemeanor [*junha*] or if a jinayet or junha is composed of several acts and each of a gang of persons perpetrates one or some of such acts with a view to the accomplishment of the offence, such persons are styled accomplices and all of them are punished as sole perpetrators.") and the 171st article of the Military Criminal Code. The relevant passages of the aforementioned articles ("An individual who, with premediation kills another, or who kills a father, mother, or grandparent with or without premediation, will be executed." "[A]n open attack with or without the use of weaponry, and the plundering or destruction of granaries, or provision stocks or wares or property, by a mob, through the breaking down of walls, or doors or by force upon persons, [shall be punishable] by execution") together, having been described herein, and in accordance with judicial authority, the aforementioned Hafız Abdullah Avni, Halit Efendi, Karmo Yusuf, Arslan, and Kagü have been sentenced to be executed.

As to the other defendants, the prosecution of Hacı Vahid-zade Riza Efendi was dismissed upon learning of his recent death. The transfer of Memdûh Bey to Malta and the combined prosecutions under the other article with his accomplice friends dictates that that prosecution be tried separately. Culpability for the aforementioned crimes having been established, it is ruled that separate legal processing be initiated for the following defendants believed to be guilty: (1) former mayor Ahmed Vefik, also the Director of Military Factories and Commander of Erzincan, (2)Major Hafı Süleyman, Former Military Director of Military Preparatory School from Trabzon; (3) Captain Ismâ'il Hakkı, Commander of the Gendarmerie Battalion of Erzincan; (4) Lieutenants Cemil and (5) Süleyman of the Erzincan Gendarmarie; (6) Gendarmarie head sergeant Halit Efendi of Erzincan; (7) Erzincan notable Yaşar Bey; (8) Gendarme "Deli" [crazy] Mehmet of Sivas; (9) Captain Asım, the Assistant Director of the Erzincan Military Preparatory School; and finally (10) Lieutenant "Cezayirli" (Algerian) Mehmet Efendi from the Internal Police of the aforementioned school.

Takvîm-i Vekâyı' *#3917, S. 5 (Mahkûmîyet)*

Erzincan Verdict (Ratification)

Mehmet Vahdeddin

As a result of the investigation and trial that have been conducted regarding the defendants, who are charged with having massacred and annihilated the Armenians of the District of Erzincan and having plundered their property during the deportation, [decisions have been reached] in regard to the following defendants:

Memdûh bin Tayyâr, age 44, born in Muğla, and the former District Governor of Erzincan, who had been previously detained at the military detention center (*tevkîfhâne*), and has [since] been sent to Malta by the Entente countries; Hafız Abdullah Avni Efendi bin Hacı bin Hacı Hüseyin, a 45-year-old resident of Erzincan's Kurşunlu neighborhood and hotel operator in Erzincan, who resides near the abode of his brother in law, Fevzi Efendi, the Sheikh of the Hüsrev Paşa dervish lodge [located] in [the] Eyüb [neighborhood of Istanbul], [who] is currently being held in the aforementioned detention center; former Parliamentary deputy Halet, who is now a fugitive from justice; Erzincanlı Hacı Vahidzade Rıza Efendi; Kırmo Yusuf, a tribal leader from Dersim and notorious bandit; Arslan, a Sergeant in the Erzincan Gendarmerie;

Keko, the tribal head and mayor of the township of Danzik, which is part of the Pülümür district of [the Province of] Erzincan.

A high degree of certainty having been attained in regard to [the aforementioned defendants] having been the perpetrators and planners of the calamities mentioned above, details of which have been recorded in the official report number 27 and dated 9 Şevval 1338 and 26 Haziran 1336 (26 June 1920), the aforenamed Hafız Abdullah Avni Efendi, Halet Efendi, and Kırmo Yûsuf are ruled guilty of [the crime] of having perpetrated and planned the aforementioned calamities.

Furthermore, as their actions fall within the purview of the 170th Article of the Imperial Penal Code for Officials and the 171st Article of the Imperial Military Penal Code and according to the provisions of paragraph 1 of the 45th Article of the former Penal Code, the aforenamed Hafız Abdullah Avni Efendi, Halet Efendi, Kırmo Yûsuf, and finally, Keko are hereby sentenced to death by execution in accordance with the terms of the aforementioned legal articles.

As it has been learned that the defendant Hacı Seyyidzâde Rızâ Efendi has passed away during the course of the trial, the civil case [against him] has been ruled dismissed.

As for Memdûh Bey, since he has been transferred to Malta and is [currently] being tried, along with his other companions, on another charge, he is to be tried separately, in order that [he] may be prosecuted together [at some time] in the future.

The following defendants are understood to have been charged with the aforementioned crimes: Mayor Ahmed Refik Bey, the former Commandant and director of the military industries in Erzincan; Major Hafız Süleyman Bey from Trabzon, the former principal of the Erzincan Military Preparatory School; Captain Ismail Hakkı, the Commander of the Ezincan Gendarmerie Regiment; Lieutenants in the Erzincan Gendarmerie Cemil and Süleyman Efendis; Gendarmerie Chief Sergeant Erzincanlı Halit Efendi; Erzincan notable Yaşar Bey; the Gendarme "Crazy Mehmet" from Sivas; Captain Asım, the Assistant Principal of the Erzincan Military Preparatory School; and Lieutenant Cezayirli Mehmet Efendi, an administrative officer at the aforementioned school.

In regard to their legal prosecution, in light of the fact that they are all [currently] in absentia, save for Hafız Abdullah Avni Efendi, who is present for trial, they are to be retried subsequent to their being apprehended [by the authorities].

This ruling and decision, which was rendered by the First Extraordinary Court Martial of Istanbul, has been ratified.

The Minister of War has been entrusted with executing this Imperial Decree.

10 Zilkade 1338 27 Temmuz 1336 (27 July 1920)

On behalf of the Grand Vizier,
Abdullah (signature)

On behalf of the Acting Minister of War,
Ahmed Hamdi (signature)

Takvîm-i Vekâyi' #3772, s. 3–6: İTC Kâtib-i Mes'ûlleri (Karar Sureti)

CUP Responsible Secretaries and Delegates Verdict

After weighing the assertions, explanations, and defenses of both sides, which were heard at length in regard to the current trial, and thoroughly studying and examining all of the documents in the case and the transcripts of the proceedings, the matter was studied thoroughly in all of its aspects in the course of the necessary deliberations.

Whereupon, as a result of the investigations carried out by the offices responsible for interrogation in regard to the Party Secretaries and Delegates of the [now-] disbanded Committee of Union and Progress (hereafter referred to as "the Committee" or "CUP"), among whose well-documented [actions include] having prepared, in the period following the armistice, the means to disrupt the peace and public order by stirring up enmity and discord in almost every part of the country, these aforementioned Party Secretaries and Delegates were apprehended. It would have been improper to allow them to cause even greater damage to the homeland by leaving them free to [conduct] villainous deeds. Upon the announcement through a circular from the Interior Ministry that they had been seized and sent under armed guard to the First Extraordinary Military Tribunal, along with the investigative records upon which their [forthcoming] prosecution is based, they were [once again] taken and, in turn, delivered over to our Military Tribunal.

The comprehensive nature of the situation, deeds, and subjects were addressed in the accusations which appeared during their trial, [which was held] upon their being sent to our Military Tribunal on the suspicion that they were accessories in the aforementioned criminal actions of the Committee [of Union and Progress]. The [suspicions revolved around] their [the party secretaries and delegates] having supported, been the active agents and the means of implementing, the broad goals and aspirations of the now defunct CUP. This organization subjected [the country] to enormous disasters by taking the overall power of the state into its usurping hand and under the reins of its administration, and through unlawful actions such as participation in the World War, profiteering [with vital commodities], deportations, massacres, banishments and expulsions of persons, and the like. The Ottoman Realms were thereby afflicted, internally, with the greatest degree of privation and all manner of calamity and externally, by the subverting of the power and prestige of the state.

The crimes and actions were examined and studied from the two [different] angles—the first collective, and the second personal and individual—and as is described later, were put on the record. After which the following [decision] was written and recorded:

We find that there are decisive proofs and clear evidence which prove that the various instances of atrocities [and] the sequence of events and the regularity of massacres indicate that they were planned by the CUP Central Committee, in connection with the Special Organization, and were prepared and facilitated by certain representatives and members of the aforementioned [Central] Committee. Namely, the following findings [which lend support to this conclusion] are set forth:

Though some of the defendants claimed that their primary duty consisted of organizing and improving the social and economic conditions of the population, improving of the conditions and housing of the poor, ensuring and realizing the election of their party's candidates by means of lawful and orderly propaganda during the elections, and ameliorating the needs of the nation by guiding and enlightening them in every matter, on the contrary, they strayed far from these stated goals;

By exercising their influence to order the confiscation of certain properties against the will of their owners, and engaging individuals from the labor battalions [to work in them], these individuals built clubhouses. They took over the residences of some Armenians who had been deported and furnished them with the plundered property [of the latter]. Not being content [with the task] to guide and enlighten during the periods of elections, and driven by self-seeking goals and aspirations, their ongoing actions within society [in fact] reflected excessive interference [in the functions of government] and oppression [of the population] by way of reliance upon the tyrannical force that they represented.

Through various means they threatened and intimidated those who, despite this policy of terror, showed [even] a modicum of opposition by displaying the civilized courage to utilize their clear legal right [of political opposition]. [What is more,] they blocked the lawful opposition that is necessary for [the proper functioning of] the Constitutional Government, and they thereby established a despotic regime that was in no way different from [that of] the absolutist regime [of Abdulhamit II].

They had the temerity to participate in [acts of] beating, insulting, illegal detention, and arrest of those who indicated in the presence of the responsible government officials that they did not have the ability to make any more payments during the collection of ["voluntary" donations for] assistance and the sale of the shares of domestic bonds. Likewise, they had the audacity to embrace the criminal decisions adopted by the CUP Central Committee, which was the locus where the vital issues of the state were [ultimately] discussed and resolved and thereby perpetrated [various] crimes, especially deportations, massacres, and the hoarding of wealth through the [illegal] seizure of property.

It is evident and apparent that the conditions surrounding the deportations, which were carried out under the Temporary Law of 14 Mayıs, [13]31 (27 May 1915), were exploited as a pretext for personal gain. Some of the aforementioned party secretaries and delegates had recourse to and activated the necessary means especially in particular in regard to the massacre and annihilation of the Armenians and the looting and plundering of their property and possessions. This was carried out by the evil and perverted gangs that the aforementioned Central Committee organized and outfitted among the [various] outlaw bands [found within] their network of organizations and [who] actively facilitated the acquisition of abandoned property.

The coded telegraph sent from Erzurum by Bahaeddin Şakir Bey, a member of the aforementioned Central Committee and the Head of the Special Organization, to the [now] fugitive Resneli Nazım Bey, [who was the] Party Secretary for [the Province of] Mamuretülaziz (Elazığ), which stated "Are the Armenians, whom you reported having been sent off, being annihilated?"

The dismissal of the former District Governor of Yozgad, Cemal Bey, for his opposition to the situation of annihilating [the Armenian deportees], which had been proposed by the Party Secretary [for the Province of] Ankara, Necati Bey, as was revealed during [the latter's] trial by our Military Tribunal for the crimes of massacre in the Provincial District of Yozgad and the County of Boğazlıyan, [and] the appointment, upon the dismissal of the aforementioned Cemal Bey, of the Boğazlıyan County Executive, Kemal, as Acting District Governor of Yozgad, who was later hanged.

As is explained further on, the fact that the Armenians of [the Province of] Kastamonu were a very small minority in relation to the overall population, and that relative to the Law on Deportation there were no antecedent violations by them, formed the basis for the firm opposition to their deportation by Governor-General Reşid Paşa ("I won't bloody my hands"), who is clearly shown to have been dismissed as a result of the persistent efforts of the Party Secretary for [the Province of] Kastamonu, Hasan Fehmi Efendi. Atif Bey, who had carried out and completed the deportation and atrocities [in] Ankara, was brought in to replace him.

The Party Secretary for [the Province of] Bolu Dr. [Ahmed] Midhat Bey's having the acting District Governor of the aforementioned provincial district, Ali İlmi Bey, dismissed for the same reasons, [namely] on account of his opposition to the Bolu deportations, which took place through the guidance and influence of [Dr. Midhat], who organized a demonstration [at which] he told the crowd, "We don't want the Armenians."

The deportation was carried out in a manner [so as] to include every part [of the country], in contradiction to the spirit behind the wording of the Law on Deportation.

[Having thus established the involvement and responsibility of the CUP Central Committee and its adjunct, the Special Organization, for the crimes in question,] we now come to [the questions of] their level of participation. [The existence of] said crimes has been proven, and, in view of the nature of the explanations for the[-ir] deeds, each one of the [defendants] was understood to have been personally and individually culpable. Nevertheless, the aforementioned crimes which were carried out in this manner cannot be attributed to all of the defendants as a whole.

From the spoken testimonies of the witnesses, the former governor of Kastamonu, Reşid Pasha, referred to Hasan Fehmi Efendi in his testimony as a "dangerous creature" and offered the following evidence in regard to the aforementioned defendant, who was the Party Secretary for [the Province of] Kastamonu:

1) Hasan Fehmi Efendi continuously enraged and incited the Muslim population [of Kastamonu] against the Armenians, poisoning the [social] environment by [uttering] such nonsense [about] the former Governor General of Kastamonu [Province], Reşid Paşa, as: "Our Governor-General is the defender of the Armenians, or more correctly, he's the governor-general of the infidels";

2) Reşid Paşa demanded from the Interior Ministry by way of [a] code[-d telegram] that, just as he had been ejected from government circles due to his having run himself ragged through his obstinate meddling in governmental affairs, Hasan Fehmi Efendi should be kicked out of the province due to his [ever]-increasing impudence;

3) One witness, retired Major Ismail Hakkı Bey, claimed to have heard that Hasan Fehmi Efendi had been among those who took very valuable possessions from the abandoned property [of the Armenian deportees];

4) Another witness, the son of the late Field Marshall Asıf Paşa, Cemal Bey, [testified as to] the presence of commercial wares in Hasan Fehmi Efendi's house and [this] at the time of the [CUP] club's burning [which] were the greatest evidence of his misuse of the abandoned property;

5) The aforementioned [defendant] was a companion of Governor-General Atıf Bey during the deportations and shared his ideas [on the operations];

6) Yet another witness, Vâhid Efendi, [claimed] that he profited quite handsomely from the abandoned property by virtue of Hasan Fehmi Efendi's agency, influence, and power during the deportations;

7) [The statements] in the memorandum of Hurşîd Bey, who is the retired Commander of the Ninth Regular Army Regiment and presently serving as district official, [in which he states] that according to [the aforementioned] Reşid Paşa, Hasan Fehmi Efendi interfered in the affairs of government and [even] took control of them during the tenure of Atıf Bey;

8) Major Mustafa Şeref Bey, who was previously [stationed] in [the Province of] Kastamonu and is today the Commander of the Gendarmerie Regiment of Silifke, testified that a rift had occurred between Governer Atıf Bey and the late Izzet Bey, who had served in the gendarmerie regiment of Kastamonu during the deportation before passing away and who had believed that the deportations would not bring about any good. [Mustafa Şeref] further testified that

Hasan Fehmi Efendi had said of the late İzzet Bey, "History and his successors shall curse İzzet Bey for having opposed the deportation of the Armenians";

9) The witnesses Cevdet and Salim Efendis and others, [who testified] that, upon joining the Commission on Abandoned Property, Hasan Fehmi Efendi entered the abandoned shops with the members of the aforementioned Commission before the public auction and, by means of his own people, removed items he needed for himself in sacks and baskets, and that [only] afterward were the shutters of the shops opened and the auction announced, and that, because Hasan Fehmi Efendi possessed greater influence than the Governor-General, [the latter] never even considered preventing his actions;

10) The accounts that have been heard of Hacı Tevfîk, a notable of Kastamonu, former Chief Secretary of the Administrative Council Besîm Bey, the professor Hoca Mehmet Efendi, the merchant Ahmed, the attorney İzzet Efendi, whose testimony was taken by deposition, and the district official Celal Bey, whose testimony was heard in court, all of which corroborate and confirm (*müeyyed ve müsbet*) the ongoing [instances of] atrocities, unauthorized interferences, and abuses.

[As for] the former Party Secretary for [the Province of] Bolu, and currently for [the Province of Bursa], Dr. Midhat Bey, although during the period in which he was Party Secretary for Bolu the Armenian population was exempted from deportation by the government on the basis of their small numbers, from the contents of the complaints [he made] in this matter and the official communications the following facts are evident:

1) Exercising his influence, [Dr. Midhat] organized a demonstration [at which] he proclaimed to the population, "We don't want the Armenians";
2) He [Dr. Midhat] had the acting District Governor of Bolu, Ali İlmî Bey, dismissed [from his post] when he [showed] opposition to the deportations;
3) He went to Düzce in order to deport the Armenians [there], as was officially communicated in the memorandum of the Office of the District Governor of Bolu;
4) When in Bursa, he also acted to facilitate the deportation [there] in this manner, and, as a result, [there were] calamities that followed from it; He also procured and accumulated monetary contributions in Gemlik in order to exercise his power and influence upon some of the city's notables, and to exercise [this] influence during the parliamentary elections as well as to assist in the purchase of the [local] CUP club.

As for CUP Inspector for [the Province of] Edirne, Abdülgani Bey, the following facts have come to light:

1) As was clear from the contents of the investigation documents attached to the memorandums from the Province of Edirne, dated 27 and 31 Tem-

muz, [1]335 (27 and 31 July 1919), [Abdülgani Bey] adopted a domineering and influential attitude and stance over government officials during the parliamentary elections for the seats in Kırkkilise and Demir Köy;

2) Sporting the title of inspector, he did not refrain from exercising his influence even as far as upon the provincial government. It has been understood that he exerted pressure to gather contributions and collection of [monetary] assistance in his own name from the [Committee for] National Defense;
3) It has been proven [by] the reports of Artin and Ohannes Altunyan, Aleksan Sarrafyan, Hayk Kürkçüyan, Leon Marakçıyan and others, whose testimonies have been recorded by the Examining Magistrate of Edirne, that:
   a) Abdülgani Bey was an influential factor in the deportations which resulted in the annihilation and destruction of a good number of Armenians;
   b) He roamed around during the deportations with gangs of armed hooligans;
   c) When the Armenians were sent off from the police station their money was taken from them on the aforementioned [Abdülgani']'s orders;
   d) He had the cassimere and textile shop of the Kazazyan brothers, which was worth one hundred thousand lira, given to his own son Hayrullah in exchange for one thousand lira, and he had the abandoned property [of the Armenian deportees] given to other followers at very low prices;
4) In the recorded testimony of the aforementioned Abdülgani Bey, it was evident that he became influential and powerful not on the basis of his humane deeds and virtue, but from his enrichment at the hands of the Armenians Avadisyan and Aleksanyan Efendis, whom [Abdülgani Bey] admitted to having exempted from the deportation through a [special] request to the governor-general. After excluding them from deportation, or more accurately, annihilation, he then took over a share in their business;
5) Although in every location, more or less every one of those deported was granted a temporary reprieve from deportation, the deportees from Edirne were left devoid of the means of subsistence when their clothing, money, and valuable possessions were taken [from them] during searches [of them], after which they were deported without delay from Edirne to Tekfûrdağı (Tekirdağ);
6) As Abdülgani Bey touched on and alluded to during his trial, these incidents were motivated by the desire for revenge that had been present [since] the occupation of Edirne;
7) Likewise, although the aforementioned Abdülgani Bey declared that the aforementioned deportation, which was conducted from Edirne, consisted of the transporting of only one convoy [and] over the period of one

night, in the communicated reply of the [government of the] Province of Edirne, his account was refuted by the statement that a portion of those, who were deported in three [separate] convoys, were sent as far as Deir Zor (Syria);

8) As a matter in furtherance of the public good and as one of a number of measures to which they resorted in order to conceal their wicked deeds, a CUP Orphanage was built with[in the confines of] the Unionist Club building. By wielding the Law of Eminent Domain as a tool, he ordered the property expropriated at a low price and then had the appraised price paid for out of the club's treasury;
9) Among these measures, he (Abdülgani Bey) undertook to decree, of his own accord, the expropriation of the house belonging to Mahtûme Hanım. Upon the entreaty to the Interior Ministry—and Abdülgani Bey admitted during questioning that [there had been such] an entreaty—by Nuri Bey's brother-in-law Ahmed Efendi, who did not accede to the aforementioned price, [Abdülgani Bey] said: "There is [only] one rich man in Edirne, and no other. Let him make [all] the entreaties [he wants], I assessed his house at three hundred lira and [he won't get] one lira more out of it";
10) He managed to acquire and set to work in the aforementioned [Unionist] club one hundred and twenty persons from the labor battalions, which had been put into service exclusively in the forced-labor construction projects during the most critical period of the army's mobilization;
11) It is understood from the communicated reply of the Ministry of War that such a situation was unprecedented in both the [Office of] General Provisioning and the aforementioned ministry.

These instances are a part of the evidence which strengthen the reports, aforementioned proofs, and circumstantial evidence regarding how the aforementioned Abdülgani Bey acquired unlawful power and influence over the affairs and operations of government.

In summation, it has been decided that the aforementioned defendants Hasan Fehmi Efendi, Dr. Midhat Bey, Abdülgani Bey, Avni Bey, Dr. Besim Zühdi Bey, Hasan Salahittin Bey, Cemal Bey, Münir Bey, Cevdet Bey, and Abdulkâdir Efendi are convicted of the crime of altering the [lawful] form of government, of which they have been accused. Furthermore, because it has not been confirmed or proven that any of the defendants, other than Hasan Fehmi [Efendi and] [Dr.] Midhat, Abdülgani, and Cevdet Beys, committed the acts of destroying the internal security [of the country], or were accessories in the acts of massacre and the plundering of property, they are acquitted of the aforementioned [charges].

As for the defendants Hasan Fehmi Efendi and Dr. Midhat and Abdülgani Beys, they are convicted of being accessories in the crimes of massacre and the plundering of property, which were committed and carried out as a result of their facilitation and support of the illegal actions of the [CUP] Central Committee, and of the deportations, [and] through their having knowingly assisted, from beginning to end, the main perpetrators in the actions that took place.

[As for] Avni Bey, the sworn testimonies of the witnesses heard [here] on this matter [averred] that, when he was a member of the commission that was formed during the period in which the domestic bonds were being registered, he assaulted and unlawfully arrested Herdem, Mağnisalı (Manisalı) Hacı Hasan, Ismail, and Mehmet from the village of Saruhan while ordering them to commit themselves to [purchase of] the shares of the domestic bonds against their will and beyond their abilities to pay.

There were also the declarations by those who have been unjustly treated, as well as his own admission that he was a member of the aforementioned commission, and that he had the audacity to undertake these illegal acts right under the nose of the responsible government officials. On the basis of this evidence, it has been decided by majority opinion that the aforementioned [defendant Avni Bey] possessed great influence, and was the perpetrator of the aforementioned acts of striking, insulting, and unlawful arrest of persons.

As for Besim Zühdi Bey, in regard to Rafail Şirpenyan Efendi's claim that [Zühdî Bey] took his carpets:

1) It has been confirmed by his own [Besim Zühdi Bey's] confession and in the course of the investigation that he did [indeed] obtain the carpets [in question];
2) The formal petitions dated 1 and 9 Teşrîn-i sânî, [13]35 (1 and 9 November 1919) and found on pages 124 and 126 of the interrogation record put forward the proposition that the matter was more one of buying and selling than of taking and seizing, especially since the carpets were later returned to their owner;
3) The prosecution's agreement that the defense claims should be considered at the close of the trial, and the defense witnesses, who by court request have been heard in this regard, have [testified] in favor of the aforementioned [defendant].

It has likewise been decided by a majority decision that this case, which is in the nature of a business transaction [that took place] before the deportations, shall be taken up and resolved by the local court. Therefore, on account of there being no further cause for their detention, the afore-named Besim Zühdi Bey, Cemal Bey, Münir Bey, and Abdulkâdir Efendi are to be released.

[As for] Cevdet Bey, although he has been indicted in regard to the Büyükdere deportations and an investigation of him has been undertaken in the Office of the Examining Magistrate, it was reported by the aforementioned office that there appeared no legal need to detain him any longer on this matter. Therefore, if there is no further cause for his detention [while] continuing the investigation in this matter, he is to be released.

Hasan Salahittin Bey is acquitted of [the crime of] hoarding and price gouging, as it could not be proven that he had undertaken [such acts]. It was nevertheless proposed by the Procurer General's Office that by participating in the abuses of Head of Provisioning Ismail Hakkı (while the latter was Head of the Directorate of Mills) and the [CUP] Central Committee member and former Commissariat (Food Supplies) Minister Kemal Bey, he had caused a number of disasters to occur. However, since he is not [currently] being tried on the [latter] issue, and this accusation would have to be written up as a memorandum to the Office of the Procurer General in order for an investigation to be undertaken, one cannot detain him on this matter, and on account of there being no further cause for detaining him, it is unanimously decided that he should be released.

As for Hayreddin and Âğâh Beys, it has been suggested that the bowl belonging to Kodayan Maksûr was found recorded as having been sold. However, as it was difficult for our court to investigate the falsification of properly clarified registries, to review account [records], or [to determine] of what sort of things the alleged abuses consisted of, and in view of the fact that upon this matter being understood as [to have consisted of] abuse of official position in accordance with the opinion of the Legal Advisor of the Finance Ministry, it was demanded, through the memorandum dated 30 Ağustos, [13]35 (30 August 1919), that the matter be taken up and resolved within the framework of the Law on Trials of Officials. In consideration of the testimony of Virjin, Âğâh Bey and Hayreddin Bey's demand for acquittal on this matter is rejected, due to the fact that they were indeed found to be jointly involved in [such abuses] and it was decided by a majority vote to return this matter to the Office of the Procuror General separately so that the requirements of the law might be carried out in regard to the demand of the Finance Ministry concerning them and [those in regard to] Hayreddin and Kosti Efendis.

Finally, as a result of [our] deliberations in regard to the punishment [of those convicted] the following decisions were reached:

The convicts Hasan Fehmi [Efendi] and [Dr.] Midhat Bey are each sentenced, according to the provisions of the 170th Article of the [Imperial] Penal Code [for Officials], to which their actions correspond, and in conformity with paragraph 2 of the 45th Article [of the aforementioned Code], to 10 years hard labor, to [be considered to have] commence[-d] from the moment of their arrest.

Abdülgani Bey's punishment shall be subject to the outcome of the trial on the Edirne deportations, in which the aforementioned is also being tried.

Avni Bey is sentenced, in accordance with the 203rd Article of [Imperial] Penal Code for Officials, to nine months imprisonment, beginning from 17 Şubat, [13]35 (17 February 1919), which was the start of his detention. Furthermore, in light of this date of his detention, the period of his sentence has been completed, and thus, if there is no further cause for his being detained, he is to be released.

This decision was rendered by a majority vote in the presence of all of the defendants other than Âğâh Bey, who is in absentia.

16 Rebî'ü'l-âhir [1]338 8 Kânûn-u Sânî [1]336 (8 January 1920)
Member, [Extraordinary Military Tribunal]
Major General (General Staff)
Mustafa Kerimi

As shall be shown in these official transcripts, we are only opposed to the decision in regard to Besim Zühdi Bey.

Member, [Extraordinary Military Tribunal]
Major General (General Staff)
Ismail Hakkı

President, [Extraordinary Military Tribunal]
Major General (General Staff)
Es'ad

Our opposition to the decision that has been adopted, firstly, from the point of view of procedure and legal practices; secondly, in regard to the matter of the description and definition of the nature of guilt; and thirdly, due to the crimes that are attributed to the persons of the defendants Hasan Fehmi [Efendi], [Dr.] Midhat Bey, and Avni Bey, shall be recorded in the transcripts, fully describing the reasons for [our] dissent.

Member, [Extraordinary Military Tribunal]
Colonel (Infantry)
Süleyman Şakir

Member, [Extraordinary Military Tribunal]
Colonel (General Staff)
İhsan

Takvîm-i Vekâyı' *#3604, S. 217–220 (Karar Sureti)*

The Key Verdict against Cabinet Ministers and Top CUP Leaders

After the assertions, explanations, and defenses of both sides had been heard in the current trial, and all of the documents in the case were thoroughly studied and examined, the requisite matters were discussed. Although both the defendants and their attorneys have denied the accusations and demanded [their] acquittals in the indictments [submitted by] the Procuror General's Office and dated 3, 20, and 22 Mayıs [13]35 and 9, 10, and 25 Haziran [13]35, the [now] disbanded CUP is presented by their moral personality, which is the suspect in numerous [illegal] actions and crimes.

Before the trials and punishments were demanded for the members of the [CUP] General Assembly, which stands in for the aforementioned moral personality and whose members are [being tried here as] the [principal] perpetrators of the crimes under discussion, circumstances appeared to necessitate a reexamination of the case regarding the aforementioned Committee. Yet, while certain individuals' deeds and actions predating the establishment of the aforementioned Committee were weighed in the balance because their intentions and designs derived from the patriotic sentiments before the [1908] Revolution remain unknown, only th[-ose] actions and deeds which have occurred since the Revolution are summarized below.

The [following facts] have been made clear from the examinations and investigations that were carried out and [from] the contents of the aforementioned indictments.

Interpreting the agitation that issued forth from the mountains [around] Resne on the ninth day of July [in] the year [1]324, as the pure water of liberty and as a heavenly cure, the Ottomans, who thirsted for liberty and justice, believed with all their hearts that [this movement] was the only sound remedy for the ailments of oppression and corruption. They labored with complete sincerity and obedience to facilitate all the actions by allowing [every] tendency and current [complete] freedom to [follow] whichever course it wished with absolutely no hindrance to its [increasing its] influence and domination. [They did this] with great indulgence, in the expectation that the raging swell would run its natural course, and in the hope that after it had run its course, it would bring justice and liberty to every corner of the vast Ottoman realms. The [people's] powers of endurance were reinforced through the sweet-sounding voices that were occasionally heard from this movement, and efforts were made to assuage the general dismay of the public by portraying each one of the many parts of the Ottoman realm that were taken [away] on one pretext or another due to political errors committed during that period as having been [the result] of the evils of the former era.

The appearance [of a situation] contrary to their hopes and expectations had grieved and afflicted the seekers of liberty, and the uninterrupted hardships and grievous outcomes of the Italian and Balkan Wars left no doubt that even though much time had passed since the restoration of liberty, no serious effort had been made to determine and pursue a course for the sound administration for the country and to discover the causes for the succession of disasters [that had befallen it]. [Even worse,] some of those who were believed to have been working toward the realization of national aspirations had instead strayed onto utterly wrong paths and been carried away by goals [stemming from] personal ambition.

These disturbing actions, which the nation had [at first] understood as the pure waters of liberty, brought the country to a sorry state, destroying, [figuratively speaking], some parts by flood, devastating others by drought. Then, reckless persons who suddenly appeared among them with ideas of their own making took advantage of this, diverting the government administration from its course. They (the Committee) created a committee of activists consisting of persons whom they would be able to secretly delude and deceive, over and over again, all the while outwardly displaying an ardent adherence to the law. Then, by consciously and tirelessly laboring to take control of the government, both through themselves and their representatives in the provinces, and finally getting the Council of Ministers [to agree to] their own opinions and decisions, they fully succeeded in [achieving] their aforementioned aims.

As was explicitly declared in the recent testimonies of [then] Finance Minister Cavid Bey, which are recorded in the transcripts of the Chamber of Deputies' Fifth Department for the dates 24–26 Teşrîn-i sânî (November) [1]334, the CUP's action committee displayed a great deal of self-righteousness and arrogance in the matter of determining and securing the fate of the nation and the country. So much so that, when it was understood by all that they [the CUP] had not even seen the need to submit to the Council of Ministers the decision to declare war, something [regarding] which not even the sovereign himself had expressed his opinion or wishes, [it was clear] that no good would result from administering matters in this manner. Even actions which the opposition had shown respect for [now] were criticized by persons of insight and intelligence. They [the CUP] ordered the uninterrupted continuation of Martial Law, [the proclamation of] which had been declared as necessary at the outset of the Revolution and which was [now] declared [again as a result of] the actions of the Committee.

After the killing of the Minister of War, Nazım Paşa, and his aide, and the toppling of the Kâmil Paşa Cabinet through a combined assault on the Sublime Porte by a group directed by the leaders of the Committee, Committee members were appointed to successive cabinet posts. The existing experienced, honorable, and capable officials were ejected from their posts. [These and other similar events] gave everyone sincere cause for complaint against the arbitrary administration and despotism, which was so widespread as to cause people to long for the [Hamidian] Period of Absolutism. Non-Muslims displayed even greater amounts of dissatisfaction. [Upon] perceiving that their [previously held] conviction that our esteemed Constitutional Regime would assure [them] security and justice was misguided, [some groups]—in particular, the Armenians—[reverted] to their previous[-ly held] opinions [that] their national aspirations could yet be attained. [What was more,] it [encouraged] all to adopt an opportunistic attitude, and the ideas of separatism and alienation were implanted in the minds of the [non-Muslim] elements [of the population], and even [in the minds] of Muslims, through the introduction of the questions of peoplehood and nationhood. [Thus] was Ottoman unity destroyed.

Furthermore, as there exists no possibility of rejecting or refuting the five points which are mentioned below and which were ordered verified by our Military Tribunal, the inner conviction has been formed by our [entire] panel that the [afore-]mentioned "Action Committee" carried out those political crimes under discussion which are attributable to and connected with the moral personality of the CUP, and in a manner that could sully the name of this Committee.

Therefore, the exigencies of justice would appear to dictate that the actions [comprising] the abovementioned crimes that were carried out in this manner cannot be charged or attributed to the Committee members as a whole. Rather, they demand that the provisions of the law be carried out against those who are implicated in participating in the aforementioned crimes according to their level of involvement as determined.

While pleading his case, the defense attorney made the following assertions:

1) The existence of political parties [derives] from the needs of the Constitutional Regime;
2) In our country today there are other parties;
3) The Liberty and Entente Party also possessed a central committee and general assembly, as well as [provincial] branches, just like the CUP, and they [too] invited individuals who were [both government] ministers and party members to their [party] assemblies.

As a result of the discussions which were held in response to these assertions, [it was determined that], while the existence of factions and parties is [indeed] necessary and vital for governments operating within a Constitutional Regime, with regard to the stages of this trial, the aforementioned arguments of the [defense] attorney cannot appear to possess any relevance for the defense because these [parties] are utterly unable to interfere with the duties belonging to the executive branch of government. Furthermore, after achieving their goals, which are directed toward securing a majority in their [respective] national assemblies, the[-se parties must] allow complete freedom of opinion and interpretation to the cabinets in which they demonstrate their confidence. There naturally emanates from this principle the dictate that the[-se parties] may not involve themselves in matters [of state] apart from laboring [to ensure] that the laws that are constructed are created in a manner in line with their own programs. They may exert pressure on those cabinets whose actions they do not agree with to resign, though not by threat [of violence] but instead by demonstrations of no-confidence and such.

[Furthermore], in regard to the parties in our country, just as it is self-evident that no party could emerge that would declare [itself to be in] a majority before the Ottoman National Assembly was opened, it is also clear that every group that would dare to act contrary to the Constitution, such as [by] trying to influence or affect the executive branch of government or by changing of the lawful form of government, would be subject to the same fate.

The [afore-]mentioned five points are as follows:

First—The evidence shows that the crimes of massacre which occurred in Trabzon, Yozgad, and Boğazlıyan, and which were verified as a result of the trials that were held in the Military Tribunal, were ordered planned and carried out by persons found among the leadership of the CUP. Furthermore, as was presented during the defense['s case], [although] there were those who became aware of the crimes after their occurrence, the[-se persons] made no effort whatsoever to prevent their repetition or stop the perpetrators of the previous crimes.

Second—It has been understood from the contents of the recorded statements of the former Grand Vizier Sa'îd Halim Paşa before the Parliament, that, although he spoke to the members of the Central Committee, whom he had invited to his mansion on the Bosporus at the beginning of the General Mobilization and explained at length that it would be very dangerous to enter the war and that the best position for the state would be neutrality (producing evidence to support this), he was unable to persuade [the others] to accept his position and the country thereby became engaged in war.

Additionally, it was admitted during the trial of the CUP Party Secretary for Trabzon, Riza Bey, that offensive assaults were made by means of armed gangs that had been organized in Trabzon, and whom he [Rızâ Bey] had sent into Russian territories before a formal declaration of war had been made. He also claimed that because war was declared before [the decision] could be properly taken under consideration by the Council of Ministers, and because it led to the resignations at that time of Cavid Bey, who was then in the Finance Ministry, Çürüksulu Mahmûd Paşa, Minister of Public Works, and Oskan Efendi, Post, Telegram and Telegraph (PTT) Minister, and the Minister of Commerce Süleyman El-Bustani, the decision to enter the war was chosen [solely] on account of its having been the [path] favored and intended by the CUP not the Council of Ministers.

Third—It emerges from the recorded testimonies of His Excellency the former Grand Vizier Ahmed İzzet Paşa that his resignation from the Ministry of War was due to the conflict arising from his opposition and reaction to the [Union and Progress] Party's interference.

Fourth—From the contents of a draft (*lâyiha*) read and enthusiastically accepted at the [1]332 (1916) [CUP Party] Congress, and from the addendum found in a memorandum arriving from the Prefecture [of Istanbul] and sent in reply to the request for an explanation in this matter, the following facts are evident: the [CUP] took over absolute control of a Chamber of Commerce, formed by the [Unionist] Delegate of Istanbul, Kemal Bey, who had been entrusted by the CUP's Istanbul Centr[-al Committee] with [all] matters concerning provisioning and whose appointment was subsequently accepted by both the [CUP] General Assembly and [party] congress, [and] followed by [additional] control of certain companies and societies along with commercial transactions, were eventually controlled [by this group]. This allowed for the confiscation from the general population of everything they possessed, and for their wealth to be handed over to a [limited] number of persons and to the aforementioned companies, actions which caused a great number of Ottoman citizens to either fall ill, become crippled, or perish entirely from starvation. In conclusion, the CUP's Istanbul Centr[-ral Committee] caused the government's defensive strength to be weakened, thereby attaining a position enabling it to interfere in tasks germane to the government.

Fifth—Former Sheikh ul-Islam Musa Kâzım Efendi's statement, in response to the question posed during the discussion in the Senate on the transferring of the Sharī'a Courts to the Ministry of Justice, stated: "Don't ask [for] my opinion. The party wants it this way, and that's the way it shall be," and his explanation and confirmation of the aforementioned matter during his trial also confirm the party's interference in state affairs.

As has been confirmed by these five points enumerated above, as understood from word of mouth and from other matters that have been revealed, the state ministers were forced, through [CUP] interference, [to act] in accordance with their [the CUP's] private aims and goals when a significant portion of state affairs were blocked by them. It has thus been made clear that through intimidation the legal framework of the Ottoman government was transformed and deformed by the creation of a fourth power above the three powers [executive, legislative, and judicial] that make up its lawful form.

Therefore, it has been decided unanimously that: former Grand Vizier Talaat Paşa, and former Minister of War Enver Efendi and former Minister of the Navy Cemal Efendi—both of whom have since been banished from the ranks of the military—and former Minister of Education Dr. Nazım Efendi, all of whom are currently fugitives and are members of the [CUP] General Assembly, who represent the moral personality of the CUP, are found guilty of having been principal perpetrators of the previously discussed crimes. As for former Minister of Finance Cavid Bey and Minister of Commerce and Agriculture Mustafa Şeref Bey, who were also members of the aforementioned assembly and are likewise fugitives, they are also found guilty of having been accessories [in the aforementioned crimes].

As for Şeyhül-islam Musa Kâzım Efendi, who was also a member of the aforementioned General Assembly and who is present for trial, it was repeatedly suggested in the declarations of [both] his attorney and of the Procuror-General that, on account of his having been a man of virtue and maturity and an accomplished scholar of religious law and of his superior character his participation in the aforementioned crimes is unthinkable. Nevertheless, the following considerations must be taken into account:

1) his presence since the beginning of the Revolution among the ranks of the leading and most influential members of the aforementioned Committee;
2) his having been a factor in preventing the correction of false beliefs and assumptions, through [his] presentation of the Committee's actions as reasonable and lawful, among the ignorant and poorly educated members of the populace despite the high opinion in which he is held by his attorney and the aforementioned procuror-general;
3) his declaration during his trial, [in response] to the question that was asked concerning certain written works and sermons whose contents were contrary to the Sharī'a Law, that he had not seen the[-se] works, even though he had [also] declared [during his trial] that he administered the CUP's department of theology and religion;
4) his admission that he made no effort whatsoever to prevent the aforementioned matters, even though he explained that he did not approve of the matters mentioned in the sermon in which they were found;
5) his likening the departure from the CUP to abandoning the Islamic faith, during the trial;
6) his proving that he possesses a mindset that cannot be reconciled with the character of virtue and maturity that was [previously] claimed [for him].

While such things might well be considered to be aggravating circumstances from the defendant's ongoing cross-examination and investigation, he was not found to be among the main authors of the crimes under discussion, due to his exclusive engagement with the Committee's department of theology and [thus], it has been decided that he was an accessory [in the crimes of which he is accused] and he is found guilty by a two-thirds vote [of the court].

As for the former member of the Senate, Rıf'at Bey, because his connection with the CUP could not be [definitively] established and as it is understood that he did not participate in the actions or crimes under discussion, the court has unanimously ruled to acquit him [of all charges]. Moreover, in case he is not being detained for any other cause of action, he shall be released from custody.

In regard to former Post and Telegraph Minister Haşim Bey, investigations have corroborated his testimony in regard to the following matters:

1) he was elected [to be Postal and Telegraph Minister] without his solicitation [for the post] while he was in Berlin:
2) despite his [attempts to] excuse [himself], he was appointed [anyway] upon his return to Istanbul;
3) because the period of his ministry did not coincide with the last years of the Unionist Cabinet, he had not initiated [any] discussions, outside of th[ose on the party's] code of internal regulations, in the General Assembly, which he [in any case] only attended three times, and even in these discussions he did not participate actively but only as a listener.

Therefore it has been decided by a majority vote to acquit him [of all charges], and, as he is not being held on any other grounds, he is to be released [from custody].

As for the matter of sentencing due to the enormity of the crimes that are [represented by] the actions of the aforementioned defendants, as per the provisions of paragraph 1 of the 45th Article of the Imperial Penal Code for Government Officials in regard to Talaat, Enver, Cemal, and Dr. Nazım, and of paragraph 2 of the aforementioned Article in regard to Cavid, Mustafa Şeref, and Musa Kâzım, and in accordance with the last paragraph of the 55th Article of the aforementioned Imperial Code and as is stated in the above-mentioned paragraphs:

"If several persons unitedly commit a felony [*jinayet*] or misdemeanor [*junha*] or if a *jinayet* or *junha* is composed of several acts and each of a gang of persons perpetrates one or some of such acts with a view to the accomplishment of the offence, such persons are styled accomplices and all of them are punished as sole perpetrators." Text of Article 45, paragraph 1.

"The person whose forcible attempt to alter, change or destroy the constitution, or the shape or form of the Government, or the system of succession of the Ottoman Empire is put to death." Article 55, paragraph 3.

"Those who are [convicted of being] accessories in the commission of a crime or offense are, in cases not specified by the law, subject to the following punishments: [In cases where] the main perpetrators are sentenced to either death or a life sentence of hard labor in exile, persons convicted as accessories shall receive temporary sentences of not less than ten years of hard labor in exile."

Upon declaration of these formulations it has been unanimously decided, in accordance with the stipulations of these legal provisions, that:

[Defendants] Talaat, Enver, Cemal, and Dr. Nazım are to be sentenced to death, Câvît, Mustafa Şeref, and Musa Kâzım are each to be sentenced to hard labor in exile for a period of 15 years, while the seized property of the fugitives, having been divested of their civil rights, shall be administered in accordance with the processing office.

Furthermore, as the decisions to acquit reached in regard to the aforementioned Rif'at and Haşim derive from matters concerning their official duties, [this decision] forms no obstacle to their being tried in the future in the High Court [of Justice].

As is understood from the ongoing investigations that former Post and Telegraph Minister Oskan Efendi and former Minister of Commerce Süleyman El-Bûstânî Efendi had gone to Europe long before [the events in question], and that due to current conditions they cannot know that they have been summoned [by the court], and even if they had notice [of the summons] it is likely that they may not possess the capability of returning here on their own, they shall be tried separately.

These decisions were rendered in the presence of [the defendants] Rif'at Bey, Haşim Bey, and Musa Kâzım Efendi, and in the absence of [the defendants] Talaat, Enver, Cemal, Dr. Nazım, Cavid, Mustafa Şeref, and Oskan Efendi and Süleyman El-Bûstânî Efendi.

6 Şeval [1]337 and 5 Temmuz [1]335 (19 July 1919)

President, Extraordinary Military Tribunal
Lieutenant General (General Staff)
Mustafa Nazım bin Ahmed

Member, Extraordinary Military Tribunal
Major General (General Staff)
Ali Nazım

Member, Extraordinary Court Martial,
Major General (Infantry)
Receb Ferdi bin Mehmet Alî

Although I participate in this decision, in light of the existing proofs and his own confessions, I am of the opinion that the aforementioned Haşim Bey is also guilty as an accessory of the 2nd degree.

Member, Extraordinary Military Tribunal
Major General (General Staff)
Mehmet Zeki

In light of the recent confessions of Musa Kâzım Efendi, although [the court was] of the opinion he was innocent in the [CUP] Central Committee's commission of crimes in the matters indicated, I am in favor [of the position] that he is himself a principal perpetrator, because by employing his theological and religious duties to serve to conceal the evil [deeds] of the aforementioned Committee, he did not prevent a single calamity nor even resign from his position, and that Haşim Bey was an accessory of the 2nd degree because according to his own admission, being wholeheartedly bound and faithful to the Central Committee, he did not object to a single calamity or crime that occurred, either at the time or earlier, and because up to the days of the trial he believed that the aforementioned committee was innocent of [any] crime.

Member, Extraordinary Military Tribunal
Major General (General Staff)
Mustafa bin Aziz Süleymân

It is verified that the seals used at the bottom of these recorded transcripts of the court are the seals of the members of the Extraordinary Military Tribunal.

5 Temmuz, [1]335 (19 July 1919)

Extraordinary Military Tribunal
Nazım

Chief of the Board of Transcripts of Extraordinary Military Tribunal
Abidin Daver

Notes

1. Translation from Ottoman Turkish into English by Vahakn N. Dadrian with the assistance of Attorney at Law Fatima Sakarya, an expert in Ottoman Turkish.
2. Memdûh Şevket later took on the last name Esendal (see p. 187).

APPENDIX

The Command Structure and the Ranks of the Ottoman Commanders

THE RANKS in Hierarchial Order			THE CORRESPONDING MILITARY UNITS	
Ottoman Titles	**English Counterparts**	**Modern Turkish**	**In Ottoman**	**In English**
Müşir	Field Marshal	Mareşal	Ordular Grubu	Army Groups
General	Field General	Orgeneral	Ordu	Army
Birinci Ferik	Lieut-General	Korgeneral	Kolordu	Army Corps
Ferik	Major-General	Tümgeneral	Fırka	Division
Mirliva	Brigadier-General	Tuğgeneral	Liva, Tugay	Brigade
Miralay	Colonel	Albay (assisted by Kaymakam, Yarbay)	Alay	Regiment
Binbaşı	Major (assisted by Adjutant Major)	Binbaşı (assisted by Kolağası)	Tabur, Müfreze	Battalion, Detachment
Yüzbaşı	Captain (assisted by First or Second Lieutenant)	Yüzbaşı (assisted by *mülazım evvel* or *mülazımi sani*, or Üsteğmen or Teğmen)	Bölük (*piyade*, *süvari*)	Company (infantry, mounted)
Teğmen	First Lieutenant	Teğmen	Takım, Müfreze	Squad, Platoon
Başçavuş	Sergeant-Major	Başçavuş		
Çavuş	Sergeant	Çavuş		
Onbaşı	Corporal	Onbaşı		

The Ottoman Provincial Hierarchy of Governors

Rank in Turkish	Rank in English	Jurisdiction in Turkish	Jurisdiction in English
Vali	Governor-General	*vilayet*	province
Mutasarrıf	District Governor	*sancak, liva*	district
Kaymakam (Kadı)	County Executive	*kaza*	county
Müdir	Administrator	*nahiye*	township
Muhtar	Headman	*karye*	village

GLOSSARY OF TERMS

Armenierverschickungen: Armenian deportations

azam cürmleri: paramount crimes

beşeriyet namına bir cinayet: crime against humanity

bizim yegâne gayemiz: our sole objective

bu derece gaddarane bir cinayet: to act with perfidy and cruelty

çetebaşıs: brigand chiefs

Çete, Chétté, çeteviye, çetekar: brigand(s)

cinayeti şahsiye: personal crimes

dalkavukluk: flattering

emri sami: high office

Encümeni Mahsus: Special Committee

gayrı insani: crimes against humanity

gayri-mesul: not responsible

hetkı ırz: rape

hissiyatı insaniye: human sentiment

ifna ve katl: kill and destroy

ihanet: treason

ihrakı mebani ve eczad: torching of corpses and buildings

imha: annihilation

Irade: imperial rescript

işkence ve eza: torture and torment

kafileler: convoys

kelek: rafts

komiteci: committee fanatics

kukla: puppet

leke: stain

mücrim: convicts

Müdafaı Hukuk: Defense of Rights movement

müfettiş: inspector

Mülkiye Müfettişi: civil inspector

murahhas: delegate

müstaceliyet: urgency

nehbi emval: plunder of properties

nehb ve yagma: plunder and theft

resmi tarih: official version

şahsen mesul: personally responsible

serseri: tramps

Sichtung: screened

Şurayı Devlet: Council of State

taktı nufus: massacre

takma: phony

tatil: suspension

tehcir: deportation

Teşkilât-ı Mahsusa: Special Organization

teshilat: facilitated

uçurumlar: cleavages

vicdan sahibi: a man of conscience

ARCHIVAL, JUDICIAL, AND PARLIAMENTARY DOCUMENTS

I. THE OTTOMAN EMPIRE AND THE TURKISH REPUBLIC

1. *TAKVIM-I VEKÂYI,* THE OFFICIAL JOURNAL OF THE TURKISH MILITARY TRIBUNAL

Issues containing the texts of the indictments, verdicts, and related criminal proceedings the tribunal effected in prosecuting the wartime mass murder of the Armenians)

Başvekalet Müdevvenat Müdüriyeti. *Düstur üçüncü tertip*, 3rd series, vol. 1 (Istanbul: Başvekalet Müdevvenat Müdüriyeti, 1929).

Preparations for the Courts-Martial
(CUP is the acronym for the Committee of Union and Progress)

The *Takvim-i Vekâyi* (*T.V*) issue numbers are presented in the first column.

3424	21 December 1918	Imperial rescript authorizing establishment of courts-martial
3427	24 December 1918	Cabinet's declaration of a law of amnesty
3430	28 December 1918	Cabinet decree extending jurisdiction to regular courts
3445	14 January 1919	Cabinet Council decision to install courts-martial in six regions
3462	15 February 1919	Cabinet Council declares CUP illegal, confiscates its properties
3491	9 March 1919	Grand Vizier Damad Ferit's decree forbidding deportation and massacre
3520	12 April 1919	Execution through hanging of Boğazlıyan's governor Kemal

The Courts-Martial against Cabinet Ministers and CUP Party Chieftains
(CC stands for Central Committee)

Issue Number	Pages	Court Session	Defendants	Type of Proceeding	Court Session Dates	Publication Dates
3540	1–14	1	Wartime cabinet ministers	Indictment and arraignment	Monday 28 April 1919 (misprinted 27 April)	Monday 5 May 1919
3543	15–31	2	Decision to postpone trial pending new evidence	Constitutional arguments re venue and competence of court-martial	Sunday 4 May 1919	Thursday 8 May 1919
3547	35–51	3	CUP leaders, mainly CUP's CC members	Interrogation	Tuesday 6 May 1919	Tuesday 13 May 1919
3549	53–66	4	CUP leaders, mainly CUP's CC members	Interrogation	Thursday 8 May 1919	Thursday 15 May 1919
3553 (3554)	67–90	5	CUP leaders, mainly CUP's CC members	Interrogation	Monday 12 May 1919 (misprinted 14 May)	Wednesday 21 May 1919
3557	91–113	6	CUP leaders, mainly CUP's CC members	Interrogation	Wednesday 14 May 1919	Sunday 25 May 1919
3561	115–126	7	CUP leaders, mainly CUP's CC members	Interrogation	Saturday 17 May 1919	Thursday 29 May 1919
3571	127–140	1	Cabinet ministers (not deported to Malta)	Reading out of new indictment	Tuesday 3 June 1919	Friday 13 June 1919
3573	141–148	2	Cabinet ministers (not deported to Malta)	Interrogation	Tuesday 3 June 1919	Thursday 12 June 1919
3575	149–155	3	Cabinet ministers (not deported to Malta)	Interrogation	Monday 9 June 1919	Sunday 15 June 1919
3577	157–159	4	Cabinet ministers (not deported to Malta)	New indictment (adding the new charge of overthrow of government)	Thursday 12 June 1919	Tuesday 17 June 1919
3586	161–164	1	CUP's responsible secretaries and delegates	Reading out of the indictment	Saturday 21 June 1919	Saturday 28 June 1919

3589	165–175	2	CUP responsible secretaries and delegates	Interrogation	Monday 23 June 1919	Saturday 5 July 1919
3593	177–183	5	Cabinet ministers (not deported to Malta)	Interrogation	Tuesday 24 June 1919	Wednesday 9 July 1919
3594	185–193	6	Cabinet ministers (not deported to Malta)	Closing arguments	Wednesday 25 June 1919	Thursday 10 July 1919
3595	195–203	7	Cabinet ministers (not deported to Malta)	Closing arguments continued	Thursday 26 June 1919	Saturday 12 July 1919
3596	204–215	3	CUP's responsible secretaries and delegates	New indictment (containing new charges)	Saturday 28 June 1919	Sunday 13 July 1919
3604	217–220	8	Cabinet ministers (present and absent)	Verdict	Saturday 5 July 1919	Tuesday 22 July 1919
3616	1–3	1	Trabzon officials	Verdict	Thursday 22 May 1919	Sunday 6 August 1919
3617	1–2	19	Yozgat officials	Verdict	Tuesday 8 April 1919	Monday 7 August 1919
3618	1–2	9	Büyükdere officials	Verdict	Saturday 24 May 1919	Wednesday 9 August 1919
3771	1–2	6	Mamüret-ül-Aziz (Harput) officials	Verdict	Tuesday 13 January 1920	Monday 9 February 1920
3772	1–6	14	CUP's responsible secretaries and delegates	Verdict	Thursday 8 January 1920	Tuesday 10 February 1920
3917	5–6	3	Erzincan officials	Verdict	Tuesday 27 July 1920	Saturday 31 July 1920
3923	2	2	Bayburt, Governor Nusret	Verdict, sultan's ratification	Tuesday 20 July 1920 Sunday 8 August 1920	Thursday 5 August 1920 In *Tercümani Hakikat*

The Orders for Deportation and Confiscation of Deportees' Possessions and Goods as Recorded in *Takvim-i Vekâyi* Issues.

"Temporary Law on Deportations," 14 (27) May 1915. Published 19 May (1 June) 1915, no. 2189.

"The 34 Instructions to Enforce that Law," 28 May (10 June) 1915. Published 28 October 1915, no. 2343.

"How to Handle the Abandoned Goods, Debts, and Credits of the Deportees," The 11 clauses of a new temporary law (just two days before the reopening of the Parliament.) 13 (26) September 1915, No. 2303. Published 14 (27) September 1915.

2. PARLIAMENTARY DOCUMENTS

Chamber of Deputies (Meclisi Mebusan)

Period (Devre) 3, Volume (Cilt) 1, Session (Içtima) 5, Sittings (Inikad) 4, 11, 14, 23, 25.

The sittings of: a. 4 (19 October 1918); b. 11 (4 November 1918); c. 14 (18 November 1918): d. 23 (9 December12 1918); e. 25 (12 December 1918).

The Senate (Meclisi Âyan)

Period 3, Volume 1, Session 1, Sittings 2, 11, 13, 14.

The sittings of: a. 2 (19 October 1918); b. 11 (21 October 1918); c. 13 (3 December 1918); d. 14 (9 December 1918).

The Transcripts of the Grand National Assembly, i.e., Parliament (*Türkiye Büyük Millet Meclisi Zabıt Ceridesi*) vol. 2 no. 2525 (30 May 1926); also, on the same topic the 27 June 1926 issue of the *Official Gazette of the Ankara Government,* i.e., *Resmi Ceride.*

Ottoman Parliament. Chamber of Deputies. *Meclis-i Mebusan Zabıt Ceridesi* [Minutes of the Chamber of Deputies]. Ankara: TBMM Basımevi, 1992.

Ottoman Parliament. Senators. *Meclis-i Ayan Zabıt Ceridesi* [Minutes of the Senate]. Ankara: TBMM Basımevi, 1990.

3. PRIME MINISTER'S GENERAL DIRECTORATE FOR ARCHIVES

Ottoman documents on the Armenians, 1915–1920

Prime Ministry. General Directorate of State Archives. Osmanlı Belgelerinde Ermeniler, 1915-1920 (Ankara: Başbakanlık Devlet Arşivleri Genel Müdürlüğü, 1994). 272 documents. Those in Latin characters are covered through pp. i–xxxix and 1–277; those in original Ottoman-Arabic script are in pp. 281–627.

4. DOCUMENTS ON STATEMENTS BY MUSTAFA KEMAL ATATÜRK

Atatürk'ün Söylev ve Demeçleri 1919-1918 [The speeches and declarations of Atatürk]. Vol. 1. Istanbul: Ministry of Education, 1945.

A Speech Delivered by Mustafa Kemal Atatürk, 1927. Istanbul: Ministry of Education, 1963.

Nutuk, Vesikalar [Speech, documents]. Vol. 3. Istanbul: Milli Eğitim, 1963.

5. TURKISH ARMY COMMANDER MEHMET VEHIP

Affidavit attesting to the centrally organized mass murder of the Armenians

Vakit, 31 March 1919 (reproducing the full text)
Jerusalem Armenian Patriarchate Archive, Series 17, File H, nos. 171–182, likewise containing the full text in its original Ottoman script.

6. ARCHIVAL DATA ON TURKISH MILITARY COMMANDERS AND PROVINCIAL OFFICIALS, 1919–1922

Görgülu, Ismet, comp. *On Yıllık Harbin Kadrosu 1912–1922* [The cadres involved in the waging of the Ten-Year Wars, 1912–1922]. Ankara: Türkish Historical Society, 1993.
Mücellidoğlu, Ali Çankaya, ed. *Yeni Mülkiye Tarihi ve Mülkiyeliler* [A new history of the Civil Service School and of its graduates]. Vols. 2, 3, 4. Ankara: Interior Ministry, 1969.
Presidency of the Turkish Republic's General Staff. *Türk Istiklal Harbine Katılan Tümen ve Daha Üst Kademelerdeki Komutanların Biyografileri* [The biographies of divisional and higher grade commanders who fought the Turkish War of Independence]. Ankara: General Staff, 1989.

7. OTTOMAN LEGAL DOCUMENTS

The Armenian Genocide: Documentation. 2 vols. Munich: Institut für Armenische Fragen, 1987–1988.
Billiotti, A., and Ahmed Sedad, trans., eds. *Législation Ottoman depuis de la Constitution.* Vol. 1. Paris: Jouve and Co., 1912.
The Imperial Ottoman Penal Code (*Usulu Muhakematı Cezaiye*). Trans. J.A.S. Bucknill and H.A.S Utidjian. Nicosia, Cyprus: Humphrey, Milford, Oxford University Press, 1913.
Kraelitz-Greifenhorst, Friedrich von. *Die Verfassungsgesetze des Osmanischen Reiches* [The constitutional laws of the Ottoman Empire]. Vienna: Forschungs Institut für Osten und Orient, 1919.
"The Ottoman Constitution (Full Text)." *The American Journal of International Law* 2, Supplement (1908). Promulgated 11/23 December 1876. (Translation in Despatch 113, 26 December 1876 MS.Records of Dept. of State) in *Diplomatic Correspondence and Foreign Relations of the US 1861-1899.* Report of 26 December 1878, p. 550 of vol. 1878.
Young, George, comp., trans., ed. *Corps de Droit Ottoman* (*Mülkiye Ceza Kanunnamesi*). Vol. 7. Oxford: Oxford University Press, 1906.

8. OTHERS

Ata, Ferudun. *Işgal Istanbul'unda Tehcir Yargılamaları.* Ankara: Türk Tarih Kurumu, 2005.

Danişmend, Ismail Hami. *Izahlı Osmanlı Tarihi Kronolojisi* [Annotated chronology of the history of the Ottoman Empire]. Vol. 4: *1703–1924.* Istanbul: Türkiye, 1961.

Demirel, Muammer. *Birinci Dünya Harbinde Erzurum ve Çevresinde Ermeni Hareketleri (1914–1918).* Ankara: Genelkurmay, 1996.

Eyyüpoğlu, Erdal Aydoğan-Ismail. *Bahaeddin Şakir Bey'in Bıraktığı Vesikalara Göre Ittihat ve Terakki.* Ankara: Alternatif Publications, 2004.

Hocaoğlu, Mehmet. *Abdülhamit Han'ın Muhtıraları: Belgeler.* [Abdül Hamit's memoranda: Documents] Istanbul: Türkiyat, 1989.

Koloğlu, Orhan. *Aydınlarımızın Bunalım Yılı 1918.* Istanbul: Boyut, 2000.

Muammer Demirel, *Birinci Dünya Harbinde Erzurum ve Çevresinde Ermeni Hareketleri* (1914-1918), Ankara, Genelkurmay, 1996.

Mazıcı, Nurşen. *Belgelerle Atatürk Döneminde Muhalefet (1919–1926).* Istanbul: Dilmen, 1984.

Örik, Nahid Sırrı. *150 Yılın Türk Meşhurları Ansiklopedisi.* Vol. 1. Istanbul: Ekicigil, 1953.

Sarıhan, Zeki. *Kurtuluş Savaşı Günlüğü.* Vol. 1. Ankara: Öğretmen Dünyası, 1982; Vol. 3. Ankara: Öğretmen, 1986.

Süslü , Azmi. *Ermeniler ve 1915 Tehcir Olayı.* Ankara: Yüzüncü Yıl Universitesi Rektörlüğü, 1990.

II. IMPERIAL GERMANY AND GERMAN OFFICIAL RECORDS

FOREIGN OFFICE (Auswärtiges Amt, i.e., A.A.), POLITICAL SECTION (Politische Abteilung, i.e., P.A.)

1. PUBLISHED COLLECTIONS

Gust, Wolfgang, comp., ed. *Der Völkermord an den Armeniern 1915/16: Dokumente aus dem Politischen Archiv des deutschen Auswärtigen Amtes.* Preface by Vahakn N. Dadrian. Springe: Klampen, 2005. Comprises 222 German official documents mostly involving official wartime correspondence between the German Foreign Office, the German Embassy at Constantinople, the wartime Ottoman capital, and the German consular officials deployed throughout the Ottoman Empire.

Lepsius, Johannes. *Bericht über die Lage des Armenischen Volkes in der Türkei.* Berlin and Potsdam: Tempel, 1916.

Lepsius, Johannes. *Der Todesgang des Armenischen Volkes.* Berlin and Potsdam: Missionary Publication, 1930.
Lepsius, Johannes, comp., ed. *Deutschland und Armenien 1914–1918: Sammlung diplomatischer Aktenstücke.* Potsdam and Berlin: Tempel, 1919. Comprises 444 official documents of the same category described under Gust, above.

2. BOTSCHAFT KONSTANTINOPEL

Documents associated with the German embassy in Istanbul, then known as Constantinople

169, no. 47 (6/26/1915)
170, no. 552 (6/28/1915)
170, A53, no. 4729 (8/14/1915)
170, no. 3841 (8/23/1915)
170, A53, no. 5263 (9/10/1915) 172, no. 93 (6/30/1916)
174, no. 10105 (11/16/1916)

3. GERMAN FOREIGN OFFICE, BERLIN

Documents involving both incoming as well as outgoing reports. In the old system they were subsumed, with respect to the Armenians, under the symbol Türkei, file no. 183. Each document had an entry number and was registered in an "entry-journal"; the entry numbers ran consecutively for each year, and in the case of the Political Section they were preceded by the letter A. Presently, however, that system has been discarded and replaced by a Registration (R) setup comprising, in this particular study, the following five documents.

R14087 (Türkei 183/38, A23991), 27 July 1915
R14088 (Türkei 183/39, A28584), 5 August 1915
R14090 (Türkei 183/41, A2888), 3 January 1916
R14092 (Türkei 183/43, A16479), 21 June 1915
R14093 (Türkei 183/44, A27741), 7 October 1916
R14104 (Türkei 183/54, A45718), 13 September 1918

4. OFFICIAL GOVERNMENTAL PUBLICATIONS

Die grosse Politik der Europäischen Kabinette 1871–1914, vol. 9, doc. no. 2184, 16 November 1884 report.
Der Weltkrieg, no. 11d secr., vol, 9, A37451, 28 November 1915.
Grosses Hauptquartier 194, Türkei 41/1, no. 763, 2 July 1916.
Politische Abteilung III/ Türkei P.O. 11, no. 3, vol. 1.
Bundesarchiv-Militärachiv (not in Berlin but Koblenz)

III. IMPERIAL AUSTRIA-HUNGARY

Ohandjanian, Artem, comp., ed. *Armenien: Der Verschwiegene Völkermord.* Vienna: Böhlau, 1989. Comprises some 130 official documents lodged in the state archive of Austria, in Vienna. Translated into Armenian by A. Ohandjanian, *1915 Twagan: Anherkelee Vugayoutiounner. Avsdriagan Vaverakreru Hayotz Tzeghasbanoutian Maseen.* Yerevan: Haysdanee Hanrabedoutiun, 1997. In English, *1915: Irrefutable Evidence. The Austrian Documents on the Armenian Genocide.* Trans. Tigran Tsulikian. Yerevan: Tigran Mets, 2004.

IV. GREAT BRITAIN

1. FOREIGN OFFICE (FO) ARCHIVES

FO 371/2781/264888, 27 December 1916
FO 371/4172/13592, 10 January 1919
FO 371/4174/118377, 18 January 1919
FO 371/4172/16321, 28 January 1919
FO 371/4173/44216, 20 March 1919
FO 371/6501/76279, 5 October 1920
FO 371/6499/E3110, 10 March 1921
FO 371/6504/E9112, 11 June 1921
FO 371/6504/E10411, 14 September 1921
FO 371/3411/210534, folio 334
FO 371/4173/84878, folio 487
FO 371/4174, folio 149
FO 371/6509/E8745, folios 23–24
FO 406/41/132278, 7 September 1919

2. DOCUMENTS PRESENTED TO VISCOUNT GREY OF FALLADON BY VISCOUNT BRYCE

Bryce, James, and Arnold Toynbee, eds. *The Treatment of Armenians in the Ottoman Empire 1915–1916.* London: His Majesty's Stationery Office, 1916. A new "uncensored" edition, compiled by Ara Sarafian, appeared in Reading, England, in 2000. It contains 150 wartime documents, a 54-page detailed analysis by Toynbee (pp. 596–649), five Annexes, an extensive Index of places referred to in the documents, and a map. In addition, the documents are identified in three separate Tables according to the genesis and type of documents.

3. BRITISH AND UN DOCUMENTS

Germany, Turkey and Armenia: A Selection of Documentary Evidence. London: J.J. Keliher, 1917.

UN War Crimes Commission, comp. *History of the United Nations War Crimes Commission and the Development of the Laws of War.* London: His Majesty's Stationery Office, 1948. Especially pp. 35, 45, 191–192, 194–197, 200–202, 569.

Yeghiayan, Vartkes. *British Foreign Office Dossiers on Turkish War Criminals.* La Verne, CA: American Armenian International College, 1991.

Yeghiayan, Vartkes, comp. *British Reports on Ethnic Cleansing in Anatolia, 1919–1922: The Armenian-Greek Section.* Los Angeles: Center for Armenian Remembrance (CAR), 2007.

V. THE UNITED STATES

1. U.S. NATIONAL ARCHIVES

Adalian, Rouben P., comp., ed. *Guide to the Armenian Genocide in the U.S. Archives, 1915–1918.* Alexandria, VA: Chadwyck-Healey, 1994. This microfiche set comprises some 37,000 pages out of a total of over 50,000 pages of documentation contained in the holdings described above, plus the Library of Congress.

The American Committee Opposed to the Lausanne Treaty. *The Lausanne Treaty: Turkey and Armenia.* New York, n.p., 1926.

Davis, Leslie A. (Wartime U.S. Consul at Harput, Turkey). *The Slaughterhouse Province: An American Diplomat's Report on the Armenian Genocide, 1915–1917,* ed. Susan K. Blair. Introduction by Susan K. Blair. New Rochelle, NY: A.D. Caratzas, 1989.

Hairapetian, Armen. "'Race Problems' and the Armenian Genocide: The State Department File," *Armenian Review* 37, no. 1–145 (Spring 1984): 41–145.

Hovannisian, Armen K. "The United States Inquiry and the Armenian Question, 1917–1919: The Archival Papers," *Armenian Review* 37, no. 1–145 (Spring 1984): 146–202.

Sarafian, Ara, comp. *United States Official Records on the Armenian Genocide 1915–1917.* Introduction by Ara Sarafian. Princeton and London: Gomidas Institute, 2004. This compilation contains 170 entries, many of which comprise multiple individual reports and documents. A large portion of these documents were serially published by Sarafian in three special issues of the *Armenian Review*: v. 1, *The Lower Euphrates* (1993); v. 2, *The Peripheries* (1994); v. 3, *The Central Lands* (1995).

2. REFERENCED AND OTHER U.S. DOCUMENTS

Record Group (R.G.) 59.867. 4016/67, 28 May 1915
R.G. 59.867.00/797½, 4 November 1915
R.G. 59.867.00/798½, 18 November 1915

Kévorkian, R.H., and Ara Sarafian. "Documents Consulaires Americains sur la déportation des Arméniens de Samsun pendant, la Primière Guerre mondiale." *Revue d'Histoire Arménienne Contemporaire* 1 (1995): 101–125.

VI. UNITED NATIONS

Messerlian, Zaven, comp. *United Nations Report, 1948.* (Article 30 of Special Rapporteur's Special Report affirming that the World War I Armenian massacres represented "the first case of genocide in the twentieth century". Reprinted from the annual *Hasg*, vols, 2 and 3 (1981–1982): 465–476.

UN Economic Social Council Offical Records. Commission on Human Rights, Sub-Commission on Prevention of Discrimination and Protection of Minorities (38th sess.). Item 57, 7, UN Doc. E/CN, 4/Sub. 2/1985/SR, 36 (1985) (summary record of 36th meeting, 29 August 1985). It is significant that Benjamin Whitaker, author of the report and a British expert-member of the subcommission renowned for his judiciousness, took eight years to research the matter and ended up with the conclusion that the Armenian Genocide is a historical fact.

VII. FRANCE AND FRENCH ARCHIVES

Beylerian, Arthur, comp., ed. *Les Grandes Puissances, L'Empire Ottoman et les Armèniens (Dans les Archives Françaises 1914–1918, Recueil de documents).* Paris: Université de Paris I, Panthéon-Sorbonne , 1983; pp. i–lxiv (Introduction by Arthur Beylerian) and 1–723, comprising 757 documents, 6 Annexes and a Chronological Listing with identification of the senders and recipients of these documents, pp. 745–768.

Nouvelle Série. Guerre Turquie 1914–1918. Arménie. 887–895..

VIII. ARMENIAN ARCHIVAL DOCUMENTS

BIBLIOTHÈQUE NUBAR, PARIS

Containing a portion of the pre-Kemalist era archives of the Armenian Patriarchate of Istanbul and the genocide-related documents assembled by Aram

Andonian. These are cited in the notes as follows: Armenian Patriarchate Archives Jerusalem, Respecting Mazhar Inquiry Commission, Series 5, 6, 10, 12, 16, 17, 21, and 25.

Kévorkian, R. H., trans., ed. *Evenements et faits observes à Constantinople par le vicariate patriarchal 1914–1916* [The events and facts of the 1914–1916 period as observed by Very Reverend Yervant Perdahjian, the vicar of the Patriarchate]. *Revue d'Histoire Arménienne Contemporaine* 1 (1995): 247–287. Archival reference for Nubar Library: Manuscript File 288/P.I. 2/6.

Kevorkian, R. H., ed. *Les Amele Tabouri ou Bataillons de Soldats-Ouvriers de l'Armée Ottomane et le Massacre des Soldats Arméniens.* (Eyewitness testimony provided by Garabed Kaprelian and recorded by Aram Andonian). *Revue d'Histoire Arménienne Contemporaire* 1 (1995): 289–303.

Kevorkian, R. H., *The Armenian Genocide. A Complete History* (London, New York: I. B. Tauris, 2011), pp. 1–5 (Introduction by R. H. Kevorkian) and main text comprising a mass of documentary material, pp. 9-811.

SELECT BIBLIOGRAPHIC SECONDARY SOURCES

BOOKS

Turkish

Ağaoğlu, Samet. *Babamın Arkadaşları.* Istanbul: Nebioğlu, 1959.

Akçam, Taner. *Siyasi Kültürümüzde Zulüm ve Işkence.* Istanbul: Iletişim, 1992.

_____. *Insan Hakları ve Ermeni Sorunu: Ittihat Terakki'den Kurtuluş Savaşı'na.* Ankara: Imge Kitabevi, 1999.

_____. *Ermeni Meselesi Hallolunmustur' Osmanlı Belgelerine Göre Savaş Yillarinda Ermenilere Yönelik Politikalar.* Istanbul: Iletisim, 2008.

Akşin, Sina. *Istanbul Hükümetleri ve Milli Mücadele.* 2 vols. Istanbul: Cem, 1983–1992.

Altınay, Ahmed Refik. *Iki Komite Iki Kıtal.* Ankara: Kabikeç, 1994.

Arıburnu, Kemal. *Milli Mücadelede Istanbul Mitingleri.* Ankara: Yeni Desen, 1975.

Atay, Falih Rıfkı. *Zeytindağı.* Istanbul: Ayyıldız, 1981.

Avcıoğlu, Doğan. *Milli Kurtuluş Tarihi.* Vol. 3, Istanbul: Ertu, 1981.

Aydemir, Şevket Süreyya. *Enver Paşa: Makedonya'dan Ortaasya'ya,* vols. 1 and 3. Istanbul: Remzi, 1972.

_____. *Tek Adam. Mustafa Kemal: 1881–1919.* Istanbul: Remzi, 1963.

Bayar, Celal. *Ben de Yazdım: Milli Mücadeleye Giriş.* Vol. 5, Istanbul: Baha, 1967.

Baytın, Arif. *Ilk Dünya Harbinde Kafkas Cephesi.* Istanbul: Vakıt, 1946.

Bayur, Yusuf Hikmet. *Türk Inkilâbı Tarihi.* Ankara: Türk Tarih Kurumu. Vol. 2, part 4 (1952); vol. 3, part 1 (1953); vol. 3, part 2 (1955); vol. 3, part 3 (1957); vol. 3, part 4 (1983).

Bilgi, Nejdet. *Boğazlıyan Kaymakamı Mehmet Kemal Bey'in Yargılanması.* Ankara: Kök, 1999.

Bıyıklıoğlu, Tevfik. *Atatürk Anadoluda, 1919–1921.* Ankara: Türkiye Işiş Bankası, 1959.

Bleda, Mithat Şükrü. *Imparatorluğun Çöküşü.* Istanbul: Remzi, 1979.

Bolayır, Enver, ed. *Talat Paşa'nın Hatıraları.* Istanbul: Güven, 1946.

Borak, Sadi. *Iktidar Kultuğundan Idam Sehpasına.* Istanbul: Yeni Matbaa, 1962.

Çankaya, Ali. *Yeni Mülkiye Tarihi ve Mülkiyeliler.* Vols. 3 and 4. Ankara: Mars, 1968–1969.

Çavdar, Tevfik. *Milli Mücadele Başlarken Sayılarla.* Istanbul: Milliyet, 1971.

_____. *Talât Paşa: Bir Örgüt Ustasının Yaşam Öyküsü.* Ankara: Dost Kitabevi, 1984.

Cemal Paşa. *Hatıralar.* Ed. B. Cemal. Istanbul: Çağdaş, 1977.

Cemil, Arif Denker. *I. Dünya Savaşında Teşkilâtı Mahsusa.* Istanbul: Arba, 1997.

_____. *Ittihadı Şeflerin Gurbet Maceraları.* Ed. Yücel Demirel. Istanbul: Arma, 1992.

Çiçek, Hikmet. *Dr. Bahattin Şakir: Ittihat ve Terakki'den Teşkilatı Mahsusa'ya Bir Türk Jakobeni.* Istanbul: Analiz Basım, 2004.

Dadrian, Vahakn N. *Ermeni Soykırımında Kurumsal Roller.* Trans. Attila Tuygan. Toplu Makaleler (Collected Articles) Series, vol. 1. Istanbul: Belge, 2004.
Erden, Ali Fuad. *Birinci Dünya Harbinde Suriye Hatıraları.* Vol. 1. Istanbul: Halk, 1954.
Erman, Azmi N. *Izmir Suikasdı ve Istiklal Mahkemeleri.* Istanbul: Temel, 1971.
Ertürk, Hüsamettin. *Iki Devrin Perde Arkası,* Ed. S.N. Tansu. Istanbul: Nurgök, 1957.
Gökbilgin, Tayyib M. *Milli Mücadele Başlarken.* Vol. 1 and 2. Ankara: Türk Tarih Kurumu, 1959. Istanbul: Analiz Basım, 2004.
Göztepe, Tarık Mümtaz. *Osmanoğullarının Son Padişahı Vahdeddin Mütareke Gayyasında.* Istanbul: Sebil, 1969.
Gürün, Kamuran. *Ermeni Dosyası.* Ankara: Türk Tarih Kurumu, 1983.
Menteşe, Halil. *Halil Menteşe' nin Anıları.* Istanbul:, Hürriyet Vakfı, 1986.
Halil Paşa (Kut). *Bitmeyen Savaş.* Ed. M. Taylan Sorgun. Istanbul: Yedigün, 1972.
Hiçyılmaz, Ergün. *Belgelerle Teşkilâtı Mahsusa.* Istanbul: Ünsal, 1979.
Inal, Mahmut Kemal. *Son Sadrazamlar.* Vol. 4. Istanbul: Dergâh, 1982.
Izzet Paşa, Ahmet. *Feryadım.* 2 vols. Istanbul: Nehir, 1992–1993.
Jaeschke, Gotthard, *Türk Kurtuluş Savaşı Kronolojisi.* Ankara: Türk Tarihi Kurumu, 1970.
Kandemir, Feridun. *Izmir Suikasdı'nın Iç Yüzü.* 2 vols. Istanbul: Ekicigil, 1955.
_____. *Istiklal Savaşında Bozguncular ve Casuslar.* Istanbul: Ağbaba, 1964.
_____. *Hatıraları ve Söylemedikleri Ile Rauf Orbay.* Istanbul: Ağbaba, 1965.
Kansu, Mazhar Müfit. *Erzurumdan Ölümüne Kadar Atatürk'le Beraber.* Vols. 1 and 2. Ankara: Türk Tarih Kurumu, 1986.
Karabekir, Kâzım. *Istiklal Harbimiz.* Istanbul: Türkiye, 1969.
_____. *Birinci Cihan Harbine Nasıl Girdik.* Vol. 2. Istanbul: Emre, 1994.
Kaynar, Reşat. *Türkiyede Hukuk Devleti Kurma Yolundaki Hareketler.* Istanbul: Tan, 1960.
Kılıc Ali. *Istiklal Mahkemsi Hatıraları.* Istanbul: Sel, 1955.
Kocahanoğlu, Osman Selim. *Ittihat ve Terrakki'nin Sorgulanması ve Yargılanması.* Istanbul: Temel, 1998.
Koçu, Reşad E., ed., *Ahmet Refik, Hayatı: Seçme Şiir ve Yazıları* (Istanbul: Semih L. Erciyas, 1938).
Koloğlu, Orhan. *Aydınlarımızın Bunalım Yılı 1918.* Istanbul: Boyut, 2000.
Küçük, Yalçın. *Türkiye Üzerine Tezler.* 2 vols. Istanbul: Tekin, 1978–1979.
Kutay, Cemal. *Birinci Dünya Harbinde Teşkilâtı Mahsusa.* Istanbul: Ercan, 1962.
_____. *Sisli Tarihimiz.* Istanbul: Özkaya, 1976.
_____. *Celal Bayar'ın Yazmadığı ve Yazmayacağı Üç Devirden Hakikatler.* Istanbul: Alioğlu, 1982.
_____. *Talat Paşa'nın Gurbet Hatıraları.* 3 vols. Istanbul: n.p., 1981.
Nadi, Yunus. *Kurtuluş Savaşı Anıları.* Istanbul: Anonim, 1978.
Nur, Riza. *Hayat ve Hatıratım.* Vol. 3. Istanbul: Işaret, 1992.
Okyar, Fethi. *Üç Devirde Bir Adam.* Ed. C. Kutay. Istanbul: Tercüman, 1980.
Sabis, Ali Ihsan. *Harp Hatıralarım.* Vol. 1 and 2. Ankara: Güneş, 1943-1951.
Şakir, Ziya. *Yakın Tarihte Üç Büyük Adam.* Istanbul: Ahmet Sait, 1946.
Samih, Aziz. *Büyük Harpte Kafkas Cephesi Hatıraları.* Ankara: Büyük Erkânıharbiye Matbaası, 1934.
Sarıhan, Zeki. *Kurtuluş Savaşı Günlüğü, vol. 2: Erzurum Kongresi'nden TBMM'ye.* Ankara: Öğretmen Dünyası Yayınları, 1984,
Selçuk, Sadi. *Esaretin Acı Hatıraları ve 37. Kafkas Tümeni'nin Trabzon Düşmandan Istirdadı.* Konya: Ülkü, 1955.

Şener, Cemal. *Topal Osman Olayı.* Istanbul: Ant, 1992.
Şimşir, Bilal. *Malta Sürgünleri.* Istanbul: Milliyet, 1976.
Talat Paşa'nın Hatıraları. Ed. Enver Bolayır. Istanbul: Güven, 1946.
Tepeyran, Ebubekir Hazım. *Zalimane Bir Idam Hükmü.* Istanbul: Milli Mecmua, 1946.
Tunaya, Tarık Zafer. *Türkiyede Siyasi Partiler, 1859–1952.* Istanbul: Doğan, 1952.
_____. *Türkiye'de Siyasal Partiler.* Istanbul: Hürriyet Vakfı. Vol. 1, 1984; vol. 2, 1986; vol. 3, 1989.
Türkgeldi, Ali Fuad. *Görüp Işittiklerim.* Ankara: Türk Tarih Kurumu, 1957 (1987).
Velidedeoğlu, Hıfzı Veldet. *Anılarım Izinde.* Vol. 1. Istanbul: Remzi, 1977.
Vardar, Galip. *Ittihad ve Terakki Içinde Dönenler.* Ed. S. N. Tansu. Istanbul: Inkilâp, 1960.
Yalman, Ahmet Emin. *Yakın Tarihte Gördüklerim ve Geçirdiklerim,* vol. 1: *(1888–1918).* Istanbul: Yenilik, 1970.

English

For documentary treatises see the compilations of Rouben Adalian, Ara Sarafian, Armen Hairapetian, Armen K. Hovannisian and Leslie A. Davis in Part V, Section 1 of the Archival, Judicial, and Parliamentary Documents, and of Viscount Bryce and Arnold Toynbee in Part IV, Section 2.

Akçam, Taner. *A Shameful Act: The Armenian Genocide and the Question of Turkish Responsibility.* New York: Metropolitan Books, 2006.
Balakian, Peter. *The Burning Tigris: The Armenian Genocide and America's Response.* New York: Harper Collins, 2003.
Balakian, Grigoris. *Armenian Golgotha: A Memoir of the Armenian Genocide, 1915-1918.* Translated by Peter Balakian with Aris Sevag. New York: Albert Knopf, 2009.
Bass, Gary Jonathan. *Stay the Hand of Vengeance: The Politics of War Crimes Tribunals.* Princeton: Princeton University Press, 2000.
Bryce, James and Arnold Toynbee, eds. *The Treatment of the Armenians in the Ottoman Empire, 1915–1916 documents presented by Viscount Grey of Fallodon by Viscount Bryce, with a preface by Ara Sarafian.* Princeton, NJ: Gomidas, 2000.
The Case of Soghomon Tehlirian. Translated by Vartkes Yeghiayan (Los Angeles: A. R. F. Varantian Gomideh, 1985).
Churchill, Winston S. *The World Crisis: The Aftermath,* vol. 5: *Armenia and the Pan-Turks.* London: T. Butterworth, 1929.
Dadrian, Vahakn N. *History of the Armenian Genocide: Ethnic Conflict from the Balkans to Anatolia to the Caucasus,* revised and enlarged 8th printing. New York and Oxford: Berghahn Books, 2006. (Russian edition, 2007; Italian edition, 2005; Greek edition, 2002; French editions, 1996, 1998.)
_____. *The Armenian Genocide in Official Turkish Records.* Special edition (in book form), *Journal of Political and Military Sociology* 22, no. 1 (Summer 1994; reprinted and revised, Spring 1995).
_____. *The Key Elements in the Turkish Denial of the Armenian Genocide.* Cambridge and Toronto, Zoryan Institute, 1999.
Derogy, Jacques. *Resistance and Revenge: The Armenian Assassination of the Turkish Leaders Responsible for the 1915 Massacres and Deportations.* New Brunswick, NJ, and London: Transaction, 1986.
Gilbert, Martin. *Winston S. Churchill,* vol. 3: *1914–1916: The Challenge of War.* Boston:

Houghton Mifflin, 1971; and *Companion*, vol. 2, part 2: *May 1915–December 1916*. Boston: Houghton Mifflin 1973.

_____. *Churchill: A Life*. New York: Henry Holt, 1991.

Helmreich, Paul. *From Paris to Sèvres: The Partition of the Ottoman Empire at the Peace Conference of 1919-1920*. Columbus: Ohio State University Press, 1974.

Hovannisian, Richard G., ed. *The Armenian Genocide: History, Politics, Ethics*. New York: St. Martins, 1992.

Kinross, Lord. *Atatürk: A Biography*. New York: W. Morrow, 1965.

Mango, Andrew *Atatürk: The Biography of the Founder of Modern Turkey*. Woodstock:, Overlook Press, 1999.

Morgenthau, Henry. *Ambassador Morgenthau's Story*. New York: Doubleday, 1918.

Nogales, Rafael de. *Four Years Beneath the Crescent*. Trans. Muna Lee. New York: Scribner's, 1926.

Shiragian, Arshavir. *The Legacy: Memoirs of an Armenian Patriot*. Boston: Hairenik Press, 1976.

Şimşir, Bilal N. *The Malta Exiles and the Armenian Question*. Ankara: Foreign Policy Institute 1985.

Willis, James F. *Prologue to Nuremberg: The Politics and Diplomacy of Punishing War Criminals of the First World War*. Westport, CT: Greenwood Press, 1982.

Woodward, W. and R. Butler, eds., *Documents on British Foreign Policy, vol. 4: (1919–1939)*. London: HMSO, 1952.

Zaven Patriarch, Der Yeghiayan. *My Patriarchal Memoirs*. Trans. Ared Misirliyan. Annotations by Vatche Ghazaryan. Barrington, RI: Mayreni, 2002.

Zürcher, Erik Jan. *The Unionist Factor: The Role of the Committee of Union and Progress in the Turkish National Movement 1905–1926*. Leiden: Brill, 1984.

_____. *Turkey: A Modern History*. London: I.B. Taurus, 1998.

German

Biehl, Wolfdeiter. *Die Kaukasus Politik der Mittelmâchter*. Teil 1: *Ihre Basis in der Orientpolitik und Ihre Aktionen 1915-1917*. Wien: H. Böhlhaus, 1975.

Gust, Wolfgang. *Der Völkermord an den Armenien: Die Tragödie des ältesten Christenvolkes der Welt*. München: Carl Hanser Verlag, 1993.

Hofmann, Tessa, ed. *Der Völkermord an den Armeniern vor Gericht: Der Prozess Talaat Pascha*. Göttingen, Wien: Gesellschaft für bedrohte Völker, 1985.

Zurlinden, Samuel. *Der Weltkrieg*. Vol. 2 (Serial parts 8, 9, 10). Zürich: Art. Institut Füssli, 1918.

French

Naslian, Mgr. Jean. *Les Mémoirs de Mgr. Jean Naslian (sur les événements politico-religieux en proche-orient de 1914 à 1918)*. Vol. 1. Beirut: Mechitarian of Vienna, 1955.

Pech, Edgar. *Les Alliés et la Turquie*. Paris: Les Presses Universitaires de France, 1925.

Armenian

Balakian, Krikoris. *Hai Koghkota*. Vol. 1. Vienna: Mechitarist, 1922.

Hovagimian, Hovagim. *Badmoutiun Haigagan Pontosee*. Beirut: Mushak, 1967.

Melidentzee, Kevork. *Nakhjirner 1915–1918*. Boston: Hairenik, 1929.
Mugurditchian, Thomas. *Dikranagerdee Nahankenn Charteru*. Cairo: Djihanian, 1919.
Teotig (Teodos Lapjinjian). *Amenoun Daretzouytzu 1916–1920* [Everyone's almanac]. Istanbul: Keshishian & Son, 1920.
Zaven Archbishop Der Yeghiayan (wartime Patriarch of Armenians of Turkey). *Badriarkagan Husherus* [Documents and testimonies]. Cairo: Nor Astgh, 1947.

ARTICLES

Turkish

Balkan, Fuat. "Beş Albaylar." *Yakın Tarihimiz* 2 (1962): 296–297.
Birinci, Ihsan. "Kâfirin Kurşunu Öldürmez." *Hayat ve Tarih* 2 (1 August 1967).
_____. "Cemiyet ve Çeteler." *Hayat ve Tarih* 2 (1 October 1971).
Ertürk, Hüsamettin, "Milli Mücadele Senelerinde Teşkilât-ı Mahsusa" Ankara Stratejik Araştırmalar ve Askerlik Tarihi Enstitüsü, Tarihsiz. In Bilge Criss, ed., *Işgal Altinda Istanbul*. Istanbul: İletişim 1983.
Hayriye Hanım. "Eşi Hayriye Hanım Talaat Paşayı Anlatıyor." *Yakın Tarihimiz* 2 (1962): 193–195.
Feridun Kandemir, "Dr. Reşit'in Intiharı," *Yakın Tarihimiz* 2 (1962): 339–340
Feridun Kandemir, "Ittihat ve Terrakki Valilerinden Doktor Reşit Beyin Son Günleri," *Resimli Tarih Mecmuası* 2 (October 1951): 1052–1055.
Karadoğan, Ismet. "Cemal Paşa'yı Ruslar Öldürmüştü." *Yakın Tarihimiz* 2 (1962): 36–38.
Kayabalı, Ismail. "Kuzey Doğu Anadolu Sınırlarının Tarihi." *Türk Kültürü* 10, no. 1 (April 1973).
Kesim, Firuz. "Cemal Paşa Nasıl Katledildi." *Yakın Tarihimiz* 2 (1962): 131–132.
Kutay, Cemal. "Izmir ve Ankara Idamları." *Türkiye Istiklal ve Hürriyet Mücadeleleri Tarihi* 20 (January 1962).
Orbay, Rauf. "Rauf Orbay'ın Hatıraları." *Yakın Tarihimiz* 1 and 3 (1962).
Özik, Nahid. "Ahmed Refik Altınay." *Yüzelli Yılın Türk Meşhurları Ansiklopedisi* (Istanbul: Ekicigil, 1953), pp. 104–105.
Sarıhan, Zeki. "1914–1918 Savaş Kabineleri Üyelerinin Görüşleri." *Saçak* 40 (May 1987): 23–29.
Silan, Necmeddin. "Ikinci Meşrutiyette Divan-ı Ali Hareketleri," part 2. *Tarih Konuşuyor* 5 (June 1966): 2469–2474.

English

American Committee Opposed to the Lausanne Treaty. *The Lausanne Treaty, Turkey and Armenia*. New York: n.p., 1926).
Bassiouni, Cherif M. "The Time Has Come for an International Criminal Court." *Indiana International and Comparative Law Review* 9, no. 1 (Spring 1991): 1–43.
Cruickshank, A. A. "The Young Turk Challenge in Postwar Turkey." *The Middle East Journal* 22 (Winter 1968): 17–28.
Dadrian, Vahakn N. "The Role of Turkish Physicians in the World War I Genocide of Ottoman Armenians." *Holocaust and Genocide Studies* 1 (1986): 169–192.

_____. "The Naim-Andonian Documents on the World War I Destruction of Ottoman Armenians: The Anatomy of a Genocide." *International Journal of Middle East Studies* 18 (August 1986): 311–359.

_____. "Genocide as a Problem of National and International Law: The World War I Armenian Case and Its Contemporary Legal Ramifications." *Yale Journal of International Law* 14 (Summer 1989): 221–334.

_____. "A Textual Analysis of the Key Indictment of the Turkish Military Tribunal Investigating the World War I Armenian Massacres." *Armenian Review* 44 (Spring 1991): 1–36.

_____. "Documentation of the Armenian Genocide in Turkish Sources." In *Genocide: A Critical Bibliographic Review*, ed. Israel Charny. Vol. 2. London: Mansell, 1991, pp. 86–138.

_____. "The Documentation of the World War I Armenian Massacres in the Proceedings of the Turkish Military Tribunal," *International Journal of Middle East Studies* 23 (November 1991): 549–576.

_____. "The Role of the Special Organization in the Armenian Genocide during the First World War." In *Minorities in Wartime*, ed. P. Panayi. Oxford: Berg, 1993, pp. 50–82.

_____. "The Law Allowing Convicts to Enroll in the Special Organization," *Journal of Political and Military Sociology* 22 (Summer 1994): 57–61.

_____. "The Historical and Legal Interconnections between the Armenian Genocide and the Jewish Holocaust: From Impunity to Retributive Justice." *Yale Journal of International Law* 23 (Summer 1998): 505–559.

_____. "The Armenian Question and the Wartime Fate of the Armenians as Documented by the Officials of the Ottoman Empire's World War I Allies: Germany and Austria-Hungary." *International Journal of Middle East Studies* 34 (February 2002): 59–85.

_____. "Impunity." *Encyclopedia of Genocide and Crimes Against Humanity* 2 (2005), pp. 489–491.

Dinkel, Christoph. "German Officers and the Armenian Genocide." *Armenian Review* 44 (Spring 1991): 77–133.

Jaeschke, Gotthard and Erich Pritsch, "Die Türkei seit dem Weltkriege 1918–1928" *Die Welt des Islams* vol. 10 (1927–1929), pp. 1–154.

Lewis, Bernard. "History-Writing and National Revival in Turkey" *Middle Eastern Affairs* 4 (1953): 218–227.

German

Baltzar, Kapitänleutnant. "Das romantische Ende der drei grossen Türken der Kriegszeit: Talaat, Enver und Dschemal Pascha. Eine Erinnerung an den 1. November 1918." *Orient Rundschau* 15 (10 November 1933): 3–4.

Jäschke, Gotthard. "Beiträge zur Geschichte des Kampfes der Türkei um Ihre Unabhängigkeit." *Die Welt des Islams* 5, no. 1–2, N.S. 5 (1958): 1–63.

Armenian

Boyadjian, Püzant. "Tebee Ayaş: Heen u Nor Husher." In *Hushartzan Abril Dasnemegee*, ed. Teotig. Istanbul, Arzuman, 1919, pp. 95–112.

Dzeroug. "Dzerougee Housheru." *Djagadamard* (2 March 1919): 3.
Keğam, Der Garabedian. "Kegham Der Garabetianee Vugayutiunu." In Garo Sassouni, *Badmoutiun Daronee Achkaree.* Beirut: Sevan, 1956, pp. 837–841.
Urhayetzee, K. A. "Urfayee Herosamardu." *Hairenik* 5 (December 1926): 99–110.

NEWSPAPERS

Turkish

Akşam
Alemdar
Ati (Ileri)
Hadisat Ictihad
Ikdam
Ileri (see *Ati* above).
Istiklal
Minber
Peyam-i Sabah
Sabah
Söz
Tasviri Efkâr
Tercümân-ı Hakikat
Tevhid-i Efkâr
Türkce Istanbul
Vakit
Yeni Gazete
Yeni Istanbul
Zaman

French

Renaissance (in French)

American

Hovagimian, Mardig, comp. *Anglo-American Select Bibliography of News and Feature Articles, Letters, and Editorials: 1915–1925.* New York, 1953. Includes texts and declarations of governmental, civic and charitable organizations, and letters from prominent educators, statesmen, clergymen, missionaries, and others, from the *New York Times.*
Kloian, Richard D., comp. *The Armenian Genocide: News Accounts from the American Press, 1915–1922.* Berkeley, CA: Anto, 1985.
Malkasian, Carneg, comp. *Newspaper clippings. 1915-1919.* (Detroit: St. John's Armenian Church Library, N.d.). Compilation of clippings from the *Detroit Free Press.*

British

Morning Post

Canadian

Armenian National Committee of Canada. *The Armenian Genocide in the Canadian Press*, vol. 1: *1915–1916*. Montreal: Armenian National Committee of Canada, 1985. Comprises news for the period March 1915–March 1916.

Peltekian, Katia Minas, comp. *The Armenian Genocide in The Halifax Herald, 1894–1922*. Halifax, Nova Scotia: Armenian Cultural Association of the Atlantic Provinces, 2000.

Australian

The Armenian Genocide as Reported in the Australian Press (May 1915–February 1917). Sydney: The Armenian National Committee, 1983.

Armenian

Ariamard
Djagadamard
Jhogovourtee Tzain
Nor Giank
Zhamanak

INDEX